Mastering Salesforce DevOps

A Practical Guide to Building Trust While Delivering Innovation

Andrew Davis
Foreword by Wade Wegner

Apress®

Mastering Salesforce DevOps: A Practical Guide to Building Trust While Delivering Innovation

Andrew Davis
San Diego, CA, USA

ISBN-13 (pbk): 978-1-4842-5472-1
https://doi.org/10.1007/978-1-4842-5473-8

ISBN-13 (electronic): 978-1-4842-5473-8

Managing Director, Apress Media LLC: Welmoed Spahr
Acquisitions Editor: Susan McDermott
Development Editor: Laura Berendson
Coordinating Editor: Rita Fernando

Cover designed by eStudioCalamar

Cover image designed by Freepik (www.freepik.com)

Distributed to the book trade worldwide by Springer Science+Business Media New York, 233 Spring Street, 6th Floor, New York, NY 10013. Phone 1-800-SPRINGER, fax (201) 348-4505, e-mail orders-ny@springer-sbm.com, or visit www.springeronline.com. Apress Media, LLC is a California LLC and the sole member (owner) is Springer Science + Business Media Finance Inc (SSBM Finance Inc). SSBM Finance Inc is a **Delaware** corporation.

For information on translations, please e-mail rights@apress.com, or visit http://www.apress.com/rights-permissions.

Apress titles may be purchased in bulk for academic, corporate, or promotional use. eBook versions and licenses are also available for most titles. For more information, reference our Print and eBook Bulk Sales web page at http://www.apress.com/bulk-sales.

Any source code or other supplementary material referenced by the author in this book is available to readers on GitHub via the book's product page, located at www.apress.com/9781484254721. For more detailed information, please visit http://www.apress.com/source-code.

Printed on acid-free paper

Advance Praise for *Mastering Salesforce DevOps*

"DevOps is the next frontier in managing Salesforce orgs for both developers and admins. This book has both the scope and depth to help any organization adapt modern software engineering and management methodologies to Salesforce. Or put another way—if you're a Salesforce developer or admin, you need to read this book now."

—Dan Appleman, Salesforce MVP; author of *Advanced Apex Programming in Salesforce*

"I was amazed at the completeness of this book. The depth and breadth presented here is not available in any single resource that I know of, not even Trailhead. It is not just the Salesforce specific portions either. The DevOps chapters provide a jumpstart for anyone who wants to understand what DevOps is and why it is critically important in today's world."

—David Brooks, VP Products, Copado Solutions; original product owner of AppExchange; one of the three founding PMs of the Force.com Platform

"Andrew Davis has written the essential reference for the next 5–10 years of Salesforce evolution. Salesforce has become a true cloud development platform, but its ecosystem of enterprise-class tools and techniques is just starting to catch up. All prospective and existing Salesforce developers should read this book if they aspire to be not just coders, but professional software engineers."

—Glenn Weinstein, Co-founder of Appirio

"This book really gets to the heart of how to properly equip a team with the tools and process to go faster with the Salesforce platform."

—Sanjay Gidwani, SVP, Copado

"In the last few years it's become clear that for companies to innovate and succeed, IT must have speed and agility like never before. Within Appirio it was Andrew who really caught the wind of the DevOps movement and pushed the entire company in that direction. The power of a performance-oriented culture is that the best ideas can come from anywhere in the company, and it was exciting to watch that unfold as we moved to promote DevOps. I'm delighted that Andrew's insights and passion for this topic are now being shared with the broader world. Those seeking to deliver maximum value from their teams and from Salesforce would be wise to read this book carefully."

—Chris Barbin, Venture Partner, GGV Capital;
Former CEO and Co-founder, Appirio

"Andrew gained experience deploying and developing SaaS applications for enterprise customers while navigating the new world of DevOps in the cloud, and put that into words that can reach readers at any technical level. This book truly delivers a thorough and practical guide to establishing DevOps for those rooted in the Salesforce platform. If you've been hesitant about implementing DevOps, or if you have tried and failed, this is the book for you."

—Katie M. Brown, Director, Methodology at Okta,
Delivery Excellence in the Cloud

"If you are using Salesforce and want to maximize your efficiency to make life easier for your teams, Andrew Davis' *Mastering Salesforce DevOps: A Practical Guide to Building Trust While Delivering Innovation* provides a thorough approach for doing that using Salesforce DevOps. In addition to providing a multitude of technical details, Andrew smartly starts with why—why use Salesforce and why use DevOps specifically for Salesforce—and honestly addresses issues people have had with Salesforce before diving into all the details to help you succeed. Andrew is the acknowledged expert on DevOps for Salesforce and shares his insights and secrets in this book to make your life as a developer, administrator, or user better."

—Dean Hering, Adjunct Associate Professor, Master of Engineering
Management Program, Duke University

"With the rapid pace of development in technology, organizations need to find ways to deliver solutions more efficiently, while retaining high quality. DevOps is an approach to software delivery that ensures both speed and quality, which is important as organizations deploy increasingly complex Salesforce.com solutions. Andrew has dedicated over a half a decade to bring structure and rigor to DevOps on this platform. This is a must-read for anyone working in the software industry!"

—Matt Henwood, Executive Vice President, Service Delivery, 7Summits

"There's never been a more important and exciting time to talk about Salesforce DevOps than right now. Expectations of getting value from an increasingly complex (and saturated) array of Salesforce clouds are high, competition is fierce, talent is scarce, and teams need to modernize to stay relevant. You want the best engine under the hood to make change happen. If you don't, you're doing it wrong. Anyone who deploys anything to production (which is everyone!) needs to read this book."

—Andres Gluecksmann, Vice President, Enable Services, Traction on Demand

"DevOps is becoming a must-have skillset for every developer in today's world. And it is especially crucial with the rapid pace of innovation on the Salesforce Platform. I think this book will become a go-to reference for Salesforce DevOps specialists seeking to leverage all the capabilities of Salesforce DX. Although this book is designed to teach how you can accelerate your Salesforce development lifecycle using CI/CD, even if you are new to Salesforce, the initial chapters will help you to understand the basics of this platform. I had the opportunity to work with Andrew for a couple of years. The best thing about working with him is how many new things you can learn from him, easily and in a very short amount of time. He's been involved with Salesforce DX since it was first announced and this book gives us access to all his learnings and research."

—Durgesh Dhoot, Platform Specialist, Salesforce

To Ashley

"May I always be a manifestation of others' good fortune"

Table of Contents

About the Author xix

About the Technical Reviewer xxi

Foreword xxiii

Acknowledgments xxv

Chapter 1: Introduction 1

Why Salesforce? 1

What Is Salesforce DX? 3

What Is DevOps? 5

The Research on DevOps 8

About This Book 9

Background 11

Part I: Foundations 13

Chapter 2: Salesforce 15

"Salesforce" vs. Salesforce 15

How Is Salesforce Different? 16

DevOps in the Salesforce World 18

What Is Salesforce DX? 19

What Are the Elements of Salesforce DX? 20

The Dev Hub 21

Scratch Orgs 21

Second-Generation Packaging 21

Metadata API vs. SFDX Source Formats 23

Salesforce Command-Line Interface (CLI) 25

Summary 25

Chapter 3: DevOps **27**

What's Driving the Need for DevOps? 29

What Is DevOps? 29

    Dev vs. Ops 30

    The Real Meaning of Agile 32

    The Three Ways of DevOps 33

    Lean Management 35

    Generative Culture 37

    Blameless Postmortems 38

The Research 39

    Business Impact of Adopting DevOps 40

How DevOps Helps 42

    Better Value, Faster, Safer, Happier 42

Measuring Performance 43

Enhancing Performance 47

    Optimizing the Value Stream 48

    Theory of Constraints 50

Enabling Change 53

    Leading Change 57

    Step 1: Create Urgency 57

    Step 2: Form a Powerful Coalition 58

    Step 3: Create a Vision for Change 59

    Step 4: Communicate the Vision 60

    Step 5: Remove Obstacles 61

    Step 6: Create Short-Term Wins 62

    Step 7: Build on the Change 63

    Step 8: Anchor the Changes in Corporate Culture 63

Summary 63

Part II: Salesforce Dev 65

Chapter 4: Developing on Salesforce 67

The Salesforce DX Dev Lifecycle 67

Development Tools 71

    The Salesforce CLI 71

    What's an Integrated Development Environment (IDE)? 71

    The Developer Console 72

    Workbench 72

    The Forthcoming Web IDE 72

    Visual Studio Code 73

    Other Salesforce IDEs 75

Metadata (Config and Code) 77

    What Is Metadata? 77

    Metadata API File Format and package.xml 77

    Converting Between Salesforce DX and Metadata API Source Formats 79

    What Metadata Should You Not Track? 79

    Retrieving Changes 81

    Making Changes 82

    Manual Changes 83

Click-Based Development on Salesforce 84

    Development—No-Code, Low-Code, and Pro-Code 84

    Declarative Development Tools 85

    Data Management 89

    The Security Model 99

Code-Based Development on Salesforce 103

    Server-Side Programming 104

    Client-Side Programming 106

Summary 108

Chapter 5: Application Architecture 109

The Importance of Modular Architecture 110

Understanding Dependencies 111

Salesforce DX Projects 113

How Salesforce DX Projects Enable Modular Architecture 113

Creating a Salesforce DX Project 115

Modular Development Techniques 116

Naming Conventions 117

Object-Oriented Programming 117

Dependency Injection 118

Event-Driven Architecture 122

Enterprise Design Patterns 124

Separation of Concerns 125

Service Layer 126

Unit of Work 127

Domain Layer 128

Selector Layer 129

Factory Method Pattern 130

Trigger Management 131

The One Trigger Rule 131

The Trigger Handler Pattern 131

The Domain Pattern 132

Modular Triggers with Dependency Injection 132

Packaging Code 133

Summary 137

Part III: Innovation Delivery 139

Chapter 6: Environment Management 141

An Org Is Not a Server 141

Different Types of Orgs 142

Which Org Should You Develop In? 146

    Why Not Develop in Production? 146

    Developing in Sandboxes 148

    The Disadvantages of Developing in Sandboxes 149

    The Benefits of Developing in Scratch Orgs 150

    Meeting in the Middle—A Sandbox Cloning Workflow 152

Org Access and Security 153

    The Dev Hub 154

    API-Based Authentication 155

    Salesforce DX Org Authorizations 158

Environment Strategy 161

    Environment Strategy Guidelines 161

    Multiple Production Orgs 162

    Identifying and Mapping Existing Orgs 167

    Identifying Requirements for Testing, Fixes, Training, and Others 169

Creating and Using Scratch Orgs 175

    General Workflow 175

    Creating Scratch Orgs 177

    Initializing Scratch Orgs 182

    Developing on Scratch Orgs 189

    Scratch Orgs As Review Apps 191

Cloning and Refreshing Sandboxes 191

    Creating, Cloning, or Refreshing Sandboxes 192

    Planning Org Refreshes 193

    Planning and Communicating Changes to Org Structure 194

    Working with Lightning Dev Pro Sandboxes 195

The Salesforce Upgrade Cycle 195

    Getting Early Access to a Release 196

    Deploying Between Environments That Are on Different Releases 197

A Behind-the-Scenes Look at Orgs 198

Summary 201

Chapter 7: The Delivery Pipeline 203

Why You Need Version Control on Salesforce 204

Version Control 205

Git Basics 206

Git Tools 209

Naming Conventions 212

Preserving Git History When Converting to Salesforce DX 216

Branching Strategy 217

Trunk, Branches, and Forks 217

Well-Known Branching Strategies 220

The Research on Branching Strategies 221

Freedom, Control, and Ease 222

Branching for Package Publishing 226

Guidelines if You Choose to Use Feature Branches 228

Branching for Org-Level Configuration 230

Deploying Individual Features 237

Forking Workflow for Large Programs 240

CI/CD and Automation 241

Automating the Delivery Process 243

CI Servers and Infrastructure 245

Configuring CI/CD 253

Example CI/CD Configuration 256

Summary 267

Chapter 8: Quality and Testing 269

Understanding Code Quality 269

Functional, Structural, and Process Quality 270

Understanding Structural Quality 271

Understanding Process Quality 275

Testing to Ensure Quality 275

Why Test? 275

What to Test? 278

Testing Terminology 278

Test Engines 282

Test Environments 282

Test Data Management 282

Fast Tests for Developers 283

Static Analysis—Linting 284

Static Analysis—Quality Gates 287

Unit Testing 291

Comprehensive Tests 297

Automated Functional Testing 298

Nonfunctional Testing 312

Manual QA and Acceptance Testing 330

Summary 335

Chapter 9: Deploying 337

Deployment Technologies 338

The Underlying Options 339

Deploying Using an IDE 345

Command-Line Scripts 346

Commercial Salesforce Tools 360

Packaging 373

Resolving Deployment Errors 380

General Approach to Debugging Deployment Errors 380

Getting Help 382

General Tips for Reducing Deployment Errors 382

Continuous Delivery 382

Why Continuous Delivery? 383

Automating Deployments 384

Deploying Configuration Data 385

Continuous Delivery Rituals 386

Deploying Across Multiple Production Orgs 387

Managing Org Differences 388

Dependency and Risk Analysis 392

Summary 392

Chapter 10: Releasing to Users **395**

Releasing by Deploying 396

Separating Deployments from Releases 398

    Permissions 398

    Layouts 399

    Dynamic Lightning Pages 400

    Feature Flags 400

    Branching by Abstraction 403

Summary 406

Part IV: Salesforce Ops (Administration) **409**

Chapter 11: Keeping the Lights On **411**

Salesforce Does the Hard Work for You 411

What Does Dev and Ops Cooperation Mean? 412

Salesforce Admin Activities 416

    User Management 416

    Security 417

    Managing Scheduled Jobs 418

    Monitoring and Observability 420

    Other Duties As Assigned 425

Summary 425

Chapter 12: Making It Better **427**

An Admin's Guide to Doing DevOps.. 428

Locking Everybody Out 431

What's Safe to Change Directly in Production?... 435

Tracking Issues and Feature Requests 436

Summary.. 437

Chapter 13: Conclusion... **439**

Bibliography **443**

Index.. **445**

About the Author

Andrew Davis is a Salesforce DevOps specialist who's passionate about helping teams deliver innovation, build trust, and improve their performance. He is a senior product manager for Copado, a leading DevOps platform for Salesforce. Before joining Copado, he worked as a developer and architect at Appirio, where he learned the joys and sorrows of release management and led the creation of Appirio DX, a set of tools to enable Salesforce CI/CD.

At different times, he led Appirio's technical governance, DevOps, and certification programs and gained 16 Salesforce certifications. An experienced teacher and public speaker, he is a regular speaker at Salesforce conferences. He lives in San Diego with his amazing wife and very cuddly dog. Follow him at `https://AndrewDavis.io` or on Twitter at AndrewDavis_io.

About the Technical Reviewer

 **John M. Daniel** has been working in the technology sector for over 20 years. During that time, he has worked in a variety of technologies and project roles. Currently, he serves as the Director of Platform Architecture at Rootstock Cloud ERP, a leading cloud-based ERP solution that is native to the Salesforce Platform. He is a Salesforce MVP and holds multiple Salesforce certifications, including Platform Developer I and II and most of the Technical Architect Designer certifications. He is currently working toward becoming a Certified Technical Architect. He loves to spend time with his family, swim and ride his Jeep at the beach, and work on open source projects such as Force-DI, AT4DX, and the DomainBuilder Framework. He co-leads his local Salesforce Developers User Group and can be found on Twitter at @ImJohnMDaniel.

Foreword

I've spent my entire career immersed in the world of software development. From early on, I fell in love with the power and the freedom that comes from being able to create magic with code. I've seen the birth of the Internet and have had the opportunity to share this passion for development with thousands of people around the world. But it didn't take long for me to realize that while writing code can be fun, it's not always the most productive way to get the job done. In fact, I've never felt more convinced about the importance of a low-code platform to enable people from every walk of life to experience that same joy and productivity I felt early in my career, creating apps using clicks and, sometimes, code. This is one of the most important things to remember about low-code: a unique and powerful low-code platform like the Lightning Platform lets you combine the power of both clicks and code to do more than you could do with either one alone.

In 2016, I left Microsoft when I was invited to reimagine the developer experience for Salesforce. I realized that this was a unique opportunity to share my love of low-code with the Salesforce community and to accelerate the pace of innovation on Salesforce by giving developers an entirely new way to build together and deliver continuously.

The DevOps movement has developed throughout our industry over the last 10 years into a rallying point for some of the most revolutionary ideas in business and technology. DevOps has a dual meaning, in that it includes a huge range of technological tools and techniques but also speaks to the importance of bringing disparate groups together. Salesforce was founded on the concept of *Ohana*, or community. Just like Salesforce has grown into one of the most passionate and collaborative communities on the planet, the DevOps movement has also inspired passion and a vision for how working together is integral to helping companies perform at levels never previously imagined.

At Dreamforce 2016, I had the privilege to go on stage to introduce Salesforce DX to the world and to share a vision that unites DevOps with the Lightning Platform for the first time. Shortly after that keynote, an earnest and persistent man started following me around the conference. As I walked to make it to a session, he introduced himself and explained that he'd been working on a similar initiative for his company, had anticipated this announcement, and implored me to let him join the pilot. Recognizing his sincerity, and that he might not leave me alone unless I relented, I invited Andrew Davis and his company, Appirio, to be the first consulting company to join the pilot for Salesforce DX.

I'm so glad I did because the rest is, as they say, history.

This book reflects the dedication and passion that Andrew brings to this topic. And it gathers in one volume all of the core ideas and values that all of us who worked on Salesforce DX have wanted to share but not had the time to write down. In this book you'll see what brought me to Salesforce back in 2016: the power of DevOps and the world's most powerful low-code platform united together. This union is expressed clearly and eloquently in this book.

We're still at the beginning of this journey, both of Salesforce DX and, in a broader sense, of this magical new world that unites the human mind with technology in ways that are both exciting and awesome. DevOps is about working together—about human beings collaborating, working toward a common vision, and using technology to be efficient even at complex activities like building software. As we take these first steps into a new world where the only certainty is change, and where technology increasingly has the ability to determine our future, it is more important than ever that we work together.

This is a technical book. But it's also a human book. It's a book about how to get things done more easily, so we have more time to do what humans do best: to solve problems creatively. It's an honor to introduce this book because I know what's between the covers is the very best of what technology today has to offer: a practical guide to building together on a platform that invites unlimited creativity.

Wade Wegner, SVP Product Management, Salesforce
Redmond, Washington
August 2019

Acknowledgments

It's been a great delight to get to know both the Salesforce community as well as the DevOps community over the last few years. As a lifelong technologist, I've always delighted in the endless puzzle-solving opportunities it presents. But I've been a human even longer than I've been a technologist, and both the Salesforce and DevOps communities are distinctively *human* communities. The degree of openness, collaboration, compassion, and enthusiasm in these communities is inspiring. And when an entire group is inspired, you find what Émile Durkheim called *collective effervescence*, a sense of joy accompanied by a softening of the boundaries between ourselves and others.

That we can be united in a common activity is one of the deepest miracles of being alive. That's also one of the special joys of being part of an organization: that it provides an opportunity for individuals to unite in a shared endeavor. As Peter Drucker said, "The purpose of an organization is to enable ordinary human beings to do extraordinary things." The cloud has enabled larger communities to collaborate in larger endeavors. And DevOps is enabling better coordination and communication in that process. It's no wonder that the Salesforce and DevOps communities are incubating visions for a better world that go far beyond technological improvement.

This book largely captures what I know about this important topic. By sharing my knowledge, I'm also sharing my ignorance, and I welcome any feedback and corrections you have to offer. Every piece of knowledge in this book has come directly or indirectly from others, principally my colleagues at Appirio. I couldn't have hoped for a better place to learn this discipline, and the people who've contributed to my education are too numerous to list.

There are no words to express my gratitude to **my wife, Ashley**, who has been endlessly patient and supportive throughout this learning process. My Sangha jewel, coach, and best friend, she's endured my endless ramblings on this topic and knows far more about both Salesforce and DevOps than she ever wanted to. **My parents and step-parents** lovingly built the foundations for me to be healthy and free and supported me unfailingly even when my decisions led me far away from them physically and culturally. And the **Kadampa community** provided the ultimate opportunity to learn humility, peace, and the joy of living a meaningful life.

ACKNOWLEDGMENTS

From **Appirio** I want to thank the Appirio DX team: **Saurabh Deep**, **Abhishek Saxena**, **Ashna Malhotra**, **Bryan Leboff**, **Rahul Agrawal**, **Katie Brown**, **Kapil Nainani**, **Sahil Batra**, and **Durgesh Dhoot**. You all believed in this vision and did the real work to make the project a reality. To **Yoni Barkan**, **Roarke Lynch**, **Rebecca Bradley**, **Halie Vining**, **Craige Ruffin**, **Erik Golden**, and **Katie Boehner**—you all are the real deal; I'm sorry we weren't able to work together longer. I'm grateful to my other mentors and teachers at Appirio, especially to **Geoff Escandon** who brought the *State of DevOps Report* to my attention and challenged the early work I was doing saying "I don't know what this is, but it's definitely not DevOps." I hope I'm getting closer.

It was **Glenn Weinstein**, **Chris Barbin**, and **Erik Duffield** at Appirio who championed this project at the highest levels and who fostered a performance-oriented culture in the company from the beginning. My coworkers at **Oath** also deserve special recognition for introducing me to continuous delivery. In particular, **Matt Hauer** dissuaded me from leading the team into branching hell and never let me ignore a broken build. **David Meyer** first challenged me to deliver "CI for the masses," a project I'm still working on. **Matt Henwood** challenged me to "let my creative juices flow" and ran interference for me as this project got off the ground. **Bob Larson** asked for some short-term assistance to set up CI/CD for a big customer; two years and thousands of deployments worth of short-term assistance gave me the confidence to write this book. I'm particularly grateful to my partners in that endeavor, **Alex Spears** (who endured the misery of being mentored by me), **Sreenath Gopal**, and **Raji Matthew**. Special mention is also due to **Lex Williams**, **Randy Wandell**, **Joe Castro**, **Andres Gluecksmann**, **Chris Bruzzi**, **Michael Press**, **Svatka Simpson**, **Neale Wooten**, **Jitendra Kothari**, **Prakash Gyamlani**, **Tommy Noe**, **Tommy Muse**, **James Wasilewski**, **Norman Krishna**, **Josh Davis**, and everyone else who supported our DevOps initiatives in a hundred ways.

It's a unique honor to work with **John M. Daniel** as the technical reviewer for this book. To have this work reviewed by a mind as sharp and experienced as his gives me far greater confidence that I'm not making this stuff up. And I'm grateful for the team at **Apress**, especially **Susan McDermott**, **Rita Fernando**, and **Laura Berendson** for affording this opportunity and for doing the hard work of bringing a book like this into existence.

Finally, to my new colleagues at **Copado**, especially **David Brooks**, **Andrew Leigh**, **Ted Elliott**, and **Federico Larsen**, the fun's just getting started. I look forward to working with you to help thousands of organizations master Salesforce DevOps.

CHAPTER 1

Introduction

This book provides a practical guide to bringing DevOps principles to Salesforce development. For those whose careers are rooted in the Salesforce world, this guide will help you adopt practices that have been proven to make life easier and teams more effective. For those who specialize in DevOps or other technologies and are tasked with adopting or supporting a Salesforce implementation, this book will allow you to translate familiar concepts into the unique language and practices of Salesforce. And for those who are already under way with optimizing your Salesforce development process, I hope that this book provides inspiration to go further, think deeper, and continue to embody excellent practices on an exceptional platform.

Why Salesforce?

Over the past 20 years, Salesforce has become the fastest growing enterprise software platform and a market leader in Sales, Service, Marketing, Integration, and custom application development among other areas.[1] Although there are many reasons why a company might adopt or consider using Salesforce, the overriding value proposition is that Salesforce provides tons of capabilities out of the box, releases new capabilities at an ambitious pace, and allows for virtually endless customization and innovation. Unlike with traditional platforms, there's no need to manage infrastructure for computing, data, network, or security and no need to invest in generic system administration that adds no value for the organization. Add to this the accessible and supportive community and learning culture based around Salesforce's Trailhead, which enables rapid onboarding and skill development, and it's easy to see the attraction of this platform.

---

[1] https://s1.q4cdn.com/454432842/files/doc_financials/2018/Salesforce-FY18-Annual-Report.pdf

© Andrew Davis 2019
A. Davis, *Mastering Salesforce DevOps*, https://doi.org/10.1007/978-1-4842-5473-8_1

Companies who adopt Salesforce do so because they don't want to manage servers, networking infrastructure, security, and the countless other aspects of application development that don't directly bring business value. When an enterprise company takes an interest in automating a new part of their workflow or storing data, they have no interest in provisioning servers or containers, let alone implementing ongoing monitoring, data backup, failover redundancy, and so forth. What they're interested in is business value. And what Salesforce delivers is the opportunity to create and deploy business value with the minimum necessary overhead. In exchange for a relatively modest subscription price, Salesforce takes care of almost every aspect of the infrastructure needed to run an application. At the same time, they have continued to expand and innovate to make the process of developing functionality easier across a broadening range of applications.

Salesforce began in 1998 with the aspirational goal to create a SaaS customer relationship management (CRM) system that was "as simple as Amazon."[2] Since then, they've become the fastest growing enterprise software company ever to reach $10 billion. And they lead the market for CRM, service automation, marketing automation, and integration. They've been recognized year after year by *Forbes* as the world's most innovative company and won their Innovator of the Decade award. *Fortune* magazine also ranked them the #1 best place to work.[3]

Salesforce's mantra throughout the 2000s was "Clicks not Code," and their logo was the "No Software" image which became embodied as SaaSy, Salesforce's first mascot. You could be a "declarative" developer using "clicks" alone and build a data model, business process automation, and user interface using drag-and-drop interfaces. This opened the door to an entire new job specialization—Salesforce Admins and "App Builders," citizen developers who were empowered to directly customize the platform to meet their company's needs.

As Salesforce grew, they recognized the need to enable custom coding on their platform and launched Apex triggers, followed by Apex classes, and Visualforce in 2008. Admins continued to configure rich business capabilities, while low-code developers and professional developers were empowered to create customizations beyond the scope of what could be built declaratively. Initially, the code developed on Salesforce was rudimentary: a few hundred lines here and there to accommodate unusual

---

[2]Marc Benioff, *Behind the Cloud* (Wiley-Blackwell, 2009).

[3]https://s1.q4cdn.com/454432842/files/doc_financials/2018/Salesforce-FY18-Annual-Report.pdf

calculations and data processing. But gradually, companies began to accumulate tens of thousands of lines of custom code, especially as legacy applications were migrated from other systems. Needless to say, the "No Software" motto no longer strictly applies.

In the decade since the launch of Apex, 150,000 companies have adopted Salesforce and moved a staggering number of legacy systems onto Salesforce. Salesforce now processes billions of transactions per day. Many of these transactions are part of the core CRM and customer service applications, but a huge number relate to custom applications, making Salesforce one of the largest Platform as a Service (PaaS) providers.

What Is Salesforce DX?

Salesforce's ease of customization has led to an unusual challenge. Whereas developers in most languages have been employing methods such as continuous delivery for a decade or two, most Salesforce customers have been slow to adopt such methods. There are two reasons for this: the Salesforce platform itself and the developers managing it.

First of all, the Salesforce platform behaves very differently from a standard server or custom application. You can't build a local instance of Salesforce on a developer's laptop, for example. Instead, Salesforce runs centrally "in the cloud," and you deploy functionality by updating a specific Salesforce instance. There are limits to what types of changes can be deployed, and tracking changes has been challenging, meaning that developers often needed to log in to a target org and make customizations manually to complete a deployment.

The other reason the Salesforce world has been slow to adopt practices such as continuous delivery is that Salesforce development is a specialized skill requiring declarative/admin skills, with programmatic/coding skills being a nice-to-have addition in many cases. Because most Salesforce developers don't do custom development on other platforms, this led to a lack of cross-pollination between ideas that were common in the Java, JavaScript, .NET, and Ruby worlds. Even when traditional developers were transplanted into a Salesforce project and reskilled to work on Apex or Lightning, they found that their customary build, test, and deploy tools were largely useless in the new Salesforce world. Instead they were provided with "change sets," an Ant Migration Tool, and very few examples of how one might build a comprehensive CI/CD pipeline for this platform. The brave few ventured into configuring complex Ant "targets" using XML and triggering them using Jenkins. But by and large, teams cobbled together a mix of manual steps and light automation, tackling deployments one at a time, and as infrequently as they could get away with.

The challenge of managing Salesforce deployments was one factor that led Salesforce to earn a very dubious accolade. In the 2017 Stack Overflow international developer survey, Salesforce tied with SharePoint as the "most dreaded platform to develop on."[4] Ouch. Needless to say, that is not one of the accomplishments Salesforce is most proud of.

When companies were using Salesforce solely for sales force automation, it could be a "shadow IT" product managed by the Sales Operations teams. But as its capabilities and adoption expanded beyond CRM, Salesforce has moved to being a core part of companies' IT infrastructure. An increasing number of CIOs and IT Directors recognized the centrality of Salesforce to their businesses and the growing complexity of their Salesforce implementations. Salesforce was increasingly fielding challenging questions in terms of how companies could adopt DevOps best practices, such as maintaining and deploying all configuration from source control.

These demands eventually led Salesforce to establish an internal tiger team known as "Salesforce DX," dedicated to improving the Salesforce Developer eXperience. The team was assembled in 2016, with several seasoned groups working in parallel on improving different aspects of the developer experience. At Dreamforce 2017, Salesforce DX went live.[5]

Prior to Salesforce DX, the only way to develop on Salesforce was org-based development, where a Salesforce org itself is the source of truth. Even if teams managed to use version control and automated deployments to update their testing and production orgs, version control necessarily lagged behind the development org. This meant that changes to the development org were often never tracked in version control, and that it was entirely possible to make changes in the development org that were difficult or impossible to track and deploy systematically. Since the org was the source of truth, anyone wanting to see the latest, integrated version of a component had to check the org, since version control could always be lagging behind.

Org-based development meant that even the most sophisticated development teams were trapped in a conundrum: they could provide each developer with their own separate org, or they could have all developers work in a single org. Separate orgs meant

---

[4]2017 Stack Overflow Developer Survey, https://insights.stackoverflow.com/survey/ 2017#technology-most-loved-dreaded-and-wanted-platforms
[5]www.salesforce.com/video/317311/

it was easy for developers to isolate their changes from the work of others, but orgs quickly got out of sync. Sharing a single org provides continuous integration (developers' work is always integrated in a single org), but it is extremely challenging to track and deploy one's own changes in isolation from the rest of the team. Vendors such as Flosum and AutoRABIT offer sophisticated synchronization tools, but the whole system is fundamentally flawed.

The most notable innovation to launch with Salesforce DX is a new type of Salesforce org called a scratch org. For the first time, scratch orgs allow a Salesforce environment to be created entirely from version control. This means that for the first time, version control can be the source of truth, rather than always lagging behind the state of development orgs. Developers can create private development environments at will, and those environments can be quickly updated from version control as other members of the team integrate their own changes.

Salesforce DX thus finally allows for source-driven development. Source-driven development in turn opens the door to adopting most of the other technological and cultural processes known broadly as DevOps. And DevOps has been shown to be a massive contributor to innovation, effectiveness, and corporate success.

What Is DevOps?

This book represents a convergence of two major movements within the IT world: the movement to Software/Platform as a Service (SaaS/PaaS) and the DevOps movement. The goal of SaaS and PaaS is to provide a scalable, global, high-performing foundation for companies to invest in their core competencies rather than having to maintain their own infrastructure. In addition, centralized SaaS applications provide powerful capabilities without introducing software upgrades, version incompatibilities, and the other headaches associated with maintaining your own software.

Salesforce provides SaaS solutions for customer relationship management (CRM), sales force automation (SFA), customer service, and more, while also offering a PaaS platform for deploying custom code (Heroku and the Lightning Platform). Salesforce DX now provides the raw capabilities to enable a DevOps workflow on Salesforce. The goal of this book is to explain how you can build a powerful and comprehensive DevOps workflow for Salesforce. The power of this can't be overstated: you can finally deploy the world's most innovative platform using the world's most effective and efficient techniques.

Within the literature and tooling providers for DevOps, there is a tremendous focus on enabling Infrastructure as a Service (IaaS) as an evolution away from managing your own servers. "DevOps solution providers" include a massive array of IaaS providers (such as AWS, Google Cloud, and Azure), as well as tools for managing software packages, database configurations, application monitoring, and so on. Almost every "DevOps tool" provider is addressing a need in the IaaS space so that organizations with legacy applications and infrastructure can begin to manage those in an efficient and orderly way.

It's interesting to note that almost all of these "DevOps tools" are helping to solve problems that simply do not exist for Salesforce users. Simply moving to Salesforce solves most every problem with infrastructure, security, monitoring, databases, performance, UI, and more. One reason Salesforce users have been so slow to adopt DevOps practices is that most of them are simply not needed. Sort of.

The reality is that functionality developed on Salesforce simply exists at a higher level: application configuration instead of infrastructure provisioning. You basically never have to worry about Oracle database patches or that Salesforce will lose your data; but that doesn't solve the problem of how to ensure that your database fields are consistent across all of your Salesforce instances. The exact same principles championed across the DevOps community are entirely applicable in the Salesforce world, they simply need to be adjusted to the particulars of the Salesforce platform.

DevOps can be understood as bringing together the practices of continuous delivery (and all that entails, such as version control) with principles of lean software engineering and an inclusive focus spanning from development to operations. DevOps builds on principles that have evolved over decades in manufacturing and software engineering and brings them together under a surprisingly catchy moniker.

Version control, continuous integration, continuous delivery, DevOps—what's that all mean? Version control is a mechanism to track and merge changes smoothly. Continuous integration means that teams should develop their work on a common master branch, minimize branching, and run automated tests after every change to the master branch. Continuous delivery means that all the configuration needed to recreate your application is stored and deployed from version control in an automated way. And DevOps means that both developers (who create new functionality) and operators/admins (who maintain production systems) should work together to optimize the flow of valuable work to end users, build software with monitoring in mind, and use the same mechanisms (such as version control) to both maintain and improve applications.

DevOps has been summarized by Jonathan Smart as "Better value, faster, safer, happier." "Better" implies continuous improvement, always striving to improve the quality of not only our work but also our processes. "Value" means using agile development and design thinking to address and adapt to the needs of end users. "Faster" means using techniques such as continuous delivery to release more quickly. "Safer" means integrating automated quality and security scanning into the development workflow. And "happier" refers to continuously improving both the development experience and the customer experience of users.

It's worth noting that the "DX" in Salesforce DX stands for "Developer Experience." The implication is that Salesforce is investing in providing a better experience for those developing on its platform, not just for its end users. Although the Admin/App Builder experience for Salesforce has always been very good, professional developers have historically been an afterthought. As a developer who moved onto the Salesforce platform, I found it confusing and frustrating that version control was not a common practice, and that Salesforce lacked sophisticated tools such as autoformatting and ESLint that make it easier to write good code in JavaScript.

In *The Phoenix Project*[6] and *The DevOps Handbook*,[7] Gene Kim popularized the idea that there are "three ways of work" or three movements that summarize DevOps. They are continuous delivery, the "left-to-right" movement of features and fixes from development into production; continuous feedback, the "right-to-left" movement of feedback from testers and production to developers; and continuous improvement, the ambition to always improve the "system of work" that is used to deliver the work itself.

Traditionally, software development was depicted as a linear process similar to an assembly line. But the DevOps community often uses variations on a circle or infinity loop as shown in Figure 1-1 to indicate that software development must be iterative and ongoing. Each stage in the development lifecycle flows into the next in an ongoing pattern. By spanning the entire lifecycle from planning and development to operation in production, DevOps promotes collaboration across teams to maximize the entire value chain or flow of valuable work to end users.

---

[6]Gene Kim, Kevin Behr, and George Spafford, *The Phoenix Project* (IT Revolution Press, 2013).
[7]Gene Kim, Patrick Debois, John Willis, and Jez Humble, *The DevOps Handbook* (IT Revolution Press, 2016).

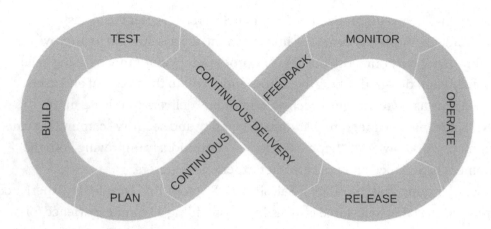

Figure 1-1. *A DevOps infinity loop*

The Research on DevOps

Since 2012, Puppet Labs has produced an annual survey and report entitled the "State of DevOps Report." That report has become increasingly methodical and influential, especially as Puppet Labs was joined by DevOps Research and Assessment (DORA) group. In 2018, the cumulative research from this report was published as the book *Accelerate* by Nicole Forsgren, Gene Kim, and Jez Humble (co-leaders of DORA).[8] In that book (as well as in the annual "State of DevOps" Reports), they provide scientific verification of long-held convictions that adopting DevOps practices predicts software delivery performance, positive organizational culture, and organizational performance (both financial and nonfinancial).

Accelerate lays out the research that use of continuous delivery (version control, CI/CD, etc.) leads to increased software delivery performance, which in turn improves corporate performance. High-performing teams are able to spend 66% more of their time doing new (constructive) work and 38% less time on issue resolution and unplanned work compared to low-performing teams. In addition, teams with high Software Development Performance (SDP) exceeded those with low SDP with

- 46 times more frequent code deployments

- 2,555 times shorter lead time from commit to deploy

- 7 times lower change failure rate (1/7 as likely for a change to fail)

- 2,604 times faster mean time to recover from downtime

---

[8]IT Revolution Press, 2018.

Software Delivery Performance also predicts corporate performance. High software delivery performers are twice as likely to exceed their commercial goals (profitability, market share, and productivity) and their noncommercial goals (quantity of goods and services, operating efficiency, customer satisfaction, quality of products or services, and achieving organization or mission goals).

Another long-standing belief in the DevOps community is that positive organizational culture leads to great results for the company. Salesforce themself has emphasized such a positive organizational culture from its outset, and many organizations in the Salesforce ecosystem such as Appirio also embody principles such as openness and philanthropy. The *State of DevOps Report* confirms the importance of culture for organizational performance. That same survey confirms that the use of continuous delivery itself predicts a positive organizational culture, high job satisfaction, high delivery performance, and employee engagement. The use of continuous delivery (version control, CI/CD, etc.) also leads to less rework, less deployment pain, and thus less burnout.

About This Book

This book is divided into four parts. **Part 1: Foundations**, provides an introduction to Salesforce and to DevOps concepts. Those new to Salesforce will find Chapter 2: Salesforce to be a helpful overview of the Salesforce platform, including core concepts and challenges that might not be obvious at first.

Those who are new to DevOps will find Chapter 3: DevOps to be a concise summary of the latest best practices and research on this topic. There is nothing in that Chapter that will be new or groundbreaking for those who are very familiar with DevOps, although it may provide a helpful recap and summary. The reason for providing a comprehensive overview of DevOps is to provide a single reference for people in the Salesforce world who may be unfamiliar with these practices. Books such as *Continuous Delivery* by Jez Humble and David Farley[9] will allow readers to go much deeper into these concepts.

The last three parts of the book cover the Salesforce development lifecycle, all summarized into three stages: development, delivery, and operations. These three stages are common to all software development, and are in fact common to manufacturing

---

[9]Jez Humble and David Farley, *Continuous Delivery: Reliable Software Releases Through Build, Test, and Deployment Automation* (Addison-Wesley Professional, 2011).

and product development in general. Things are made, then they're shipped, and finally they're used. Along the way, they're generally *bought* as well, which implies that what is being created has value.

The only reason things are made is in the hope that they will bring greater benefit than they cost to make or buy. The difference between the benefit something brings and the cost of making it is known as value added. Lean software development, and lean practices in general, talk extensively about value creation, value streams, and value-added steps, in contrast to what is known as waste. The goal of DevOps is to reduce waste, and to enable teams to deliver value as effectively as possible.

Thus when we talk about development, delivery, and operations, we are primarily talking about the stages in which value is created (in the form of new software functionality), delivered (including testing and deployment), and realized or experienced by end users. **Part 2: Salesforce Dev** provides a concise overview of how to maximize the ease of developing on Salesforce and the quality of the work. Of particular interest is how to develop so that the subsequent testing, deployments, and operations can be as successful as possible. The very definition of DevOps implies that developers keep operation in mind. That means that things are developed so they can be delivered as quickly as possible and operated successfully, and that defects can be discovered and features improved in the most efficient way.

Part 3: Innovation Delivery covers the stages in which Salesforce DX really shines. Software deployments in general are painful; and Salesforce deployments have been notoriously painful. The pain of deployments drives people to do them as infrequently as possible. This means that in addition to being delayed to once a week or once a month (or less), deployments are done in large batches. A fundamental concept in lean software development is to develop and deploy in small batches. This enables the highest value features or fixes to be deployed as soon as possible, reduces the risk and impact of each deployment, and opens the door to fast feedback.

Deployments aren't just about moving functionality into production; moving functionality into testing environments also requires deployments. So delays in deployment imply delays in testing. Delaying the start of testing doesn't always mean that go-live can be delayed, so the QA and testing process in Salesforce projects is often squeezed. The high pressure to test quickly to avoid further delays in feature delivery has meant that the entire testing ecosystem in Salesforce is generally underdeveloped, with an overemphasis on repetitive manual testing. Part 3: Innovation Delivery provides an overview of how to deploy, test, and release Salesforce features, including both older technologies and the newer capabilities such as unlocked packages that Salesforce DX provides.

Part 4: Salesforce Ops (Administration) is on operations, or how Salesforce capabilities are used in production. As many people have commented, software spends most of its life in production, so it makes sense to consider that phase carefully, including how to measure and detect issues as quickly as possible. On many platforms, operations is equivalent to administration. But in the Salesforce world, the term "Admin" is overloaded to mean both "keeping the lights on" and building new capabilities declaratively. Salesforce's "Awesome Admins" are thus responsible for the majority of development on the platform, in the form of adding objects and fields to the database, modifying business logic declaratively, and changing the UI through layouts. The tension between developers and operations in Salesforce is ironically the opposite of how it is on most platforms. On most platforms, it is the admins who are screaming to keep the system stable and running, while developers are clamoring to release new capabilities. In Salesforce, however, it is admins who are more likely to make changes directly in production at the behest of users and to be reluctant to follow the disciplined deployment processes that developers are forced to adhere to. Locking admins out of production (at least in the sense of preventing them from changing the database, business logic, or UI) is actually a requirement for realizing the goals of DevOps. But for this to be palatable, there has to be a smooth and admin-friendly process in place whereby small declarative changes can easily be made, committed, and deployed to production. Thus the final section speaks to how admins can participate in the DevOps process.

For some companies who have adopted continuous delivery for Salesforce, the first skill new Salesforce admins are taught is how to use Git, so that they can make their changes in a development environment, but track and deploy them by themselves. And for those who are skeptical whether their admins will ever adopt Git, we'll discuss the variety of options available to help Admins keep their orgs stable while still churning out business value at the speed of clicks.

Background

This book arose out of a 4-year focus on the Salesforce development lifecycle, especially Salesforce DX, while working at Appirio. Appirio is a consulting company focused exclusively on cloud technologies, primarily Salesforce. From the beginning, the company has emphasized effective development processes and worked hard to bring customers the most value in the shortest amount of time. I joined Appirio in 2014 as a technical consultant and very soon began evangelizing the use of version control and continuous integration for Salesforce. At the time those practices were quite rare on Salesforce projects. But my colleagues and mentors at Appirio regularly encouraged me that this was indeed a critical need across most projects. My focus became how to adapt these practices to the peculiarities of Salesforce and to help others do the same.

In 2017, after 2 years of working on side projects related to code quality and development automation, Appirio agreed to establish an internal team known as Appirio DX to focus on tooling, training, and evangelism to bring DevOps principles to all of our projects. In 2018 we released Appirio DX as a commercial tool that could be used by anyone to help ease the Salesforce development process. In 2019 I joined Copado, one of the leading DevOps tool providers for Salesforce, to work on the next generation of their platform.

I've been inspired by Appirio and Copado's commitment to empowering developers and admins, and am grateful for their providing an environment in which I could learn so much and be free to chase the wild but important idea that DevOps is critical to delivering innovation while building and maintaining trust.

PART I

Foundations

Before getting into the details of how to implement DevOps on the Salesforce platform, it's important to establish some foundations. What is Salesforce, and how is it different from other kinds of application or platform? And what do we mean when we talk about DevOps?

CHAPTER 2

Salesforce

It's important to clarify what we mean by "Salesforce" in this book, since the company has grown by acquisition, and the techniques shared in this book do not apply to all of the products that now fall under the Salesforce brand.

What makes Salesforce different? How is DevOps done in the Salesforce world? What is Salesforce DX? And how does it facilitate DevOps on Salesforce?

"Salesforce" vs. Salesforce

Salesforce is a vast and growing company with a vast and growing suite of products. It's a challenge even to keep up with the names of the various products that Salesforce releases or attains through acquisition.

The focus of this book is on what's known internally at Salesforce as "Salesforce Core." Salesforce Core consists of Sales Cloud (the core CRM application), as well as Service Cloud (for customer support), Community Cloud (to create customer-facing web applications), and the Lightning Platform (previously known as `Force.com`). The first three of these constitute the SaaS part of Salesforce, while the Lightning Platform constitutes the PaaS component. All of these components of Salesforce Core work together seamlessly.

In the architecture of Salesforce, "Salesforce Core" is a massive, multi-gigabyte JAR file that is deployed across data centers and "Pods" around the world to allow secure multitenant access to customers via the Internet.

© Andrew Davis 2019
A. Davis, *Mastering Salesforce DevOps*, https://doi.org/10.1007/978-1-4842-5473-8_2

The "markitecture" of Salesforce (how Salesforce is presented externally by their marketing department) depicts a vast and cohesive range of other products such as Tableau, Heroku, Marketing Cloud, and Commerce Cloud, but these are all truly separate products, generally the result of acquisitions. Sharing data or functionality between these products and Salesforce Core requires some type of integration.

Although Salesforce is working hard to integrate these products in a way that is transparent to customers, these other products are developed and deployed in fundamentally different ways. For example, the methods of developing and deploying customizations to Marketing Cloud or Commerce Cloud are entirely different from the way customizations are developed and deployed to Salesforce Core.

Therefore, throughout this book, whenever we refer to "Salesforce," we are referring either to the company itself or to this Core platform, and not to any of these other products.

How Is Salesforce Different?

As mentioned earlier, Salesforce provides both SaaS (Software as a Service) and a PaaS (Platform as a Service). By contrast, much of the focus elsewhere in the DevOps world is in moving from on-premise infrastructure to using IaaS (Infrastructure as a Service). Figure 2-1 shows an illustration of the differences between these four modes and how they represent progressive simplifications of what companies themselves have to manage.

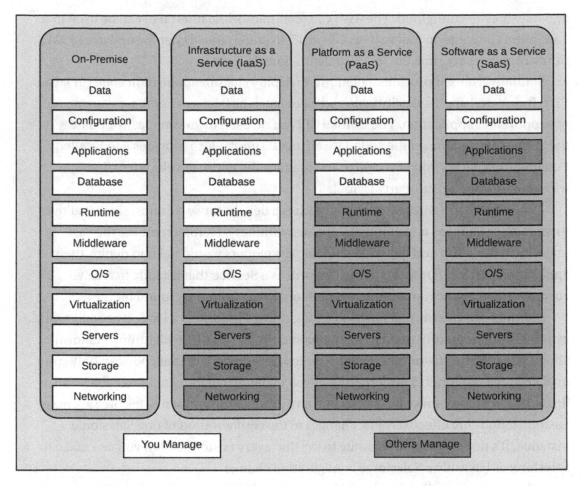

Figure 2-1. *On-premise systems require you to manage all of the resources yourself. IaaS, PaaS, and SaaS delegate progressively*

Managing the Salesforce development lifecycle requires a unique skillset and approach compared to most other platforms. You can say that the DevOps movement was jointly realized by both developers (working in traditional languages such as Java) and system admins or operators (working on traditional infrastructure such as servers and databases). There are thus a vast range of well-established tools and techniques in the DevOps world for developing and deploying code and for managing and updating infrastructure. Unfortunately, almost none of them can directly be used for Salesforce.

To illustrate this, let's look at how teams would manage infrastructure using AWS or deploy an application onto Heroku (a PaaS product also owned by Salesforce). Every aspect of AWS infrastructure can be represented using JSON configuration. JSON can be used to define which AWS services are used, which data centers they are running in, and how they're configured. The AWS CLI (command-line interface) can be used in a continuous integration tool such as GitLab CI to automatically deploy updates to AWS infrastructure every time the JSON configuration changes.

Similarly, Heroku provides a platform to deploy custom application code (in Java, PHP, Ruby, etc.) and to specify which services (such as Postgres databases) are needed to support that application. The Heroku CLI can be used to automatically update the application whenever the codebase changes. Heroku also provides a tool called Pipelines that allows you to visualize and manage the entire development lifecycle without requiring a third-party CI tool.

AWS's "infrastructure as code" approach is a delight for sysadmins, since it allows them to track changes and automate updates. Similarly, Heroku removes the vast majority of the setup and dependencies that developers would need to deploy their applications. Heroku provides a true Platform as a Service that is ready to receive custom-coded applications built in a traditional way: from the ground up.

Although we can say that Salesforce's Lightning Platform is a PaaS, it actually works extremely different from true PaaS systems such as Heroku. The Lightning Platform allows you to write custom server-side or client-side code, but that code can only run on Salesforce. Although Salesforce allows you to define custom database tables and fields, that schema cannot be loaded into any database other than Salesforce's. These customizations are effectively just changes to the configuration of one Salesforce instance. It's therefore more accurate to say that every customization you can make to Salesforce is basically a Salesforce configuration change.

Salesforce is actually just a big application that happens to allow for infinite customization. But this means that the tools used for managing other IaaS and PaaS products cannot be used to customize Salesforce. Fortunately, however, the release of Salesforce DX means that the *techniques and principles* used with other technologies can now be ported over to Salesforce. That is the focus of this book.

DevOps in the Salesforce World

Moving from on-premise CRM software to Salesforce removes the need for servers and manual software upgrades. Consolidating customer support and online community management onto the CRM platform removes the need to integrate sales, support, and community applications. Migrating legacy applications onto the Salesforce platform allows those applications to share data and processes with the rest of the business.

Because moving to the cloud dramatically simplifies many of the challenges in delivering IT functionality, many Salesforce customers have been able to innovate quickly without having DevOps practices in place. But even without the hassle of managing servers and building software from scratch, the inevitable growth of complexity eventually causes companies to struggle with issues like orgs getting out of sync and delays in deploying functionality.

Salesforce solves so many IT headaches, it's almost easy to overlook the fact that it's created some new ones.

Salesforce has unleashed the ability for companies to focus on their core competencies, instead of struggling to provide basic IT services. Salesforce admins and developers are empowered to spend their time directly creating business value. But with multiple Salesforce admins and developers working at companies year after year, more and more Salesforce customers are finding themselves drowning in all of that "business value."

If you have tens of thousands of components, each providing business value, but no systematic way of tracking, managing, or deploying them, you now have a new form of business pain and chaos. Far too much of a good thing.

What Is Salesforce DX?

Salesforce DX is an initiative begun by Salesforce in 2016 and that launched publicly at Dreamforce 2017. "DX" here stands for Developer eXperience. The goal of the initiative is to reenvision the developer experience on Salesforce with a focus on how to empower the Salesforce development community with the tools and processes needed to develop safely and effectively.

Salesforce DX is a very broad initiative, including several teams at Salesforce focused on environment management, custom coding, developer tooling, APIs, and more. Although the Salesforce DX teams tackle very diverse needs, their main focus (at least initially) is to improve the developer tooling and development lifecycle.

The tools and capabilities included in Salesforce DX are made available for free to all Salesforce customers. In that sense, Salesforce DX is an important complement to Trailhead, Salesforce's free, self-paced, gamified, interactive learning platform. Trailhead is also a major investment for the corporation. Together these are intended to support the growth of skilled Salesforce professionals and to make it easier for those workers to build and innovate on the platform. These multiyear strategic initiatives help ensure that talent shortages and worker inefficiency will not be the limiting factor on the company's aggressive 30% annual growth.

What Are the Elements of Salesforce DX?

Salesforce DX is a new way of developing and collaborating on Salesforce. At its heart are two main concepts:

- Version control is the source of truth for each project. Development is done principally in scratch orgs (temporary Salesforce environments created from version control) as opposed to Developer sandboxes. Scratch orgs are discussed more in Chapter 6: Environment Management.

- Code and metadata should be subdivided into packages representing discrete functionality. This reduces complexity and allows packages to be developed and deployed independently of one another. unlocked packages are discussed more in Chapter 9: Deploying. In addition, Salesforce DX includes new developer tools: the Salesforce CLI and a set of extensions for the Visual Studio Code IDE. The Salesforce CLI replaces an earlier set of Ant-based tools called the Ant Migration Tool, while the VS Code extensions replace the original Force.com IDE built on Eclipse. Salesforce's choice to build on Visual Studio Code was prescient, since that free tool has come to dominate the code editor marketplace.

All of these capabilities and tools are built on top of Salesforce's existing APIs such as the Metadata API, and so continuing to improve those APIs has also been the responsibility of the DX team. A persistent challenge for teams hoping to automate their development lifecycle has been that some configuration settings can't be deployed automatically. Meanwhile, the platform continues to expand its capabilities. Many Einstein and Community capabilities were not initially supported by the APIs. A major victory for the DX team was enforcing automated processes behind the scenes to ensure that all new features on the platform are API accessible when they are released.

In addition, the DX teams have done a significant amount of developer outreach and evangelism to help customers understand how to take advantage of these capabilities. It's my hope that this book can also be of benefit in this effort.

The Dev Hub

Some aspects of Salesforce DX are installed on a developer's local machine or CI runner, while other aspects are capabilities built on top of Salesforce itself. The capabilities built into Salesforce include the ability to create new, ephemeral Salesforce orgs called scratch orgs and also to create and publish versions of unlocked packages. To make use of these, a development team needs to designate a production Salesforce org to be a Dev Hub and enable the "Dev Hub" setting in that org.

Enabling Dev Hub has no risk or side effects to the org. And since scratch orgs created from that org carry no data or metadata, giving developers access to a Dev Hub does not constitute a security risk. There is even a free license type called "Free Limited Access License" that can be enabled in a production org to allow developers or consultants to use a Dev Hub even if they wouldn't otherwise have a user license in that org. This license type does not expose any data or metadata in the production org; it just gives access to use the Dev Hub functionality.

Each developer also needs appropriate permissions on that Dev Hub (see "Permissions Needed to Use the Dev Hub" in Chapter 6: Environment Management). For training purposes, Developer Edition orgs, including those created in Trailhead, can be used as Dev Hubs, although their limits are too restrictive for production use.

Scratch Orgs

As mentioned, scratch orgs are temporary, disposable environments similar to virtual machines. They are populated with code and metadata stored in version control and can be used to support development, testing, and continuous integration. These orgs live for only 7 days by default, although they can be configured to live up to 30 days. Scratch orgs are used for source-driven development, while sandboxes remain useful as long-running test environments. Packages and metadata are developed in scratch orgs and can be deployed to sandboxes and production using CI/CD.

Second-Generation Packaging

One of the most important characteristics of our bodies is the existence of many internal organs that each perform specialized functions while also working together as a whole. Well-organized software follows a similar pattern, known as modular architecture. The division of software into independent modules is a long-standing best practice that makes software easier to understand, maintain, and update.

Modular architecture in software exists at many levels, such as methods, classes, files, and packages. Each of these represents a layer of abstraction that brings similar benefits. The general idea is that the details of what is *inside* the module should not concern other parts of the system *outside* the module. What is of concern is the *interface* between that module and the rest of the system, for example, the input parameters and return values for a method. This allows each module a degree of independence, to be internally changed and refactored, as long as they don't change their interface with the rest of the system. Similarly, when viewed from outside the module, all that matters is its interface. By hiding the underlying details, the whole system becomes easier to understand and work with.

Modules that comprise collections of many files that all perform related functions are called packages. Most if not all high-level software languages support different types of packages such as JavaScript modules, Ruby Gems, or .NET NuGet packages. This type of packaging is enormously helpful for developers since it allows them to build on pre-packaged solutions such as any of the 800,000 JavaScript modules on NPM[1] rather than attempting to recreate such solutions themselves.

Salesforce has long supported the creation and installation of managed and unmanaged packages on its platform. Managed packages are typically used by ISVs to create commercial applications, since they hide their internal IP and prevent most functionality from being modified. Unmanaged packages are often used as a mechanism to share or install groups of related functionality. The AppExchange has been a market-leading business "app store" since its inception,[2] and most of the "apps" available there are in fact managed or unmanaged packages that can be installed in a Salesforce org.

The challenge is that although unmanaged packages can be used to install related functionality, the metadata within that package does not remain part of that package. The package exists like a cardboard shipping container that does not perform any useful function once it has been delivered and unpacked.

The challenge with managed packages is that the method for creating and updating them is very challenging, involving the use of a separate Developer Edition org, packaging orgs, namespaces, and so on. For these reasons, few enterprises build or use managed packages to migrate functionality between their environments.

The consequence is that although most Salesforce orgs make use of commercial managed packages to extend their org's functionality, homegrown customizations to

---

orgs are almost never organized into packages. It's common for large enterprises to have tens of thousands of unpackaged pieces of metadata (classes, objects, fields, Flows, etc.) that exist together as an undifferentiated collection.

Some organizations have disciplined themselves to use pseudo-namespace prefixes to distinguish related pieces of functionality, but for the most part it is not easy to see which pieces of metadata are closely related to one another without taking time to inspect their contents.

To address these problems, Salesforce DX introduces two types of second-generation packages: unlocked packages and second-generation managed packages. The former is mostly for use by enterprises, since it does not hide its contents or prevent them from being modified after they've been installed. The latter is a more flexible successor to managed packages, designed for ISVs to be able to deploy and update functionality while still retaining control over most of the contents of those packages.

This book is mostly oriented toward helping enterprises to manage their customizations, and so we discuss unlocked packages at great length. Fortunately, the methods for creating and deploying unlocked packages and second-generation managed packages are almost identical so most of the content in this book is relevant to second-generation managed packages as well.

Metadata API vs. SFDX Source Formats

Another important innovation in Salesforce DX was recognizing that the file format made available by the Metadata API was not conducive to team development in version control. It's common for standard Salesforce objects like the Account object to be used by many applications and extensively customized. Those objects are represented by the Metadata API as XML files that can grow to tens or hundreds of thousands of lines long. Naturally, developers working collaboratively on these objects frequently encounter merge conflicts, issues with sorting tags, and invalid XML.

Salesforce DX brought a new project structure and source file format. Salesforce DX source format uses different file extensions and folder structure compared to the Metadata API format that Salesforce developers are accustomed to. Salesforce DX also provides a new source shape that breaks down large files to make them easier to manage with a version control system. Listing 2-1 shows the traditional Metadata API file structure, while Listing 2-2 shows the equivalent files converted into the "source" format. Note that -meta.xml is used as the file suffix for XML files, and the complex .object files have been decomposed into their subcomponents.

Listing 2-1. The traditional "Metadata API" structure of Salesforce files

```
src
├── applications
│   └── DreamHouse.app
├── layouts
│   ├── Broker__c-Broker Layout.layout
│   └── Property__c-Property Layout.layout
├── objects
│   ├── Bot_Command__c.object
│   ├── Broker__c.object
│   ├── Property_Favorite__c.object
│   └── Property__c.object
└── package.xml
```

Listing 2-2. The new "Source" structure of Salesforce files

```
force-org
└── main
    └── default
        ├── applications
        │   └── DreamHouse.app-meta.xml
        ├── layouts
        │   ├── Broker__c-Broker Layout.layout-meta.xml
        │   └── Property__c-Property Layout.layout-meta.xml
        └── objects
            └── Broker__c
                ├── Broker__c.object-meta.xml
                ├── compactLayouts
                │   └── Broker_Compact.compactLayout-meta.xml
                ├── fields
                │   ├── Email__c.field-meta.xml
                │   ├── Mobile_Phone__c.field-meta.xml
                │   └── Title__c.field-meta.xml
                └── listViews
                    └── All.listView-meta.xml
```

You can read in detail about this format in the Salesforce DX Developer's Guide.[3]

Salesforce Command-Line Interface (CLI)

The Salesforce CLI is a powerful command-line interface that simplifies development and build automation when working with your Salesforce org. Based on the Heroku CLI, the Salesforce team built a flexible, open source CLI engine called OCLIF, the Open CLI Framework. The Salesforce CLI was the first tool built on OCLIF, although other tools have followed.

The Salesforce CLI allows common Salesforce API commands to be called from the command line and also encapsulates complex processes like synchronizing source with a scratch org in concise commands. Importantly it also allows the output from those commands to be exported in JSON format so that it can easily be parsed and possibly passed as input to other commands.

The Salesforce CLI can be used directly on the command line, included in scripts such as CI jobs, and is also the underlying engine powering the Visual Studio Code extensions.

Summary

Salesforce is an extremely powerful and versatile platform. But it's unique in many ways and it hasn't been easy for professional developers to adapt their tools and techniques to working on this platform.

Salesforce DX is a major strategic initiative from Salesforce to ensure that industry best practices such as DevOps and modular architecture are possible on the platform. Salesforce DX includes many components such as scratch orgs, unlocked packages, and the Salesforce CLI. It also encompasses many teams such as the Apex and API teams working behind the scenes to empower these capabilities.

The significance of this shift to DevOps is explained in detail in the next chapter.

---

[3]https://developer.salesforce.com/docs/atlas.en-us.sfdx_dev.meta/sfdx_dev/sfdx_dev_source_file_format.htm

CHAPTER 3

DevOps

DevOps has become a trending topic in the tech industry over the last decade, gaining the attention of both developers and the C-suite. Despite some legitimate debate over what it does and does not entail, this interest in DevOps has elevated the discussion around software development practices and the impact they can have on how businesses rise and fall. Figure 3-1 gives one indication of the acceleration of interest in the topic of DevOps over time.

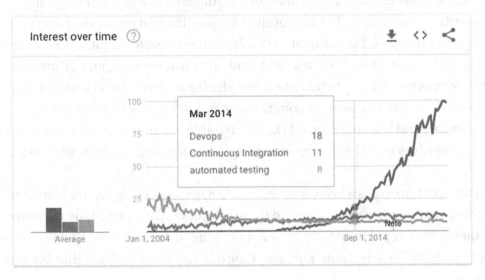

Figure 3-1. *Google Trends ranking showing the acceleration of interest in DevOps compared to related terms*

The practice of DevOps is to regard IT processes as central to a business's ability to deliver value to its customers and to continually improve the process of delivering new functionality while ensuring quality and stability. DevOps is a portmanteau of the terms "Dev" (Development) and "Ops" (Operations). The term implies collaboration between these teams, where they're motivated by the shared goal to enhance both innovation

© Andrew Davis 2019
A. Davis, *Mastering Salesforce DevOps*, https://doi.org/10.1007/978-1-4842-5473-8_3

and stability. Achieving this goal involves integrating long-standing development practices—such as continuous integration, continuous delivery, automated testing, and infrastructure as code. As such, it's become a catch-all term for development process improvements both new and old.

In practice, DevOps is not something you're ever "done with." In that sense it's like "collaboration" or "efficiency"—a principle to adopt and a goal to always improve upon. One core metric used to determine successful implementation of DevOps is called "lead time"—how long does it take your organization to deploy a single line of code to production? It is important that any changes delivered to production be well tested and made in a controlled way. But increased delays in delivering features to production mean greater delays in getting feedback. Delayed feedback means that improvements and bug fixes are delayed, causing inefficient context switching as developers repeatedly revisit work that they may not have touched for days, weeks, or even months.

There are many examples of companies like Amazon, Google, and Etsy who continuously deliver innovation as a result of automating and optimizing their development processes. For companies like these, their development processes are central to their businesses. And their CEOs and other leaders recognize IT process improvement as being every bit as critical as reducing their overhead and building market share. There are also many companies in industries like communication, manufacturing, and banking (Capital One is a notable example), who have shifted to viewing themselves as technology companies, with technological innovation as a core competency.[1]

This chapter provides a brief overview of DevOps, especially for the benefit of Salesforce practitioners who are new to these concepts. There are many excellent books that delve deeply into this topic—among others, *Accelerate* by Nicole Forsgren, *The DevOps Handbook* by Gene Kim, and *Continuous Delivery* by Jez Humble and David Farley.

---

[1]https://hbr.org/2016/04/you-dont-have-to-be-a-software-company-to-think-like-one

What's Driving the Need for DevOps?

Some companies have been automating and optimizing their code development processes for decades, while others have only recently begun to consider this. Probably the best industry-wide survey of DevOps maturity is the *State of DevOps Report*[2] by Puppet Labs and DORA (DevOps Research and Assessment, now part of Google Cloud). The *State of DevOps Report* shows striking differences between DevOps "haves" and "have-nots." High-performing DevOps teams deploy far more frequently and have vastly shorter cycle times (lead time for changes), fewer failures, and quicker recovery from failures compared to low-performing teams.

At the heart of DevOps is the process of continuous improvement, inspired by the Japanese process of *kaizen*. The implication is that you should get started now, while adopting a discipline of continuous improvement, coupled with the playfulness and flexibility to innovate and experiment. The first and most important step is to capture the state of all of your systems in version control and to perform all your deployments using continuous delivery to ensure that changes are always tracked. These practices set the foundation for increasingly refined automation.

What Is DevOps?

DevOps is a term for a group of concepts that, while not all new, have catalyzed into a movement and are rapidly spreading throughout the technical community. Like any new and popular term, people have somewhat confused and sometimes contradictory impressions of what it is. While a lot of discussions about DevOps focus on the specific tooling or technical implementations, the core meaning relates to the people that develop and maintain technical systems and the culture that surrounds this process. An infinity loop, as shown in Figure 3-2, is often used to illustrate the ongoing rhythm of activities that make up the DevOps process.

---

[2]https://puppet.com/resources/whitepaper/state-of-devops-report

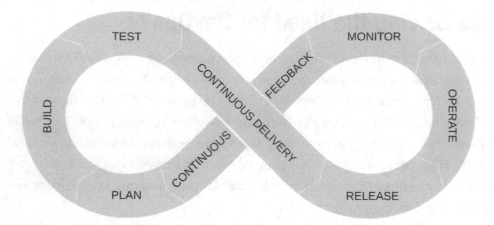

Figure 3-2. *A DevOps infinity loop*

Dev vs. Ops

Working with cloud applications like Salesforce greatly simplifies the requirements for delivering capabilities. In a sense, Salesforce itself takes the place of the "Operations" team that keeps the production system running. Salesforce Admins largely work as declarative developers, building new capabilities rather than just keeping the lights on and keeping performance tuned. But to understand the DevOps challenge, we can think about development and operations needs in a traditional enterprise.

A critical need for businesses is the ability to innovate and develop new functionality for their customers and employees. This is the role of the Development team.

Another critical need is for existing systems to be stable, reliable, and secure. This is the role of the Operations team, which typically consists of system admins, database admins, web site admins, and so on. Their main job is to make sure servers are up and running, SLAs are being met, the application is performing as expected, and so on.

There's a natural tension between the need for innovation (change) and the need for stability. Developers want and need to keep changing the system, while the Operations team wants and needs the system to remain as static as possible so that they can optimize performance and reduce the risk that change brings.

In large organizations, these teams had historically worked in silos which isolated the Development teams from QA and Ops. QA and Ops typically deal with huge numbers of applications and features, sometimes with little understanding of the business purpose and value of the software they were enabling.

The end goal for all of these teams is customer satisfaction, but specific goals for "Devs" include fixing bugs fast and creating new features, whereas for their "Ops" counterparts, the goals might be to maintain 99.99% server uptimes. These goals can often be in conflict with one another, leading to inefficiency and finger-pointing when things go wrong.

Chronic conflict between the Dev and IT operations teams is a recipe for failure for the IT teams as well as the organization they serve.

The concept of DevOps is founded on building a culture of collaboration, communication, and automation between teams that may have historically functioned in silos. The goal is for both Developers and Operations to share responsibility for facilitating innovation while still ensuring stability.

The generative culture promoted in the DevOps community emphasizes values such as ownership and accountability. Developers and operations teams collaborate closely, share many responsibilities, and combine their workflows. This reduces inefficiencies and saves time (e.g., writing code that takes into account the environment in which it is run). Figure 3-3 depicts DevOps as uniting the focus and activities of these previously disparate teams.

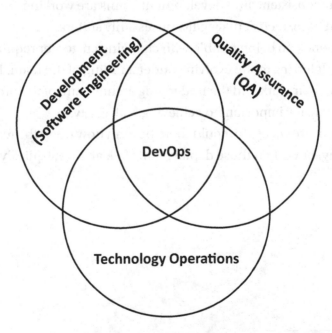

Figure 3-3. *DevOps brings together activities that were traditionally done by independent development, QA, and IT operations teams*

The Real Meaning of Agile

In the book *Accelerate*,[3] the authors make the point that

> *at the time the Agile Manifesto was published in 2001, Extreme Programming (XP) was one of the most popular Agile frameworks. In contrast to Scrum, XP prescribes a number of technical practices such as test-driven development and continuous integration … Many Agile adoptions have treated technical practices as secondary compared to the management and team practices that some Agile frameworks emphasize. Our research shows that technical practices play a vital role in achieving these outcomes.*

The Agile Manifesto itself promotes 12 principles,[4] the first of which is that "Our highest priority is to satisfy the customer through early and continuous delivery of valuable software." And the ninth of which states "Continuous attention to technical excellence and good design enhances agility."

To the extent that most development teams organize their work into sprints, and craft their requirements in the form of user stories, "Agile" has become the dominant practice for delivering software. But if deployments require hours or days of preparation, environments are inconsistent, and development teams are working on differing versions of the codebase, then actual agility necessarily suffers.

Real agility depends on being nimble with changing customer requirements and on promoting and deferring to the evolving understanding of the team. But the systems the team uses to do their work and the underlying architecture of the products they're building are also critically important to achieving real agility.

What better measures of agility could there be than how often the team is able to deploy, how quickly, how often those deployments fail, and how quickly the team can recover?

---

[3]Nicole Forsgren, Jez Humble, and Gene Kim, *Accelerate: The Science of Lean Software and Devops Building and Scaling High Performing Technology Organizations* (IT Revolution Press, 2018): p. 41.

[4]https://agilemanifesto.org/principles.html

The Three Ways of DevOps

In his books *The Phoenix Project* and *The DevOps Handbook*, Gene Kim popularized the concept of the Three Ways of DevOps. You can find excellent explanations in those books or in blog posts such as this one.[5] The basic idea is depicted in Figure 3-4. I like to summarize these Three Ways as continuous delivery, continuous feedback, and continuous improvement.

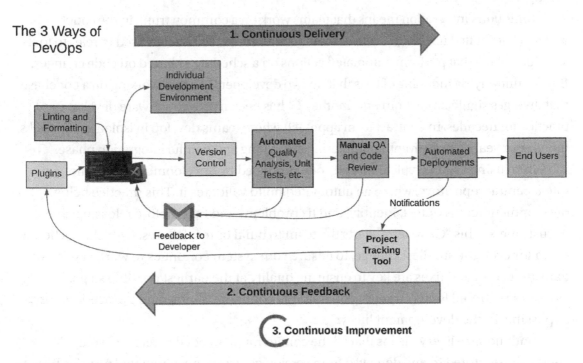

Figure 3-4. *DevOps can be characterized by "Three Ways" of working, illustrated in this diagram*

Continuous Delivery

The First Way is the left-to-right flow of work from Development to QA to IT Operations to Customer. To understand the process of continuous delivery, it helps to understand some basic concepts involved in this process.

---

[5]https://itrevolution.com/the-three-ways-principles-underpinning-devops/

The foundation for continuous delivery (and thus for implementing DevOps) is the use of version control. Version control is a mechanism to track and merge changes smoothly. There are many types of version control, but the most common type used by developers today is Git. The use of version control provides many benefits, but it also opens the door to all of the practices mentioned later. The reason for this is that code stored in version control can be accessed by automated scripts, with each commit tracked in version control reflecting an iterative improvement that is a candidate for testing and deploying.

Continuous integration means that teams work on a common trunk in the codebase and run automated tests with every commit to that trunk. "CI" is often used to refer to tools such as Jenkins that perform automated actions on a schedule or based on code changes. But the underlying meaning of CI is that no two developers are ever working on a codebase that diverges significantly from one another. CI has been a proven software development practice for decades, in contrast to an approach where teams develop in isolation for weeks, months, or years before eventually entering into a long and painful integration phase.

When using CI, it is typical that all code produced by development teams merges into a central repository, where an automated build validates it. This practice helps development teams detect, identify, and fix problems and bugs before releasing changes to customers. This "CI system" alerts the team to build or test failures, with checks being rerun for even the smallest change, to ensure your system continues to work flawlessly. Early detection and fixes are key to ensuring quality at the earliest possible stage. Developers should focus on setting up a simple continuous integration process as early as possible in the development lifecycle.

Continuous delivery means that all the configuration needed to recreate your application is stored in and deployed from version control in an automated way. It's based on the preceding two practices and is the main technical capability at the heart of DevOps.

As mentioned earlier, DevOps is based on the practice of continuous delivery. DevOps brings together continuous delivery with lean management to maximize the throughput of valuable software and the stability of systems at the same time. That is, "move fast and don't break things!"

Continuous Feedback

The Second Way is the feedback cycle going from right to left; the constant flow of feedback at all stages of the value stream to ensure we can prevent problems from happening again or enable faster detection and recovery. The necessary processes include the creation of fast automated test suites, monitoring the security, quality, and reliability of the work being passed through the pipelines and failing the pipeline as soon as a test fails, ensuring the code is always in a deployable state.

Continuous Improvement

The continuous delivery and feedback systems described earlier are called the "system of work"—the mechanism that enables valuable work to flow to production. With any changing system, entropy causes things to break down over time, there is no remaining the same. Only by applying effort to continuously improve the "system of work" can it continue to support and empower the whole organization. DevOps demands continual experimentation to improve the "system of work", and to prioritize this system above the work itself. Maturing the DevOps pipeline involves taking risks and learning from success and failure. The necessary practices include creating a culture of innovation, risk taking, and high trust.

Lean Management

DevOps basically combines two movements: the technical practices of continuous delivery and the practice of Lean management and Lean product development that originated with Toyota. The Toyota Production System set the world standard for how to mass produce a top-quality product. And their product development processes set the world standard for how to quickly innovate to satisfy customers' diverse needs. Lean Software Development was born from the realization that applying the same practices to software development increased quality and thereby company performance.

There are two pillars of the Lean approach (whether manufacturing or software): just-in-time and stop-the-line. Just-in-time is focused on speed, throughput, and efficiency. With software, the idea is to minimize the time required to deliver a requested feature through steps like automating deployments and identifying other bottlenecks in the process that don't add value. One key to fast delivery is to break work into small batches. As each small batch is completed, it can be released, which is why the frequency of releases is an excellent indicator of whether teams are following this approach.

Stop-the-line means that as soon as any defect or abnormality is found, the production line (or deployment pipeline) stops and the top priority becomes identifying and uprooting the source of the problem to ensure it doesn't happen again. The focus here is on stability and quality. With software, this is accomplished through building in checkpoints such as automated testing and validations, and rerunning those every time the codebase changes. The idea is to make the system autonomic, like your autonomic nervous system, where your reflexes recoil from fire without your having to consciously think about it. Having a culture of blameless postmortems is a clear foundation for this kind of approach.

The amount of time a customer spends waiting for a feature to be delivered is called Lead Time. What's happening while the customer waits? Three things:

- Valuable work is being done.

- Work is being done that (in retrospect) doesn't add value
  (and sometimes isn't even necessary).

- The feature is waiting on someone else to build/review/test/deploy it.

It's sometimes hard to tell which actions add value and which actions don't. But it's always the case that time spent waiting doesn't add any value. The fastest sustainable speed at which all of the valuable work could be done is called the Process Time. The difference between the Lead Time and the Process Time is one of the main types of waste.

If you think of the lifecycle of groceries, they're first grown or manufactured, then they're stored or shipped, then eventually they're bought and used. The more time elapses between being grown and being used, the more likely they are to go bad. Software also ages quickly. More importantly, the longer the lead time, the longer it takes to get feedback from actual users. Building software is extremely complex, and the only reliable way to ensure things are built well is to get feedback quickly and repeatedly.

The essence of DevOps (and Lean software development) is to eliminate waste, especially time spent waiting. Reducing lead times allows for fast feedback, fast feedback allows for innovation, and innovation enables success.

One of the easiest ways to eliminate wasted time is to automate your deployments using continuous delivery. Implementing continuous delivery on Salesforce is one of the main focuses of this book.

Generative Culture

In his study of safety cultures, sociologist Ron Westrum famously categorized organizational cultures into pathological, bureaucratic, or generative.[6] Pathological cultures are oriented around gaining and maintaining power. To maintain power, groups and individuals in pathological organizations tend to limit knowledge sharing and retain tight control over their areas of responsibility.

Bureaucratic cultures are rule oriented, with a focus on applying rules consistently across the organization. Bureaucratic cultures have an emphasis on fairness and on following processes.

Generative cultures, by contrast, are performance oriented. The focus in generative cultures is on getting the job done, rather than emphasizing control or process. Control is still important in generative cultures, as are rules and processes; but they are important only in serving the larger mission of organizational effectiveness.

The term DevOps itself indicates collaboration between Dev and Ops. By extension, DevOps involves collaboration with the QA teams, security teams, as well as business owners and subject-matter experts. The origins of DevOps in lean manufacturing imply looking at the entire software delivery chain strategically, to gradually improve the flow of work. The adoption of new development tools and best practices is done as a means to improve the entire system and thus requires the team to work together for the benefit of all.

For these reasons, Westrum's generative culture model is an excellent description of a culture conducive to DevOps. DevOps requires collaboration between different teams as well as learning and experimentation to optimize software delivery. For many companies, the biggest challenge to adopting DevOps is establishing an open, performance-oriented culture that allows for such continuous improvement.

The 2018 State of DevOps survey asked respondents about their team's culture and their organization's culture. The survey analysis concluded that a generative culture is indeed indicative of better company performance. Importantly, it also found that adopting DevOps practices such as continuous delivery actually drives further cultural improvements by reducing the barriers to innovation and collaboration.

---

[6]Ron Westrum, "A typology of Organisational Cultures," *Quality and Safety in Health Care* 13, no. suppl 2 (2004): ii22-ii27.

Blameless Postmortems

One manifestation of such a generative culture is an absence of finger-pointing. Development of a strong "safety culture" is recognized as important across many industries, notably healthcare, manufacturing, and transportation. In the aftermath of any incident (whether a train crash or an outage in an IT system), blameless postmortems should be conducted to determine how such incidents can be averted in future. Rather than ever settling on "human error" as a root cause, emphasis should be placed on the circumstances that allowed that error to occur. Human error itself has root causes, and a rich safety culture builds in protections that allow imperfect humans to nevertheless avoid such risks and dangers.

A powerful example of a blameless postmortem followed a headline-generating outage for Amazon Web Services. AWS has become the computing infrastructure for an enormous number of companies. On February 28, 2017, the S3 storage service in AWS's main region went offline for 4 hours. This took a large number of major Internet companies like Quora and Trello offline during that time, since S3 is used to host web site files among many other things. AWS soon released a postmortem of that event,[7] in which they identified that a typo from one of their admins triggered a chain of other problems.

Although human error was involved, nowhere in their analysis did they cite "human error" as a factor, let alone a root cause. Rather they dug deeper to ask what other circumstances allowed this mistake to unfold. They implemented several new protections and safety checks as a result. Despite the PR problems caused by this incident, there was no implication that the admin responsible was fired or disciplined. Rather energy was invested in further improving AWS to eliminate the risk of this kind of incident happening again in future.

A dramatic example of the long-term impact of improving safety culture can be found by looking at automobile fatalities in the United States over time. Figure 3-5 shows the dramatic increase in the number of miles driven per year, juxtaposed with the progressive reduction in risk of fatalities from automobile travel, along with a few practices that helped bring about these improvements. Blameless postmortems provide the opportunity for IT teams to make similar progress to build systems that are increasingly resilient, even as the velocity of innovation continues to increase.

---

[7]https://aws.amazon.com/message/41926/

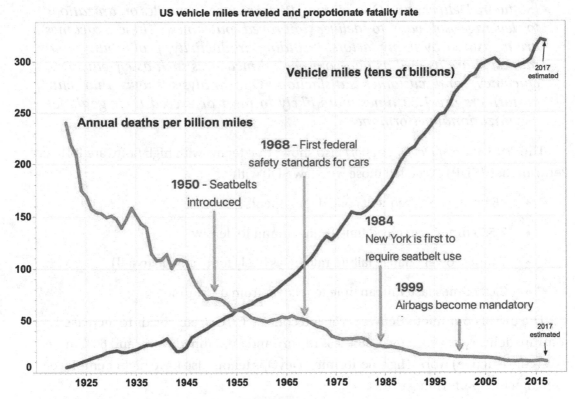

Figure 3-5. *Progress on automobile safety in the United States over time*[8]

The IT industry still has much to learn from the systematic improvements in quality and worker safety that have been implemented through such long-standing safety cultures.

The Research

The use of DevOps (continuous delivery and lean software development) has been shown to improve Software Delivery Performance (how fast you can release functionality in a stable way). According to the *2018 State of DevOps Report*

---

[8]National Highway Traffic Safety Administration.

[Software Delivery and Operational] Performance ... enables organizations to leverage software to deliver improved outcomes. These outcomes are measured by many factors, including productivity, profitability, and market share as well as non-commercial measures such as effectiveness, efficiency, and customer satisfaction. Our analysis shows that elite performers are 1.53 times more likely to meet or exceed their goals for organizational performance.

The *2018 State of DevOps Report* also shows that teams with high Software Delivery Performance (SDP) exceeded those with low SDP with

- 46 times more frequent code deployments

- 2,555 times faster lead time from commit to deploy

- 7 times lower change failure rate (⅐ as likely for a change to fail)

- 2,604 times faster mean time to recover from downtime

The use of continuous delivery (version control, CI/CD, etc.) leads to increased software delivery performance, 38% less rework and unplanned work, and 66% more new (constructive) work. High-performing DevOps teams also have higher employee NPS than low-performing teams.

Business Impact of Adopting DevOps

The *State of DevOps Report* affirms the positive impact that adopting DevOps has on businesses. These studies validate that organizations with high-performing DevOps processes outperform their peers financially by enabling faster time to market for features and increased customer satisfaction, market share, employee productivity and happiness thus allowing them to win in an increasingly competitive economy.

As shown in Table 3-1, organizations like Amazon, Google, Twitter, Facebook, and Etsy embody DevOps processes and routinely deploy hundreds or even thousands of production changes per day while still preserving world-class "reliability, stability, and security." These organizations are more agile, and the time required to go from code committed to successfully running in production is an average of 8,000 times faster. In contrast, organizations that require weeks or months to deploy software are at a significant disadvantage.

Table 3-1. *Software Delivery Performance metrics from some industry-leading software companies*[9]

Company	Deployment Frequency	Deployment Lead Time	Reliability	Customer Responsiveness
Amazon	23,000/day	Minutes	High	High
Google	5,500/day	Minutes	High	High
Netflix	500/day	Minutes	High	High
Facebook	1/day	Hours	High	High
Twitter	3/week	Hours	High	High
Typical Enterprise	Once every 9 months	Months or quarters	Low/medium	Low/medium

Not only do these organizations do more work, they also have far better outcomes. When they deploy code, it is twice as likely to run successfully (i.e., without causing a production outage or service impairment), and when a change fails and results in an incident, the time required to resolve the incident is far faster.

With DevOps in place, instead of deployments being performed only at nights or on weekends, full of stress and chaos, these organizations are deploying code throughout the business day without most people even noticing.

Developers get feedback on their work constantly: linting tools, automated unit, acceptance, integration tests, and other build validations run continually in production-like environments. This gives continuous assurance that the code and environments will work as designed and that code is always in a deployable state.

---

[9]Gene Kim, Kevin Behr, and George Spafford, *The Phoenix Project: A Novel about It, Devops, and Helping Your Business Win* (IT Revolution Press, 2013), 380.

How DevOps Helps

The *State of DevOps Report* confirms the importance of technical practices such as continuous delivery in improving software delivery performance and thus company performance. But that same survey also speaks to the benefits that come directly to teams adopting these practices. The use of continuous delivery itself drives a positive organizational culture, high job satisfaction, and higher employee engagement.

In addition, the use of continuous delivery (version control, CI/CD, etc.) leads to less rework, less deployment pain, and thus less burnout. This is a virtuous cycle. Practices that benefit the development team also benefit the customer; and happier customers in turn make the development team more engaged.

Better Value, Faster, Safer, Happier

Jonathan Smart, who led Barclays Bank on a journey of enterprise-wide DevOps transformation, summarized DevOps as "Better value, faster, safer, happier."[10]

Better means always striving to improve the quality of our work and our products. This implies continuous improvement.

Value means using agile development and design thinking to address and adapt to the needs of end users. The focus here is on delivering the desired results to end users and improving their experience. Software is not "done" until it's in the hands of users, the ones who actually experience value from it.

Faster means using techniques such as continuous delivery to release more quickly. Speed matters; life is short. The more time elapses between requesting something and getting it, the less time that solution will remain valuable. The more time between creating something and getting feedback on it, the more time is wasted in waiting and inevitably forgetting how to improve it.

Coupling increasingly frequent releases with increasingly automated testing allows you to innovate for customers faster, adapt to changing markets better, and improve your product faster. The quicker you can release new features and fix bugs, the faster you can respond to your customers' needs and build competitive advantage.

---

[10]https://medium.com/@jonathansmart1/want-to-do-an-agile-transformation-dont-focus-on-flow-quality-happiness-safety-and-value-11e01ee8f8f3

Safer means focusing on stability and integrating automated quality and security scanning into the development workflow. Just as when driving in a car, speed only matters if you can arrive safely. Safety means that the solutions we deliver will work and that they won't break other things. Safety implies testing, or quality assurance. Testing means testing that the software does what it's supposed to do, is resilient against changing conditions, and doesn't introduce regression failures (break things that used to work). Safer also implies security, which is an aspect of structural quality.

Automated testing gives confidence that each change is functional and safe. Monitoring and logging practices help teams stay informed of performance or issues in real time.

And **happier** refers to continuously improving the development experience and the customer experience of users. We're humans developing for humans. The experience should be increasingly positive for the developers creating functionality and increasingly positive for the end users consuming it.

Note that all of these terms are relative and subjective. This implies an ongoing process, where value is flowing from developers to end users (from creators to consumers), and the whole process is improving on an ongoing basis. We all want better and better experiences. Wisdom dictates that if we focus on improving our actions, our experiences will naturally improve. And so wisely, we strive to improve ourselves and our teams, so that together we can do a better and better job.

The team with the fastest feedback loop is the team that thrives. Full transparency and seamless communication enable DevOps teams to minimize downtime and resolve issues faster than ever before.

Measuring Performance

One of the main contributions of the *State of DevOps Report* has been to focus consistently on the same key metrics year after year. Although the questions in their survey have evolved and new conclusions have emerged over time, the four key metrics used as benchmarks have remained in place:

1. Lead time (from code committed to code deployed)

2. Deployment frequency (to production)

3. Change Fail Percentage (for production deployments)

4. Mean Time to Restore (from a production failure)

The book *Accelerate* provides a detailed explanation of each of these metrics and why they were chosen; those points are summarized here.

The first two of these metrics pertain to innovation and the fast release of new capabilities. The third and fourth metrics pertain to stability and the reduction of defects and downtime. As such, these metrics align with the dual goals of DevOps, to "move fast, and not break things."

These also align with the two core principles of Lean management, derived from the Toyota Production System: "just-in-time" and "stop-the-line." As mentioned earlier, just-in-time is the principle that maximum efficiency comes from reducing waste in the system of work and that the way to reduce waste is to optimize the system to handle smaller and smaller batches and to deliver them with increasing speed. "Stop-the-line" means that the system of work is tuned not just to expedite delivery but also to immediately identify defects to prevent them from being released, thus increasing the quality of the product and reducing the likelihood of production failures.

Lead Time is important because the shorter the lead time, the more quickly feedback can be received on the software, and thus the faster innovation and improvements can be released. *Accelerate* shares that one challenge in measuring Lead Time is that it consists of two parts: time to develop a feature and time to deliver it. The time to develop a feature begins from the moment a feature is requested, but there are some legitimate reasons why a feature might be deprioritized and remain in a product's backlog for months or years. There is a high inherent variability in the amount of time it takes to go from "feature requested" to "feature developed." Thus Lead Time in the *State of DevOps Report* focuses on measuring only the time to deliver a feature once it has been developed. The software delivery part of the lifecycle is an important part of the total lead time and is also much more consistent. By measuring the Lead Time from code committed to code deployed, you can begin to experiment with process improvements that will reduce waiting and inefficiency and thus enable faster feedback.

Deployment frequency is the frequency of how often code or configuration changes are deployed to production. Deployment frequency is important since it is inversely related to batch size. Teams that deploy to production once per month necessarily deploy a larger batch of changes in each deployment than teams who deploy once per week. All changes are not created equal. Within any batch of changes, there will be some which are extremely valuable, and others that are almost insignificant. Large batch sizes imply that valuable features are waiting in line with all the other changes, thus delaying the delivery of value and benefit. Large batches also increase the risk of deployment failures and make it much harder to diagnose which of the many changes was responsible if a failure occurs. Teams naturally tend to batch changes together when deployments are painful and tedious. By measuring deployment frequency, you can track your team's progress as you work on making deployments less painful and enabling smaller batch sizes.

Change Fail Percentage measures how frequently a deployment to production fails. Failure here means that a deployment causes a system outage or degradation or requires a subsequent hotfix or rollback. Modern software systems are complex, fast-changing systems, so some amount of failure is inevitable. Traditionally it's been felt that there's a tradeoff between frequency of changes and stability of systems, but the highly effective teams identified in the *State of DevOps Report* are characterized by both a high rate of innovation and a low rate of failures. Measuring failure rate allows the team to track and tune their processes to ensure that their testing processes weed out most failures before they occur.

Mean Time to Restore (MTTR) is closely related to the Lead Time to release features. In effect, teams that can quickly release features can also quickly release patches. Time to Restore indicates the amount of time that a production system remains down, in a degraded state, or with nonworking functionality. Such incidents are typically stressful situations and often have financial implications. Resolving such incidents quickly is a key priority for operations teams. Measuring this metric allows your team to set a baseline on time to recover and to work to resolve incidents with increasing speed.

The *2018 State of DevOps Report* added a fifth metric, System Uptime, which is inversely related to how much time teams spend recovering from failures. The System Uptime metric is an important addition for several reasons. First of all, it aligns with the traditional priorities and key performance indicators of sysadmins (the operations team). The number one goal of sysadmins is Keeping the Lights On or ensuring that systems remain available. The reason for this is simple: the business depends on these systems, and when the systems go down, the business goes down. Outages are expensive.

Tracking System Uptime is also central to the discipline of Site Reliability Engineering (SRE). SRE is the evolution of the traditional sysadmin role, expanded to encompass "web-scale" or "cloud-scale" systems where one engineer might be responsible for managing 10,000 servers. SRE emerged from Google, who shared their practices in the influential book *Site Reliability Engineering*.[11] One innovation shared in that book is the concept of an "error budget,"[12] which is the recognition that there is a tradeoff between reliability and innovation and that there are acceptable levels of downtime.

> *Put simply, a user on a 99% reliable smartphone cannot tell the difference between 99.99% and 99.999% service reliability! With this in mind, rather than simply maximizing uptime, Site Reliability Engineering seeks to balance the risk of unavailability with the goals of rapid innovation and efficient service operations, so that users' overall happiness—with features, service, and performance—is optimized.[13]*

The *State of DevOps Report* shows how these five metrics are interrelated, illustrated in Figure 3-6. The timer starts on Lead Time the moment a developer finishes and commits a feature to version control. How quickly that feature is released depends on the team's deployment frequency. While frequent deployments are key to fast innovation, they also increase the risk of failures in production. Change Fail Percentage measures this risk, although frequent small deployments tend to reduce the risk of any given change. If a change fails, the key issue is then the Mean Time to Restore service. The final metric on availability captures the net stability of the production system.

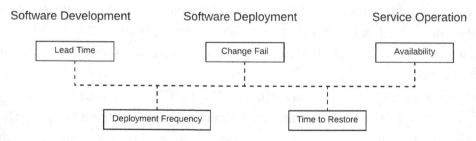

Figure 3-6. *How the five key software delivery and operations performance metrics tie together*

[11]Betsy Beyer, Chris Jones, Jennifer Petoff, and Niall Richard Murphy, *Site Reliability Engineering: How Google Runs Production Systems* (O'Reilly Media, 2016).

[12]https://landing.google.com/sre/sre-book/chapters/embracing-risk/

[13]*Site Reliability Engineering*, Chapter 3.

Together, these metrics constitute a team's **Software Delivery Performance**. The goal of any DevOps initiative should be to improve Software Delivery Performance by strategically developing specific capabilities such as continuous delivery and the use of automated testing.

How your team measures these capabilities is another challenge. But *Accelerate* makes a compelling argument for the validity of surveys. Automated metrics can be implemented over time, although the mechanism to do this will depend on how you do your deployments. Salesforce production orgs track past deployments, but it's not currently possible to query those deployments, and so you would need to measure deployment frequency (for example) using the tools you use to perform the deployments. Salesforce publishes their own service uptime on `https://trust.salesforce.com`, but that gives no indication of whether critical custom services that your team has built are in a working state or not.

Surveys provide a reasonable proxy for these metrics, especially if responses are given by members of the team in different roles. Guidelines for administering such surveys are beyond the scope of this book, but your teams' honest responses are the most critical factor. Avoid any policies that could incent the team to exaggerate their answers up or down. Never use these surveys to reward or punish; they should be used simply to inform. Allow teams to track their own progress and to challenge themselves to improve for their own benefit and for the benefit of the organization. As it says in the *Agile Manifesto,* "At regular intervals, the team reflects on how to become more effective, then tunes and adjusts its behavior accordingly."

Enhancing Performance

High software delivery performance is associated with objective improvements in corporate performance (both commercial and noncommercial) and subjective improvements to deployment pain, burnout, and employee satisfaction. It's therefore in the best interest of everyone in an organization to strive to improve their software delivery performance by monitoring the metrics mentioned earlier.

What methods are available to improve software delivery performance? The research from the *State of DevOps Report* has identified 32 factors that drive this performance. The book *Accelerate* categorizes those factors into five groups:

1. Continuous delivery

2. Architecture

3. Product and process

4. Lean management and monitoring

5. Cultural

In this book, we'll focus almost entirely on how to implement technical practices related to architecture and continuous delivery, with some references to monitoring as well. As such, our goal here is not to provide a comprehensive prescription for all the cultural, management, and process improvements that might be needed, but to at least provide more guidance and definition on how a high-functioning Salesforce implementation would be architected, deployed, monitored, and maintained.

This chapter provides a brief summary of the cultural and lean management practices necessary for success, but for further guidance the reader is encouraged to look at the many excellent books, articles, and talks that are available on these topics.

Optimizing the Value Stream

A fundamental concept in Lean software management is to understand the software development and delivery process in terms of how each aspect of the process contributes (or does not contribute) to value for the end user. As mentioned earlier, value reflects the benefit that the end user receives and would be willing to pay for. As software moves through the development and delivery process, different individuals and teams add value through their contributions. Their ongoing contributions to the process are described as flowing into a "value stream" that delivers ongoing value to end users.

Value Stream Mapping is a key tool in lean management. This involves mapping each stage of the development and delivery process and then gathering three metrics from each stage: lead time, process time, and percent complete and accurate. Lead time is the total amount of time that it takes from a work item entering that stage until it leaves that stage. Process time is the amount of time that would be required for that activity if it could be performed without interruption. And percent complete and accurate is the percentage of the output from that stage that can be used, as is, without requiring rework or clarification. The goal of this mapping is to identify slowdowns where work items spend time waiting or could be completed more efficiently, as well as stages that suffer from quality issues. It's also possible that this process uncovers steps that don't add much value and can be eliminated or simplified. The core concept of lean management is to assess this process and identify how to eliminate waste from this system, to maximize the flow of value.

The potential technical improvements that can be made to a software product or to the way of working on that software product are limitless. This book alone introduces a huge range of possible improvements to the way code is written or developed, the way it's tested, packaged, deployed, and monitored. But it is unwise to assume that adopting DevOps means that we should simultaneously take on all of these improvements or make improvements arbitrarily. Instead, the goal should be to identify the bottlenecks in the system that limit the overall flow of value and to optimize the system around those bottlenecks.

Begin by identifying the current state value map, and then craft a future state value map that aims to increase the percent complete and accurate of the final product or reduce the amount of waste (lead time where no process is being performed). For more guidance, see the book *Lean Enterprise: How High Performance Organizations Innovate at Scale*[14] or *Value Stream Mapping: How to Visualize Work and Align Leadership for Organizational Transformation.*[15]

It can be very challenging to discern where to begin such a process. One complementary approach known as the *theory of constraints* can provide a practical simplification to help target priority areas for improvement.

---

[14]Jez Humble, Joanne Molesky, and Barry O'Reilly, *Lean Enterprise: How High Performance Organizations Innovate at Scale* (O'Reilly Media, 2015).

[15]Karen Martin and Mike Osterling, *Value Stream Mapping: How to Visualize Work and Align Leadership for Organizational Transformation* (McGraw-Hill, 2013).

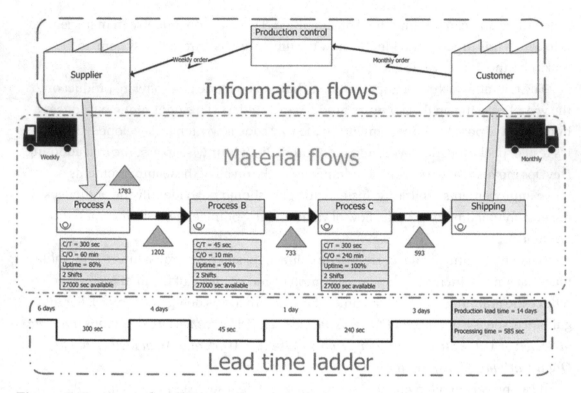

Figure 3-7. A sample value stream map

Theory of Constraints

The concept known as the theory of constraints was introduced and popularized by Eliyahu M. Goldratt in his book *The Goal*.[16] That book is cited extensively in DevOps literature and emphasizes a fourfold approach to optimizing the flow of value through a system:

1. Identify the constraint

2. Exploit the constraint

3. Subordinate and synchronize to the constraint

4. Elevate the performance of the constraint

---

[16]Eliyahu M Goldratt and Jeff Cox, *The goal: a process of ongoing improvement* (North River Press, 2004).

In layman's terms, the idea is that the overall performance of any system at any given time will always be limited by a single constraint. In a software development process, the constraint might be that there are not enough developers, or that the testing process takes too long, or that the deployment process can only be done at certain times, or that there is not any additional demand from customers, and so on. The most important point to note is that **improvements to any part of the system other than this constraint will not yield any significant benefit**. For this reason, the most critical step to making overall improvements is to first identify the constraint.

Identifying the constraint on a system can be a challenging process, combining measurement, intuition, and experimentation. One approach to identifying the constraint is to look for a buildup of "inventory" in a system, since this tends to indicate a point where the process slows down. The concept of inventory is borrowed from manufacturing, but can be extended to the software development process and relabeled as "work in progress." Where does work in progress (WIP) accumulate in your development process? You can ask your team questions like how large is the backlog for developers? How many pieces of work are waiting for review by a tech lead? How much work is waiting to be tested? How many items are waiting to be deployed? Asking questions like this and observing trends over time can help you home in on the main constraint in your process.

Once the constraint has been identified, the biggest improvement that can be made is to **exploit that constraint**—to make sure that it is fully utilized. At the time that Goldratt wrote *The Goal*, it was common in manufacturing to focus on getting maximum utilization from every single system involved in a manufacturing process. The equivalent in a software team is ensuring that everyone is busy all the time. But in practice this local optimization of each part of the system *does not* optimize the performance of the overall system, because overall performance is always defined by a single constraint. It is that constraint that needs to be optimized, getting the maximum sustainable productivity out of that constraint.

The third stage is to **subordinate and synchronize to the constraint**. This means that every other part of the system should be seen as a means to enable and support the constraint. The priority for other systems should be to ensure that the constraint is never waiting on "raw materials" (such as specifications for work) and that the work produced by the constraint is quickly whisked away to the next phase of the process.

For example, if you determine that the capacity of the development team is the limiting factor on your ability to deliver value, then the other individuals or processes that contribute to the value stream—business analysis, architecture, testing, and deployment—should ensure that the developers can be made as effective as possible. That means ensuring that they have a backlog of work and clear architectural guidance, and that once their work is complete, it can be tested and deployed as quickly as possible. Importantly, releasing quickly also allows bugs to be identified quickly so that developers can address those while the relevant code is still fresh in their minds.

Having identified the constraint, the second and third stages of optimization function to maximize the throughput of the constraint (first by using it fully and then by organizing everything else around it). It is entirely possible that through making these optimizations, the original constraint ceases to be the constraint. By definition, the constraints on a system are subject to moving and changing as conditions evolve. This is why it's important to begin by mapping the entire value stream and continuing to monitor each component of it to gain insight into your overall flow. If you find that the constraint has changed, then you have just achieved the first level of optimization for that new constraint: identifying it. Your task then becomes how to exploit the new constraint, and so forth.

If a constraint persists despite your maximizing its throughput, you have only one remaining option: to **elevate the performance of that constraint**. When your constraint is one or more individuals, elevating the performance of that constraint might take the form of giving them better tools, training or coaching them, hiring additional team members, or even replacing them and moving them to a different role if necessary.

This fourfold process is a continual dance. There is never a time when there is not some constraint on a system. Even when the market itself is your constraint, your practice is the same: to exploit that market, subordinate your other activities to feeding market demand, and finally work to elevate demand through marketing and publicity.

Even the optimization process itself is subject to unseen constraints. It takes time, effort, and situational awareness to understand how your value stream is performing; and it can take time, effort, and money to make the changes necessary to improve that performance.

From the point of view of the theory of constraints, this continual dance is the essence of effective management.

Enabling Change

Suffice it to say, implementing or improving any of these capabilities is a change management process that relies on human communication, learning, and experimentation.

Industry surveys conducted by McKinsey[17] indicate that only 25% of transformation initiatives have been very or completely successful; however, organizations that take multiple parallel actions to improve and especially those which emphasize communication have a 79% success rate. In any case, the DevOps journey is not one that is ever "done." The point is to provide a clear vision for your team about areas for possible improvement; to provide training, examples, and encouragement to help them understand how to proceed; and to proceed systematically and incrementally with a process of continuous improvement.

It's helpful to consider the *law of diffusion of innovation*, first introduced by Everett Rogers in 1962[18] and concisely summarized in this diagram. According to this widely cited model, individuals adopt a new process (such as DevOps or Salesforce DX in this case) at different rates. A small few individuals fall into the Innovators category. They are the ones who initially experiment with a technology and lay the early foundations for others to follow. They are followed by early adopters, who tend to copy more than innovate, but who are nevertheless bold and enthusiastic about taking on this new process. Innovators and early adopters may only account for 16% of a total population. But they are truly trailblazers and open the door for subsequent adoption. At these early stages, it may seem that adoption levels are very low, which can be disheartening for those trying to champion change. But these initial stages of adoption are the foundation that eventually leads to a tipping point as the early majority and late majority begin to follow suit. The "S" shaped curve in this diagram shows total adoption and depicts how the slow early phases give way to a period of fast diffusion as the majority gets on board.

---

[17]www.mckinsey.com/business-functions/organization/our-insights/how-to-beat-the-transformation-odds

[18]Everett Rogers, *Diffusion of Innovations*, 5th Edition (Simon and Schuster, 2003).

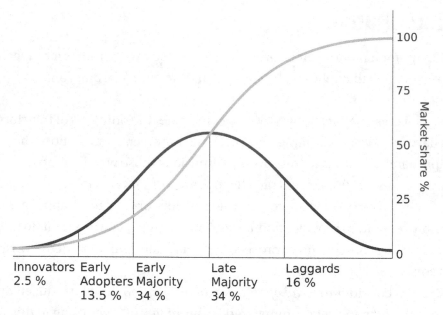

Figure 3-8. *An illustration of the law of diffusion of innovation. Eagerness to adopt a new technology or practice typically follows a bell curve distribution across a population. The cumulative increase in adoption follows an S curve (the integral of the bell curve)*[19]

This law of diffusion of innovation has been the basis for many other analyses. Two relevant observations that are frequently made are that there is a tipping point in this system at which adoption becomes self-sustaining, but also that there is a chasm that needs to be crossed when you transition to majority adoption.

First, the good news. Once you have gained adoption from the innovators and the early adopters (the initial 16% of your target population), you have reached a tipping point where adoption can become self-sustaining, as shown in Figure 3-9. As the early and late majority begin to adopt these processes, the momentum of word-of-mouth marketing and other network effects begins to take hold. People begin to follow this process because it starts to become standard practice. Their friends are doing it; other teams are doing it; the team they used to be on did it, and so on. Malcolm Gladwell's bestselling book *The Tipping Point*[20] was based partly on these same ideas.

---

[19]Image source: `https://commons.wikimedia.org/wiki/File:Diffusion_of_ideas.svg`

[20]Malcolm Gladwell, *The Tipping Point: How Little Things Can Make a Big Difference* (Back Bay Books, 2002).

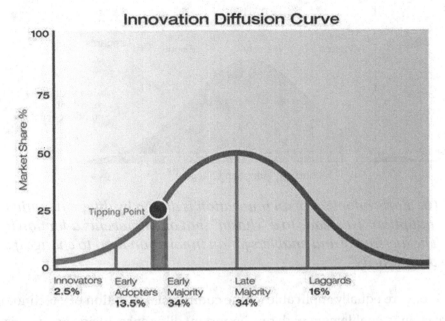

Figure 3-9. *As the early majority begins to embrace an innovation, adoption reaches a tipping point where further adoption tends to become self-sustaining[21]*

Now for the bad news. While there will always be people who explore and experiment with new approaches, Geoffrey Moore pointed out in *Crossing the Chasm*[22] that for new and disruptive technologies, there is a chasm that exists between the early adopters and majority adoption, illustrated in Figure 3-10. Many very promising technologies have achieved adoption from a small corps of aficionados, but never managed to get wide market adoption. Moore explains that this is because there is a markedly different psychodynamic between innovators and the bulk of the population. To cross this chasm, Moore argues, you must reconsider your target market for each stage and tailor your marketing message and medium differently when appealing to the majority.

---

[21]Source: (CC) Gavin Llewellyn, www.flickr.com/photos/gavinjllewellyn/6353463087

[22]Geoffrey A. Moore, *Crossing the Chasm: Marketing and Selling Technology Products to Mainstream Customers.* (HarperBusiness, 1991).

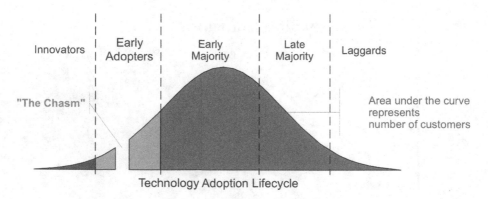

Figure 3-10. *Early adoption of an innovation is driven by different motivators than later adoption. This leads to a "chasm" that often prevents adoption by the majority. The messaging and enablers for an innovation need to change if it is to appeal to the majority*[23]

These ideas are equally applicable for the commercial adoption of a technology or for internal change enablement with one important difference. Inside an organization there is always the possibility of making a change mandatory, tracking and rewarding based on adoption metrics, and so on. As much as they might wish for it, such options are not available to those marketing commercial products!

Nevertheless, effective change inside an organization is most powerful and sustainable when it's driven by intrinsic motivators—when people feel that the new process truly benefits them and their team. To take this organic approach, at the beginning, you should seek to attract and appeal to potential DevOps innovators within your company, working to enable them. As you get adoption from this initial group, you can gradually shift your focus to gaining broader adoption by considering different strategies as you begin to roll out change across more and more teams.

DevOps in general and Salesforce DX in particular represent a paradigm shift for Salesforce developers. There are significant changes to behavior that are required for teams to shift from making and deploying changes in an ad hoc or manual way to tracking and automating this process. Those charged with leading change in their organization should take heart and emphasize getting buy-in from innovators and early adopters while encouraging them to share their experience with others around them. They then become the basis on which you can begin to work toward majority adoption,

---

[23]Figure source: `https://upload.wikimedia.org/wikipedia/commons/d/d3/Technology-Adoption-Lifecycle.png`

amplifying those early success stories and building a network of support that can help these changes take hold in the rest of your company.

Leading Change

If you are in charge of a small team of Salesforce developers, you may be able to lead adoption of Salesforce DX in a simple and organic way just by piloting its usage and demonstrating some of its benefits. But if change needs to happen across a large and distributed organization, you have entered into the realm of organizational change management. If you have access to experts in organizational change, you should lean on them for advice on succeeding at this process.

A leading voice in organizational change management is John Kotter, whose book *Leading Change*[24] has been an important and influential guide for many organizational initiatives. Kotter defines an eight-stage process by which effective change takes place. The eight-stage process for leading effective change[25] is shared here, together with some notes on the relevance to improving DevOps processes.

Step 1: Create Urgency

None of us act unless there's a need to. Especially when it comes to changing habitual behaviors and learning new practices, the motivation for change must be strong to overcome our inertia. The same holds true for organizations. Organizational change derives from a sense of urgency, and the first step in effecting broad change is to stimulate this sense of urgency in your leadership team.

Kotter suggests that for change to be successful, 75% of a company's management needs to "buy into" the change. When it comes to DevOps, this mostly pertains to the managers responsible for overseeing development teams. But changes in process can sometimes involve temporary slowdowns as a team learns new practices.[26] There needs to be a commitment from anyone who is a stakeholder in the development process, including project managers, internal customers, and even external customers if you are a consulting company doing development at their behest.

---

[24]John P Kotter, *Leading Change* (Harvard Business Review Press, 2012).
[25]See `www.mindtools.com/pages/article/newPPM_82.htm` for another explanation of this process.
[26]This is sometimes called a "J curve" or the valley of despair. Things get a bit worse before they can get much better.

Urgency is built from understanding the problems implicit in the current approach and the benefits of adopting a new approach. The *State of DevOps Report* provides compelling statistics on the impact of adopting DevOps practices, and I've touted those statistics hundreds of times to thousands of listeners to help gain buy-in and motivation.

It's important for you to also identify risks and opportunities that are specific to your company. In Chapter 12: Making It Better, I share Lex Williams' story of Salesforce's own DevOps adoption. Their technical team had been arguing for years that production changes should only be made through a continuous delivery system. But it was only once they started documenting the financial cost of outages arising from ad hoc production changes that they managed to get executive approval to adopt that kind of governance.

Begin to track metrics on how long it takes your teams to deploy to production, merge codebases, perform regression tests, and so on. Take note of how often one team is prevented from deploying critical changes because they have to wait on other teams to complete their work. Gather statistics and explanations to support your vague sense that processes could be more efficient or effective than they currently are. These arguments form the basis for convincing other stakeholders of the need for change.

At the same time, these analyses need to be honest, and you need to listen to counterpoints and have dialog around the need for change as well as possible risks. There are indeed risks associated with change. But by discussing costs and benefits clearly and honestly, you can help yourself and others discern when the risks of not making these improvements outweigh the risks of making them.

Step 2: Form a Powerful Coalition

The first step is the most important, and you should spend time to make sure you have won organizational support before proceeding. But buy-in from management is only the beginning. You now need to gather others who can act as change agents within the company.

Change takes leadership. But leadership happens in many ways, at many levels. You need to find influential people across your organization who are similarly committed to seeing these changes take root. These people may or may not hold traditional leadership roles. Their influence may instead derive from their length of time at the company, their technical expertise, their passion, or their social connections.

Connect with these people to form a coalition. Ask them to commit to helping bring about this change, and work on building trust and collaboration within this initial group. It is helpful to ensure that you have a broad mix of people from different roles and different groups within your organization. For example, at Appirio, we began our DX initiative with a survey of all our technical consultants in which we asked them "which Appirian has helped you the most to improve your coding skills." This survey helped us to identify influencers across different levels and geographic regions. We brought these people together as evangelists, giving them early access to training and demos as we began to promote Salesforce DX.

Step 3: Create a Vision for Change

Humans are remarkably good at telling and remembering stories. And the most effective communicators rely on stories to convey the essence of complex messages in memorable and impactful ways. Salesforce has poured a phenomenal amount of money into their sales and marketing efforts; and marketing is fundamentally about storytelling.

The tagline for Salesforce DX is "Build together and deliver continuously with a modern Salesforce developer experience."[27] That succinct statement creates a vision, which itself inspires change. "Build together" speaks to collaboration and promises easy collaborative development even across large and distributed teams. "Deliver continuously" speaks to easing deployments and helping end users get ongoing value from development. "A modern developer experience" speaks to the promise of replacing tedious manual processes with powerful and automated tools.

What is the vision for modernizing your own Salesforce development experience?

Think about the values that are most important for this initiative. Are you most concerned about speed? Security? Reliability? Ease of debugging?

Based on these values, write out a one- or two-sentence summary of what the future looks like once these changes are in place. This becomes the vision statement for your change.

---

[27]https://developer.salesforce.com/platform/dx

Next craft a strategy to achieve that vision. The strategy adds detail that you'll need as you begin to roll out changes. But the first step in your strategy is to regularly reinforce the vision and ensure that everyone in your change coalition is able to articulate this vision and some key aspects of the strategy. This is the message that you need to build and amplify. It needs to be clear, simple, and compelling so that the story can be told, remembered, and retold again and again throughout the organization.

Step 4: Communicate the Vision

Having gathered support from management, built a coalition of change agents, and established a clear and compelling vision for change, you now need to communicate that vision repeatedly across many channels.

People are subjected to many messages and stories every day. In a busy company, even attendance at ongoing training or all-hands meetings may be limited. So for a message to gain traction, it needs to be heard repeatedly, across different mediums, over a prolonged period. At one point in the Appirio DX initiative, I recognized that many people in our organization lacked grounding in some basic DevOps concepts. So I initiated a "DevOps December" campaign to reinforce some basic DevOps ideas across many channels.

We began the campaign somewhat quietly with posts on our internal Chatter group. But my manager encouraged me that we should reiterate these messages across different channels. "I want people to have DevOps coming out of their ears. I want them to hear about this so much that I start getting complaints!" he said. I happily obliged and sent out daily "byte-sized" updates by both email and Chatter, along with an appearance on a company all-hands call, several open webinars, and a dozen small group meetings. Eventually, he did receive complaints, so we limited the volume and distribution a bit. But we were both delighted with the impact and the reach. No one at the company escaped that December without learning a bit about DevOps.

This formal messaging is not the only way to reinforce the vision. Your actions speak louder than words. So embed these concepts into how you work. Call out teams who are adopting parts of these practices and highlight the benefit they're receiving. Invite people from those teams to talk about their process. Look for examples in other technologies and share those to bring inspiration.

Tie everything back to the vision. And look for opportunities to incent people to move toward this goal, rewarding them when they do.

Step 5: Remove Obstacles

Repeated communication represents the "happy path" of sharing the vision for change. But it's entirely natural for you to encounter obstacles as you move toward this goal. Those obstacles may be in the form of skeptics or naysayers who emphasize the shortcomings with the new process or downplay the need for change. There may also be processes or structures in place that get in the way of change.

I've encountered senior technical architects who have said that it will never be possible for us to get all of our teams using version control, or that Salesforce DX is not mature enough or a high enough priority for most teams to adopt. Such voices can represent healthy skepticism, but in many cases they are simply based on these individuals' own inertia or lack of experience with this new way of working.

Listen to skeptics, and make sure you're understanding the doubts and risks being expressed. But be on the lookout for voices and processes that are actively standing in the way of change and figure out how to overcome these. Help educate these skeptics if their concerns are not valid. Or help them understand how the benefits of change outweigh the disadvantages. There is a learning curve to adopting version control. But every developer I've talked to who has worked extensively with version control and continuous delivery would never go back to their old way of working and would want these systems in place on any project they were on in future.

If the obstacles relate to time challenges, the need for training, gaps in tooling, and so on then address those obstacles appropriately.

Kotter's eight steps to effective change were originally based on his analysis of how change efforts *failed* in organizations. Having studied dozens of transformation efforts across 15 years, he wrote an article called "Leading Change: Why Transformation Efforts Fail" in which he identified that change efforts fail for one of eight reasons, which are the converse of these eight steps for effective change. Your role in leading change is to identify any obstacles to transformation and uproot them rather than letting them undermine the success of your effort.

Step 6: Create Short-Term Wins

Success begets success.

One important conclusion from the law of diffusion of innovation is that Salesforce's Trailhead motto is not strictly true. We're *not* all trailblazers, at least not in every aspect of our lives. Most people, most of the time, are trail **followers**. And there's nothing wrong with that.

When it comes to implementing Salesforce DX or other DevOps initiatives, you can expect at most 2.5% of the population to be true trailblazers. To extend the analogy, these are the innovators who tromp through the wilderness and blaze (mark) trees to show others where to go. They're followed by the equally intrepid 13.5% of early adopters who by analogy are perhaps clearing the trail and ensuring that it's increasingly easy to follow.

What these trailblazers offer are examples of successes, small and large. And it is these successes that you need to amplify, advertise, and celebrate. Keep track of these successes and share them.

My brother is an extremely seasoned mountaineer, who has traversed almost every terrain you can imagine. But for myself and the majority of the population, the best we'll do is hiking well-marked trails, while staying in range of cellphone towers that allow us to double-check Google Maps. It's the same with most of the development teams at our organization. Their adoption will come when they see clear examples of other teams that have succeeded.

You can strategically choose small early wins to build everyone's confidence in this process. Nowhere is this more important than with refactoring your codebase to make use of Salesforce DX unlocked packages. Many people have tried and failed to convert their entire org into a single massive package. But the most effective approach is to first build a single relatively simple package and ensure you can deploy it across all of your orgs. Unlocked packages make it easy to add unpackaged metadata into a package, so once teams have established initial success with that process, they can build on that strength as their packages grow and multiply.

Create short-term targets, especially quick wins that you can confidently achieve. This gives everyone on the team increased confidence and helps pacify critics and those who might oppose your efforts.

Step 7: Build on the Change

Kotter argues that many change projects fail because victory is declared too early. Quick wins are only the beginning of what needs to be done to achieve long-term change, and your goal here is to effect a deep and lasting change in approach.

On the basis of your initial successes, keep building. Continue to set targets for training and adoption. And importantly, encourage teams to track their own development and delivery metrics and practice continuous improvement.

Consider establishing a center of excellence around DevOps or Salesforce DX practices. This provides the opportunity for disparate teams to share their challenges and successes. This kind of ongoing knowledge transfer is important.

Step 8: Anchor the Changes in Corporate Culture

The final stage is to ensure that these practices become embedded in corporate culture, so that they can become self-sustaining and are simply the way the company operates.

When I joined Appirio, the organization had an extremely well-established performance-oriented culture. From day one the executive team championed open communication, transparency, collaboration, and efficiency. In addition, the agile practices of working in sprints, using user stories, and so forth are second nature. There is still work to do to embed DevOps practices into the culture and to ensure they are as natural to the organization in the future as sprints and user stories are today.

It's important to see the broader context in which these practices exist, so that even sales and business people recognize that a reason our organizations can be so effective is that we empower our developers and continuously optimize and automate our software delivery processes. It is only when such practices become part of your corporate DNA that you can have confidence that this change effort will outlive any of the original instigators, and be passed from generation to generation of the organization, despite the constant churn and turnover many IT organizations face.

Summary

DevOps is a rich and growing area in the IT world. The foundations of DevOps have their roots in early automation that developers enacted to facilitate their own workflow. But the practices continue to mature, become clarified, and grow in adoption.

DevOps combines the management and cultural practices of lean software development with the many technical practices that enable continuous delivery. Its business impacts have been analyzed extensively through the *State of DevOps Reports* and other studies, which conclude that these practices bring benefits that reach far beyond the development team.

Because software development and delivery is increasingly central to achieving organizational missions, the significance of DevOps is growing as well. Organizations that implement the various capabilities that lead to high software delivery performance are twice as likely to meet or exceed their commercial and noncommercial goals.

The business benefits of using SaaS systems like Salesforce are very well established. But DevOps practices are not yet common in the Salesforce world. There is an enormous amount that Salesforce practitioners can learn from the experience and successes achieved elsewhere in the DevOps world. Salesforce DX unlocks the door to combining the benefits of SaaS with the benefits of DevOps and allowing our development teams to be as effective as possible.

PART II

Salesforce Dev

To illustrate the DevOps lifecycle, this part of the book summarizes how to build applications on the Salesforce platform, while Part 4: Salesforce Ops (Administration) summarizes administering Salesforce in production. Building things right and running them wisely are the two most important aspects of the development lifecycle, but in this book we touch on them only briefly. The vast majority of the book, Part 3: Innovation Delivery, covers the stages of deployment and testing that unite development and operations. Less has been written about that critical topic, but there are enormous efficiencies to be gained from doing it right.

Developing on the Salesforce platform is generally fun and straightforward, and there is an amazing array of learning resources available to help. Salesforce's developer documentation is excellent, as are Trailhead and the thousands of presentations given at Salesforce conferences and events every year. In addition, there is a wealth of books, blogs, tweets, and StackExchange posts you can find to educate you or help you untangle complex problems.

Although this section is brief, we introduce key concepts in development and architecture along with recommendations for where you can learn more.

CHAPTER 4

Developing on Salesforce

Developing on Salesforce means configuring the platform to meet the needs of your organization. It can take the form of clicks or code, but is frequently a combination of the two. The scope can range from tiny changes to sophisticated applications.

Here, we'll briefly introduce the Salesforce DX development lifecycle. We'll then look at development tools, click-based development, and code-based development. In the next chapter, we'll look at application architecture to introduce important principles to help you structure your development in a flexible and scalable way.

The Salesforce DX Dev Lifecycle

The basic elements of the Salesforce DX development lifecycle are a Salesforce development org, an IDE or code editor, version control, and a CI tool to perform automated tasks like deployments. Version control and CI tools are discussed at length in Chapter 7: The Delivery Pipeline, and the types and purposes of different Salesforce orgs are discussed in Chapter 6: Environment Management.

Salesforce has enabled sandbox development environments for many years. With DX, there are now two additional ways to create development environments: scratch orgs and cloned sandboxes. Scratch orgs are a flagship feature of Salesforce DX. They are short-lived orgs you create "from scratch" based on code and configuration stored in version control. Cloned sandboxes can allow developers to clone an integration sandbox that has work still under development, instead of only being able to clone the production org. The Salesforce CLI now makes it possible to clone a sandbox and automatically log in from the command line.

Changes made in that development environment need to be synced to version control so that automated processes can test and deploy those changes. One of the most helpful features of scratch orgs is the ability to perform a simple `source:push` and `source:pull` command to synchronize metadata between version control and your org.

© Andrew Davis 2019
A. Davis, *Mastering Salesforce DevOps*, https://doi.org/10.1007/978-1-4842-5473-8_4

That capability will soon also be available when developing on sandboxes. Changes can also be retrieved from sandboxes using either `source:retrieve` or `mdapi:retrieve`, depending on whether you are storing metadata in the "Source" format or the original "Metadata API" format mentioned in Chapter 2: Salesforce.

Salesforce developers typically have to modify multiple aspects of Salesforce to create a solution. For example, a typical feature might involve changes to a Lightning Web Component, an Apex class, a custom object, a Lightning record page, and a permission set. To deploy that feature to another environment, it's necessary to isolate all of the related metadata changes. But it's entirely possible to make changes in the Salesforce Setup UI without being sure what type(s) of metadata you're modifying.

If you're the lone developer in an org, working on a single feature, it's relatively easy to distinguish the metadata for that feature, especially if you're using version control. Just retrieve all the metadata and check for changes in that org since you began developing; whatever has changed must pertain to that feature. When dealing with small volumes of changes, small teams, and a moderate pace of innovation, it's not hard to manage Salesforce changes and deploy them across environments. But as teams begin to scale up, the pre-DX workflow begins to suffer from many limitations.

As soon as you put multiple developers in a single development org, it becomes much harder to isolate and deploy their changes independently. But when developers are working on separate orgs, integration is delayed and it becomes much harder for them to build on the work of others. Scratch orgs address this need by making it trivial to create a fresh new Salesforce environment that is up to speed with the metadata stored in version control. As you update your code repository, you can push those changes to your org, and as you make changes in the org, you can pull them down into version control without having to enumerate each type of metadata. Thus, if possible, you should develop in scratch orgs.

Unfortunately, it's still not practical for every team to use scratch orgs, and so you may find you need to keep using sandboxes for development. One very promising workflow is to automate the cloning of developer sandboxes from a single integration sandbox and then deploy changes as they're ready from those developer sandboxes into that integration org using a CI process. Recent updates to the Salesforce CLI make it possible to automate sandbox cloning and login.

One way or another, your job as a developer is to make changes in your development org, to commit them correctly to version control, and then to monitor automated tests and deployments to ensure your feature can be deployed without error. Setting up such automation is the topic of later chapters, but once it's set up, developers can adopt this rhythm: build, commit, monitor.

Since version control is critical to this process, before beginning development, you must establish a code repository for your team. If a project has already been created, you'll need to clone that project to your local machine before proceeding.

There are two Salesforce DX development models: the org development model and the package development model. The org development model is the default approach, but the two are complementary. Your team may gradually migrate most of your metadata into packages, but there will always remain the need to manage some org-level metadata through the org development model. You can find a nice introduction to these different models on Trailhead at `https://trailhead.salesforce.com/content/learn/modules/application-lifecycle-and-development-models`.

The options available for developing on Salesforce are in flux, and most Salesforce developers are still getting up to speed on foundational concepts such as version control. This means that there's more variety in the development workflow than there was just a few years ago, and the optimal workflow of the future is not yet clear. This book attempts to present a comprehensive picture of the options, but expect things to evolve over the coming years.

If you are using the org development model, you will probably have a single repository representing all aspects of the org's metadata that are managed by the development team. Chapter 7: The Delivery Pipeline provides recommendations on an appropriate branching structure for this model.

If you are using the package development model, you will probably have one repository for org-level metadata and one or more repositories for managing package metadata. Dividing your code across multiple repositories makes it easier to set up automation for each repository, but can easily get confusing as to which repository contains which metadata.

The package development workflow lends itself to a simpler Git branching structure than the org development workflow. Until you develop tooling that can dynamically determine which packages have changed and should have new versions published, separate packages should be developed in separate code repositories.

The package development model implies that you are using scratch orgs. If you are using scratch orgs, you will need to periodically recreate these scratch orgs to ensure that they are clean and reflect the latest version of the codebase. If you are working with a complex set of metadata and package dependencies, you may find the scratch org creation process takes a long time (up to an hour or more), so you may want to periodically precreate scratch orgs for upcoming work. The forthcoming Scratch Org Snapshots capability allows you to perform scratch org creation in advance and take a Snapshot of that org. The Snapshot can then be used to quickly create new orgs that are fully provisioned.

For those accustomed to working in long-lived sandboxes, it can feel frustrating to have to periodically recreate an entire development org. The purpose of recreating scratch orgs is to ensure that the entire application is fully represented in version control. This allows others on the team to create identical environments, and knowing all your dependencies limits the chances of confusion about why your applications don't work properly in testing and production environments.

Subtle variations between the orgs used for development and testing are a massive source of risk, confusion, and inefficiency. This is a hidden challenge that often goes unnoticed, and the time spent debugging these variations between orgs is generally not accounted for. But every moment spent debugging out-of-sync orgs is waste. Though it may seem like a radical solution, the regular destruction and recreation of scratch orgs is key to ensuring an efficient overall workflow.

You should commit changes to the code repository after each significant change. If you are making changes on a feature branch in Git, all of those changes will be associated with the name of that branch, and so your branch naming strategy can be a way of linking a work ticket number to a group of many changes.

When your development is complete and you're ready for review, you will merge it into your shared master branch (or create a merge request if your team requires that). Developing in scratch orgs unlocks the possibility of creating "Review Apps" so that other members of the team can review the developer's work in a live scratch org.

Review Apps are environments created dynamically from version control that provide an isolated environment to review features that may still be under development. The concept was popularized by Heroku. Review Apps should be used for most QA and testing activities, but they only contain the test data that you deploy and are generally not connected to external systems, so some testing might need to be done in an SIT org instead.

Many of the topics presented in this brief overview are covered in more detail in later chapters.

Development Tools

Some aspects of Salesforce development are done directly inside the Salesforce Setup UI, while other aspects are best handled with developer-specific tools. The critical step of externalizing changes in Salesforce to a version control system is always done outside of Salesforce. This section gives a brief introduction to key Salesforce development tools and how they are used.

The Salesforce CLI

The Salesforce CLI can be downloaded from `https://developer.salesforce.com/tools/sfdxcli`. This command-line interface is an essential part of your DX toolkit. Many Salesforce CLI commands will only run inside a Salesforce DX project. A Salesforce DX project is one which contains a file called `sfdx-project.json`. That file is used to store information about the folders and packages in your project.

You can quickly scaffold a new project by using the `sfdx project:create` command, or you can clone one of the sample repositories from the Salesforce DX Developer Guide to be able to use a CI system like CircleCI. All of these project templates contain `sfdx-project.json` along with other helpful files.

You can get help for any CLI command by adding the `-h` or `--help` parameter. You can also find detailed help in the Salesforce CLI Command Reference. The CLI commands also allow you to export their results in JSON format by adding the `--json` parameter. This capability unlocks the possibility of automating complex processes by extracting the results from one command and passing them as parameters to other commands. See the section on "Command-Line Scripts" in Chapter 9: Deploying for advice.

What's an Integrated Development Environment (IDE)?

An IDE is a code editor which brings together all the tools that developers need to write, track, debug, test, and deploy code. Some IDEs are built for a particular language (e.g., PyCharm is specific to Python), whereas others (like Eclipse and IntelliJ) support multiple languages. An IDE provides a code editor, but also offers things like syntax highlighting, code completion, debugging, and more. Most IDEs are extensible, allowing you to install plugins which add new functionality.

The Developer Console

The Dev Console is a web-based IDE that is built into Salesforce. It's accessible from the gear icon in the upper right of each Salesforce org. It provides a convenient way to edit Apex, Visualforce, or Lightning Components. It also allows you to review debug logs, set checkpoints, and run anonymous Apex or SOQL queries among other capabilities.

It does not provide you a way to track metadata in version control, do deployments, or work with Lightning Web Components, and it's no longer under active development. For certain tasks, like using logs to analyze performance, optimizing queries using the query plan, or checking Visualforce ViewState, the Developer Console is still my go-to tool, so it's worth becoming familiar with its capabilities, although it will become less relevant over time.

Workbench

Workbench is an unofficial Salesforce tool hosted at `https://workbench.`
`developerforce.com`. It provides a user interface for numerous developer-focused tools. In particular, it provides a simple way to navigate Salesforce's various APIs and to test out API commands. Workbench exposes the Metadata API's ability to deploy or retrieve metadata and to describe metadata such as custom objects. It exposes the bulk API's ability to retrieve or modify data. And it allows you to execute SOQL or SOSL queries and anonymous Apex.

Workbench may never become part of your daily workflow, but it's important to know it exists, as it's the right tool for a wide variety of jobs.

The Forthcoming Web IDE

If this were a Salesforce conference, I would insert a forward-looking statement slide at this point. The Salesforce DX team is working on a web-based IDE that will encapsulate the capabilities of the Developer Console and Workbench (and thus allow those tools to be retired). At the same time, the Web IDE will allow teams to store complete sets of project files, run Salesforce CLI and Git commands, and interact with both Salesforce orgs and code repositories.

The initial goal is to get feature parity with the Developer Console and Workbench. Eventually this will provide a convenient IDE for teams who aren't able or don't wish to use desktop development tools.

Visual Studio Code

Salesforce built the original Force.com IDE on Eclipse, an open source IDE popular among Java developers. In 2018, Salesforce retired that IDE and began building a set of extensions on top of Visual Studio Code.

Visual Studio Code (VS Code) is a rare success story among developer tools. It's an open source code editor that first appeared in 2015. Within 3 short years, it became the world's most popular development environment.[1]

VS Code is the product of Microsoft, a company whose success and wealth have been built around proprietary commercial tools. Microsoft has not historically been well loved by the open source community, but VS Code is one of many such contributions[2] made under Satya Nadella's guidance. VS Code may even be reducing the number of people willing to pay for Microsoft's commercial code editors.

Whatever the history, Microsoft has built an editor that has won the hearts and minds of millions of developers. And by making the tool open source, they are benefitting from an amazing stream of innovation from hundreds of citizen developers who have contributed features and bug fixes. Not to mention the thousands of companies like Salesforce who have built extensions for VS Code.

So, what is VS Code? Why has it become so popular? And why, in particular, is it the new chosen platform for Salesforce to build their IDE on?

Visual Studio Code is a free, open source, cross-platform, multilingual IDE. VS Code has the speed and simplicity of Sublime Text, with the power and tool set of Eclipse or paid IDEs like IntelliJ. It's fast, simple, and clean; there's a fast-growing set of extensions for it; and it's adding new features every month.

Because it's popular, it's attracting innovation. In its short lifetime, VS Code has become the world's most popular IDE, with more than 50% of developers worldwide adopting it. Salesforce has deprecated the Force.com IDE and is solely focused on building tools for VS Code.

- Visual Studio Code is fast and can be installed on Windows, Mac, or Linux machines.

- It has support/extensions for 72+ programming languages out of the box.

---

[1]https://insights.stackoverflow.com/survey/2018/#development-environments-and-tools
[2]www.zdnet.com/article/microsoft-open-sources-its-entire-patent-portfolio/

- It gives built-in syntax highlighting and bracket matching in your code, as well as easy code navigation.

- It has a built-in terminal and a stepwise debugger that supports many languages, including the new Apex Debugger and Apex Replay Debugger.

- It supports Git natively so you can view diffs, commit, sync, and perform all the essential source control commands without leaving the editor.

- It has a wise set of defaults but is extensively configurable.

There are many blogs that have done "bake offs" or detailed feature comparisons between other popular editors (like Vim, Eclipse, Sublime Text, Atom, and TextMate). We won't repeat all of the details here, but instead just summarize some of the main comparisons as follows:

- It's more user-friendly than old-school editors like Vim, Emacs, Nano, Pico, and so on (anyone remember Edlin?).

- It's faster and more flexible than Eclipse.

- It has more robust built-in developer tools (like version control and debugging) compared to Sublime or Atom.

- It's also faster and handles large files better than Atom.

- It has far richer capabilities (like syntax highlighting and autoformatting) compared to TextMate, BBedit, or Notepad.

- It's free-er than IntelliJ or (the original, commercial) Visual Studio!

While Salesforce itself lives "in the cloud," professional developers tend to write code for Salesforce using desktop tools. For a long time, the Force.com IDE based on Eclipse was the standard Salesforce development environment. With the preview release of Salesforce DX in 2016, Salesforce launched a Force.com IDE 2.0, also based on Eclipse. But before long, they changed course, deprecated the Force.com IDE and are now exclusively promoting VS Code as their official editor.

One reason for the change of heart is the architecture that VS Code is built on. VS Code is built using Electron, a framework that allows you to build Windows, Mac, and Linux desktop applications using HTML, CSS, and JavaScript. This means that to improve the user interface or add automation to VS Code, you can use the same technologies used to build web sites—the most common IT skillset in the world.[3] VS Code also uses the innovative concept of Language Servers—which allowed Salesforce to build a generic language server for Apex and Lightning[4] that can in theory be ported to Atom, Eclipse, or any other IDE that supports Language Server Protocol (LSP).

In the meantime, Salesforce was aware that MavensMate (especially in conjunction with Sublime Text) had become the open source editor of choice for many Salesforce developers who preferred its speed and simplicity to the older, rigid structure enforced by Eclipse. Sublime Text's simplicity was a key inspiration for VS Code's clean UI.

So by Dreamforce 2017, Salesforce had officially retired the Force.com IDE (including the newer IDE 2.0), in favor of VS Code.

In the meantime, Salesforce has continued to roll out innovation on top of VS code, and the VS Code team themselves have been releasing new features at a phenomenal pace.

VS Code should be your default choice for a Salesforce IDE. You can use it on your existing Salesforce orgs using the new metadata deploy and retrieve commands. This gives you a chance to get used to tools like the Apex Replay Debugger (a superior way to handle debug logs), test management tool, and more.

Despite these developments, VS Code still has frustrating gaps, especially for those developing on sandboxes. As of this writing, it does not provide any warning if you are pushing updates to a sandbox that will overwrite others' work. Those limitations will eventually go away, but you should also seriously consider one of the IDEs mentioned below in the meantime.

Other Salesforce IDEs

There are currently two commercial IDEs for Salesforce that provide extremely robust capabilities: The Welkin Suite and Illuminated Cloud. The Welkin Suite is based on Microsoft's Visual Studio (the commercial one, not VS Code) but is downloaded as a standalone application. Illuminated Cloud is a plugin for the IntelliJ and WebStorm IDEs by JetBrains.

---

[3]https://insights.stackoverflow.com/
survey/2018/#technology-programming-scripting-and-markup-languages
[4]https://youtu.be/eBOVoYOb2V8?t=861

Both Visual Studio and IntelliJ are exceptional development environments and are loved by millions of developers. They both now offer free tiers, but their popularity has been eclipsed as VS Code's has exploded.

Illuminated Cloud and The Welkin Suite fill major gaps in the Salesforce extensions for VS Code. They both charge an annual fee, but will quickly pay for themselves in terms of time and agony saved for each developer. The Welkin Suite is somewhat more expensive, but is supported by a larger team of developers. Illuminated Cloud is the work of Scott Wells, who has supported it tirelessly and has an amazing knowledge of the platform and the challenges faced by developers.

Both of these tools innovate extensively and continue to have promising futures, even as Salesforce evolves their free alternative. The Welkin Suite created a replay debugger several years before this was available in VS Code. And Illuminated Cloud combines IntelliJ's excellent features such as code completion and task management integration with support for all Salesforce languages, metadata types, and development models.

In addition to these, it's worth mentioning three other tools. ForceCode[5] was one of the earliest VS Code extensions for Salesforce. It was created by John Nelson while working for CodeScience. The project had been deprecated after Salesforce released their extensions for VS Code, but I learned recently that it has come back to life. Among other good qualities, it helps compare your local copy of code with the latest version in your Salesforce org and includes tools to manage the process of building complex single-page apps using JavaScript frameworks and deploying them to the Salesforce platform.

MavensMate is now retired but was largely responsible for convincing the Salesforce developer ecosystem that there were faster and simpler alternatives to the Force.com IDE. Joe Ferraro labored for years to provide MavensMate, doing an enormous service to the Salesforce developer community.

Aside.io is a web-based IDE that was also very popular with my colleagues. It has the benefit of not requiring any local software installation. But as a result, it does not provide a method to interface with version control. Aside.io may be discontinued soon, but its founder has committed to open sourcing the project if possible.

---

[5]https://marketplace.visualstudio.com/items?itemName=JohnAaronNelson

Metadata (Config and Code)

For those new to Salesforce development, it's useful to reiterate that Salesforce does not allow for local development because changes are necessarily compiled and run on a Salesforce instance and cannot be run locally. Lightning Web Components are some exception to that, and LWC local development capability is now available. The JavaScript used in static resources is also available for local development, but these are typically only small parts of a Salesforce application.

What is possible, however, is to download your Salesforce configuration as metadata that can be stored, tracked, updated, and deployed back to a Salesforce instance.

What Is Metadata?

Most Salesforce customizations are represented as metadata components. These metadata components are files that can be retrieved from the server (Salesforce instance) and modified locally, then saved back to the server or deployed to another environment. A detailed list of available metadata items can be found in the Metadata API documentation.[6]

These metadata files are largely stored as XML, although some are code, and some new types are JSON. It's this metadata representation that can be stored in version control and is the basis for automated processes such as static analysis and automated deployments.

Metadata API File Format and `package.xml`

As explained in Chapter 9: Deploying, the key technology that enables retrieving and deploying metadata from a Salesforce org is the Metadata API. The Metadata API uses a file called `package.xml` to enumerate the metadata that should be deployed or retrieved. Some developer tools like MavensMate rely on this file as a representation of the metadata in your org.

The use of `package.xml` can lead to confusing results if there's a mismatch between its contents and the metadata files you're working with. So an increasing number of tools are doing away with this file and instead automatically generating it as needed.

---

[6]https://developer.salesforce.com/docs/atlas.en-us.api_meta.meta/api_meta/
meta_types_list.htm

For example, the Salesforce DX source format does not include this file at all. Nevertheless, it's dynamically generated behind the scenes when communicating with the Metadata API.

The Metadata API explicitly deals with files using an src/ directory that contains the package.xml file itself as well as the individual metadata for the project. These files are organized into folders based on the type of metadata as shown in Listing 4-1. Each metadata item is its own file within that folder.

Listing 4-1. The native Metadata API file and folder structure

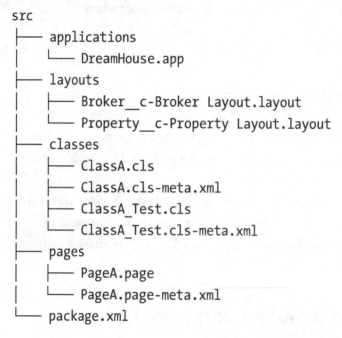

```
src
├── applications
│   └── DreamHouse.app
├── layouts
│   ├── Broker__c-Broker Layout.layout
│   └── Property__c-Property Layout.layout
├── classes
│   ├── ClassA.cls
│   ├── ClassA.cls-meta.xml
│   ├── ClassA_Test.cls
│   └── ClassA_Test.cls-meta.xml
├── pages
│   ├── PageA.page
│   └── PageA.page-meta.xml
└── package.xml
```

Note that some metadata types like applications and layouts have a single metadata file to represent a single item, while other types like classes and pages use two or more files. Files like ClassA.cls contain the actual metadata body (in this case an Apex class), while files like ClassA.cls-meta.xml are called "sidecar files" and store some accompanying metadata. Sidecar files are typically very small XML files.

One of the innovations of the Salesforce DX source format is the ability to group related metadata into subfolders that can eventually be published as packages. That is not possible in the native Metadata API format and is a key benefit of moving to Salesforce DX.

Converting Between Salesforce DX and Metadata API Source Formats

There are special commands to convert between the Salesforce DX metadata format and the Metadata API format. The Salesforce DX Developer Guide and some Trailhead modules[7] and video tutorials[8] describe this process in more detail. Here we provide just a brief overview.

sfdx force:project:create allows you to create a new set of project files in the Salesforce DX format. But it's often the case that you want to convert an existing set of metadata files into Salesforce DX "source format."

sfdx force:mdapi:convert operates on projects stored in the native Metadata API format and converts them to the "source format." All files in the src directory are converted into files in the default folder specified in sfdx-project.json (typically force-app/main/default/). Large .object files are decomposed into smaller components, zipped static resources are decompressed, and so forth. Initially these files are not grouped into subdirectories, but after being converted, you can create subdirectories to group metadata into packages.

sfdx force:source:convert performs the opposite conversion, taking metadata files in the SFDX source format and converting them into the native Metadata API format. Even if you have grouped your source format metadata into many subfolders, once converted into the Metadata API format, they will all be in a single src/ folder. This process will autogenerate the package.xml file mentioned earlier. Note that this is a "lossy" conversion; if you convert these files back to the DX source format, you will lose the folder structure.

What Metadata Should You Not Track?

The main goal of this book is to provide advice on building a CI/CD pipeline for Salesforce. That pipeline becomes a delivery vehicle for metadata to allow it to be built in a development environment, promoted for testing, and finally delivered to production.

---

[7]https://trailhead.salesforce.com/en/modules/sfdx_app_dev/units/sfdx_app_dev_deploy
[8]www.youtube.com/watch?v=6lNG6iFVGQg&list=PLp3OcEU4IpnBX2yZWJw7jjMXvsFIltM57&index=2

There are however types of metadata such as those shown in Table 4-1 that generally should not be included in the code repository and CI/CD process. There can be temporary and long-term exceptions to this rule depending on the needs of the project team. Think of the things that you include in the CI/CD process as being "controlled by developers and admins," as opposed to being "controlled by end users." The essence of continuous delivery is being able to reliably recreate development, testing, and production environments and code. And for this reason all core functionality (custom objects and fields, business logic, even page layouts) should be controlled by this development process. But functionality like reports and dashboards are a great example of metadata that can safely be controlled by business users, since they may need to change frequently and with rare exceptions changing them will not cause side effects elsewhere in the system.

If you exclude these items from your code repository, you should also add them to your `.forceignore` file to prevent them from sneaking back in.

Table 4-1. *Types of metadata that might be excluded from CI/CD*

Metadata Type	Reason to Exclude from CI/CD
Certificate	Certificates are generally environment-specific and should be kept secure.
ConnectedApp	Connected Apps are generally environment-specific. If you automate their deployment, you will need to dynamically replace some parameters.
Dashboard	These are often changed frequently by users in production and should not go through the development lifecycle unless they are a dependency for your code or metadata.
Document	These are often changed frequently by users in production and should not go through the development lifecycle unless they are a dependency for your code or metadata.
EmailTemplate	These are often changed frequently by users in production and should not go through the development lifecycle unless they are a dependency for your code or metadata. An exception is VisualForce email templates or other templates that use embedded code and may require a careful development process.

(continued)

Table 4-1. (*continued*)

Metadata Type	Reason to Exclude from CI/CD
InstalledPackage	You can't control the installation order. Use `sfdx package` commands to install packages instead.
Layout	When following the package development model, page layouts can be problematic. They should be managed at the org level for any objects that straddle multiple packages.
NamedCredential	Named Credentials are generally environment-specific. If you automate their deployment, you will need to dynamically replace some parameters.
PlatformCachePartition	These are typically environment-specific.
Profile	Profiles are the fussiest of all metadata types, as explained below. Without special automation, you will find it easier to manage these manually.
Report	These are often changed frequently by users in production and should not go through the development lifecycle unless they are a dependency for your code or metadata.
SamlSsoConfig	SAML SSO Configuration is usually environment-specific. If you automate their deployment, you will need to dynamically replace some parameters.
Site	The Site metadata type represents Communities, but is stored as a binary file and can change unpredictably, making it a poor candidate for CI/CD.

Retrieving Changes

After modifying items in a development org, you need to retrieve those changes and merge them into your local working directory so that you can track changes and deploy them using CI/CD.

The Salesforce CLI and the different IDEs mentioned earlier all provide mechanisms to retrieve metadata. The commercial Salesforce release management tools introduced in Chapter 9: Deploying also provide mechanisms for doing this.

The way the Metadata API behaves can make retrieving metadata very awkward without the help of a specialized tool. This is especially true when working in the native Metadata API format. A single `.object` file can contain hundreds of child metadata items. If you request to retrieve one of those child items, such as a field, your request will overwrite the entire `.object` file with just the metadata for that one item.

Profiles are famously awkward to deal with. A profile can contain thousands of permission details such as field-level security. But when you issue a simple retrieve command for a profile, it will retrieve only the small subset called "user permissions." To retrieve the field-level security part of a profile, you have to retrieve both the profile and the appropriate field. As mentioned earlier, this will overwrite the local metadata file for the object and will also overwrite any other permissions in the profile file. Even more confusingly, to retrieve the page layout assignment for a particular record type, you have to retrieve the profile, the page layout, and the particular record type. I could go on.

Why such bizarre and unfortunate behavior? It's because the Metadata API was not originally designed to create a single representation of the org that was suitable to be stored in version control. This is one of the key reasons why it's important to use tools that are specialized for Salesforce development, and one of the key reasons why naively attempting to build a Salesforce CI/CD process without specialized tools will end in tears.

Adopting a specialized Salesforce IDE or release management tool will pay for itself very quickly (especially if you use the free ones!). These tools have solved these problems and allow you to follow a rational workflow for retrieving, tracking, and deploying metadata.

The Salesforce DX source synchronization process for scratch orgs also addresses these challenges. The SFDX source format is designed to store metadata for use in version control and automated deployments. And the source synchronization capability of scratch orgs handles complex retrieves and merges automagically.

Making Changes

Changes to a Salesforce org can be made either using the Salesforce UI or by modifying the metadata in your local IDE and compiling it to the Salesforce org.

Most configuration changes should be made with the UI to ensure that the metadata remains coherent, while most code changes are made from the IDE. The Salesforce-specific IDEs perform a two-step process when saving. They first save your file locally and then attempt to deploy them to your development org. If the deployment is unsuccessful, you will receive an error that prompts you to fix your change. In the case of code files, deploying your metadata files will also compile your code and show you any compile-time errors. If the deployment is successful, your update will be saved to the org.

Note that you have to remain attentive to any errors returned by your IDE. It's entirely possible to commit local metadata files to version control in an invalid format, which will cause downstream failures if you attempt to deploy them. It's the developer's responsibility to ensure that they can make a successful round-trip from their local metadata file to the Salesforce org and back.

Salesforce DX scratch orgs and source synchronization address these challenges. Scratch orgs are generally designed for a single user or for limited collaboration between one dev, one admin, and maybe people testing or demoing new features. This bypasses the challenge of possibly overwriting others' work in a shared sandbox.

The source synchronization process also makes deployments to scratch orgs very fast and simple. Local metadata is first analyzed to see if it has changed (using a timestamp and a hash), and only metadata that has been changed is pushed, which makes the deployments much faster. There's no need to specify which specific files should be pushed to the scratch org; every changed file will be pushed using a single command.

Manual Changes

Almost all of the steps required for a deployment can be automated using metadata and the Salesforce CLI, although it takes time to get familiar with the way that UI changes are represented in metadata. There are however some changes that cannot be tracked or deployed in this way. When manual configuration is needed for functionality to work, developers or admins should track and document the required steps in whatever project tracking tool is being used. The instructions should be as detailed as necessary for whoever will eventually perform those manual steps.

It's at this point that the dreams of fully automated deployments bump up against a more manual reality. As mentioned in Chapter 9: Deploying, many of the things that people think are manual steps can in fact be automated. And the Salesforce Metadata API teams keep working on addressing gaps in the metadata.

Traditionally, when developing on sandboxes, developers need to have extensive knowledge of many different metadata types and do research to determine if and how that metadata can be downloaded. The source synchronization process available in scratch orgs and soon also in sandboxes addresses this problem by automatically identifying what was changed through the Setup UI and downloading the appropriate metadata. The productivity gains from this cannot be overstated.

Click-Based Development on Salesforce

There are roughly 250 different types of Salesforce metadata that are configured declaratively, using "clicks not code," on the Salesforce platform. This configuration can be as simple as toggling settings and as complex as using sophisticated "Builders" to create complex UIs, data models, and business logic. The App Builder, Schema Builder, Flow Builder, Process Builder, and Community Builder provide drag-and-drop components for these purposes, each with their own configurable settings.

The degree to which Salesforce can be configured in this way is a defining characteristic of the platform. It means that even code-based Salesforce developers need to be familiar with at least the basic declarative configuration tools. It also means that one can spend their entire career building and customizing Salesforce and never leave the Salesforce UI.

Development—No-Code, Low-Code, and Pro-Code

Salesforce sometimes distinguishes three types of developers—no-code, low-code, or pro-code—based on their skills and preferred tools. The term "developer" implies someone who creates something systematically and by phases. This is certainly true of those who code, since the process involves extensive testing and iteration. But it's equally true of those who use graphical tools. The initial iteration of a Flow might be quite simple. It then needs to be tested, edge cases need to be identified, logic can be added, and so forth.

It's worth remembering that code itself is a user interface—it's just a text-based UI rather than a graphical one. The history of computer science is largely the history of building increasingly high-level abstractions to make logic more clear for humans. Assembly language was created to free people from having to write numeric instructions in machine code. Higher-level languages like C freed people from having to deal with esoteric assembly language. Languages like JavaScript layer on further abstractions and simplifications, eliminate the process of compiling code, and give access to hundreds of thousands of prebuilt modules that encapsulate solutions to common problems.

Each transition to a higher level has made the language more accessible, at the cost of some performance. Those who are familiar with working at lower levels of abstraction can boast of building more optimized solutions. But a performance cost is often a very worthwhile sacrifice for a solution that is easier to understand and maintain over time.

And so in Salesforce, "pro-code" developers are those who are comfortable or prefer working directly with Apex, Visualforce, Lightning, or Salesforce APIs. "Low-code" developers are those who are more comfortable working with declarative tools, but who are nevertheless comfortable creating or maintaining small and strategic bits of code. And "no-code" developers are those who build and maintain customizations entirely using declarative tools.

"No-code" developers are extremely common in the Salesforce world. But the idea of developing without code is still a nascent movement in the IT world. Graphical abstractions for UI and data models are extremely common, for example, with tools that allow you to build web pages without dipping into HTML or build relational databases visually. Graphical abstractions of logic are less common; but even the most sophisticated programmers often crave and create visual representations of complex code like UML diagrams. In this respect, the future is already here on the Salesforce platform.

Salesforce Flows actually use Visualforce or Lightning to generate pages. In that sense, Flows are truly higher-order abstractions built over top Salesforce coding technology. As with other abstractions, Flows and Processes do not perform as well as pure Apex or Lightning solutions, and their metadata format is arcane. But they allow business processes to be visualized and edited by a far larger group of users, which is a massive boon for maintainability. They are one of many examples where Salesforce is democratizing development. While pure coders may be dismissive of solutions that trade efficiency for simplicity, history shows that this can be a massive strategic advantage.

But don't expect code to go away anytime soon. Salesforce themselves had to retreat from their original "clicks not code" motto. And "pro-code" development options like Web Components, Git, and CI/CD are becoming increasingly easy and popular on Salesforce. Just as I would have been hard-pressed to write this book using graphical tools, there's often no substitute for the freedom and flexibility of text-based code to express complex scenarios.

Declarative Development Tools

Entire books have been written about Salesforce declarative tools like Community Builder, so I'm making no attempt to cover that topic exhaustively here.

What matters for our purposes is that any declarative changes that are made in Salesforce need to be converted into a textual form if they are to be tracked in version control and migrated to other environments using the tools described in Chapter 9: Deploying. This is the job of the Metadata API, described in detail in that chapter. The Metadata API provides a text-based representation of declarative configuration, mostly in XML, that can be inspected, tracked, and deployed to other environments.

In most cases, the purpose of capturing declarative configuration as text is simply to retrieve it from one Salesforce environment and deploy it to another environment. Along the way, there certainly is manual or automated processing that can be done on that metadata, some of which is described later in this book. But just as the declarative tools themselves range from simple to complex, so too does this metadata representation. I feel extremely comfortable viewing and updating the XML that describes custom objects, fields, and validation rules. But I don't know anyone who regularly edits the metadata representations of Flows and Processes.

There are countless tips and tricks that could be shared about working with declarative metadata; some of these I know, many of them I don't. So I'll constrain this discussion to a few points about a few of the most complex declarative Builders.

Lightning App Builder

The Lightning App Builder is a way to create UIs by assembling Lightning Components. From a metadata point of view, the final result of using the App Builder is a metadata item of type `Flexipage`. This is an XML representation of the page that includes the page layout, the components on the page, component properties, and some other metadata such as platform actions available for that page. This metadata is stored in a single file and is easy to version and deploy.

Community Builder

Community Builder is similar to Lightning App Builder in that it is used to create and configure user interfaces with drag-and-drop elements. But it adds considerable sophistication in that it can be used to create entire Communities—multipage web sites—and to define the overarching structure of the site as well as individual pages. Community Builder is a massive area of growth and focus for Salesforce, and they're working on a unified "Experience" model that can also encompass the web site builders associated with Marketing Cloud and Commerce Cloud.

One massive disadvantage of Community pages is that until recently they didn't have human-readable metadata contents. That's changing with the release of the

ExperienceBundle metadata type, although that's still in Developer Preview as of this writing. In marked contrast to most Salesforce metadata, ExperienceBundles are stored as JSON files. Salesforce began in 1998 and is mostly written in Java, the most promising programming language from that time. Salesforce also relies heavily on the data storage and exchange formats which were popular at that time, XML and SOAP, which are very well supported by Java. JSON is a newer and simpler standard that has grown in popularity alongside JavaScript, since it allows for smaller and more readable files, which can be parsed natively by JavaScript.

Although it's currently possible to deploy entire communities using the Site, Network, and SiteDotCom metadata types, the Site is stored as a binary file which changes each time it's retrieved, and so isn't suitable for version control or continuous delivery. As ExperienceBundles become widely adopted, it should become possible to selectively deploy aspects of a Community without redeploying the entire thing. Until then, teams must either deploy the entire Site or manually migrate Community configuration from one Salesforce org to another.

Process and Flow Builders

Process Builder is used to create business logic that is triggered by an event such as a record update. Processes are necessarily linear sequences of steps that are performed one after another, although there are an increasing number of available options.

Flow Builder is used to create more complex logic and can also be used to create user interfaces and to define data flow across screens. Processes are built on the same underlying technology as Flows, and they are both retrieved using the metadata type Flow.

For many releases, managing Flow metadata also required managing metadata for FlowDefinition. Each Flow or Process version was stored as a separate Flow file, and a corresponding FlowDefinition file specified which version of the flow was active. Since Winter '19, only the active Flow version is retrieved, FlowDefinitions are not needed, and Flows can be deployed as active under certain circumstances. Since Flow versions update the same filename, you can keep a clear history of changes in version control.

Flows and Processes are one of a small number of metadata types where Salesforce manages version numbers internally and allows versions to be updated or rolled back from the Setup UI.

This is a very powerful capability for many reasons. First, Flows are asynchronous and may be waiting for user input for many minutes. Flows store the user's state in a

`FlowInterview` object, along with which version of the Flow is being used. Even if a different version is activated while a user is still progressing through that Flow, they will be able to complete the process using the same Flow version they started with.

Second, this allows for versions of a Flow to be deployed without being immediately released. As explained in Chapter 10: Releasing to Users, the ability to deploy without releasing is a key capability that enables continuous delivery. While Flow versions do not allow you to release to only a subset of users, they certainly enable you to roll out or roll back a flow version on your own schedule, regardless of when they were deployed to an org.

Finally, Flow versions provide a form of declarative version control. The use of traditional version control is still far from ubiquitous on Salesforce. Declarative developers building Processes and Flows are grappling with complex logic and UIs that might take days or weeks to build. As with code-based development, it's invaluable to be able to take a snapshot of your work and begin experimenting with a new approach, confident that you can always roll back to a previous version. By dispensing with `FlowDefinition` metadata, Salesforce is making it easier to manage Flows using traditional version control like Git while still preserving the declarative versioning of Flows.

There's one final sense in which Flows and Processes are unique among declarative metadata. Salesforce has begun to enforce code coverage requirements on these, just as they do with Apex code. As we'll discuss in Chapter 8: Quality and Testing, Apex tests are not limited to only validating Apex code. They can validate any form of backend business logic in Salesforce, including validation and workflow rules, Processes, and autolaunched Flows (those which don't require a UI).

The only case when code coverage is required for Processes and Flows is when they are deployed as Active. By default, they are deployed in a Draft status and have to be manually activated. You can enable the ability to deploy these as active from **Setup ➤ Process Automation Settings ➤ Deploy processes and flows as active**. If you choose this option, then you must ensure that you have Apex tests that exercise these flows. For example, if a Process is triggered any time you create or update an Opportunity with a particular record type, you must have an Apex test that performs such an action.

This is a fairly soft requirement, in that not every logical execution scenario has to be tested. So it doesn't require tests that are as detailed as those which test Apex classes or triggers, where 75% of all the *lines* have to be covered. But you have to at least touch those Flows and Processes.

Data Management

The very core of Salesforce is a relational database that can be easily managed using clicks not code. This is the earliest configurable part of the platform and is still the most heavily used. Admins can use graphical tools to define objects and fields, connect them to other database objects, place them on page layouts, and define who can see them.

A complete explanation of this topic is far outside the scope of this book, but it's worth mentioning a few points that have an impact on the overall flow of changes from development to production.

Managing the Schema

"Schema" is a fancy name for the data structures in a relational database. In the simplest terms, it defines what data you want to store and how that data is related to other data. In a traditional database, you define spreadsheet-like tables to hold each category of data, in which each "row" is a record, each "column" is a field, and some special columns can be "lookup relationships" to rows in other tables. In Salesforce, tables are referred to as "Objects" (like the Account Object) because the definition of that object includes far more than just the data structure.

Creating a new schema object or field is typically done using multistep wizards, and this is often the first configuration activity that Salesforce admins and devs will learn. For the impatient, Salesforce provides a Schema Builder that allows you to create objects and fields quickly while bypassing nonessential steps in the wizard.

Although this process is relatively quick and easy, it can have big impacts on the rest of the org. UI, reporting, and business logic are built around displaying, analyzing, and manipulating data, and so the schema is fundamental to most other customizations.

When people first begin to set up version control and continuous delivery for Salesforce, it's tempting to only track code. Code is certainly the most important candidate for version control, but code in Salesforce is largely built for retrieving and manipulating database objects, and so without tracking the schema you don't have a complete picture stored in version control. If you attempt to automatically deploy code to later environments, your deployments will fail unless the necessary objects and fields are already in place.

For these reasons, you should manage the schema in your testing and production environments using version control and a continuous delivery process. You should not allow any manual changes to the schema in those environments, unless you have a high tolerance for confusion and inefficiency. You can and should modify objects and fields in a development environment and deploy from there along with the rest of your configuration.

As mentioned, there's a lot more to Salesforce objects than just a data table. This is reflected in the `object` metadata format, which includes fields, validation rules, compact layouts, and record types among other components. It's for this reason that critical objects in your data model like Accounts can easily have an object metadata file that grows to tens or hundreds of thousands of lines. Version control tools like Git excel at managing and merging line-by-line changes to code files. But the default `diff` tool included with Git gets extremely confused when comparing repetitive blocks of XML metadata, making such large files very hard for teams to manage and collaborate on.

The Salesforce DX source format "decomposes" each object file into a folder, with files for each child component organized into subfolders by metadata type. Breaking large XML metadata into many files makes it straightforward for teams to manage and deploy the schema collaboratively.

Changing the Schema

Most schema changes lend themselves well to being propagated from dev to test to production. There is, however, one caveat and two big exceptions. The caveat is that some seemingly innocent schema changes can cause data loss or other problems. The two exceptions where schema changes can't (or shouldn't) be propagated automatically are when changing the object/field names and when changing field types.

It is important to emphasize to your developers and admins that their changes can and will have an impact on production data and users, and that it is their responsibility to envision not only the end state that they want to build but also the impact of any changes to existing functionality. It's important to facilitate the free flow of innovation, but here are just a few examples where schema changes require a skeptical eye:

- Increasing the length of a field is usually safe, but decreasing its length can truncate data and cause data loss.

- Increasing the length of a field can cause problems if you're integrating with external systems and those systems truncate or refuse to accept longer data values.

- Adding validation rules is part of business logic and must be tested carefully since it can cause Apex tests and integrations to break.

- Disabling field or object history tracking will delete that historical data unless you're using Salesforce Shield.

- Making a field required can also break Apex tests and integrations and is not a deployable change unless that field is populated for every record in the target org.

Don't Change DeveloperNames

The two types of schema change that are truly problematic in a continuous delivery process are changing object/field names and changing field types. Every type of Salesforce metadata, including objects and fields, has a DeveloperName (aka API name) that uniquely identifies it. That name is usually created dynamically when you specify the label or display name for the metadata. For example, if I create a field labeled "Implementation Manager," the New Custom Field Wizard will suggest the field name `Implementation_Manager__c`. When you retrieve the metadata for that new field, the field name appears as the `<fullName>` property in the XML and the name of the field file if you're using the Salesforce DX source format.

Let's say you decide to change the label for that field to "Success Manager." It's tempting to also want to change the field name to `Success_Manager__c`. If you've already deployed this field to other environments, **DON'T CHANGE ITS NAME**. Take a cue from Salesforce, who regularly rebrands their features, but doesn't change their names on the backend. Einstein Analytics is still known as `Wave` in the metadata. Communities and Sites were rebranded a decade ago, but are still referenced as `Picasso` in some parts of the metadata. The list goes on and on.

The problem with changing developer names is that when you deploy the new name, it's created as an entirely new field, object, and so on. It's treated as something new and unknown; none of the data is carried over from the old object. Not only that, but you'll have to update any code, formulas, or external integrations that relied on it. **DON'T DO IT**, change the field *label* to update the UI, but leave the underlying field name the way it is. You can add an explanatory note in the field description if you think that will help.

Changing Field Types

What about changing field types? A groan is arising from the depths of my heart when I think about this activity; it's generally a big pain to propagate these changes. Here are some recommendations about addressing this.

First, the basics: every field in a Salesforce object has a field type. There are currently 23 possible field types including text, picklist, number, lookup relationship, and formula. Field types determine the storage size for fields and provide built-in data validation: you can't put text in a number field, lookup relationship fields have to point to another record, and so on. Twenty-three types of fields means there are theoretically $23 * 22 = 506$ permutations of field type changes. But there are limitations on this, so, for example, it's not possible to change a field from a formula into any other type or from any other type into a formula. Salesforce provides a help article outlining those restrictions and the cases in which data loss can occur, such as changing from a text field to a number field.[9] That article is an important reference when considering a field type change.

Why would you ever need or want to change the type of a field? There's always uncertainty in the development process. One common example is changing from a text field (which allows any value) to a picklist field (where only certain values are valid) or vice versa. The team may create a text field to store a particular value, but later realize that it's important to standardize the options to improve data quality and generate better reports.

The book *Refactoring Databases*[10] arose from the recognition that data models need to evolve over time and introduced the concept of "evolutionary database development" to address this challenging process. They provide numerous recommendations, not all of which are relevant for Salesforce, but some of which can be summarized here.

1. Delay creating (or at least deploying) objects and fields until you are actually ready to use them. It's very easy to modify your schema in your development org, but can be challenging to propagate changes, especially if you're already storing data.

2. Think long and hard about whether you actually need to change the type of a field. I've facilitated field type changes for developers, only to facilitate changing them back, and then changing them once again. Such indecision can strain your friendships.

---

[9]https://help.salesforce.com/articleView?id=notes_on_changing_custom_field_types.htm

[10]Scott W. Ambler and Pramodkumar J. Sadalage, *Refactoring Databases: Evolutionary Database Design* (Addison-Wesley Professional, 2006).

3. Experiment with the field type change in your development environment to see if it's even possible. Create a new field of the original type, and then change that field to see if it's permitted and what warnings are displayed. Delete that field when you're done.

4. Assess the risk of data loss from any field change, and get sign-off from the appropriate business stakeholders on the change.

5. Assess whether any external integrations connect to this field, to ensure they won't break or introduce bad data.

6. If you decide to proceed, you can change the field type in your development environment and attempt to deploy it. Some field type changes can be successfully propagated using the Metadata API. If your deployment succeeds, you're lucky.

7. If your deployment does not succeed, you have two options: manually change the field type or create a new field and migrate data.

8. You can manually change the field type in all other environments as a way of propagating this change. This is tedious once you become accustomed to continuous delivery, but may be your simplest option. The problem with this is if you have a long lead time to get changes into production, since it may require careful choreography to facilitate a large release and also to make manual changes such as field type changes, especially if those changes are required for work done weeks or months in the past. This is one of many arguments for doing small and frequent releases.

9. You can also create a new field of the new type and then migrate or synchronize data from the old field. This is necessary for certain field type changes, especially if the field is heavily referenced by code or other configuration. Migrating data from the old field to the new field can be done using a data management tool or by using batch or anonymous Apex, depending on how much data you need to move. Batch Apex can be used to iterate across thousands or millions of records. You query records which have the old field populated and the new field empty, and you copy

values from the old field to the new field, transforming them along the way. The Metadata API allows you to mark the old field as deprecated if you want and eventually to delete it.

10. In circumstances where you need to change a heavily used field in a production environment without incurring downtime, you can actually create a data synchronization between the old and new fields. This is the most elegant solution and could involve Apex, Processes, or Workflow rules to update the new field with the old value and the old field with the new value whenever they change. While complicated, this allows for true refactoring and enables you to deploy a complete process from development to production without requiring any manual steps. Needless to say, you should test the heck out of this process before deploying it. Once it's in place and your refactoring is complete, you can delete the old field.

Bulk Database Operations

In addition to field type changes, there may be other bulk database operations you need to perform. Many of my colleagues at Appirio specialized in transforming and migrating data from legacy systems into Salesforce, and for this there are specialized tools and skills you might need. The Salesforce data management applications Odaseva and OwnBackup both provide a wealth of tools that you might use to perform large-scale data operations. The free Salesforce Data Loader and MuleSoft's dataloader.io are excellent no-frills options to help with this process, especially in combination with clever use of spreadsheets for data transformations.

As mentioned earlier, the use of anonymous Apex and batch Apex are both excellent methods to perform bulk database operations, although you should approach this with due caution. Anonymous Apex allows you to build an Apex script so you can query, transform, and create/update/delete data as needed. Such scripts should generally be stored in version control (so you don't forget what you did), but are generally run through the developer console or the Salesforce CLI. Test such scripts very carefully. Anonymous Apex allows you to transform up to 10,000 records at a time (the DML limit). Combined with a query that is smart enough to know which records have not been processed, you can script or manually trigger iterations of this code until the job is done.

Batch Apex handles the iterations for you and is designed to process large volumes of data over time. Batch Apex is an Apex class that uses the `Database.Batchable` interface to define `start`, `execute`, and `finish` methods that iterate across your database 200 records at a time. This can be used either for one-time or ongoing processing as needed.

Data Backup

Unless you're unusually paranoid, you don't need to back up your data out of fear that Salesforce will lose it. They have excellent redundant backup systems that distribute the backup across multiple data centers. What you need to worry about is the actions of your users and yourself. Remember those bulk database operations I just mentioned? Remember how I said you should test them extremely well? I think you're getting the picture.

While unlikely, you could be subject to malicious users or hackers who intentionally delete data. More likely, unwitting users or admins might make sweeping changes that cause data loss or corruption. And it's also possible for developers to introduce batch Apex, processes, triggers, workflows, or integrations that cause sweeping and undesired changes.

For all of these reasons, data backup is important. Your free option is the monthly export service accessible in **Setup ➤ Data ➤ Data Export**. That will generate a one-time or scheduled downloadable backup. You should practice and ensure you have the skills on hand to restore some or all of that data in an emergency. Your concierge options are data management services such as AutoRABIT Vault, OwnBackup, or Odaseva who can provide data backup and recovery tools and services.

Configuration Data Management

One of the weakest links in the continuous delivery systems I have built and seen for Salesforce is the management of configuration data. Salesforce release managers and release management tools generally specialize in migrating configuration **metadata**. The Salesforce Metadata API provides a mechanism for retrieving and deploying this metadata. While there are some complexities in this process, Salesforce actually takes care of most of the complexity for you. When you do a deployment, Salesforce checks the validity of your code and configuration, ensures referential integrity and idempotency, assesses differences, sequences the metadata loads, and more. There's an enormous amount of intelligence being leveraged behind the scenes.

If you need to migrate complex configuration data, you will need to address those problems of data sequencing and referential integrity on your own. The tools and techniques for this are unfamiliar to most Salesforce release managers and so have been an afterthought for many teams.

Unfortunately, large managed packages such as Rootstock ERP, nCino, Vlocity, FinancialForce, and Salesforce CPQ require extremely complex configuration data to operate. If you use any of these packages, it's important for your team to establish tools and expertise to facilitate migrating this data, so that you can use your sandboxes to develop this configuration as well. The reason to manage configuration data in your release management process is twofold: first, that configuration data can determine logical pathways that actually affect the behavior of your applications, and second it allows you to develop and test changes to this data before migrating it to production.

To my knowledge, among the packages listed earlier, only Vlocity has built its own configuration data migration tool, Vlocity Build.[11] Prodly Moover has carved out a niche for itself as a tool that specializes in migrating such complex data. Some of the Salesforce release management tools like AutoRABIT, Gearset, and Copado have also begun to develop excellent tools to help in this process. Where these release management tools have an advantage over Prodly is that they can choreograph this data load along with releases. I haven't personally been involved with creating a highly automated configuration data release process from scratch, although it's certainly possible to do so. If you opt to code such a process yourself rather than relying on a commercial tool, here are some suggested steps you'll need to undertake to complete that script:

1. Recognize that data migrations require you to address all the steps mentioned earlier that the Metadata API does for you.

2. Recognize that the skills and experience for doing this will lie with data migration specialists and that there will need to be some logic built into the process as well.

3. Salesforce record IDs and Auto-number fields can vary from org to org, so you can't rely upon those to represent the lookup relationships between objects when you migrate data to other orgs. Therefore, there must be external IDs on all of the objects in the configuration data model so that you can establish uniqueness

---

[11]https://github.com/vlocityinc/vlocity_build

and define relationships between records in a way that's org independent. Configuration objects in managed packages should have external IDs in place already, but if you've built your own configuration objects, there needs to be at least one required, unique, external ID field on each of them.

4. Assuming the exported configuration data spans multiple objects, the result will be multiple data tables that express their record identity and relationships through external IDs. Those files then need to be loaded in sequence into the target orgs, with parent records being loaded before child records. The Bulk API provides intelligent ways to organize the loading of parent records and child records. But dealing with the Bulk API will require you to do some coding and build some familiarity with its capabilities. The Salesforce CLI introduces the possibility of `data:tree:export` and `data:tree:import` to store and transfer structured data, especially configuration and sample data, using the REST API's Composite resource endpoint. Unfortunately, those commands are limited to 200 records across all trees in one call. This means that to manage large and complex data structures across multiple orgs with minimal overhead, you will need to stitch together many such calls to represent one or more complex data trees. Prepare to do some coding, or retreat to one of the commercial tools mentioned earlier.

5. Retrieving and loading these complex trees from one org to another is clearly a challenge in its own right. If you make careful use of external IDs, marking them required and unique, then you can ensure idempotency any time you load this data in. Idempotency means that if you perform the same actions many times, you will always get the same results. In data migration, this is the same as doing an upsert, matching on external IDs, so that you will create any records that need to be created, but you will never create duplicate records, no matter how many times the data load is run.

6. The only remaining improvement is a performance improvement, so you'll need to assess whether this improvement is even beneficial enough to perform. If you're truly managing large, complex data, it can take a long time to extract, transform, and load that data between orgs. You can make a performance improvement by only retrieving and loading data that has changed since you last checked it. One trick for doing this is to use the REST API's "Get Updated" calls to see if any configuration has been updated since you last checked. This requires tracking and recalling the last time you ran the retrieval or deployment and then generating a coherent set of record updates based on the results from your query. For example, you can run a "Get Updated" call to check each configuration object for record updates since you last ran the command. You can then update the Git repository or database where you're storing this data to track the changes or proceed immediately to deploying those changes. When deploying the changes, you need to query your target org to see if configuration changes have been made in that org. You'll need to have logic to decide whether to preserve the configuration in the target org or in the source org, but if you're driving your configuration through your delivery pipeline, you'll always favor the source org. Based on knowing what changed in the target org, you can know what data to reset to the desired values. Based on knowing what changed in the source org, you'll know what data you need to migrate from source to target. The result of combining these data sets is the data set you need to migrate, which may be significantly smaller than your configuration data set.

This whole process is clearly complicated, which is why I believe this is still a nascent idea among most Salesforce development teams. But the same factors that have driven teams to seek a deployment workflow for metadata will increasingly apply to data in complex orgs. Configuration data changes can be too risky to make directly in production orgs, so they should first be done in development orgs. Those changes sometimes need to be complex, spanning multiple objects, which leads to the need to manage and migrate complex data. This is tedious and error prone for an individual to migrate; therefore an automated process is important. Therefore building this capability is important to enable our teams to not just configure but to configure safely and efficiently using a migration process to separate development from deployment.

The Security Model

The Salesforce security model is another complex topic to which I'll just offer a brief introduction and some tips to help smooth the development workflow. To make things simple, we can divide this into four topics: infrastructure security, login and identity, admin access, and user access.

Infrastructure Security

Infrastructure security refers to securing the underlying servers, networks, and data stores for an organization. This is a massive area of concern for most IT teams, a massive area of risk and liability for most companies, and one of the important areas that Salesforce handles for you. `http://trust.salesforce.com` can provide you plenty of information on Salesforce's infrastructure security protocols, certifications, and track record, but needless to say, they do an excellent job of handling this for you.

Login and Identity

Login and identity is handled by Salesforce through a variety of mechanisms. Salesforce provides a wide range of Identity and Access Management (IAM) options such as single sign-on (SSO), various types of OAuth, API access, multifactor authentication (MFA), and so on. Whereas infrastructure security is opaque to Salesforce customers, IAM is highly configurable on Salesforce, and customers take joint responsibility to ensure that this is handled correctly. Salesforce does allow you to track and deploy certain aspects of your IAM configuration between environments, and it can be helpful to manage this in your code repository along with other types of org metadata.

Metadata that defines login and identity is shown in Table 4-2. Notice that there's some overlap with the list of metadata in Table 4-1 that you *might not* want to deploy using CI/CD. The reason for this is that this metadata will need to have some variable substitution done if you want to deploy it automatically, and that might not be possible in your first iteration of CI/CD.

Table 4-2. *Types of metadata used to manage login and identity*

Metadata Type	What It Controls and How to Manage It
SecuritySettings	Includes organization-wide security settings such as trusted IP ranges as well as login session settings such as how soon users are logged out after becoming inactive.
ConnectedApp	Defines your OAuth Connected Apps including their callback URLs and consumer keys. The consumer secret is an important part of this definition, but is not stored in metadata for security reasons.
AuthProvider	Defines social sign-on providers like OpenIdConnect and Facebook that can be used to authenticate users. Social sign-on is typically used to authenticate Community users, as opposed to regular Salesforce users, although OpenIdConnect is becoming increasingly common in the enterprise. For example, Microsoft Azure Active Directory is a cloud-based identity provider which uses OpenIdConnect for SSO.
SamlSsoConfig	Defines your SAML SSO configuration, including the login URLs and validation certificate. SAML 2.0 has traditionally been the enterprise standard for SSO, but OpenIdConnect is increasingly common for enterprise use.

Some aspects of login and identity security are also handled by Profiles, and Login Flows can also affect this. Profiles can be used to specify login IP ranges and times on a per-user basis. Login Flows provide sophisticated authentication options such as calling out to third-party authentication services and assigning temporary session-based permissions.

For teams that are just getting started tracking their Salesforce code and configuration in version control, it may seem like overkill to track this kind of metadata in the repository. In fact in some cases, this metadata needs to vary slightly for different environments. For example, Connected Apps in sandboxes might have different endpoints that point to sandbox versions of other systems. But it is precisely because this configuration is so important that it makes sense to track and deploy it from version control. Many changes to login and identity should be tested in a sandbox first, and in any case, it's extremely helpful to see a history of changes. An errant admin could readily break integrations, but having version control provides you the ability to roll back and monitor changes. Automating the deployment of some of these metadata types requires that you have the ability to dynamically substitute values as part of your deployment process. This is a native capability of tools like Copado, but we provide an overview of how you can build this yourself in "Managing Org Differences" in Chapter 9: Deploying.

Admin Access

Admin access refers to ensuring that only the appropriate people have permission to make certain changes in your org. Remember that everything in Salesforce is defined by configuration and that even custom code on Salesforce is a form of configuration. You can think of admin access as configuration security, or "what you can/can't do in the Salesforce Setup UI."

Salesforce provides a built-in System Administrator profile which possesses "God Mode" privileges in your org. Needless to say, you should be very selective in who is given this profile. Most users would be assigned the out-of-the-box "Standard User" profile, which typically provides the ability to use Salesforce and see data, but not to change configuration.

Admin access and user access are the two areas where admins have the most ability to tune Salesforce to meet their organizational needs. Most organizations will eventually find the need to make a copy of the System Administrator profile and the Standard User profile and begin to customize these according to the needs of their organization.

The traditional method of providing access to control configuration has been through the use of Profiles. But as mentioned earlier, Profiles are a nightmare to manage in version control and typically don't provide the right level of granularity that teams need. Permission Sets should be your preferred method to manage permissions. You should keep profile permissions extremely thin and instead use permission sets to determine both "admin"- and "user"-level access. If possible, limit your use of profiles to defining things like login IP ranges which can't be defined in Permission Sets. More details on this are provided in Chapter 11: Keeping the Lights On.

User Access

Whereas admin access determines who can do what in the Salesforce Setup UI, user access refers to what end users can access or modify inside the Salesforce application itself. Data security defines which users have create, read, update, or delete (CRUD) permissions on Salesforce data objects. User access also defines who can use particular Apex classes, applications, Visualforce pages, and standard Salesforce applications like

Service Cloud and Knowledge. Permissions in Salesforce are always **additive**, meaning that the default is for users to have no permissions, but they gain permissions as a result of their profile, user settings, permission sets, and permission set licenses.

As mentioned, all of the admin and user access privileges are defined using profiles or (preferably) permission sets. Permission sets can and should be tracked in version control and deployed as part of your release management process. This provides history tracking on changes to these and ensures that permissions can be tested thoroughly before being deployed to production.

One of the most common failure modes for custom Salesforce applications is for developers to not deploy appropriate permissions along with other metadata. Developers can and should have System Administrator privileges in their own development environment. Such unobstructed access allows them to build capabilities without restriction. But it also makes it easy for developers to forget that end users will need explicit permissions to use what the developer has built.

Developers and testers should use the "Login As" capability to log in to their development and testing environments as one of the target users to ensure those users will have access. If a developer creates a custom application, a new object, with new fields, a tab for that object, a Visualforce page, and an Apex controller for that page, users will need permissions for each of those components. Thus as the complexity of an org increases, so too does the complexity of user permissions.

If you use profiles to manage permissions and you want to give all profiles access to this custom application, then you will need to assign those permissions to every profile. Permission sets thus help you follow the DRY maxim, "don't repeat yourself." You can define permissions for this new custom application in a single permission set and then assign that permission set to all users in the org.

Profiles and Permission Sets are both metadata and can be deployed between environments. But which users are assigned those profiles and permission sets cannot be deployed in the same way. This means that when deploying a new permission set to production, you will either need to manually assign this to all users or preferably write a bit of anonymous Apex to query all User IDs and create PermissionSetAssignment records for each user to assign the new permission set to them.

Salesforce is working on the concept of "Permission Set Groups," which is currently in Pilot. This provides a much more elegant alternative. You attach multiple permission sets to a permission set group and then assign a large group of users to that single Permission Set Group. Permission set groups provide a simple way to bulk assign permissions consistently to a group of users. They can be updated by adding or removing permission sets to a group, and those permission sets can be used across multiple permission set groups.

Permission Set Groups are not accessible via the Metadata API in the pilot, and so you would still need to add any new permission sets to the group manually. If this is eventually made accessible through the Metadata API, then developers will have the ability to create new permission sets in a development environment, add them to the appropriate permission set group, and deploy those permissions all the way to users in production.

A new type of Permission Set called a "Muting Permission Set" is also in pilot. Muting Permission Sets can be added to a Permission Set Group and provide the ability to "Mute" permissions. To my knowledge, this is the first example of Salesforce enabling a **negative** permission on the platform. The explicit purpose of this is to inhibit permissions that would otherwise be given to members of the group by other Permission Sets in that same group. It might be possible to use this for security purposes to ensure that members of the group are never given powerful admin privileges such as "Modify All Data," but this use case is not mentioned in the documentation.

Code-Based Development on Salesforce

Salesforce allows for both server-side programming and client-side programming on Salesforce. Apex triggers, Apex classes, and Visualforce are all server-side programming options. Although Visualforce pages include dynamic JavaScript, they are compiled and sent from the server like PHP. Client-side programming includes Lightning Web Components and Lightning Aura Components, but might also include the use of complex JavaScript inside of Visualforce.

This section is very brief, since there are so many other references on how to write high-quality code for Salesforce. You should also refer to the discussions about static analysis and unit testing in Chapter 8: Quality and Testing and to the discussion of "Monitoring and Observability" in Chapter 11: Keeping the Lights On.

Server-Side Programming

Server-side programming in Salesforce allows direct access to the underlying Salesforce data model, and a large part of its purpose is to allow for queries, processing, and transformation on this data that cannot be done through clicks alone. Visualforce provides the ability to build custom user interfaces, although Lightning Web Components are now the preferred method to do this.

Apex

Apex is a strongly typed language, similar to Java, that provides native access to some underlying Salesforce capabilities. The most obvious native capability in Apex is the ability to work with Salesforce data as first-class Objects. So, for example, you can perform a query on Accounts and then perform actions on that data without having to explicitly define an "Account" object. Although Apex compiles down to Java behind the scenes, its most notable limitation is that you can't use third-party Java libraries or some advanced features of that language.

Salesforce runs Apex on the core platform, and Apex can't be compiled or run outside of a Salesforce org. The limitations on the language are largely to ensure that it can run safely in a multitenant environment without causing excess load or accessing things that would compromise the security of the platform.

There are actually two kinds of Apex metadata: triggers and classes. Triggers are a concept borrowed from other relational databases and allow custom code to be run as part of a database transaction (insert, update, delete, or undelete). Apex classes are more flexible than triggers, since they allow the use of methods, interfaces, global variables, and so on. Triggers were the first form of custom code allowed on the platform and have a very strictly defined format that does not allow the use of methods or some other capabilities of Apex classes.

Salesforce executes Apex in the context of a transaction. To ensure that no single transaction goes out of control and soaks up excessive system resources, Salesforce strictly enforces governor limits on heap size, CPU time, number of SOQL and DML statements, and so on. These governor limits are uncomfortable for developers accustomed to running code on their own servers, but are a design constraint that encourages code to be performant and balances freedom with the needs of other users on the platform.

Each Apex class or trigger runs using a specified version of the Salesforce API. This wise design decision allows Salesforce to make breaking changes in a new version of

Apex without impacting code that was written previously. When downloaded, this API version is shown in a "sidecar file" that has the same name as the class or trigger with an added -meta.xml suffix. As a best practice, classes and triggers should periodically be reviewed and upgraded to the latest API version to ensure optimal runtime performance. In most cases, updating the API version is a trivial change, but it's possible to face compilation errors, and this is a good reason to write good quality Apex unit tests to ensure behavior remains unchanged even if you update the API version.

It is essential to avoid hardcoding IDs in Apex code or anywhere else. Record IDs are typically different in each environment. Instead, ensure your logic can dynamically identify the proper data to operate against and not fail.

Visualforce

Visualforce allows you to create completely custom user interfaces, using an HTML-like syntax to display information and invite user input and actions. Visualforce also excels in giving access to Salesforce's internal data model through the use of Standard Controllers or Controller Extensions. A Visualforce page that uses a Standard Controller for Account allows you to create, access, and update Accounts without any other backend code. This page can override the standard record detail or record edit page in Salesforce, thus providing an alternative user interface for working with any Salesforce object.

There are many other capabilities of Visualforce, but it's fallen out of favor since it's relatively slow compared to Lightning-based pages. Visualforce pages have to be rendered on Salesforce, and their state is transferred back and forth from the browser each time you perform an action or move to a new page. There are also strict limitations to the size of this Viewstate that make them unsuitable for editing large amounts of data.

Scripting and Anonymous Apex

There are other ways to execute Apex such as creating custom REST and SOAP services. But one form of Apex worth mentioning here is "anonymous Apex," which is not stored on the server but can nevertheless be run on demand.

Among the many uses of anonymous Apex is the ability to automate predeployment and postdeployment steps in the process of building and delivering an application. Anonymous Apex has the ability to query, transform, and update data, and this includes system-level data such as permission set assignments.

As mentioned earlier, governor limits make anonymous Apex unsuitable to perform massive or long-running data transformations such as migrating data between fields on more than 10,000 records at a time. For this purpose, you can use batch Apex. But there are many practical one-time activities that you can perform using anonymous Apex, such as creating or removing scheduled jobs, triggering batch Apex to run, modifying User Role assignments, and so forth.

Although anonymous Apex is not persisted inside of Salesforce, you can and should save such scripts in your code repositories. This allows for reuse and also provides a clear audit trail should you or someone else need to review the changes that were made.

Client-Side Programming

Client-side programming involves systems where the bulk of processing and state management happens inside the user's client, either a web browser or the Salesforce mobile app. Lightning Web Components are now the recommended way of creating custom user interfaces, and they provide many benefits over Visualforce. Salesforce's original Lightning Component technology was based on an open source framework known as Aura. Although it's a bit confusing and frustrating for developers to have to learn new technologies, it's par for the course, and there are good reasons why Lightning Web Components have come into being. There are also a variety of other ways to connect to Salesforce from a web client, such as JavaScript Remoting.

Lightning Web Components

Most people who were using the Internet in the late 1990s and early 2000s were aware of the "Browser Wars," when Internet Explorer competed with Firefox and eventually Chrome for market dominance. But only web developers are familiar with the "Framework Wars" that pitted Angular against React and a hundred other frameworks to provide a more robust way to build applications on the Web.

Web Components are a standards-based alternative to custom JavaScript frameworks that are natively supported by modern web browsers. Unlike custom frameworks like Angular and React, Web Components provide native execution that allows them to run quickly and a consistent syntax that allows developers to reuse their skills more easily. Salesforce was a participant in developing the open standard for Web Components, and Lightning Web Components are an implementation of the standard that is optimized for working with Salesforce.

Lightning Web Components were announced in late 2018, but Salesforce had been quietly rewriting their entire Lightning user interface in LWC for a year or more. This enabled much faster performance and gave Salesforce the confidence that it was possible for customers to mix Lightning Components and Lightning Web Components together on the same page. Salesforce themselves had been refactoring the application in that way for over a year!

Lightning Aura Components

The original Lightning Component framework was based on an open source project called Aura, inspired by AngularJS. Like other code built on custom frameworks, Lightning Aura Components require the browser to do more work, since they have to be compiled into native JavaScript, adding significant amounts of execution overhead.

The vision for Lightning Aura Components is powerful and inspiring, since it allows organizations to build custom UI components using the same technology used to create Salesforce's own UI. Salesforce Classic is a fundamentally different technology than Visualforce. And Visualforce pages actually run in a separate domain to ensure transaction security and prevent custom Visualforce code from scraping data that it should not have access to.

By creating Lightning Aura Components, Salesforce opened the door to a long-term vision in which developers could seamlessly mix custom components with built-in components, even down to overriding a single field. That vision has not yet been fully realized, and Salesforce is still making incremental improvements to balance flexibility with security. But the Salesforce UI is far more responsive and performant today than before Lightning was rolled out.

JavaScript Remoting, S-Controls, and API Access

There are other client-side coding options on Salesforce that predate Lightning Components. Three official options are JavaScript Remoting, Visualforce Remote Objects, and S-controls. JavaScript Remoting is a technique that allows Visualforce pages to host complex JavaScript applications that can store state on the client side while still sending and receiving data from Salesforce using an Apex controller. Visualforce Remote Objects allow you to create a JavaScript representation of Salesforce objects so you can create, retrieve, and update Salesforce data using client-side JavaScript. S-controls were deprecated many years ago, but were Salesforce's first foray into allowing custom coding.

They allow you to create custom HTML and JavaScript in an iFrame, which can access Salesforce data using the standard Salesforce API.

Salesforce's API is also what enables a variety of other third-party custom code solutions such as Restforce for Ruby and Simple Salesforce for Python. These prebuilt libraries provide convenient wrappers around the REST API that allow teams familiar with those languages to work with Salesforce data and trigger Salesforce operations. The most significant such library is JSForce for JavaScript. JSForce is now the engine used by the Salesforce CLI to communicate with Salesforce and is also at the heart of many other JavaScript, TypeScript, and Node.js libraries for Salesforce.

Summary

This has been a brief introduction to the process of developing on Salesforce. The Salesforce DX team is responsible for a huge portion of the Salesforce platform, including developer tooling. This developer tooling has been evolving rapidly since the introduction of Salesforce DX, although there are still some key improvements needed. While most Salesforce developers focus on the actual technologies used to build on the platform with clicks and code, we introduced key concepts about the Metadata API that are important for facilitating the entire DevOps process.

We gave a brief summary of the click-based and code-based options for building on the platform, but we intentionally focused on those aspects most relevant to automating deployments to other orgs.

Much has been written about developing on Salesforce, but far less has been said about how to make the release management process easier. Perhaps that's because the people with the knowledge and skill to manage that process are too busy doing releases to take the time to share that knowledge. Or perhaps they're so burned out by following manual processes that they don't want to think or talk about the subject any more. I've somehow been fortunate enough to gain release management experience and live to tell about it, especially about how the process can be made easier.

Hidden in between the topics of building and releasing is the topic of architecture. It's fair to say that you must control your architecture, or it will control you. Salesforce makes it easy to build, which implies that it also makes it easy to build badly. If you're just beginning down the path of configuring Salesforce, now is the time to study carefully the techniques in the next chapter so you can build your org in a scalable and modular way. If that time has long since passed, then hopefully the techniques in the next chapter can provide you ideas on how to dig yourself out of technical debt.

CHAPTER 5

Application Architecture

In the business world, it's common to distinguish between strategy and tactics, two terms borrowed from the military. Strategy refers to high-level decisions that fundamentally determine the landscape in which you operate. In military planning, strategy dictates where to move armies, how to attract and train armies, what kinds of weapons to invest in, and so on. In business planning, strategy dictates what markets to pursue, whether to invest in onshore talent or outsource, what new products to develop, and so on. By contrast, tactics dictate how to succeed on a small scale. In the military, tactics refers to the skills and tools needed for an individual to survive and win in activities such as hand-to-hand combat. In the business world, tactics address topics such as how to organize teams, motivate employees, communicate to customers, and so on.

This distinction extends to the world of Salesforce DevOps. Part 1 of this book speaks to the overall strategy you can apply to drive innovation and continuous improvement for your organization using Salesforce. Parts 3 and 4 of this book speak to the tactics of setting up a delivery pipeline as the mechanism to deliver innovation safely and get feedback from production.

Although Part 2 of the book (you are here ↓) covers developing on Salesforce, I've said very little about how to actually develop on Salesforce. How to develop on Salesforce is a **tactical** discussion. It's a complex topic, but one that is very well covered in Salesforce's documentation and endless other books, blogs, and talks. What is not as commonly understood is how to architect Salesforce applications in such a way that they allow for continual innovation and lend themselves to being packaged and deployed independently. On the level of coding, this is a **strategic** topic.

Martin Fowler described architecture as "those aspects of a system that are difficult to change." There's not a clear-cut distinction between a developer and an architect, but the expectation is that an architect has sufficient experience and understanding to make decisions at the outset of a project that the team will not come to regret. Just as the role of a military general is to get armies to the correct battlefield so they don't waste their effort and skill fighting the wrong battles, the role of a Salesforce architect is to be a strategist

A. Davis, *Mastering Salesforce DevOps*, https://doi.org/10.1007/978-1-4842-5473-8_5

and hold a wise vision of the system being designed so that development teams can build and deploy their applications in a scalable way.

The *State of DevOps Reports* identify application architecture (especially loosely coupled architecture) as one of the key enablers of continuous delivery and thus one of the key drivers for delivering value to the organization.

We'll begin by looking at modular architecture and how dependencies arise and then look at various techniques for modularizing your code.

The Importance of Modular Architecture

The architecture of your software and the services it depends on can be a significant barrier to increasing both the tempo and stability of the release process and the systems delivered. ... We found that high performance is possible with all kinds of systems, provided that systems – and the teams that build and maintain them – are loosely coupled. ... The biggest contributor to continuous delivery in the 2017 [State of DevOps] analysis – larger even than test and deployment automation – is whether ... the architecture of the system is designed to enable teams to test, deploy, and change their systems without dependencies on other teams. In other words, architecture and teams are loosely coupled.[1]

—Accelerate: Building and Scaling High Performing Technology Organizations

A vivid indication of the impact of modular architecture on team performance can be inferred from Figure 5-1. This graph, taken from the *2015 State of DevOps Report*, shows a very surprising effect. In general, as the size of a development team increases, the traditional expectation is that the number of deploys per day would decrease due to the increasing complexity of the application. That trend is seen in the "Low Performers" trend line, which shows deployments per developer decreasing as the team size approaches 100 people. What is surprising is that "High Performers" (the high-performing software organizations mentioned previously) actually record a dramatic increase in the number of deployments per day per developer as the team size increases. Such performance increases are only possible with a loosely coupled architecture, one that is free from complex interdependencies between teams and packages.

---

[1]Nicole Forsgren, Jez Humble, and Gene Kim, *Accelerate: The Science of Lean Software and Devops Building and Scaling High Performing Technology Organizations* (IT Revolution Press, 2018), 76.

Figure 5-1 doesn't depict data for low-performing teams with more than 100 people, and it doesn't depict data for medium-performing teams of 1,000 people. This is presumably just a gap in their sample data, but if you extrapolate those curves, it hints at a possible conclusion: it may be impossible to scale your team beyond a certain size unless you have enabled that team to deliver software effectively. DevOps is sometimes felt to be easier to do at smaller scales. It's certainly easier to implement new processes while you're small. But this graph may be indicating that it's only through implementing DevOps principles that you'll *be able* to scale your business without sinking into crippling inefficiencies.

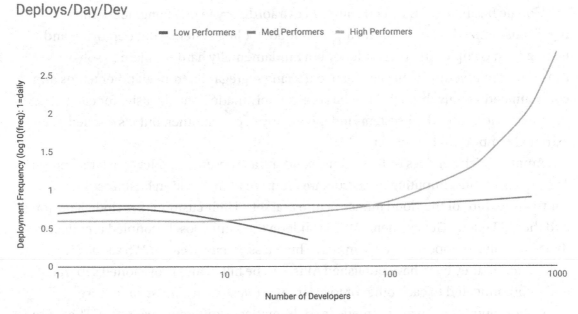

Figure 5-1. *Number of deployments per day per developer. 2015 State of DevOps Report*

Understanding Dependencies

Salesforce metadata, like any system, is interconnected with other components. Each time a piece of metadata references another piece of metadata, it establishes a dependency on that component. The net result of this is a tangled web of dependencies like that shown in Figure 5-6. Such a dependency network is known as "tight coupling," where different parts of the system have definite dependencies on other parts of the system. The opposite of this is "loose coupling" in which multiple systems can interact with one another but don't depend on one another.

Tightly coupled architecture is a characteristic of many systems, not only Salesforce, that have evolved over time without taking care to avoid this risk. One famous example and counterexample was given by Steve Yegge[2] and widely shared by Jez Humble and others in the DevOps community. Yegge's "Platform Rant" contrasted Google's architecture with that of Amazon, both his former employers. While clearly complimentary to Google, Steve Yegge pointed out that Amazon did an extraordinary job of enforcing strict separation between their systems with communication only through published APIs. By contrast, Google maintains a single code repository containing 2 billion lines of code and 86 TB of data,[3] within which there is little or no isolation between sections of code.

Google has made this work through an extraordinary team of engineers and highly customized version control and developer tooling systems. But deploying and testing such complex interdependency is a fundamentally hard problem to solve. Amazon's architecture, with each team enforcing segregation from all other teams and communicating only through APIs, has presumably made it much easier for each of their teams to evolve their systems independently of one another, but it's also led to an extremely important byproduct: AWS.

Amazon Web Services is the leading cloud infrastructure provider by a large margin. They support the computing infrastructure for more than a million businesses[4] and control one third of the cloud infrastructure market.[5] Their customers include Salesforce and the US Federal Government. AWS is built on the same loosely coupled architecture that was built to support their eCommerce business. Because each AWS service is independent, they each have published APIs, can be billed and provisioned separately, and interconnected to each other or to external services with almost equal ease.

Google and Amazon are dramatic (and dramatically different) examples. There are benefits and tradeoffs to both a tightly coupled and a loosely coupled approach. But it is important to recognize that although superficially it may look like Google has a tightly coupled architecture, they do not. Their underlying tooling allows their 25,000 active developers to collaborate on a common trunk, but commits can be automatically rolled back, dependencies can be automatically analyzed, regression testing is performed

---

[2]https://gist.github.com/chitchcock/1281611

[3]https://cacm.acm.org/magazines/2016/7/204032-why-google-stores-billions-of-lines-of-code-in-a-single-repository/fulltext

[4]https://expandedramblings.com/index.php/amazon-web-services-statistics-facts/

[5]www.canalys.com/newsroom/cloud-market-share-q4-2018-and-full-year-2018

automatically, and so forth. So in effect, Google achieves loose coupling on the fly through the miraculous use of tooling automation.

Barring some miraculous, not-yet-invented tooling, your fastest path to delivering innovation quickly and safely to your users will be to try to constrain the interdependencies in your system so that portions of the codebase maintained by different teams are not tightly dependent on one another. This is the meaning of building a modular, loosely coupled architecture.

Many of the following techniques are focused on Apex classes and triggers, since these are the most complex type of metadata and the ones which provide the most creative options for loose coupling. Where possible, I've offered suggestions for other metadata types as well.

Salesforce DX Projects

A discussion of Salesforce application architecture begins with a look at Salesforce DX projects, since it's these projects that open the door to building with a modular architecture.

How Salesforce DX Projects Enable Modular Architecture

The Salesforce DX project structure was introduced earlier, but there are a few aspects of this project structure that are worth looking at in more detail, since they enable special capabilities.

Salesforce faced a major challenge when envisioning Salesforce DX as a new way of building and managing applications. On one hand, they needed to ensure backward compatibility with teams using legacy tools. They also needed to accommodate customers whose development teams used a mix of old and new tools. They were also aware of the cost and complexity of building and testing entirely new APIs for managing application metadata.

One of the first big challenges was how to enable teams to store metadata in folders. Folders are not exactly a novel concept in computer operating systems, but the concept was never built into the Metadata API, since it was not built to handle source-driven development. What the Salesforce DX team came up with was a compromise that continues to use the Metadata API to communicate with Salesforce, but allows teams to divide metadata into folders on their local development environment and route metadata changes back and forth between those local folders and their development org.

Those folders allow teams to begin to group related metadata together. This provides information on which metadata components are more closely related, but can also be used to segregate areas of responsibility between different teams. More importantly, those folders form the basis for being able to build multiple packages in a single code repository.

Scientists hypothesize that the earliest single-celled organisms began as organic molecules isolated inside a sphere of phospholipids that separated their contents from the water surrounding it. Gradually this lipid sphere became the plasma membrane that surrounds complex cells capable of reproduction. Salesforce DX folders are like this lipid sphere that provides a gentle division between certain groups of metadata. Packages are the full evolution of this division that allow groups of metadata to become autonomous units that can be deployed and upgraded on their own.

The key file that defines a Salesforce DX project is the `sfdx-project.json` file contained in the project root. When an SFDX project is first created, this file specifies a single default package folder called `force-app/` and creates metadata in `force-app/main/default`. Importantly, you can immediately begin segregating metadata into different subfolders inside of `force-app/` even without changing the `sfdx-project.json` file.

The `sfdx-project.json` file becomes more important when you begin to define actual second-generation packages inside your code repository. In this case, each package must be associated with a specific folder, and there should be no overlap between these package folders. For example, you might define a package called `main` that is associated with the folder `force-app/main/default` and a second folder called `sales` associated with the folder `force-app/sales`. One package must remain the "default" package, since any newly created metadata will be downloaded and stored in this default package until it's moved elsewhere.

The Package Directories section in `sfdx-project.json` allows you to specify dependencies, either on other packages in the same project or on packages defined elsewhere. They can also specify environment requirements by linking to a scratch org definition file.

Scratch org definition files are another important feature of the Salesforce DX project format. They specify the characteristics of a scratch org and are used in the package publishing process to explicitly state the edition, features, and settings that must be in place for the package to work.

To evolve your Salesforce org configuration from an unstructured collection of metadata (the "happy soup") to a well-ordered set of interdependent packages is one of the biggest architectural challenges on Salesforce today. We can perhaps take inspiration from the evolution of life on earth, where it took 750 million years for single-celled organisms to evolve from a primordial soup. With packaging we do have the benefit of intelligent design, including the techniques shared in the remainder of this chapter. Even if it takes your team a few years to accomplish, you will be well ahead of Mother Nature.

Creating a Salesforce DX Project

If you're starting a new project, you can start using Salesforce DX from the very beginning. Developing using scratch orgs allows you to develop in your own private environment while easily integrating changes from the rest of the team. Dividing your codebase into unlocked packages allows separate teams to develop and release independently, with confidence that every aspect of the application is included.

For teams moving an existing org over to Salesforce DX, there are two main challenges to be overcome. First of all, it's difficult to untangle all of an org's metadata into logical packages. Second, complex orgs defy attempts to recreate all the underlying dependencies in scratch orgs. Much of the rest of the chapter talks about techniques that can help you to decouple dependencies to allow you to build discrete packages. But this undertaking requires time and care, so what you'll find here are suggestions and guidelines rather than simple solutions.

You'll first want to decide on which Dev Hub to use, and enable access for all collaborators. See "The Dev Hub" in Chapter 6: Environment Management. In general, it's important for the whole team to use the same Dev Hub so that they can all access and update the packages created during the development process, as well as capabilities such as org shapes, namespaces, and scratch org snapshots, all of which are stored on the Dev Hub.

The Salesforce CLI provides a command `sfdx force:project:create` that creates or "scaffolds" the basic files needed to use Salesforce DX. You can use that folder structure as a starting-off point. If you have been tracking existing metadata using version control, you may want to see the section "Preserving Git History When Converting to Salesforce DX" in Chapter 7: The Delivery Pipeline for tips on converting without losing history.

As discussed in Chapter 7: The Delivery Pipeline, there are different branching strategies and different CI/CD jobs for managing org-level metadata compared to managing Salesforce DX package metadata. For this reason, your life will be far simpler if you have at least two separate code repositories: one for org-level metadata and one for packaged metadata. You can then have separate code repositories for each package, which may simplify the package publishing process. With a bit of automation, you can also combine multiple packages into a single repository as described in the same chapter.

I recommend you create a single parent folder to hold these multiple repositories on your local machine and a team/group/project in your version control system to give everyone on the development team access to all these repositories. It can be tempting to want to strictly segregate the codebase between different teams, but this generally just causes confusion and inefficiency. Salesforce metadata can interact in complex ways. It's important for anyone on any of your teams to be able to see what code and configuration has been defined, so they can reuse that, interface with it successfully, and hopefully help with refactoring across package boundaries as your team's needs evolve. If you don't trust someone enough to give them access to your organization's codebase, you probably shouldn't have hired them. If you want your team to be efficient and collaborative, you'll need to promote trust as an internal core value. Version control enables tracking who made which changes and rolling back mistaken changes.

Part 3: Innovation Delivery details how to create a continuous integration system that will be used by your entire team for testing and deployments. When you set up your local development environment, you'll connect to the Dev Hub and development environments using your personal credentials. When setting up the CI systems, you should use the credentials for an integration user. Providing your personal credentials to set up a CI system may constitute a security risk in some cases or cause a service interruption if your personal user account is deactivated. Using an Integration user to run automated jobs on each Salesforce org in your delivery pipeline avoids these issues.

Modular Development Techniques

So what are some of the modular development techniques that can be employed on the Salesforce platform? We first look at some oldies but goodies, before moving to some of the newer and more powerful techniques.

Naming Conventions

Naming conventions are a "poor man's packaging." Nevertheless, they have been one of the few available methods to segment metadata in Salesforce and thus deserve recognition. Martin Fowler famously remarked that "Any fool can write code that a computer can understand. Good programmers write code that humans can understand." Naming things is a big part of that, and naming Classes and other metadata begins to bring sense and structure to an otherwise chaotic system.

Naming conventions in Salesforce generally take the form of prefixes and suffixes. Prefixes include the use of "fake namespaces" that often represent a department or group of capabilities. Salesforce packages can take advantage of real namespaces like SBQQ__ that are separated from the metadata name by two underscores. But any team can create fake namespaces like HR_ separated from the metadata name by a single underscore. As you begin to move your organization's metadata into Salesforce DX package folders, you may be able to use such fake namespaces as clues left by previous developers about which metadata belongs together.

The use of suffixes in metadata names is typically to indicate the specific function of a Class rather than which application it belongs to. By convention Apex tests should have the same name as the classes they test, but with the suffix Test. Visualforce controllers will ideally have the suffix Controller; Schedulable Apex will ideally have a suffix Schedule; and so forth.

None of these prefix or suffix conventions are enforced, but it is a good convention for your team to adopt and adhere to wherever possible.

Object-Oriented Programming

Object-oriented programming is in fact an example of modular design. Fortunately, this capability is baked into Apex and is already in widespread use, but it's worth recalling its benefits. The purpose of object-oriented design is to centralize data and capabilities inside objects, to promote interaction between objects as opposed to disconnected variables and functions, and to allow for sophisticated techniques such as inheritance.

Apex classes are just that—they are object-oriented classes that are usually instantiated into objects. Their functions are actually methods attached to the class, the variables defined in those classes are local variables by default, and so on. Teams who are already making wise use of Apex's object-oriented architecture will find it easier to adopt some of the techniques described later, such as dependency injection, packaging, and separation of concerns.

An important aspect of object-oriented programming that's not commonly used by most Salesforce programmers is the use of inheritance and interfaces to create classes that share common characteristics. Inheritance is a requirement for using Dependency Injection, since it allows you to write code based on the generic behavior of classes, even if you don't know which specific class will be used when your code is run.

Dependency Injection

Dependency Injection (DI) is a sophisticated programming technique that began to gain significant attention when Salesforce DX introduced unlocked packages. DI truly allows for modular architecture by allowing you to define dependencies at runtime, as opposed to when the code is compiled.

The example used here is borrowed from Philippe Ozil's excellent blog post "Breaking Runtime Dependencies with Dependency Injection,"[6] and I refer you to that post for a more clear and detailed explanation. Other seminal contributions on this topic come from Andrew Fawcett,[7] Douglas Ayers,[8] and Jesse Altman,[9] as well as from John Daniel, the technical reviewer for this book.

Normally, when you make a reference from an Apex class called `MyClass` to another class, you do so by specifying the other class' name and the method you want to access such as `OtherClass.doSomething()`. When you save your class, the Apex compiler checks to ensure that there is in fact a class called `OtherClass` that contains a method called `doSomething`. This establishes a hard dependency from `MyClass` to `OtherClass`.

Normally this is not a problem, but it leads to several limitations. First, there is no flexibility built into that approach: `MyClass` simply depends on `OtherClass` to execute some processes. This means that the behavior cannot vary per environment, be configured at runtime, behave differently as part of an Apex test, and so on. Second, it

---

[6]https://developer.salesforce.com/blogs/2019/07/breaking-runtime-dependencies-with-dependency-injection.html

[7]https://andyinthecloud.com/2018/07/15/managing-dependency-injection-within-salesforce/

[8]https://douglascayers.com/2018/08/29/adopting-dependency-injection/

[9]http://jessealtman.com/2014/03/dependency-injection-in-apex/

means that `OtherClass` must be present in the environment when `MyClass` is saved. This can prevent the two classes from being separated into different packages that can be deployed independently.

Ozil's article shows how to use the concept of Inversion of Control to access other classes indirectly instead of hardcoding references directly. Listing 5-1 shows a code snippet in which `OrderingService` directly depends on `FedExService`. Inversion of Control adds a layer of abstraction to return the `ShippingService` indirectly as shown in Listing 5-2. This gives additional flexibility at the expense of some added complexity.

Ozil then shows how this code can be refactored further so that the dependencies can be determined at runtime. Dependency injection uses the Apex `Type` class to dynamically create an instance of the appropriate ShippingService as shown in Listing 5-3. That example shows how a ShippingService class can be specified at runtime using Custom Metadata.

Using Custom Metadata to specify dependencies dynamically is a very robust solution and one that is used by the Force-DI package[10] cocreated by Andrew Fawcett, Douglas Ayers, and John Daniel. Custom Metadata can be created and deployed from a development environment to production, but can also be overridden in a particular environment if appropriate. Custom Metadata records can also be distributed across multiple packages as long as the Custom Metadata type is defined in a common package dependency.

The Force-DI package supports dependency injection in Apex, Visualforce, Lightning, and Flows, and can be used as a foundation for your own code. The package defines a Custom Metadata type to store references to the metadata you want to call at runtime. Where you want to use dependency injection, you pass an instance of the `di_Injector` class as a parameter and use that to access the metadata that has been configured for that org.

One of the most broadly applicable use cases for this is when creating Triggers that rely on code from multiple unlocked packages. This use case is discussed in the section "Modular Triggers with Dependency Injection".

---

[10]`https://github.com/afawcett/force-di`

119

Listing 5-1. OrderingService has an explicit dependency on FedExService (from Philippe Ozil's blog post)

```
public class OrderingService {

  private FedExService shippingService = new FedExService();

  public void ship(Order order) {
    // Do something...

    // Use the shipping service to generate a tracking number
    String trackingNumber = shippingService.generateTrackingNumber();

    // Do some other things...
  }
}
```

Listing 5-2. OrderingService refactored to use inversion of control to determine the ShippingService indirectly (from Philippe Ozil's blog post)

```
public class DHLImpl implements ShippingService {
  public String generateTrackingNumber() {
    return 'DHL-XXXX';
  }
}

public class FedExImpl implements ShippingService {
  public String generateTrackingNumber() {
    return 'FEX-XXXX';
  }
}

public class ShippingStrategy {
  public static ShippingService getShippingService(Order order) {
    // Use FedEx in the US or DHL otherwise
    if (order.ShippingCountry == 'United States') {
      return new FedExImpl();
    }
```

```
    else {
      return new DHLImpl();
    }
  }
}

public class OrderingService {
  public void ship(Order order) {
    // Do something...

    // Get the appropriate shipping service
    // We only see the interface here, not the implementation class
    ShippingService shipping = ShippingStrategy.
    getShippingService(order);

    // Use the shipping service to generate a tracking number
    String trackingNumber = shipping.generateTrackingNumber();

    // Do some other things...
  }
}
```

Listing 5-3. OrderingService refactored to use dependency injection to determine the behavior at runtime (from Philippe Ozil's blog post)

```
public class Injector {
  public static Object instantiate(String className) {
    // Load the Type corresponding to the class name
    Type t = Type.forName(className);
    // Create a new instance of the class
    // and return it as an Object
    return t.newInstance();
  }
}

// Get the service implementation from a custom metadata type
// ServiceImplementation.load() runs a SOQL query to retrieve the
   metadata
Service_Implementation__mdt services = ServiceImplementation.load();
```

```
// Inject the shipping service implementation
// (services.shipping is either FedExImpl, DHLImpl or any other
implementation)
ShippingService shipping = (ShippingService)Injector.
instantiate(services.shipping);

// Use the shipping service to generate a tracking number
String trackingNumber = shipping.generateTrackingNumber();
```

Event-Driven Architecture

Event-driven architecture is an ultimate example of loosely coupled architecture. In this model, components communicate by passing events as opposed to being directly connected to one another. One system will **publish** an event, and other systems can **subscribe** to categories of events that they're interested in. For this reason, it's sometimes also called a "pub-sub architecture." Typically, there's also a common **event bus** where those events are stored for a period of time. The event bus provides a shared platform for event publishers and subscribers and can provide capabilities like unique message IDs, sequencing, and event playback.

As an analogy, I can subscribe to an email list to receive information about webinars I might be interested to attend. My relationship with those webinars is "loosely coupled": if I don't attend, the webinar will still go on; and if they don't have the webinar, my life will still go on. I can subscribe or unsubscribe based on my interests and take action as appropriate.

The first event-driven architecture to become popular in Salesforce was Lightning Events, introduced in 2015, which provide a way to pass messages between Lightning Components in the same browser window. This architecture means that you can have one Lightning Component that responds immediately to events emitted from another Lightning Component, but neither of them will break if the other is not present. This architecture is extremely flexible and powerful, since you could potentially have a large number of publishers and subscribers, all interacting with one another, but without tightly coupled relationships.

Just 2 years later, in 2017, a second event-driven architecture, platform events, was introduced to Salesforce developers. Whereas Lightning Events exist only in a user's browser, platform events are exchanged on the Salesforce platform itself and provide a way to exchange messages between standard Salesforce components, custom components, and external systems. This is broadly referred to as the Salesforce Enterprise Messaging Platform (EMP), which hosts a common message bus on the Salesforce platform that systems can use to exchange messages.

Enterprise Service Buses (ESBs) have been popular for many years as an integration strategy between external systems. ESBs provide the same benefits described earlier by enabling external systems to have a loosely coupled relationship. The need for ESBs was driven by the rapid increase in complexity that comes from trying to integrate multiple systems that might each have different data formats. As shown in Figure 5-2, if you have to create direct integrations between n systems, you will have to create $n * (n - 1)$ direct integrations. If you have access to two-way "Point-to-point connectors" (such as a Salesforce to SAP connector), you will need $n * (n - 1)/2$ of these connectors. But if you use an ESB, you simply need n ESB connectors for each of n systems. The reduction in complexity is dramatic when you're connecting more than three systems. The same simplification holds true for the Enterprise Messaging Platform.

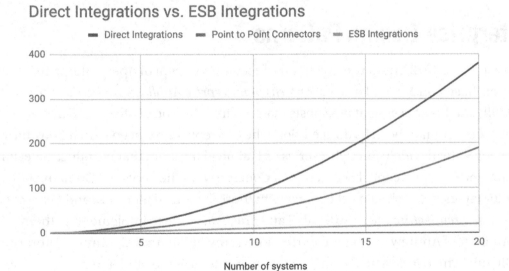

Figure 5-2. *Using an Enterprise Messaging Bus (ESB) requires far fewer integrations as system complexity increases*

Salesforce is increasingly emphasizing the use of the enterprise messaging platform, in part to address the need for data integration within its own sprawling portfolio of applications. Commerce Cloud, Marketing Cloud, and Salesforce's core platform have no native integration. Salesforce is beginning to use this event-driven architecture to ensure that these systems can keep their data in sync. A simple event like a user changing their email address should ideally propagate across all of these systems. This is one reason why Salesforce is rolling out Change Data Capture capabilities to autogenerate events when important data is changed.

Using an event-driven architecture is a way to enable components in one package to communicate with components in another package. But dependency injection has benefits that make it more suitable in some circumstances. One of the benefits of Salesforce is that it performs business logic in transactions, so that if there's a problem, the entire transaction can be rolled back. Dependency injection allows you to take advantage of this so that components from across multiple packages can combine in a single transaction. It's now possible to delay sending platform events until after a transaction completes successfully, which prevents firing events prematurely for activities that might end up getting rolled back. But the publisher of an event and the subscriber to an event would still use two different transactions, thus making them perhaps *too loosely* coupled for some scenarios.

Enterprise Design Patterns

At Dreamforce 2012, Andrew Fawcett introduced the concept of Apex Enterprise Design Patterns, based on Martin Fowler's *Patterns of Enterprise Application Architecture*. That talk and his subsequent blog posts matured into the book *Force.com Enterprise Architecture*, soon to be in its third edition. The concepts introduced in that book have now been spread widely through a series of Trailhead modules that introduce Salesforce developers to the concept of Separation of Concerns and the Service,[11] Domain, and Selector layers.[12] You should get familiar with those Trailhead modules, and *Force.com Enterprise Architecture* is a very detailed and practical guide to implementing them.

Another of Andrew Fawcett's contributions is the FFLib Apex Commons[13] library on GitHub, which is designed to make these patterns easier to implement. This section contains just a brief summary of this topic as encouragement to consider using these patterns if you are dealing with a complex and growing codebase.

---

[11]https://trailhead.salesforce.com/content/learn/modules/apex_patterns_sl
[12]https://trailhead.salesforce.com/content/learn/modules/apex_patterns_dsl
[13]https://github.com/financialforcedev/fflib-apex-common

Separation of Concerns

The fundamental concept behind these enterprise design patterns is that you should have a clear separation of concerns when you write code. In general, there are four layers for you to consider:

- Presentation Layer—Provides the user interface

- Business Logic Layer—Services that manage calculations and other business logic

- Database Layer—Mechanisms to store data, the data model, and the stored data itself

- Data Access Layer—Selectors that allow you to retrieve from a database

This separation of concerns can be understood by considering different kinds of Salesforce metadata. Components like Page Layouts and the Lightning App Builder form part of the presentation layer, but don't allow you to customize business logic. Components like Validation Rules, Processes, and Workflow Rules allow business logic to be customized. The Salesforce object model itself, along with standard record edit pages, is part of the database layer. And Reports and Dashboards are part of the data access layer.

A common counterexample that does **not** employ separation of concerns is writing an Apex controller for Lightning or Visualforce that mixes together tools to manage the UI, handle calculations, update data, and access data. The reason this is an anti-pattern is that it hides business logic inside what seems to just be a controller for the user interface and prevents that logic from being reused if people access the data through a different channel such as the API. It also means that data access and updates are defined only in this one controller, even though other code in your org may require similar methods.

Separation of concerns allows for a clear logical distinction between parts of your system that handle these different jobs. Importantly, it also makes it easier to separate parts of your code across multiple packages, as described in the following sections.

Service Layer

The Service layer helps you form a clear and strict encapsulation of code implementing business tasks, calculations and processes. It's important to ensure that the Service layer is ready for use in different contexts, such as mobile applications, UI forms, rich web UIs, and numerous APIs. It must remain pure and abstract to endure the changing times and demands ahead of it.[14]

—Trailhead module "Learn Service Layer Principles"

As shown in Figure 5-3, the service layer centralizes business logic in a single place that can be accessed by many other types of component. Your business logic is one of the most critical customizations you can make on Salesforce. Calculations, logical conditions, and relationships between data can be business critical and sensitive to small mistakes. If that logic is distributed across many parts of your codebase, it makes it hard to understand and even harder to maintain. Where logic is defined using code, each group of logic should be held in a single service class.

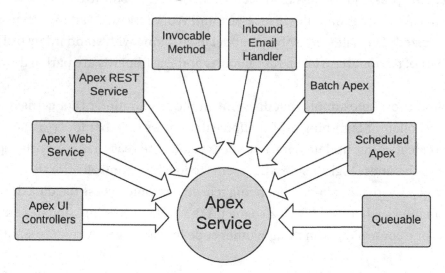

Figure 5-3. *The service layer provides services for many types of component*

For example, maybe you dynamically generate a commission on Opportunities that come from a channel partner. You should create a `PartnerCommissionService` that

---

[14]https://trailhead.salesforce.com/en/content/learn/modules/apex_patterns_sl/
apex_patterns_sl_learn_sl_principles

centralizes the logic for that calculation. This service can then be used by Visualforce controllers, Lightning controllers, the API, Visual Flows, and so on. If you update the calculations, you only have to update that in a single place.

Implementing a service layer is generally simply a matter of copying code into a central place and updating references to point to that service class for their calculations. It's the first place for you to start if you want to implement these enterprise patterns, and it generally does not require much refactoring.

Unit of Work

The Unit of Work concept is a way to help manage database transactions and bulkification when implementing a service layer. As it says in the Trailhead module, "it's not a requirement for implementing a service layer, but it can help."

Whereas implementing service classes is generally quite simple, implementing the Unit of Work pattern, Domain Layer, and Selector Layer generally requires some specialized code to help them to work. This is where the FFLib Apex Commons package becomes particularly valuable, since it predefines interfaces and classes that can be used to implement this.

The basic idea of a unit of work is to allow a group of records to be passed from one class to another, being modified and updated as needed, before finally being committed to the database in a single transaction. The FFLib module enables you to manage parent-child relationships, bulkifies database operations, wraps multiple database updates in a single transaction to enable rollbacks, and more.

The reason this becomes relevant when building a modular architecture is that the Unit of Work object also provides a common data type for passing records between classes from multiple packages. The same is true with the following Domain and Selector layers: they provide an abstraction on top of DML and SOQL that allows multiple packages to collaborate on database transactions and queries.

These techniques add some overhead and complexity to your codebase, but reduce overhead and complexity as your project scales up. It's therefore important to become familiar with implementing these patterns so that you can make a more accurate cost-benefit assessment for each project. The Trailhead module on Separation of Concerns provides a chart[15] to help discern whether your project's scale justifies this approach.

---

[15]https://trailhead.salesforce.com/en/content/learn/modules/apex_patterns_sl/
apex_patterns_sl_soc

Domain Layer

As mentioned, the Domain Layer is an abstraction on top of DML that allows you to manage validation, defaulting, and trigger handling logic in a single place that can be used by any class involved in updating data. The FFLib module provides interfaces and helpers for implementing a domain layer.

The basic idea is that there are some scenarios in which you need to apply a complex process consistently in both Triggers and in other DML updates. The domain layer provides this ability, as well as an object-oriented wrapper for dealing with native Salesforce objects. The FFLib naming convention is to name the Domain objects similarly to the native objects they represent. For example, you could use a Domain object called `Opportunities` that is a wrapper around the native Salesforce `Opportunity` object. This wrapper gives you access to additional methods and properties and allows you to attach logic (such as the `.applyDiscount` method shown in Figure 5-4) to the object when that's appropriate.

It's easy to misunderstand the Domain Layer as just another variation on trigger handlers. But it's actually much more than this. It provides a place to centralize business logic that is specific to a particular object, rather than allowing that logic to be distributed in ways that are difficult to understand or maintain.

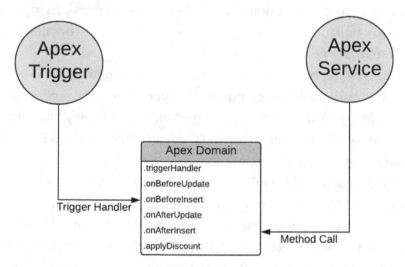

Figure 5-4. *The Domain Layer provides a wrapper around DML for both triggers and services*

Selector Layer

The Selector Layer is part of the data access layer used to retrieve data from a database. In Apex this means it's a wrapper around SOQL. Importantly, the Selector Layer provides an object-oriented wrapper around queries that allows for many helpful capabilities. When query definitions are distributed across many different classes, it becomes challenging to maintain them if fields change or new fields or filters become required. A Selector class addresses that by allowing you to specify the base query in a single place. It also allows queries to be passed between classes so that they can be modified if, for example, a class requires an additional field to be queried. Figure 5-5 shows how multiple classes can make use of a single Selector class.

Selectors allow you to use a "fluent syntax" in which multiple methods can be chained together to modify the query as shown in Listing 5-4. This becomes particularly powerful when passing Selectors across classes from different packages. Classes using the Selector can have confidence that all of the required fields have been selected and that appropriate row-level security has been enforced, and they can add requests for additional fields they may need to the same query before it is executed.

Listing 5-4. An example of Selector syntax showing multiple methods chained together (from Trailhead)

```
public List<OpportunityInfo> selectOpportunityInfo(Set<Id> idSet) {
  List<OpportunityInfo> opportunityInfos = new List<OpportunityInfo>();
  for(Opportunity opportunity : Database.query(
      newQueryFactory(false).
        selectField(Opportunity.Id).
        selectField(Opportunity.Amount).
        selectField(Opportunity.StageName).
        selectField('Account.Name').
        selectField('Account.AccountNumber').
        selectField('Account.Owner.Name').
        setCondition('id in :idSet').
        toSOQL())))
    opportunityInfos.add(new OpportunityInfo(opportunity));
  return opportunityInfos;
}
```

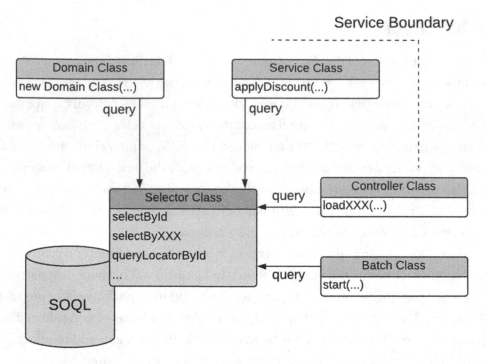

Figure 5-5. *The Selector Layer provides a common way to perform queries*

Factory Method Pattern

Implicit in the preceding patterns is the use of the Factory Method or "Application Factory" pattern. This is another example of Inversion of Control. The general idea is that instead of directly instantiating objects using, for example, new Opportunity(), you create methods that will return the object(s) you need. Listing 5-2 uses that approach when returning ShippingService. Adding this kind of indirection allows you to create mock interfaces for unit testing, polymorphic methods that determine their behavior at runtime, and allow you to gather repetitive boilerplate code in a single underlying method. The details of this are described briefly in a 2015 presentation by Andrew Fawcett.[16]

This is only a brief introduction to these topics. It is included here because of how helpful these patterns can be for dividing code across multiple packages. You should refer to Trailhead and Force.com *Enterprise Architecture* for a comprehensive guide.

---

[16]www.slideshare.net/andyinthecloud/building-strong-foundations-apex-enterprise-patterns/12

Trigger Management

Apex triggers allow for complex logic to be executed every time a database record is modified. As such, they're an extremely important part of the platform and are in widespread use across the Salesforce world. There are two main challenges related to Apex triggers, one old and one new. The old challenge has been a concern since I first encountered the language: how should you structure your triggers to make them maintainable and flexible? The general answer to that is to have one trigger per object and to delegate all the trigger logic to one or more trigger handlers. That advice worked well enough until we encountered the new challenge: if there should only be one trigger per object, how can we manage triggers if we need logic to be loosely coupled and distributed across multiple packages?

We'll first look at the classic "One Trigger Rule" before looking at strategies for handling triggers in a modular way.

The One Trigger Rule

Salesforce does not provide a way to determine the order in which triggers will execute. If you have more than one trigger on a single object, you can't predetermine the order in which those triggers will fire. When designing trigger logic, it's easy to encounter situations where you assume that processes happen in a particular order. But this can lead to very confusing scenarios in which a trigger seems to behave correctly sometimes but not other times.

It's also common to need to reference other data in your trigger using queries, and to iterate through records in a trigger, processing them one by one. Having more than one trigger can lead to redundant queries and redundant loops. All of these issues are addressed by having a single trigger for each object. Note that managed packages may supply their own triggers, but this isn't normally a concern.

The Trigger Handler Pattern

Triggers suffer from other limitations, such as the inability to define methods in them or to use most object-oriented design patterns. As a result, it's generally recommended to have little or no logic inside the trigger itself, but instead to create a trigger handler class that can hold all of this logic.

There are a number of common needs for triggers that are also well served by using a trigger handler. One common need is the ability to quickly disable triggers for certain users or at certain times. Trigger execution will slow data writes, so they're usually undesirable when loading large volumes of data. It's sometimes also not desirable to execute triggers when data is written as part of an integration.

Common trigger handler patterns, such as the "Comprehensive Trigger Template" by Mike Leach,[17] provide the ability to easily disable triggers for a period of time or for a particular user. Using Hierarchical Custom Settings for this purpose is useful since it allows you to determine the behavior for the entire organization or override that by profile or by user. This template also allows you to specify some processing to be delegated to @Future methods so they can be performed asynchronously and not count against governor limits.

The use of trigger handler patterns is probably the earliest widespread use of software design patterns in the Salesforce community.

The Domain Pattern

The use of the Domain pattern described earlier provides an alternative to using trigger handlers. The Domain pattern provides an object-oriented way to ensure that logic that should be associated with an object is always associated with that object, whether it's accessed through a trigger or through a service class.

Modular Triggers with Dependency Injection

The concept of Dependency Injection introduced earlier becomes particularly important as a way to manage trigger behavior where the logic is distributed across multiple Apex classes.

A very effective pattern is to use Custom Metadata records to track the names of classes that should be executed in a trigger context and the order in which they should execute. Multiple packages can contribute Custom Metadata records to register themselves to execute when a particular trigger runs. An admin on that org can modify the order of execution if desired.

---

[17]https://gist.github.com/abd3/a4a8a6b4476440adcfdea290de47948d

When a trigger runs, it first queries the Custom Metadata records (which is fast and "free" since they're stored in the platform cache), retrieves the list and order of the handler classes, and then executes them in order.

This provides loose coupling between the trigger and the handler classes, but still allows all of the execution to happen in a single transaction and to succeed or fail as a unit. John Daniel, the technical reviewer for this book, did much of the groundbreaking work to show how to modularize your codebase into packages. He created a sample project illustrating the techniques used in this process at `https://github.com/ImJohnMDaniel/at4dx`.

Packaging Code

The previous discussions about developing a modular, loosely coupled architecture all culminate in the topic of packaging. With the arrival of Salesforce DX, it's finally possible for enterprise developers to build packages (principally unlocked packages) on Salesforce.

Packages perform many functions and are one of the recurring themes throughout this book. Principally, they define a clear organizational unit for the codebase that makes the code easier to understand. They help ensure that your codebase is loosely coupled and thus easier to test and easier to deploy. They also help to ensure the integrity of groups of metadata, thus allowing them to be deployed consistently across orgs, including to more than one production org.

Building Salesforce packages requires that the metadata going into those packages can be decoupled from all other metadata except for that which is included in the package dependencies. This is a challenging problem, and is the reason that migration to packaging has been slow. It's also the reason I've taken the time to summarize some of the most promising techniques to achieve a modular architecture.

Building your metadata into packages doesn't perfectly guarantee that your code is loosely coupled, and you can encounter unexpected behavior if the versions of your packages are out of sync between different orgs. Nevertheless, keeping track of package version numbers is infinitely easier than keeping track of subtle variations between unpackaged metadata spread across many orgs.

Salesforce DX allows you to specify package dependencies in the `sfdx-project.json` file as shown in Listing 5-5. Note there are two valid syntaxes. The first uses an alias like `industry@0.1.0.12546` to point to an ID; this syntax is used when the package is not included in the same project folder. The second syntax is to specify both the `package` and a `versionNumber`; this syntax is only valid for packages that exist on the same Dev Hub.

Listing 5-5. An `sfdx-project.json` file showing package dependencies

```
"packageDirectories": [
  {
    "path": "force-app/healthcase",
    "package": "healthcare",
    "versionName": "ver 0.1",
    "versionNumber": "0.1.0.NEXT",
    "dependencies": [
      {
        "package": "industry@0.1.0.12546"
      },
      {
        "package": "schema",
        "versionNumber": "0.1.0.LATEST"
      }
    ]
  },
  {
    "path": "force-app/schema",
    "package": "schema",
    "versionName": "ver 0.1",
    "versionNumber": "0.1.0.NEXT",
    "default": true
  }
],
"packageAliases": {
  "industry@0.1.0.12546": "04t1T000000703YQAQ",
  "schema": "0Ho6F000000XZIpSAO"
}
```

Specifying package dependencies is one of the most important aspects of packaging. Figure 5-6 shows the actual metadata dependencies in one Salesforce org I worked on (this org was large, but by no means the most complex I've seen). Each node in the graph represents a piece of metadata such as a class or field, and each edge in the graph represents a dependency (small arrows show the direction of the dependency).

This level of complexity is impossible for humans to reason about, which means that it's difficult or impossible to understand the implications of changing a piece of metadata. When making changes is risky, innovation is stifled and teams delay activities like refactoring or reorganizing the code.

Figure 5-6. *Actual metadata dependencies in a large Salesforce org*

Contrast this with Figure 5-7, which shows the same org's metadata after refactoring it into packages and the interrelationships between packages. Each of these packages may contain their own complexity, but that complexity is hidden from view and somewhat irrelevant to other packages. This means that the implications of making a change to one of the packages are much clearer.

Since in Figure 5-7 the "base-metadata" package is depended on (directly or indirectly) by all of the other packages, changes to it should be made with care. But since no other packages depend on the "Account Planning" or "Customer Community" packages, the teams responsible for those packages don't need to worry about causing side effects in other packages. There is still complexity in this diagram, but it's trivial compared to the metadata dependencies in unpackaged metadata shown in Figure 5-6. Simplifying dependencies in this way makes it much easier to understand the risks associated with changing packages.

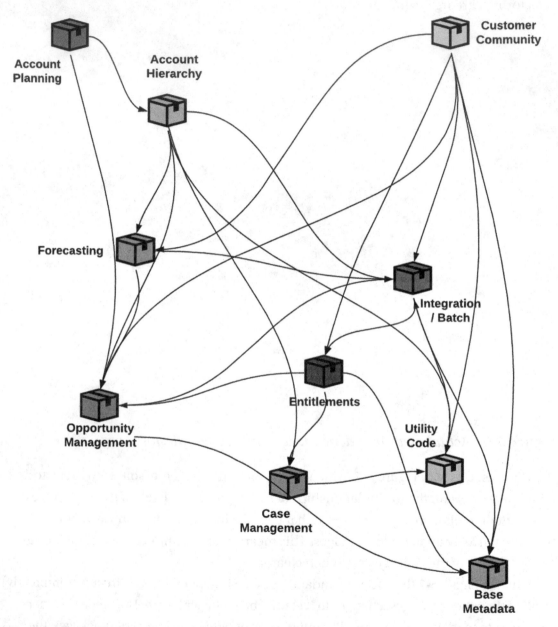

Figure 5-7. *A depiction of package dependencies*

Summary

Refactoring metadata so that it can be built into unlocked packages is the single most challenging aspect of adopting Salesforce DX. But it is also the most beneficial.

To some degree, the refactoring process can be undertaken gradually. If you are beginning work on a new application with limited dependencies on other metadata, that might provide an opportunity to begin working with unlocked packages. There is some tooling required to make this process easier, much of which is described in later chapters. There are many human factors involved in such an effort as well.

If your team works on a relatively independent part of the Salesforce codebase, it may be possible to get started independently. But in most cases, you'll soon find that you need to store and modify some common metadata like Account fields that are also shared with other teams. Therefore, typically the entire development organization first needs to move together onto a common delivery pipeline to deploy metadata at the org level.

The process of setting up a delivery pipeline, working with version control, setting up CI/CD, automated testing, deployments, and releases is the topic of Part 3: Innovation Delivery. Even once your entire org is refactored into packages, you'll still need to manage some metadata at the org level; therefore, it's beneficial to set up an org-level CI/CD pipeline from the very beginning. Ideally you should set this up using the Salesforce DX file format so you can benefit from easier merges, better filenames, and the ability to create folders for metadata.

You can then set up one or more delivery pipelines for packages and begin the process of migrating metadata out of your org-level repository and into your package repository(s). Keep returning to and experimenting with the architectural techniques introduced in this chapter as you go through that process. It is not easy to refactor a codebase in this way, and so it's also important that you keep clear goals for the process for both the development and business teams.

Your long-term goal in this process is to continually increase your team's ability to develop and release functionality for the business quickly, safely, and sustainably. Keep metrics on your starting-off point, and periodically check in on whether your refactoring efforts are enabling you to deploy more quickly and reduce the incidence of failures. DevOps is a process of continual improvement. Your architecture is a key factor in enabling or inhibiting your team's ability to continually improve.

PART III

Innovation Delivery

Software delivery is the phase of the software development lifecycle in between development and operation. It's the phase in between something being created and that thing being used. In this book, I refer to this phase as "Innovation Delivery" to emphasize that much of what we're delivering in Salesforce are non-code changes. To use the analogy of groceries, things are first grown or manufactured, then they're picked, shipped, and stored, and finally they are purchased and consumed. Software delivery is analogous to the picking, shipping, and storing phase.

This analogy is important in illustrating that this middle phase doesn't add much value, and in fact it often adds risk and waste. The longer things are held in storage, and the longer it takes to ship them, the shorter their eventual useful life and the more chance that they'll go bad or get out of date. Whereas manufacturing adds value (transforms raw materials into a valuable finished product), shipping rarely adds much value. It simply makes that valuable thing available for use.

The essence of Lean management is to identify and eliminate waste from the system. To eliminate waste, you first need to understand the system as a value chain, a series of interconnected steps, each of which contributes value to the finished product. Within a value chain, there are typically steps that do not add any value. Those steps are deemed "waste." Since DevOps incorporates Lean management, we can say that the goal of DevOps is also to eliminate waste in a system. And much of this waste can be found in the Innovation Delivery phase, which is why DevOps puts such strong emphasis on understanding and improving this phase.

Innovation delivery consists of environment management, creating a delivery pipeline, testing, deploying, and releasing. Although we've spent considerable time in this book explaining development techniques that enable DevOps, we've done so largely in the spirit of enabling success in this delivery phase. It is in this phase that DevOps techniques such as continuous delivery really shine, and it's this phase that is the heart of this book and the phase where the innovations of Salesforce DX have the biggest impact.

CHAPTER 6

Environment Management

Careful application development demands different environments to play different roles such as development, testing, training, and production. The software delivery lifecycle is largely a process of promoting changes through these environments, and thus it's important to begin with an overview of the different types of Salesforce environments and how to manage them.

An Org Is Not a Server

Although this is obvious to Salesforce veterans, it's an important clarification to make for anyone new to the platform. A Salesforce org is not a server. It's also not something that you can ever run on your local machine or on your corporate network. It's also not something that you can provision for yourself on a cloud infrastructure provider such as Google Cloud or AWS.

All Salesforce development, testing, and use take place in a Salesforce org, and Salesforce orgs can only ever be provisioned by Salesforce, in one of their own data centers, accessible only via the public Internet. Got it?

We'll discuss more of the underlying architecture in "A Behind-the-scenes Look at Salesforce Orgs." The way that orgs exist was a strategic decision by Salesforce that ensures that they can control the infrastructure, the upgrade process, and access to the underlying intellectual property. There are never outdated versions of Salesforce running behind a corporate firewall. Throughout most of the year, there is only one version of Salesforce running in the world. During the Seasonal Upgrade Period

© Andrew Davis 2019
A. Davis, *Mastering Salesforce DevOps*, https://doi.org/10.1007/978-1-4842-5473-8_6

(described later in the section on "The Salesforce Upgrade Cycle") and during times when patch releases are being rolled out, there are two versions of Salesforce running, as orgs are upgraded in batches.

Another reason why orgs exist in this way is that there are no orgs. Sound like a Buddhist paradox? What I mean by this is that not only is an org not a server; it's not a virtual machine; it's not a cluster; and it's not a container. It's actually just a unique ID that allows Salesforce to isolate the data and metadata that belong to one customer from the data and metadata of all other customers. In general, Salesforce can be seen as a single massive application, running on a single massive database, with all customers' data in that same database, segregated by a single Org ID such as 00DB00000001Tax.

Many layers of carefully crafted security, application, and database optimization are then used to generate a unique experience in each Salesforce org, so that it appears to function as a completely independent instance. Even Salesforce support have no access to data within a customer's org unless they are explicitly granted access on behalf of a specific user for a period of time.

Thus, when we talk about environment management, the process is somewhat different from the process on other platforms. It's nevertheless still important to distinguish different types of org and to provision different orgs for different purposes.

Different Types of Orgs

For practical purposes, there are only three types of Salesforce orgs that most people need to know about: production orgs, sandboxes, and scratch orgs. These different types of orgs behave in almost identical ways, but have different limits (such as the amount of data and records they can hold) and may have different features enabled.

Salesforce production orgs are the ones you pay for. They come with different features depending on which edition and licenses you buy. The first distinction is between the different editions of Salesforce such as Essentials, Professional, Enterprise, and Unlimited. Each edition is progressively more expensive but offers increasing capabilities and higher limits on data storage, number of sandboxes, and so on.

There are also free editions used for training and demonstration purposes such as Developer Edition and Partner Edition. A single org is always of a particular edition. Since Essentials and Professional editions do not support custom code or API access, they are rarely used by large organizations. Enterprise edition is the most common.

Orgs are priced on a per-user basis, and there are also different user license types available, the most common being Sales Cloud User, Service Cloud User, and Platform User licenses. Each user has exactly one user license. Whereas the edition unlocks certain capabilities (such as API access) across the entire org, user licenses allow different users to access different types of data and capabilities. A common scenario would be for a company to have an Enterprise Edition org in which the salespeople are assigned Sales Cloud licenses, and the customer support representatives and their managers are assigned Service Cloud licenses. In addition, there may be employees who are assigned only Platform licenses so they can make use of certain custom Salesforce applications. Meanwhile all employees of the company might have access to Chatter Free licenses so that they could at least collaborate using Chatter, and customers of the company may have licenses to use a self-service community created from that Salesforce org.

Figure 6-1 shows the 2019 pricing for Sales Cloud user licenses.

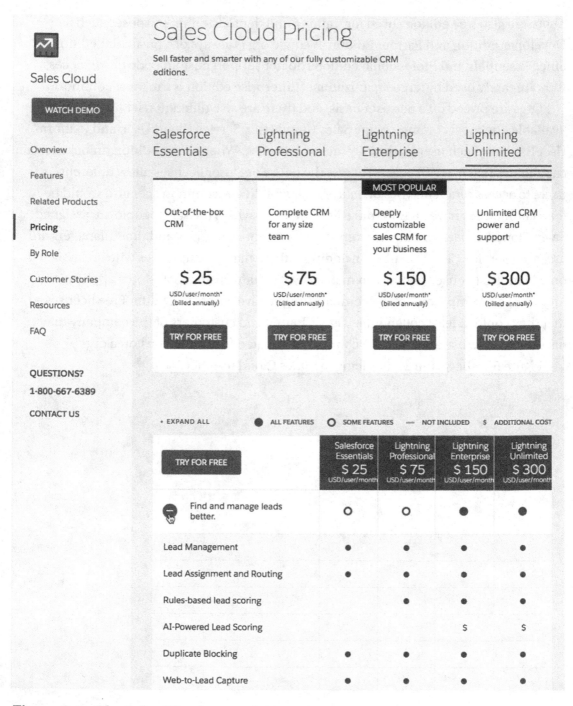

Figure 6-1. *The Sales Cloud user pricing page*

Developer Edition orgs are a special type of production org that are free and intended for use by developers. You can sign up for a Developer Edition org at `https://developer.salesforce.com/signup`. Developer Edition orgs have access to almost every capability that is available on Salesforce, making them ideal places for developers and admins to learn and experiment. Available features include Sales Cloud, Service Cloud, and Community Cloud as well as add-ons such as Work.com, Identity, Knowledge, Data.com, and Live Agent that would normally be paid add-ons to a Salesforce org. Developer Edition orgs have strict limits on the amount of data stored, API requests, and active users, so they can't be used for any significant business activity. Developer Edition orgs are updated on the same schedule as Salesforce production orgs. Salesforce partners can also get access to Partner Edition orgs, which are identical to Developer Edition orgs but with higher limits.

The second main type of Salesforce orgs are sandboxes. Sandboxes are long-lived development, testing, or training environments that are associated with a particular production org. Until recently, sandboxes were necessarily created as clones of the production org (having the same metadata and configuration as the production org). It is now also possible to clone one sandbox from another, which opens up entirely new workflows (see the section "Cloning and Refreshing Sandboxes").

Sandboxes also come in different sizes, each with varying levels of data storage: Developer, Developer Pro, Partial Copy, and Full Copy. The most inexpensive type of sandbox is a Developer sandbox (not to be confused with Developer Edition orgs, which are actually production orgs). Developer sandboxes cloned from the production org have the exact same metadata as the production org but do not contain *any* data from that org. Developer sandboxes that are cloned from other Developer sandboxes *do* contain a copy of the data from the source org, which allows an organization to establish certain orgs as templates from which other orgs can be cloned.

Developer Pro sandboxes have slightly higher data storage limits. Partial Copy sandboxes have substantially higher data storage limits than Developer sandboxes and also can receive a partial subset of production data copied into them when they are refreshed from production. Full Copy sandboxes allow the entire database from a production org to be replicated and are typically used as staging orgs where functionality can be tested against real data conditions prior to being deployed to production. Different editions of Salesforce come with different numbers and types of sandboxes, but customers can pay to get more. For example, Unlimited Edition includes one free full sandbox, for other editions it's a paid add-on.

The final type of org is also the newest type: scratch orgs. Scratch orgs are a key part of the Salesforce DX workflow. Scratch orgs are similar to sandboxes, since they are necessarily created from and associated with a production org. A production org that has been enabled to create scratch orgs is called a Dev Hub and is discussed more in the next section. Like sandboxes, scratch orgs are used for development, testing, training, or demos but, unlike sandboxes, scratch orgs contain no data or metadata from the production org and are short-lived orgs that are deleted after a period of time (7 days by default).

Scratch orgs also possess two important characteristics that make them ideal for a DevOps workflow: their characteristics (Edition, Features, Settings, Name) can be defined in a configuration file, and their metadata can be easily synced with version control. Even their short lifespans should be viewed as a feature, not a limitation: this design constraint forces teams to not rely on an org being their source of truth, but instead to capture all relevant configuration in version control. We'll discuss scratch orgs in more detail later in this chapter, but it's important to note that they do not replace sandboxes but rather complement them. There are disadvantages to using sandboxes as development environments, but they are still useful as long-lived testing and training environments.

Salesforce recently announced a new type of sandbox, Lightning Developer Pro sandboxes. These have identical characteristics to Dev Pro sandboxes, but can be created and destroyed using API commands, similar to scratch orgs. Unlike scratch orgs, these orgs begin as a clone of an existing org (generally your production org), which means they have all of the features, settings, managed packages, and metadata of their source org. Thus they don't require teams to refactor their orgs into packages, but nevertheless provide a short-lived development environment that can be used to make and test incremental changes.

Which Org Should You Develop In?

Given these different types of orgs, how and where should you develop new functionality?

Why Not Develop in Production?

Small organizations, organizations that are new to Salesforce, and those with loose governance and less restrictive security requirements might be doing development work directly in production. Most types of Salesforce "development" don't involve code, and changes such as adding a new field to an object are almost always safe. Even code-based development in Salesforce is not as risky as directly changing code on, say, a production web server. For example, in most cases a coding error in one Apex class will only impact a limited part of your org, whereas in a traditional application, a coding error could cause the entire app or site to fail.

It's partly for this reason that most organizations persist in doing some "development" directly in production. However, there are always dangers to doing this.

It's entirely possible to cook your meals and eat them right out of the pot, standing in the kitchen; it's efficient and minimizes the time you spend washing dishes. Most of the time though, people opt to move from the kitchen to the dining table to enjoy what's been prepared, even if they live alone. The more important the situation and the more people are involved, the more important it is to segregate these activities. Even the cleanest kitchens get messy quickly. Thus in most restaurants, chefs prepare food in the kitchen, waiters deliver it to the table, and patrons enjoy it without ever seeing where it was made.

Just as you can eat straight out of the pot, you can develop directly in production. But development environments are no more clean than kitchens, developer changes are no more safe than working with knives or fire, and an org that changes or breaks unpredictably is no more pleasant for your users than the noise and bustle of a short-order grill.

Just as a well-run restaurant develops a smooth flow of sending orders to the kitchen and food to the table, it's important to optimize the process of building in a development environment and deploying to production.

What are the dangers of developing directly in production?

1. Making changes without testing can lead to application failures, data loss, or corruption.

2. The risk of making changes inhibits innovations that might bring benefit but which require iteration and testing.

3. Changes are hard to track. Most metadata shows who last modified it and when, but does not show what changed or the history of changes. Salesforce provides a setup audit trail, but it does not show much detail.

4. Untracked changes are hard to reverse. It's difficult or impossible to reverse changes when you don't have their history.

5. Changes in production are not propagated to other testing or development orgs unless those orgs are refreshed, which wipes out any changes in them.

6. This practice may violate compliance laws such as SOX, HIPAA, or PCI-DSS. Instead, changes should be made in a development environment, tracked in version control, and deployed to production using a CI/CD system.

Developing in Sandboxes

As mentioned in Chapter 2: Salesforce, prior to the arrival of Salesforce DX, the normal workflow for Salesforce was for a team to do all of their development in one or more Developer sandbox and then to migrate those changes to the testing and production org(s). As of this writing, that is still the most common workflow for teams, since for complex orgs the migration to Salesforce DX usually requires some care and time.

When developing using sandboxes, the team creates one or more Developer or Developer Pro sandboxes, each of which contains an exact copy of production metadata. Teams then make their code or config changes in that org and use some mechanism to capture those changes and deploy them to testing, training, and production orgs.

Salesforce's Development Lifecycle Guide (now deprecated) recommended creating one Developer sandbox for each developer, and some guides still recommend this. The benefit of having one Developer sandbox per developer is that the sandbox contains only the changes made by that developer. It therefore gives the developer total control over that org and makes it relatively easy to identify all of the metadata touched during development, so that metadata can be moved to other orgs.

There are, however, major disadvantages to every developer having their own sandbox. Synchronizing changes between orgs requires deployments, and performing multidirectional deployments between many developer orgs requires substantial time, repetitive manual changes, and deployment error resolution and brings ample risk of overwrites. This generally prevents continuous integration, since it effectively isolates each developer in orgs that invariably become more different from one another over time.

By contrast, forcing developers to develop in a single, shared Developer sandbox ensures that each developer's work is continuously being integrated with the work of every other developer. Unfortunately, it also makes it difficult to isolate which changes belong to which feature, and so difficult to deploy features independently.

Developing in sandboxes is Org-based development, wherein a Salesforce org itself is the source of truth. If all development is done in a single, shared Developer sandbox, that org becomes the unquestionable source for the latest state of the config and code. If developers make conflicting changes, those conflicts are generally recognized and resolved very quickly. This also brings a risk of having your work overwritten, which gives plenty of incentive to start using version control!

Integrating conflicting changes requires developers to pause and communicate to resolve the conflict. When developers communicate and resolve conflicts on a daily basis, during the actual development process, each developer can more easily remember and articulate the reasons why their changes are important and so can more easily find a resolution. Developing in independent sandboxes over weeks or months causes potential conflicts to accumulate, while developers gradually forget the detailed reasons behind each change. This makes integration painful and far more risky. It also makes it very difficult for anyone to make small iterative changes to improve the entire codebase (refactoring), since old versions of the code will creep back in during integration.

Isolating teams into separate sandboxes brings the same risks as isolating individual developers in their own sandboxes. Parallel work streams, such as simultaneous Sales Cloud and Service Cloud implementations, will face the same problems if they delay integrating their codebases. It's tempting to have teams develop in parallel so they avoid the risk of conflicting changes. But delaying conflict resolution until close to go-live is a far riskier strategy.

Developing in a shared developer sandbox thus ensures a type of continuous integration, a recognized best practice in software development. There are nevertheless major disadvantages to developing in sandboxes compared to using scratch orgs for this purpose.

The Disadvantages of Developing in Sandboxes

The purpose of developing is to deliver innovations that benefit production users. The purpose of using a separate development environment is to innovate safely. Safe innovation also requires that each change be tracked so that it can always be rolled back. And in general, small, frequent innovations are safer to deploy and easier to debug. Developing in this way implies the use of version control and continuous delivery.

It is possible to use version control and continuous delivery when doing sandbox-based development, by capturing changes from the development environments in version control and then using continuous delivery to update testing and production orgs. But in this scenario, version control necessarily lags behind the development org, so development sandboxes are the actual source of truth.

Sandboxes are basically immortal. Unless you refresh or delete them, they will remain for as long as your production org remains. They always start as a replica of their source org (usually production), and they continue to accumulate changes until they are refreshed or deleted. But because the sandbox itself holds the latest features under development, refreshing the org means losing any changes that you have not already saved or deployed. Development has to stop (or move to a new sandbox), and you have to be able to copy or restore all of the work that was under development. Unless teams are particularly disciplined about refreshing developer sandboxes, the simplest, safest option chosen by most teams is to never refresh the development org. But with every passing day, the Developer sandbox becomes further and further out of sync with production.

Development is a messy process. Just as a craftsman's wood shop accumulates sawdust and scraps, development environments accumulate cruft—duplicate fields, half-finished customizations that were eventually abandoned, and so on. Large organizations have enormous amounts of customizations and complex architectures. Long-lived Developer sandboxes contain all that complexity, plus the accretion of months or years of half-baked or unneeded changes.

Even if a team is using version control to deploy changes to their test and production orgs, many changes in the development org may never be tracked in version control. There are also some changes that can be made in an org that may be critical for functionality but that can't be tracked in version control. This can lead to difficult to debug problems when you finally attempt to deploy a feature or application that has been under development for a long time.

The Benefits of Developing in Scratch Orgs

Scratch orgs offer enormous benefits for team development. But the team needs to understand these benefits and the implied changes to their workflow if they are to become comfortable developing in scratch orgs.

For those familiar with developing in long-lived sandboxes, developing in a scratch org, which expires after several days, is disconcerting. Developing in such an ephemeral environment is truly a paradigm shift, but you should understand this as a feature, not a bug. The short lifespan of a scratch org is a design constraint that forces developers to not rely on the org, but instead to persist their work in version control. There is no better motivator for developers to use version control than the threat that their development environment will soon disappear.

Scratch orgs can be configured to persist for up to 30 days, but as a rule teams should strive to create automated setup processes that make creating new orgs a fast and trivial process.

Unlike sandboxes, scratch orgs do not inherit any data, metadata, features, or preferences from the Dev Hub that creates them. As explained later in this chapter, Salesforce is planning to release capabilities for creating scratch orgs from Snapshots and creating scratch orgs from an Org Shape, but in general scratch orgs are created entirely from configuration stored in version control. That means there's no ambiguity about what features, settings, packages, or metadata are required to create an application in a scratch org. Because everything is recorded in version control, customizations can be easily recreated in another scratch org or deployed to other orgs as metadata or as packaged applications.

Scratch orgs also support "source synchronization," which means you can just run `sfdx force:source:pull` and `sfdx force:source:push` to synchronize metadata between version control and your org. With org-based development, developers use metadata retrieve commands to "pull" metadata from these orgs and metadata deploy commands to "push" metadata to these orgs. But deploying your team's changes into a private Developer sandbox requires struggling through deployment errors and risks overwriting your own customizations. And picking your own changes out of the fast-changing ocean of unpackaged metadata in a shared Developer sandbox requires deep expertise in the different types of Salesforce metadata.

Source synchronization means that you do not need to be an expert in Salesforce metadata. Open a scratch org, make changes, pull down the source for those changes, review it to remove any cruft or unneeded changes, commit it, and then merge your work with the team's code repository. Every developer can have a private development environment, can track their changes with confidence, and easily share customizations with the rest of the team.

Since the entire team is generally pushing and pulling source many times a day, deployment errors and conflicts are spotted very quickly. Without this workflow, it can take days or weeks before deployment errors reveal to teams that their commits to version control contained missing or invalid metadata.

Scratch orgs complement sandboxes but do not replace them. Because sandboxes are production-like environments, they remain useful as long-running test environments. Sandboxes for integration testing can be configured with stable integrations to external systems. Sandboxes for testing production hotfixes can be refreshed as frequently as needed. Sandboxes for training can be recreated with real production data in a Partial Copy sandbox. And Full Copy sandboxes can be used as staging environments to ensure that customizations are performant and able to handle the diversity of production data.

As of this writing, scratch org snapshots are not yet available. This means that it can be challenging or impossible to quickly provision scratch orgs for teams building on top of large managed packages, extensive and fast-changing configuration data, or settings that are not supported in scratch orgs. My view and hope is that this is a transitional time and that developing in scratch orgs will gradually become viable for even the most complex orgs.

Meeting in the Middle—A Sandbox Cloning Workflow

Scratch orgs are built "from the ground up," beginning with an empty org. Scratch orgs give you complete confidence that you know what's in your org, why it's there, and that you can recreate it whenever necessary. But organizations may struggle to build packages and record all the org preferences from their existing orgs. And complex orgs can require more than an hour to install the necessary packages, additional time to deploy metadata, and significant data loads to establish meaningful sample data.

Sandboxes are established "from the top down," in that they're always cloned from an existing org, complete with preferences, packages, and metadata. That means teams can immediately get started using them for development, testing, or training.

Salesforce DX is a growing technology, and the Salesforce DX team is working to enable a wider array of options to enable efficient workflows for development and release. Enabling scratch org snapshots allows teams to build a template org from the ground up and then create working orgs from that template very quickly. Similarly, enabling fast sandbox cloning, source synchronization in sandboxes, and automated authentication means that sandboxes can also begin to be part of an efficient and automated workflow.

For teams working on complex orgs, a sandbox cloning workflow can provide a mechanism for each developer to have their own environment that can be regularly integrated with changes from the rest of the team.

The key to this is to establish an integration sandbox that receives deployments from all of the developers and to regularly recreate development environments by cloning this integration sandbox. The cloning and authentication of this integration environment can be automated using the Salesforce CLI as explained in "Postcreation Sandbox Login." Changes that developers make in their individual sandboxes should be tracked in version control and deployed to the integration environment on an ongoing basis. Teams can use trunk-based development to ensure that their changes are expedited to the integration org, or feature branches to ensure that everyone's changes can be validated and reviewed. But the key to efficiency with this workflow is to regularly recreate those developer sandboxes to ensure they stay up to date and don't accumulate cruft.

Org Access and Security

Salesforce Orgs are accessible (and secured) in many ways. The most common methods of access are through the login user interface (`https://login.salesforce.com`, or `https://test.salesforce.com` for sandboxes and scratch orgs) and via APIs. Whether users log in interactively or via the API, access is always associated with a particular username and limited by that user's permissions. Usernames must be unique across all Salesforce orgs and are in the form of email addresses, although they do not need to correlate with actual email addresses. Users can be created and deactivated, but can never be deleted. Whenever a sandbox is created or refreshed, user accounts are created in that sandbox for every user that exists in the source org from which it was created. Sandbox usernames are autogenerated by appending the sandbox name to the source username. For example, if a user's production username was user1@production. org, when a sandbox called UAT is created from that production org, it will contain a user account with username user1@production.org.UAT. User's email addresses are automatically modified to prevent sandboxes from accidentally emailing users (and possibly confusing users). Email sending is also disabled by default in sandboxes.

Sandbox user accounts have the same profile, licenses, permission sets, and password as the user account in the source org. This means that if a user knows the name of a sandbox, they can log in to that sandbox by going to `https://test.salesforce.com`, appending the sandbox name to their production username, and using their production password. Users who log in using SSO may not even know their production passwords, however, and SSO has to be set up separately for each sandbox. The correlation between sandbox user accounts and production user accounts provides a convenient way for admins to direct users to log in to a sandbox for testing or training if needed. Because a user's permissions are also copied from the source org, even on full copy sandboxes the user will not be able to access data that they were not allowed access to in production. But it is important to understand this behavior, and data security in full and partial copy sandboxes should be considered alongside data security in production orgs.

Scratch orgs behave in a very different way. Scratch orgs are not created from a production org or sandbox. Because they contain no metadata or data from a long-lived org, their security is not as big a concern. The user who creates a scratch org automatically gets sysadmin access in that org, which allows them to use that environment for development without any restrictions. A typical first step after creating a scratch org is to populate that scratch org with metadata and test data stored in version control. But access to view and edit that metadata and test data is controlled by the version control system itself; Salesforce doesn't create any additional restrictions.

Just as scratch orgs don't contain any metadata or data from a source org, they also don't contain any user accounts aside from a single sysadmin user. It's possible however to use Salesforce CLI commands to create user accounts in a scratch org so that applications can be reviewed and tested from the point of view of users with different permissions.

The Dev Hub

Salesforce DX capabilities such as creating scratch orgs and publishing versions of Unlocked or Managed packages depend on a Dev Hub. A Dev Hub is a Salesforce production org that has special capabilities enabled. All paid Salesforce orgs and free Developer Edition Orgs can function as Dev Hubs. For training purposes, you can use your own Developer Edition org, but this allows only a small number of scratch orgs and packages. For business work, you should designate a production org that the development team has access to and enable Dev Hub on that org. For example, Appirio's internal development teams use Appirio's production org as their Dev Hub, but for customer projects we used the customer's production org as the Dev Hub. Developers should never be given access to edit metadata in production orgs (see "Locking Everybody Out" in Chapter 12: Making It Better), but there is no security risk with giving them permission to use the production org as a Dev Hub.

Permissions Needed to Use the Dev Hub

To use an org as a Dev Hub, that capability first needs to be enabled by going to `Setup UI ➤ Dev Hub`. For a user to make use of the Dev Hub, they then need several specific permissions. Administrators have these permissions automatically, but you shouldn't give your developers Admin rights in production. Add the necessary permissions to a permission set or profile, following the steps in the Salesforce DX Setup Guide. Permissions include

- Create and delete scratch orgs

- Create and update second-generation packages

When a package version is created, it is in the "beta" status and cannot be installed in a production org. To enable users to mark a package version as "Released" so that it can be installed in a production org, you need to enable the system permission `Promote a package version to released`.

What if developers don't have access to the production orgs? In these cases, Salesforce support can enable "Free Limited Access Licenses" in that production org. These secure licenses allow access to the Dev Hub, but do not allow any other data, login, or API access. Developers can be safely assigned this type of user license, even when they have no other access.

API-Based Authentication

While most user interactions with Salesforce involve users logging in manually and then viewing and editing the org interactively, automated processes are usually based on API access. Salesforce provides a very rich set of REST and SOAP-based APIs to access data and metadata and to trigger operations. Their robust API has allowed for the creation of a vast number of integrations from other enterprise software providers, as well as from tools specific to Salesforce. Since the technical processes in DevOps focus largely on automation, you'll be directly or indirectly exploiting these APIs as you refine your development workflow.

The most common API workflow involves using the REST API based on OAuth 2.0 authentication. The OAuth 2.0 flow for authenticating against Salesforce can be briefly summarized as follows:

1. Prompted by user actions, a local tool or third-party service requests access to Salesforce on the user's behalf.

2. The user is redirected to Salesforce and logs in.

3. Salesforce then presents an *authorization* screen similar to Figure 6-2 asking whether the third-party tool should be allowed access to Salesforce on the user's behalf. This screen specifies which permissions ("grants") are being requested on behalf of the user. Some apps require limited permissions such as "Access your basic information" (e.g., name, username, email), whereas others may request more permissions. Apply appropriate care when authorizing an app—you may be giving it permission to access all of your data and manage Salesforce on your behalf.

4. If you allow access, Salesforce will then send the third-party application an **Access Token** on your behalf. That access token is used to read data and perform actions on Salesforce on your behalf, subject to the limits of whatever permissions you gave in the authorization page.

5. Importantly, if you approve the permission "Perform requests on your behalf at any time," the application will be given a **Refresh Token** that allows it to reconnect to Salesforce at any future time. The Refresh Token is used to request a fresh Access Token whenever an Access Token has expired.

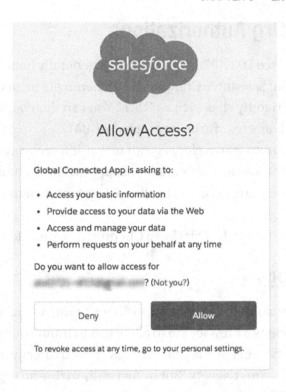

Figure 6-2. *An OAuth authorization prompt requesting full access to your account*

At any point, you can view the applications that were authorized using your credentials by visiting Settings ➤ My Personal Information ➤ Connections. To see the OAuth connections for all users across the org, admins can go to Setup UI ➤ Apps ➤ Connected Apps ➤ Connected Apps OAuth Usage.

OAuth 2.0 authentication is considered more secure than username/password authentication, because the permissions for an OAuth Connected App can be tuned carefully, monitored, and revoked if needed. Sharing your Salesforce username and password with a third-party app is fundamentally less secure, so when given the chance you should give strong preference to tools that use OAuth.

For long-running integrations between Salesforce and another system, you should always create and use an integration user and perform the authentications as the integration user. Using an integration user ensures that the connection is not disabled as a result of the user who initially set up the integration leaving the organization. It also enables multiple users to monitor the activity of the integration user account.

Salesforce DX Org Authorizations

In the context of Salesforce DX, API authentication is generally handled using the Salesforce CLI. Using the Salesforce CLI, you can authenticate to an org, and save your org connection with a friendly alias such as "UAT." You can then perform commands using those aliases such as `sfdx force:org:open -u UAT`.

The Salesforce CLI provides developers with many different ways of authorizing Salesforce orgs. Some of these methods are more appropriate for manual use by developers, whereas others are designed to allow CI systems to autonomously perform actions on Salesforce orgs.

The main **auth** commands the Salesforce CLI provides are as follows.

force:auth:web:login

This is the typical method for authorizing orgs when working with Salesforce CLI commands locally. It opens a browser tab to allow you to input your credentials to authorize the org. This type of login is generally never used directly in automated processes such as continuous delivery. But by first authorizing an org locally, you can then access an Auth URL for that org that can be used in automated processes.

force:auth:sfdxurl:store

The simplest way to enable API access to Salesforce as part of an automated workflow is to take advantage of a special string called an Auth URL that the Salesforce CLI generates.

This one URL contains all the information necessary to access an org on a user's behalf, including the endpoint URL, OAuth Client ID, and refresh token.

Auth URLs have the format: `force://clientId:clientSecret:refreshToken@instanceUrl`

To get the Auth URL for an org, follow these steps:

1. Authorize the org whose Auth URL you need using `sfdx force:auth:web:login -a OrgAlias`. By default, this command opens `https://login.salesforce.com`. If your org uses a custom domain or you need to authorize a sandbox, specify the `-r` parameter with the custom domain.

```
$ sfdx force:auth:web:login -a OrgAlias -r https://test.
salesforce.com
$ sfdx force:auth:web:login -a OrgAlias -r https://myDomain.
my.salesforce.com
```

2. Log in with your credentials and authorize the Global Connected
    App.

3. Once you've successfully authorized the org, close that browser
    tab and run `sfdx force:org:display -u <OrgAlias> --verbose`
    command (substituting the appropriate OrgAlias) as shown in
    Figure 6-3.

4. This will display the Auth URL for the org.

5. Your CI system will have some mechanism for storing secrets. You
    can then add that Auth URL as a secret variable in your CI system
    to connect to that org. It is extremely important to secure this Auth
    URL, and any other access credentials, as you would a password.
    CI systems should all provide a mechanism for storing secrets.
    These should never be hardcoded or included in the repository.

6. In a CI job, you will first need to write that secret variable to a
    temporary file, then read it into the Salesforce CLI from that file
    using the command:

```
sfdx force:auth:sfdxurl:store -f  -s -a MyDefaultOrg
```

7. Finish by including a command to delete that temporary file.

8. In your CI job, you can then perform commands such as `sfdx
    force:apex:test:run` to, for example, run Apex tests in the
    default org that you authorized.

```
             $ sfdx force:org:display -u Devhub  --verbose
  ►     sfdx-cli: update available from 6.12.0 to 6.13.0-3bc8bd73d8
Using resolved username                            from alias Devhub

=== Org Description
KEY                     VALUE
_____         _____
                        _____
_____

Access Token            00D7F00
YENawvX8Z8nxuSAoIK6jusD2_
Alias                   Devhub
Client Id               SalesforceDevelopmentExperience
Connected Status        Connected
Id                      00D7F00
Instance Url            https://fighter-enterprise-6780.my.salesforce.com
Sfdx Auth Url           force://SalesforceDevelopmentExperience:1384510088588713504:5A
```

Figure 6-3. *Getting an Auth URL for use in automated processes*

auth:jwt:grant

This method is recommended by Salesforce in the Salesforce DX Developer Guide and in the Trailhead module entitled "Continuous Integration Using Salesforce DX." It is also a method useful for authorizing orgs to be used in CI context. The benefits of this method compared to the "Auth URL" approach are that

- Credentials are stored in three pieces (key, clientID, and user) instead of a single token, which some might argue is more secure.

- A custom Connected App is created for each org, and special security restrictions can be applied to that Connected App.

The disadvantages of this method are that

- Setup is more complex and time-consuming.

- The username can easily be spoofed by supplying the username of any user who is assigned to that Connected App.

This method should be used for orgs where security is of particular concern. To use this method, follow the instructions in the Salesforce DX Developer Guide.[1] We recommend that you assign only a single integration user to the custom Connected App to avoid the risk of user spoofing. Separate Connected Apps can be created for each integration.

---

[1]https://developer.salesforce.com/docs/atlas.en-us.sfdx_dev.meta/sfdx_dev/sfdx_dev_auth_jwt_flow.htm

Postcreation Sandbox Login

Salesforce recently introduced a new form of authentication related to sandbox cloning or refreshes. The Salesforce CLI allows you to request a new sandbox to be created, cloned, or refreshed. Sandboxes are always associated with a particular production org, which is typically also the org used as a Dev Hub for Salesforce DX scratch orgs and packages. You can initiate a sandbox clone (from production or another sandbox) using `sfdx force:org:clone`. You can then track the progress of that clone using `sfdx force:org:status`. Once the sandbox is ready, Salesforce automatically authenticates you to that org. The actual authentication is performed using an OAuth connection from the production org to the sandbox, but the tokens are passed securely to the user who requested the sandbox to be created, allowing them to immediately log in or perform actions on that sandbox.

Environment Strategy

What Salesforce orgs and sandboxes do you need to put in place to support your development, testing, and training activities?

Environment Strategy Guidelines

An effective delivery pipeline lets innovation flow from development to production. The foundation for that is a sensible environment strategy. Having multiple environments is critical for allowing development and testing to happen in an orderly way. But every extra environment increases the complexity of your delivery process, which can cause confusion, extra work, and delays. Therefore the basic guideline is to use the minimum number of orgs possible and keep the connections as simple as possible. Resist the need to add more orgs for as long as possible.

This rule does not apply to scratch orgs. Since they are temporary environments created from version control, they don't add any complexity to the development process. But the rule *does apply* to code repositories and long-running branches in those repositories. Every code repository and long-running branch increases complexity in the development workflow and increases the overhead required to keep things in sync. Your life will be simpler and happier if you can have one code repository, one main branch, and a small number of long-lived sandboxes. Branching strategy is thus related

161

to environment strategy, and the two need to harmonize (see Chapter 7: The Delivery Pipeline for more on branching strategy).

Multiple Production Orgs

For every production org, there needs to be an environment strategy to manage the development, testing, and training process. If you have multiple production orgs that share common functionality, there needs to be a coordinated process for delivering that shared functionality to all the orgs. Managing multiple production orgs greatly increases the complexity of the overall environment strategy.

There are generally three reasons why an organization would have multiple production orgs:

1. This was a deliberate architectural decision.

2. One company using Salesforce acquired or merged with another company using Salesforce.

3. Different business units bought Salesforce at different times without an overarching strategy.

Multiple Production Orgs As an Intentional Architecture

Why is having multiple production orgs sometimes the best architecture? Sharing a production org allows teams to share data and to share common business processes. If multiple business units do not need shared data and have entirely different business processes from one another, then it can make sense for them to have multiple production orgs. A clear example is when a holding company owns multiple different businesses (say, a book publisher and a software company) that do not interact and don't share common processes. It is almost inevitable though that a time will come when the executive leadership of the parent company might want real-time reporting from across both business units. It's also quite likely that management might want to consolidate some departments across both groups such that there later develops a need for consolidated processes between them.

It is extremely important to make the appropriate decision up front about how many production orgs to have. Greg Cook provides important guidance for the org architecture decision process in the Salesforce Developer Blog "Enterprise Architecture: Single-org versus Multi-org Strategy."[2] I strongly suggest you study that article when making this decision, since it's extremely difficult to change later. He references this 2 x 2 matrix from the book *Enterprise Architecture as Strategy*[3] shown in Figure 6-4.

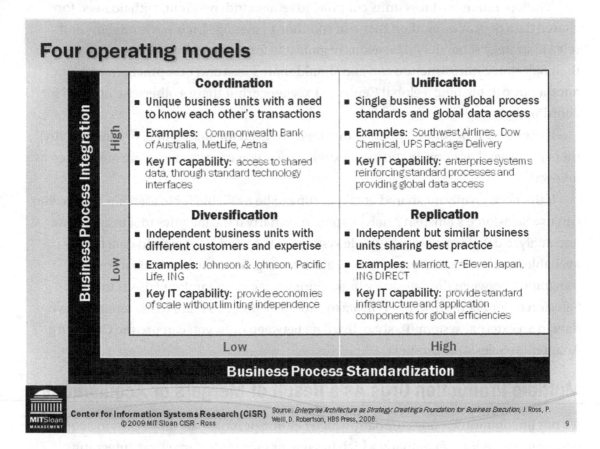

Figure 6-4.   The balance between business process integration and standardization should determine the org strategy. (Reproduced with permission from MIT Sloan CISR)

In this diagram, high "Business Process Integration" implies the need to share common data, while high "Business Process Standardization" implies the need to share common processes by sharing Salesforce metadata. Since that blog post was first published, Salesforce has added new mechanisms for aggregating and analyzing data

---

[2]https://developer.salesforce.com/blogs/developer-relations/2014/10/enterprise-architecture-multi-org-strategy.html

[3]Enterprise Architecture as Strategy: Creating a Foundation for Business Execution by Jeanne W. Ross, Peter Weill, and David Robertson, Harvard Business School Press, 2006.

across orgs (Einstein Analytics), new mechanisms for sharing data (Salesforce Connect), and new mechanisms for sharing metadata (unlocked packages), which can make it much easier to manage multiple production orgs.

If independent business units continue to remain independent, with no need for shared data or processes, then they can continue to manage their environments and release strategy separately. The teams responsible for maintaining and developing their Salesforce infrastructure can and should share ideas and best practices with one another by establishing a global Center of Excellence, but there's otherwise no need for coordination.

If over time it becomes apparent that there's a need for shared data or functionality, there are several options. In the most extreme case, you can pursue an org merge (see as follows).

If the need is only for shared data reporting to be available for leadership review, you can use Salesforce's Einstein Analytics or a third-party data analytics tool to aggregate and analyze data from across multiple systems. If the need is for certain data to be available in real time to users of either Salesforce org, then you can build a custom integration between the Salesforce orgs. The easiest option for doing this is to use Salesforce Connect, which uses OData to allow Salesforce to read/write/report on live data in an external system. To share live data between orgs, you can use the Cross-Org Adapter for Salesforce Connect.

Multiple Production Orgs As a Result of Mergers or Acquisitions

It's not uncommon for one company which has one or more Salesforce orgs to acquire or merge with another company which has one or more Salesforce orgs. Integrating IT systems is a massive part of M&A, and integrating or merging Salesforce orgs is no exception. See the following for more.

Multiple Production Orgs As a Result of Department-Level Purchases

It's not uncommon, especially in large, dispersed organizations, for different departments to have purchased and to maintain separate Salesforce orgs to support their independent needs. Although Salesforce increasingly markets itself as a way to integrate all of your enterprise data, its origin is as a CRM and sales force automation tool. Different sales organizations across the company might maintain a "shadow

IT" infrastructure inside their business unit as an alternative to coordinating through corporate IT. Corporate IT may be seen as overly restrictive, requiring too long an approval process, or not having the budget or enthusiasm for taking on new projects. It's also not unheard of for Salesforce Account Executives to conspire in this approach to help them get their foot in the door with a particular customer and to gradually build a presence in an organization.

Whatever the reason, it's important to bring these initiatives out of the shadows and to establish a global Salesforce Center of Excellence to decide on the best path forward. It's in the best interest of all teams to coordinate their activities and to decide on the most efficient global architecture. Such discussions might conclude that it's beneficial for different divisions to maintain separate Salesforce orgs; the point is that this should be an intentional decision.

Merging Production Orgs

God help you if you ever need to merge production orgs. You're looking at a long, complex process that will require careful architecture and careful work. You should plan to commit significant time and resources or seek out a qualified consulting partner to help you with the process. Salesforce provides many mechanisms such as record types to segregate data and business processes, but you will need to design all of this carefully to meet the needs of the different business units.

My colleagues at Appirio have been involved in many org merges, including one multiyear org merge that resulted from a corporate merger. Shortly after the project completed, they were reengaged for a complex org split after those organizations decided to separate again!

Splitting Production Orgs

Splitting orgs is simpler than merging orgs, but is still a process that should be considered carefully (Figure 6-5). Salesforce support may be able to authorize a behind-the-scenes clone of a production org, for example, using what's known as a DOT ("Default Organization Template"). There are also third-party products, such as Sesame Software's Relational Junction, that can help with this process.

Figure 6-5. *My suggested confirmation prompt before splitting orgs*

The main point is that once an org is split, the two environments will naturally diverge from one another over time. Reversing the operation would require an org merge.

An org split requires that the metadata, data, and any integrations be migrated. Users will generally be using one org or the other, so their accounts should be deactivated on the org they are not using. If users need to access and use both orgs, this is one of many signs that you may not actually want to do an org split. Instead you can consider segregating different processes using record types or some other mechanism.

Coordinating Multiple Production Orgs

As mentioned earlier, there are new mechanisms available to coordinate data that's spread across multiple orgs and to harmonize processes that are shared across multiple orgs. Data reporting and analytics needs can be addressed by numerous business intelligence tools. Salesforce offers their proprietary Einstein Analytics tool for this purpose. This offers native integration with Salesforce, although it is limited to pulling fresh data once per hour. Salesforce has rich REST and SOAP APIs, which allow for efficient retrieval of recently modified data by specifying "If-Modified-Since" headers in the API calls. This has made it easy for most enterprise data analytics tools to build Salesforce connectors.

Salesforce Connect, and in particular the Cross-Org Adapter for Salesforce Connect, provides a mechanism to make data from one Salesforce org accessible inside another org. That data can be used in lookups, automation, Apex code, reports, and so on. The data can be read, searched, and modified. Reporting can be slow, and there are numerous limitations on that integration, but it's a much more powerful type of integration than earlier options such as Salesforce to Salesforce.

Finally, if a company has multiple production orgs (separated perhaps by geography) but wants common customizations across orgs, that's an ideal use case for unlocked packages. Unlocked packages are discussed in detail in Chapter 9: Deploying, but they allow a team to build a package of code and customization and then to syndicate it to multiple orgs. They are useful even when moving customizations to a single testing and production environment. They are infinitely more useful if you must maintain multiple production orgs. As mentioned earlier, even if orgs start with the same configuration, "configuration drift" is inevitable unless org updates are managed strictly through a continuous delivery process. When that customization is bundled into packages, it further reduces configuration drift, since a single package version is guaranteed to be consistent across all orgs.

Using second-generation managed packages is another option that is now far more accessible to enterprise developers. The original managed package process required the use of Developer orgs, Packaging Orgs, and various forms of sorcery generally only used by ISVs building for the AppExchange. Second-generation managed packages are built and function much the same as unlocked packages, although it's very important to understand their differences.

Managed packages prevent users from modifying metadata in the receiving org and obscure the contents of metadata such as Apex classes. To allow end users some degree of configurability, managed package components such as page layouts are not upgradeable. This makes managed packages less desirable in enterprises that want central control over all orgs, but more useful where an enterprise wants to provide common functionality but allow independent teams some ability to customize. In most cases, however, enterprises should be locking everybody out of the production orgs (see Chapter 12: Making It Better), so deploying unlocked packages (and updating them as needed) should provide sufficient protection against configuration drift.

Identifying and Mapping Existing Orgs

The environment strategy is the foundation for the release management process. If a team is experiencing problems with release management, there are often also problems with the environments. And environments that are outdated or out of sync are always a potential source of confusion and problems. If you happen to join an existing project and are charged with mapping and rationalizing existing environments, you can follow these tips to determine the existing structure before proceeding to make changes.

The focus here is on identifying all of the active development, testing, training, and production environments. To the degree that you find unused orgs or excessive complexity, your goal will be to simplify the environment layout by deleting those orgs (after triple-checking that they are in fact entirely unused).

The best way to determine whether an org is actually in use is by logging into that org and going to Setup ➤ Identity ➤ Login History to see whether anyone (other than you) has logged into the org. This screen provides a definitive list of every authentication against the org, including API-based read or write access. If no one has logged into the org for a long time, that indicates it's not in use by users or integrations and so is almost certainly a candidate for deletion.

By all means, ask the team if they have any existing documentation on the orgs in use. But as with everything in software development, reality trumps documentation. For each production org, you can visit the "Environments" section in the Setup UI to see a list of all sandboxes associated with that org. For each sandbox, you will see the name of the sandbox, the sandbox type, the last refreshed date, and a link that allows you to log in to that org.

If in any supporting documentation, you see indications that the team is using Developer Edition orgs, or some other type of org other than sandboxes or scratch orgs, you should view those with suspicion. Developer Edition orgs are a key part of the original managed package workflow, but otherwise should not be used as part of an enterprise development workflow. Enterprise admins have no centralized control over such environments, and they may constitute a security concern.

If the team is using a third-party release management tool like Gearset or Copado, check those systems to see what orgs are currently authorized and how they are connected to enable metadata deployments.

If the team is using change sets for their deployments, the deployment pathways are defined under "Setup ➤ Environments ➤ Deploy ➤ Deployment Settings." Each production org and their related sandboxes can be connected to each other to allow incoming change sets, outgoing change sets, or neither. To see all of the relationships, you have to log in to each org. The number of possible combinations increases geometrically based on the number of orgs. The lack of a single overview of relationships between orgs is one of many reasons why change sets don't lend themselves to fast-paced, large-scale development. In practice it's not necessary to map or control all of these relationships, just the ones leading into production. As you move to scratch orgs, you will probably also be able to delete many existing sandboxes.

If your team is using an IDE or desktop scripts to manage deployments, there's no easy way to determine all of the pathways that code and configuration may be flowing in your orgs. Establishing a clear CI/CD process will remedy that.

The purpose of building a list of active orgs and their connections is to begin to gain control over what, for many organizations, is an unruly development process. By reducing the total number of orgs that you're managing, you also greatly simplify the process of ensuring those orgs remain up to date.

Identifying Requirements for Testing, Fixes, Training, and Others

Creating a clean and rational org structure begins with determining the requirements you'll need to serve. At a minimum, you will need scratch orgs for development, one sandbox for testing integrated changes, and your production org. There are many legitimate reasons to add more environments than that, but every additional org adds complexity and requires some time to keep in sync. The benefit of adding additional orgs must be balanced against the cost of maintaining them.

The reasons for needing additional environments can be divided into these categories:

1. Developing new functionality

2. Testing functionality under development

3. Testing large volumes of data for integrations and data migrations

4. Training users

5. Resolving bugs/issues

Environment Requirements for Development

For the reasons mentioned earlier, developing new functionality should ideally be done using scratch orgs instead of sandboxes.

Despite the benefits of scratch orgs, teams who are managing massive amounts of customizations may not be able to migrate to scratch orgs in the near term. Make a plan to help your teams transition to using scratch orgs, but you may need to maintain one or more developer sandboxes during that transition.

Scratch orgs can also be used when developing custom integrations with external systems. Because scratch orgs are short-lived, their connections to external systems may have to be recreated every time a scratch org expires. It might be tempting to develop integrations such as custom Apex REST services in a sandbox that is integrated with an external test environment. Instead, practice "design by contract" by writing Apex Mocks in a scratch org to simulate requests and responses from that external system. This allows for test-driven development of those REST services and ensures robust test coverage. Then use a CI/CD process to migrate the service to an integrated sandbox for integration testing.

Environment Requirements for Testing

Testing functionality under development is itself a vast topic. Different types of testing bring different demands for test environments. This is explained in more detail in the "Test Environments" section in Chapter 8: Quality and Testing. The general strategy to support these demands is to "shift left" as much as possible and to try to batch multiple different demands into a small number of environments. "Shifting left" is a general DevOps strategy, illustrated in Figure 6-6. Visualize your development environments arranged from left to right, with the developer workstation on the far left, followed by scratch orgs, then a CI/CD server, testing sandboxes, and finally production on the far right. If a test is currently being performed in a testing sandbox, shifting that test to the left, so that it is done in a scratch org, allows the test to be performed earlier in the development process. This greatly reduces the time required to identify and resolve issues.

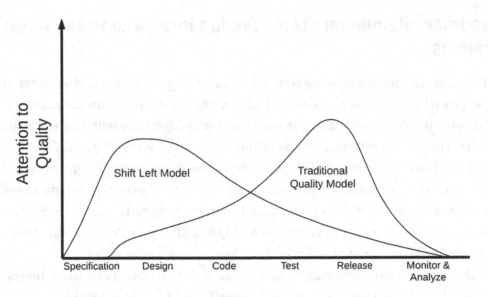

Figure 6-6. _"Shifting left" reduces overall costs by performing testing earlier in the development lifecycle_

Testing can be divided into static analysis, code reviews, unit testing, automated and manual acceptance testing, integration testing, and performance testing. Details about the environments needed for these tests are shared in Chapter 8: Quality and Testing, but these can be summarized as follows:

1. Static analysis and code reviews don't require a Salesforce org.

2. Apex unit tests and Lightning Component tests should be run both in development orgs and in other testing orgs.

3. Unit tests for JavaScript in static resources may be executable in the CI server.

4. Automated acceptance tests can be run in scratch orgs, but generally should be run in fully integrated orgs with full sample data.

5. Manual acceptance tests by the internal QA team should be run in scratch orgs; UAT should be performed in fully integrated orgs with full sample data.

6. Performance tests should be performed in a partial or full sandbox but require prior authorization from Salesforce.

Environment Requirements for Testing Integrations and Data Migrations

Salesforce integrations are ongoing connections allowing Salesforce to share data or functionality with some external system. Data migrations are one-time movements of data into or out of Salesforce. Salesforce's integration documentation explains that integrations might be performed at one of four layers, depicted in Figure 6-7.[4]

Most integrations are done at the "logic" layer, where an external system is required to get complete functionality. In this case, data is transferred between systems using APIs as part of a business process. For example, an order might be created in Salesforce and then a corresponding order created in a CPQ or ERP system. That system then sends data such as the price, order number, or order status back to Salesforce.

It's also possible to do integrations at the data layer (e.g., using External Objects), at the UI layer (e.g., using Canvas), or at the Security layer (e.g., SAML SSO).[5]

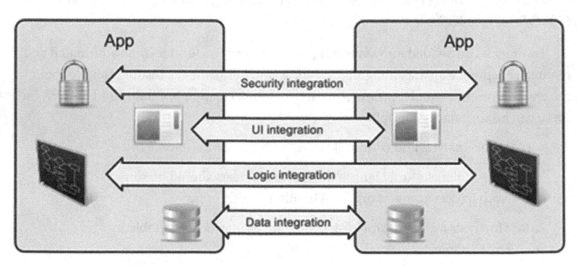

Figure 6-7. *Integration can be performed at different levels*

Can you ever use a production version of that external system for testing? If Salesforce is only reading data from that system, and there is zero possibility that the external system will be written to, and if there are no concerns about any data in the external system being exposed to someone who shouldn't have access, then it might be

---

[4]https://developer.salesforce.com/page/Integration

[5]https://developer.salesforce.com/blogs/developer-relations/2015/06/integrating-force-com.html

acceptable to test the integration against a production system. But that's rarely the case unless you're integrating with a public read-only service such as Google Maps or the US Postal Service's address validation service. In all other cases, these integrations require a test instance of the external system.

Not all platforms are as generous as Salesforce in providing sandbox or test environments. This means that the availability of test instances of external systems might be a limiting factor in what Salesforce environments you can support. If you're building a two-way integration with a product that has only three instances—development, test, and production—then you can only have three Salesforce environments integrated with this system. If you want the development instance to be available to your developers, then you have only one nonproduction instance left to use. You'll have to choose whether to make that available to your UAT testing environment, to your training environment, or to some other environment.

Environments where there are multiple external systems integrating will generally benefit from having a middleware tool in place. In those instances also, there should be development, testing, and production instances of the middleware, each connecting the appropriate environments.

For any kind of large-scale data import into Salesforce, you will almost certainly need a separate partial or full sandbox to test in. Scratch orgs and Developer sandboxes have extremely limited data volumes (200 MB). Developer Pro sandboxes allow 1 GB, Partial Copy sandboxes allow 5 GB, and full sandboxes give the same storage amount as the production org. Most Salesforce records require 2 kB of storage space, which means that a Partial Copy sandbox can store 2.5 million records. If your data migration is larger than that, you'll need a Full Copy sandbox, which might require that your organization buy an additional one.

Like software development, data migration is an iterative process that will likely require multiple attempts. Your data team will need the freedom to delete and reimport data multiple times before they have satisfactorily resolved all issues with character encoding (hint: use UTF-8), field length, relationships, picklist values, and so on. Do everyone a favor and put them in their own environment.

For small-scale testing of integrations or small migrations of new data, you might be able to safely reuse your UAT sandbox for this purpose. That allows the UAT environment to be fully integrated, available for end user testing, and also available for the integration team to validate their work. But this approach requires care, and you should make a clear segregation between the records that the integration team is touching and the records being used by your UAT testers.

Environment Requirements for Training

To support employee onboarding or when training your employees in new processes, it's customary to provide a dedicated training environment. In some cases, this can be the same as the UAT testing environment. If you can clearly demarcate training data from business data, you might also be able to do training in production. Even when you're rolling out new functionality, in some cases you can use feature flags (see Chapter 10: Releasing to Users) to deploy that functionality to production. Record types can be used to enable distinct layouts or business logic, and so users can be trained on forthcoming features by providing them training data that uses a new record type that exhibits different behavior. When you're ready to roll out the new processes on all data, just change the record types of your existing data.

If none of these scenarios are suitable, you may need a dedicated environment for training. You should include this training environment in your delivery pipeline so that its metadata is automatically updated at the same time as your other environments. This reduces the burden involved in maintaining a separate environment.

Environment Requirements for Resolving Bugs/Issues

Most bugs discovered in production are minor enough that they can be logged and fixed by the development team as part of their normal release process. However issues that cause downtime or data corruption require immediate fixes.

Your goal should be to handle even critical production hotfixes through your normal delivery pipeline without creating a separate process for this. The speed with which the development team can restore production systems and the speed with which new updates can be deployed are two of the five key metrics for measuring your software delivery performance (see Chapter 3: DevOps).

The practice of continuous delivery means that the master branch of your repository is always able to be released to production. If you've achieved this, then your normal, linear delivery pipeline will also be the conduit through which emergency bug fixes can be deployed. Developers will always be working on half-baked functionality, but that functionality should be hidden behind Feature Flags such that it can be safely deployed without releasing.

If your release process is not yet at this point, it may be tempting to bypass your CI/CD pipeline entirely in an emergency. This is inevitably a bad idea, since it means that you are making changes in a panicked state of mind *without tracking those changes* in version control. There are many horror stories of teams making problems worse by implementing hasty and untracked changes.

Some of the most difficult-to-debug production issues involve data issues. Since full sandboxes can only be refreshed every 30 days, it's not always easy to debug these issues outside of production. But accessing debug logs requires "View All Data" permission, which is not something that developers should have in production. To address this, you can consider having a separate hotfix environment.

Teams doing periodic major releases often maintain a partial sandbox as a separate hotfix environment. Immediately after the production deployment, they refresh this sandbox to ensure its metadata and at least a subset of its data are in sync with production. This environment can be connected to your CI/CD system so that changes made to a particular branch (e.g., "hotfix") will be deployed to this environment. If there is a problem, you can create a hotfix branch off of the master/production branch and push urgent changes to this environment for testing. If the fix is successful, it can then be put into the delivery pipeline so that all environments (including production) get updated.

Creating and Using Scratch Orgs

The short-lived nature of scratch orgs makes them an ideal environment for development, demos, and most types of testing. How do you create and use scratch orgs for these purposes?

General Workflow

The main body of your Salesforce metadata should ideally be built in scratch orgs, published as unlocked packages, and installed and kept up to date in testing and production environments. Metadata that cannot or should not live inside a package should be managed at the org level.

Salesforce DX introduces the concept of unlocked packages. Unlocked packages allow related functionality to be compiled and deployed together as a single unit. Packages are versioned, and the Setup UI shows what metadata is in a particular package, in which version of the package it was added (or deprecated), and which package each piece of metadata belongs to. Importantly, packages also allow for metadata deletions to be safely propagated from development to production.

Thus unlocked packages are generally the best method of moving features from development to sandboxes and production orgs.

Some types of metadata, like org Settings and Profiles, apply to an entire org and not to any one package. They therefore need to be managed using the metadata deploy and retrieve commands. The main reason certain types of metadata cannot be included in packages is that it could lead to situations where multiple packages have conflicting configuration, with no way to discern which should take precedence.

Packages cannot include Setting metadata. But you can specify the Settings that are required in the target org by specifying a `definitionFile` for that package. The definitionFile is a scratch org definition file that specifies features and settings that should be present in an org. This file is used in the background during the package version creation process. It also allows you to explicitly state the environment dependencies for every package rather than just implicitly depending on certain features or settings. This explicit definition makes it very clear how orgs must be configured before receiving this package.

Grouping metadata into folders allows you to logically organize your metadata, which is a capability that was sorely lacking before DX. Depending on the needs of your project, you can store multiple packages in one repository, although in most cases it will be easier to automate your workflow if each package is in its own repository. The source "synchronization" capability of scratch orgs means that developers can easily sync changes from the org's Setup UI to their local machines without having to be experts in deciphering the different types of metadata. Once downloaded, that metadata can be viewed, edited, and tracked in version control in the developer's IDE.

Tracking changes using version control allows developers to easily merge their work with others on their team, so that scratch orgs can be independent of one another but also easily synchronized with recent changes from others.

Building packages ensures that metadata is guaranteed to be identical across orgs, and means that deployment errors can be resolved during the package publishing process as opposed to recurring every time the same metadata is deployed to different environments.

Managing org-level metadata (along with which version of different packages is installed) in a central org-level repository allows central control and visibility of org-level configuration and differences. Org configuration can be identical across orgs where appropriate, and can also vary if needed.

Creating Scratch Orgs

Scratch orgs are created by sending an org creation request to a Dev Hub. The creation request must reference a scratch org definition file, which determines the initial characteristics of the org. Creation requests are typically made using the Salesforce CLI, although Salesforce's VS Code extension and an increasing number of third-party tools provide wrappers around that process.

Since the purpose of scratch orgs is to build new functionality destined for a production org, you need to use the scratch org definition file (such as shown in Listing 6-1) to match the characteristics of the target org. Applications always depend on certain underlying functionality in their Salesforce org; the scratch org definition file makes those dependencies explicit. Those developing managed packages will likely need to test using multiple scratch org definition files to simulate a variety of different installation orgs. Those developing for a particular business may only need a single scratch org definition file, although if that business has multiple production orgs, or is experimenting with enabling certain features, they too may need multiple scratch org definition files. Don't worry, they're short and easy to create.

Listing 6-1. Sample scratch org definition file

```
{
    "orgName": "Acme",
    "edition": "Enterprise",
    "features": ["Communities", "ServiceCloud", "Chatbot"],
    "settings": {
        "orgPreferenceSettings": {
            "networksEnabled": true,
            "s1DesktopEnabled": true,
            "s1EncryptedStoragePref2": false
        },
        "omniChannelSettings": {
            "enableOmniChannel": true
        },
```

```
    "caseSettings": {
        "systemUserEmail": "support@acme.com"
    }
  }
}
```

There are a number of optional configurations in a scratch org definition file, such as the `orgName`. But the most important configurations to understand are `edition`, `features`, and `settings`. There are also two other significant configuration options that as of Spring 2019 are still in pilot: `sourceOrg` and snapshot.

The `edition` option corresponds to the Salesforce edition, explained earlier in the section "Different Types of Orgs," and simply allows the user to select "Developer," "Enterprise," "Group," or "Professional." Unlimited edition orgs are just Enterprise edition orgs with higher limits. Match the edition to your target org. For example, Developer edition orgs have many features enabled that would otherwise only be available as paid add-ons. If you build a feature based on Work.com capabilities in a Developer Edition org, don't expect that to work in an Enterprise org that does not have Work.com installed.

The `features` option generally corresponds to paid features that are not available in every org, whereas the `settings` option corresponds to org configuration that is available for free, but may need to be enabled in an org. For example, the `SalesWave` feature can't just be turned on in any Salesforce org … that's a paid capability that would normally require your organization to have purchased Einstein Analytics. Fortunately for developers, you **can** create a scratch org that has Sales Wave enabled, so you can build apps on top of those capabilities. As an aside, there is often a disconnect between the backend/developer names for things in Salesforce and their current marketing names. Sales Wave is now called "Einstein Analytics for Sales Cloud Einstein," but the older name `SalesWave` remains on the backend to ensure that developer-built integrations don't break.

The `settings` configuration allows you to specify any setting that is available in the Metadata API (see `https://developer.salesforce.com/docs/atlas.en-us.api_meta.meta/api_meta/meta_settings.htm`). These are configuration options that can be specified through the setup UI.

When you are initially migrating from org-based development to source-based development, expect to spend some time adjusting the features and settings in your scratch org definition file until you can get your metadata deploying successfully to your new scratch org. For example, I spent several hours trying to diagnose why I was getting `Variable does not exist: Suffix` errors when trying to push metadata to a scratch org. Eventually, I found that there is a `nameSettings` metadata item that allowed me to specify `enableNameSuffix`.

Although this kind of debugging can be tedious, for those familiar with Salesforce release management, this will feel familiar. Identifying missing dependencies or differences in org configuration is one of the most common challenges in Salesforce release management. The massive change that Salesforce DX brings, however, is that instead of having to repeatedly diagnose and resolve obscure deployment errors every time you move metadata to a new org, those errors can be resolved up front while defining your scratch org configuration and getting your packages to publish. Once those dependencies are made explicit, it is straightforward to confirm that the necessary features and settings are in place before attempting to install a package.

The `sourceOrg` and `snapshot` configuration options relate to two features that are still in Pilot as of this writing: Org Shape and Scratch Org Snapshots. Although there is an enormous amount of configuration that can be defined through features and settings, there are some kinds of configuration like org-wide email addresses that have lingered for many years without an easy way to automate their setup. Gaps in the Metadata API mean that in some cases a scratch org can't be completely defined from source and that manual steps are required to complete setup.

Salesforce has responded to that gap in several ways. First, they've now put in place an automated process to ensure that any new features are fully covered by the Metadata API. The Metadata Coverage Report (`https://developer.salesforce.com/docs/metadata-coverage/`) is dynamically generated from that automated process. Second, they continue to work with the engineering teams responsible for different parts of the platform to help them ensure that their configuration can be controlled using the Metadata API. Finally, to bypass those gaps, Org Shape and Scratch Org Snapshots allow scratch orgs to be created based on templates, instead of being based on an Edition.

Org Shape and Scratch Org Snapshots

Certain features of a production org are not yet available in scratch org definition files. Similarly, for some production orgs, Salesforce may have approved increased limits (number of custom objects, lines of Apex code, etc.) compared to what is standard for a particular edition. And there are also many settings that can't be represented in the Metadata API and thus are not supported in scratch org definition files. Thus it may not be possible to replicate some characteristics of production orgs using just scratch org definition files.

Org Shape creates a template based on a particular production org that can be used to create a scratch org. The org shape mimics the features, limits, and settings of your production org without the extraneous data and metadata. This means that org shape does not contain data or metadata, but is otherwise identical to the characteristics of a production org. This allows scratch orgs to be created with features or settings that cannot be represented in scratch org definition files. When creating a scratch org based on org shape, a reference to the shape ID is used in place of specifying an `edition` in the scratch org definition file. Note that org shape is not automatically updated when the production org's settings are updated; you'll need to recreate the shape.

By contrast, Scratch Org Snapshots create templates based on the configuration of a particular scratch org. You first create a scratch org, then manually adjust its settings, then capture a snapshot which you can then use to create other scratch orgs. Just like with org shape, when creating a scratch org based on a snapshot, a reference to the snapshot is used in place of specifying an `edition` in the scratch org definition file.

Scratch org snapshots work similar to org shape, with some very nice additional characteristics. First of all, you can create a scratch org based on org shape and then capture a snapshot of that! This allows you to begin by capturing the characteristics of your production (target) org and then modify those as needed and use that as the foundation for your development and testing environments. Further, you can also install managed packages and other metadata in the scratch org, add data for testing and configuration, and capture a snapshot that includes all of that customization.

The installation of dependent packages is one of the most time-consuming aspects of scratch org initialization. Large managed packages such as Vlocity can take up to 30 minutes to install, making scratch org setup time-consuming and burdensome. The forthcoming Scratch Org Snapshots feature will help address this issue. A scratch org can be created and configured, and have managed packages and other metadata loaded into it. You can then take a snapshot of that org and use that snapshot as the template for creating new scratch orgs. Scratch orgs created in this fashion have the managed packages in place, thus greatly speeding the setup process.

Table 6-1 summarizes which aspects of an org are (and are not) carried over to different representations of an org.

Table 6-1. *How an org is created determines which aspects of the org are populated*

Org Aspect	Full Sandbox Copy	Partial Sandbox Copy	Developer Sandbox Copy	Scratch Org Snapshot	Scratch Org Shape	Scratch Org Definition File
Can be the basis for Scratch Orgs				✓	✓	✓
Can be the basis for packages				✓		✓
Edition	✓	✓	✓	✓	✓	
Features	✓	✓	✓	✓	✓	✓
Org limit overrides	✓	✓	✓	✓	✓	Partial
Settings supported by the Metadata API	✓	✓	✓	✓	✓	✓
Settings not in the Metadata API	✓	✓	✓	✓		
Managed packages	✓	✓	✓	✓		
Metadata	✓	✓	✓	✓		
Partial data	✓	✓				
Full data	✓					

Although org shape and snapshots are extremely useful, they are not a substitute for capturing and deploying configuration from version control. To the degree possible, the settings and packages in a snapshot should be specified in your configuration files, and you should automate the build process for your snapshot. Thus you can use the snapshot to speed up scratch org creation while still having confidence that you know the characteristics of that snapshot and how they evolve over time.

Using either org shape or snapshots makes the underlying configuration opaque, in that you are not explicitly stating the features and settings that a package requires. But when defining packages and orgs based on these templates, you can also explicitly specify features and settings that you require. This allows you to use the org template to address gaps in the Metadata API while still being as explicit as possible about the required org configuration. Tracking every aspect of org configuration in version control provides traceability and makes it easy to move those packages to other orgs in the future.

Scratch org snapshots are extremely powerful. But you should be careful about what you include and do not include in the snapshot itself. Your snapshot should contain only the underlying dependencies that your project is building upon, not any of the metadata that your team may need to update. For example, they can and should contain third-party managed packages and metadata that is common to other teams and not under active development. The idea is to include all the foundations for your team's own customizations, but not to include the actual metadata for your project. Instead, push that metadata from version control to the scratch org you create from the snapshot. That ensures that if you need to delete or modify any of that metadata, your version control system remains the source of truth.

Initializing Scratch Orgs

When a scratch org is first created, it has an edition, features, settings, and one dynamically created admin user. To proceed with developing on scratch orgs, there are several other steps that are required. In most cases, those setup steps are

1. Install dependent packages

2. Push metadata

3. Create additional user accounts

4. Load sample or testing data

5. Run additional setup scripts

Install Dependent Packages

Whereas the scratch org definition file defines the scratch org's characteristics, Salesforce DX projects also contain an `sfdx-project.json` file that defines your package configuration. Listing 6-2 shows an example of this file. Salesforce DX project metadata is grouped into folders called "packages" based on the expectation that this metadata will be built into individual packages, versioned and installed in target orgs.

The most common initial step for initializing a scratch org is to install other package dependencies. You may be making use of functionality tied to the Marketing Cloud Connector, in which case you'll need to install the latest version of that managed package. The `sfdx-project.json` file allows each package to define other packages on which they depend. These package dependencies are specified using an alias, with the alias defined in one place in the file. For external package dependencies, you specify the alias using the ID of a particular package version. If one package in your project depends on other packages in the same project, those dependencies should also be specified, but in this case they can reference the package by name and specify a `versionNumber` for that package.

Listing 6-2. Sample `sfdx-project.json` configuration file

```
{
    "namespace": "",
    "sfdcLoginUrl": "https://login.salesforce.com",
    "sourceApiVersion": "43.0",
    "packageDirectories": [
        {
            "path": "util",
            "default": true,
            "package": "Expense Manager - Util",
            "versionName": "Spring '18",
            "versionDescription": "Welcome to Spring 2018 Release of Expense
            Manager Util Package",
            "versionNumber": "4.7.0.NEXT",
            "definitionFile": "config/scratch-org-def.json"
        },
```

```json
{
    "path": "exp-core",
    "default": false,
    "package": "Expense Manager",
    "versionName": "v 3.2",
    "versionDescription": "Spring 2018 Release",
    "versionNumber": "3.2.0.NEXT",
    "definitionFile": "config/scratch-org-def.json",
    "dependencies": [
        {
            "package": "Expense Manager - Util",
            "versionNumber": "4.7.0.LATEST"
        },
        {
            "package" : "External Apex Library - 1.0.0.4"
        }
    ]
}
],
"packageAliases": {
    "Expense Manager - Util": "0HoB00000004CFpKAM",
    "External Apex Library - 1.0.0.4": "04tB0000000IB1EIAW",
    "Expense Manager": "0HoB00000004CFuKAM"}
}
```

Although this is a highly requested feature, as of this writing, Salesforce does not automatically install dependent packages for you as part of scratch org setup. You can write scripts to automate the scratch org setup process or use third-party tools such as Appirio DX, the Texei plugin,[6] or the Rootstock dependency utility[7] to manage this.

As mentioned previously, to speed the scratch org creation process, you can use a scratch org snapshot that has these managed packages already installed.

---

[6]https://github.com/texei/texei-sfdx-plugin
[7]www.npmjs.com/package/rstk-sfdx-package-utils

Push Metadata

After installing packages, your typical next step will be to push the metadata for your packages to the scratch org. Your local metadata typically depends on other packages, whereas user permissions and data depend on your metadata; thus the order of these stages is important.

The Salesforce DX command for pushing your source metadata to a scratch org is `sfdx force:source:push`. The command allows you to specify which scratch org you want to push to, but does not allow you to limit the metadata that you are pushing.

Pushing metadata and installing dependent packages both take time. If you're dealing with a small org, the process may only take a few minutes. But as your org's complexity grows, the initial setup time for a scratch org will grow as well. If you find that your scratch org creation is taking more than 10 minutes, you might consider mechanisms to initialize your scratch org with only the subset of functionality relevant to your current work. The larger your team and more complex your org, the more likely you are to need a selective process for initializing these orgs.

The simplest method for narrowing the scope of metadata in a scratch org is to divide your codebase into several repositories. If you have two relatively independent teams developing functionality for your org (e.g., sales cloud vs. service cloud), you might have three code repositories, one for each team, and one for shared functionality. The repository governing shared functionality can be built as a package that is then installed as an external dependency for the two team-specific repositories. Each team repository otherwise stands alone, allowing the creation of a scratch org with just the functionality needed for that team. Even when code is divided into multiple repositories, you can easily work across multiple folders by adding them to a single workspace in your IDE. Visual Studio Code and most other IDEs allow multiproject workspaces, although not all extensions fully support this.

It's worth noting that if you want to limit the metadata that is pushed to a scratch org or ignore non-metadata files present in the same folders, you can use a `.forceignore` file like that shown in Listing 6-3. The `.forceignore` file has a syntax similar to the `.gitignore` file used with Git. Metadata files or folders listed in a `.forceignore` file will not be pushed or pulled from that scratch org.

Listing 6-3. Sample `.forceignore` file

```
# Specify a relative path to a directory from the project root
helloWorld/main/default/classes

# Specify a wildcard directory - any directory named "classes" is
excluded
classes

# Specify file extensions
.cls
.pdf

# Specify a specific file
helloWorld/main/default/HelloWorld.cls
```

Create Additional User Accounts

Pushing metadata to the scratch org establishes the basic capabilities of that org. But Salesforce's flexible permission system means that different users can have substantially different views and access, even in the same org. Proper testing requires that you impersonate the user permissions of the users you are developing for, and to do this you may want to create additional user accounts in your scratch org.

The Salesforce CLI provides the `sfdx force:user:create` command for creating users. When running this command, you can add a `--setalias` parameter to create a short name that can be used to refer to that user in subsequent commands.

Similar to the previously mentioned SFDX configuration files, Salesforce also makes available a user definition file such as the one shown in Listing 6-4 that can be used to create users that fit standard personas. You specify this using a `--definitionfile` parameter.

Listing 6-4. Sample user definition file

```
{
    "Username": "tester1@sfdx.org",
    "LastName": "Hobbs",
    "Email": "tester1@sfdx.org",
    "Alias": "tester1",
    "TimeZoneSidKey": "America/Denver",
```

```
    "LocaleSidKey": "en_US",
    "EmailEncodingKey": "UTF-8",
    "LanguageLocaleKey": "en_US",
    "profileName": "Standard Platform User",
    "permsets": ["Dreamhouse", "Cloudhouse"],
    "generatePassword": true
}
```

You will typically want to omit the "Username" property and allow Salesforce to autogenerate this, since it needs to be unique across all Salesforce orgs. The other properties in this file, especially the `profileName` and `permsets`, allow you to specify the permissions assigned to this user, thus defining their level of access and how the org behaves for them.

As you develop features in service of your users, spend time refining these user definition files, and make them available to your developers and testers so that they can easily view the org from the point of view of these sample users.

Load Sample or Testing Data

One major difference between scratch orgs and sandboxes is that scratch orgs contain no metadata or data from a production org. Scratch org definition files have a property `hasSampleData` that can be used to populate the scratch org with data similar to that in developer edition orgs. But you will want to curate appropriate sets of sample data for your organization.

The Salesforce CLI provides several data-related commands for exporting and importing modest amounts of data for development and testing.

`sfdx force:data:tree` commands should be your first approach. These commands handle the challenge of creating related records in a single step, without the need to explicitly specify external IDs. If you wanted to manually load some related Accounts, Contacts, and Cases, you would first need to create the Accounts, get their IDs, and then create the Contacts, specifying their Account IDs, and then create the Cases, specifying their Contact IDs. `sfdx force:data:tree` allows you to export and import a JSON file that expresses hierarchical data without using IDs. The data tree API processes these files and handles the process for you.

To use this command, generate appropriate testing data in an org, and then run the sfdx `force:data:tree:export` command, specifying a SOQL query to export the data. By using subqueries like `sfdx force:data:tree:export -p -q "SELECT Id, Name,`

(SELECT Id, LastName, FirstName FROM Contacts) FROM Account", you can export data, including multiple levels of relationships. The result of this query is one JSON file for each object and another JSON file to specify the relationship between each object. Although IDs are specified in the query, they are ignored when creating this data tree so that the records can be inserted into any org.

Once you've exported that data, you can then import it using the sfdx force:data:tree:import command, which takes the generated files as input and inserts corresponding records, establishing relationships between them.

As your org evolves, plan to manage this sample data alongside the code, regularly updating it to capture the diversity of objects and data you are working with. This will never substitute for testing in a staging sandbox against a full volume of production-like data, but it allows you to provide realistic data to your developers and testers and to add special cases as they are discovered.

The sfdx force:data:tree commands are extremely convenient but are limited to importing 200 records at a time. If you need to import larger volumes of data, you can use commands such as sfdx force:data:bulk which is a complete wrapper around the Bulk API. The Bulk API is the mechanism used for importing or exporting large volumes of data (thousands or millions of records).

The Salesforce CLI provides an additional set of commands sfdx force:data:record for modifying individual records. If appropriate, those can be added to setup scripts to fine-tune data as needed.

One important use of data loading is to populate configuration data that is not stored in custom metadata. See "Configuration Data Management" in Chapter 4: Developing on Salesforce.

Run Additional Setup Scripts

Even all of the preceding steps are sometimes not sufficient to complete the org setup process. As the icing on the cake, you can run additional scripts to complete the setup. The most common kinds of scripts are anonymous Apex and Selenium UI automation scripts.

Anonymous Apex are blocks of Apex code that are executed in an org but not stored in that org. They can be run from the developer console, but can also be run using the Salesforce CLI's sfdx force:apex:execute command. Any kind of setup scripts should be stored in your code repository along with your code. You can then use that command by specifying the Apex code file and the user to execute as. Anonymous Apex is particularly useful if you want to query a group of records and do some simple batch processing on them.

Selenium is the most common type of UI automation, although there are other types such as Tosca and Provar. Selenium is most commonly used for UI testing, but can also be used to script activities that can only be done through the UI. Org shape and scratch org snapshots may be able to address limitations in the scratch org setup process by capturing settings that are not supported by the Metadata API and allowing you to create scratch orgs based on manually configured orgs. But until those are generally available, you can use Selenium automation for this purpose.

Selenium scripts use the web browser to simulate user actions such as logging into an org, navigating to a particular page, and changing a setting. They require care to craft in such a way that they continue to work even as Salesforce rolls out updates. UI automation is notoriously brittle, so you will do well to get help from someone who is experienced with building resilient Selenium scripts for Salesforce testing. As with anonymous Apex, these scripts should be stored in your code repository to ensure they are versioned and can be updated along with your source code and configuration as your org evolves.

Developing on Scratch Orgs

Scratch orgs provide two main characteristics that make them ideal for development. First, because they can be created entirely from configuration stored in version control, they behave and can be recreated in a predictable way. In other words, they are always in a "known" state, unlike long-lived sandboxes which might be modified by other users in ways that have unpredictable impact. Second, they allow for simple "source synchronization" that can synchronize the org configuration with your local file system (and thus with version control) in a single step. Source synchronization allows the state of the application to evolve in a controlled way that is tracked in version control.

For developers who are accustomed to working in long-lived developer sandboxes, this means that their development workflow has at least one additional step: they need to periodically recreate a development scratch org. Whether developers create development scratch orgs many times per day, once per week, or once per month (the maximum lifespan of a scratch org) depends on several factors, outlined here.

First, do you need different types of scratch orgs to work on different applications? If your org is complex enough to require different setup paths for different applications, then developers may need to create multiple scratch orgs to work on those different applications. They may find themselves recreating these orgs as they move between different work items.

Second, how long does your scratch org take to create, and have you completely automated the setup? Until capabilities such as scratch org snapshots are generally available, teams may find that it takes tens of minutes or up to an hour or more for automated package installations to complete. If on top of that there are manual configuration steps that have to be performed, this will add to the setup time and make recreating orgs regularly an inefficient process. This challenge should push teams to look at additional automation such as Selenium UI automation, but may also decrease the frequency that orgs are created.

Finally, if developers are using a feature branch workflow, where features are developed in separate version control branches which each require review and approval, this leads to the need to create multiple independent scratch orgs, one per branch, to ensure that each feature branch is truly distinct from each other. For teams that are just getting started with using version control, and need to ensure rigorous testing and approval of each feature in isolation, a feature branch workflow can be helpful. However it is not as efficient as trunk-based development (continuous integration) and tends to limit refactoring and collaboration and lead to increased merge conflicts.

Once the developer creates the scratch org, they can then make code changes on their local machine and run an `sfdx force:source:push` to push them to the scratch org. As they make changes in the org itself, they can run `sfdx force:source:pull` to pull those configuration changes into their local codebase. Salesforce's extensions for VS Code recently introduced a compile on save functionality that will automatically push local source to the scratch org when files are updated. This is particularly helpful when pulling or merging changes from shared version control, since this triggers a push when the local source is updated. A variation on this is the capability included in Appirio DX which watches the scratch org for changes and periodically runs synchronization.

Scratch orgs are generally intended to be worked on by one developer at a time. But there are some cases where collaborating in a scratch org can be useful. If the click-based developers on your team don't have an easy way to create scratch orgs and capture changes in version control, they may need to partner with code-based developers who can provision such an environment for them and capture their changes in version control. This can be a good way to force collaboration within the team and for these two developers to work together using their complementary skillset.

Development in a scratch org is otherwise identical to development in any other Salesforce environment. Other sections of this book such as Part 2: Salesforce Dev provide an overview of how to approach development with the whole dev lifecycle in mind.

Scratch Orgs As Review Apps

In addition to their use as development environments, scratch orgs are well suited to be used as review apps. Review apps are environments created dynamically from version control that provide an isolated environment to review features that may still be under development. The concept was popularized by Heroku.

A review app is simply a scratch org that is created for testing or evaluation purposes and is not intended for development. As such, they are perfect for performing quality analysis, functional review, or demos.

An important characteristic of a review app is that they should be self-service. A tester, reviewer, or person giving a demo should be able to create a review app for themselves with minimal difficulty and without relying on developers for assistance. If you are not using a commercial tool, you can build such a capability using a manual job in your CI system that runs the same setup script that your developers use to create their development environment. After initializing the org, generate a one-click login URL by running `sfdx force:org:open --urlonly`. Reviewers can execute that CI job to initialize an org, which they can open directly using that login URL.

Cloning and Refreshing Sandboxes

For most of Salesforce's history, there has been only one path for creating or "refreshing" a development or testing environment: creating a sandbox that is a copy of the production environment. This greatly limited the possible ways that sandboxes could be managed.

Fortunately, with the arrival of Salesforce DX, there are now a diversity of org creation and refresh options. For example, it's recently become possible to clone one sandbox from another, and Lightning Dev Pro sandboxes will make it possible to create and destroy sandboxes dynamically as needed. Having discussed scratch orgs, we can now look at the options for sandboxes and how they can be used beneficially.

Sandboxes are managed from the Sandboxes section in the Setup UI in your production org. That screen shows a list of your existing sandboxes, along with options to create, clone, refresh, and delete sandboxes.

Creating, Cloning, or Refreshing Sandboxes

In essence, creating, cloning, and refreshing sandboxes all do the same thing. All of these actions replace the sandbox with a new copy based on a source org. If a new sandbox is being created from production, this is called "creating a sandbox." If a new sandbox is being created from another sandbox, this is called "cloning a sandbox." And if an existing sandbox is being refreshed, either from production or from another sandbox, this is called "refreshing the sandbox."

Refreshing a sandbox is equivalent to destroying that sandbox and recreating it. The only thing that is preserved during a sandbox refresh is the name of that sandbox and its type (Developer, etc.).

In all of these cases, the features, limits, settings, and metadata of the source org are recreated in the target org. To what extent **data** is also copied depends on the situation.

Cloning or refreshing a sandbox from another sandbox requires that both sandboxes be of the same type, and a complete copy of the source sandbox's data is made into the target sandbox. If you are creating or refreshing a sandbox from **production**, data may or may not be copied, depending on the type of your target sandbox.

Full copy sandboxes receive a complete copy of the production org's data. Creating, cloning, or refreshing full copy sandboxes can take a very long time (a day or two) if the source org contains large volumes of data. Salesforce also limits these updates so that the org can only be refreshed once every 29 days.

Partial copy sandboxes created from production receive a subset of production data, based on a filter called a sandbox template. The sandbox template is used to determine which objects' data will be copied and how many records. This allows for a faster creation and refresh process, and partial copy sandboxes can be refreshed as often as once every 5 days.

Developer and Developer Pro sandboxes created from production do not receive any data. Their creation is generally quite fast, and they can be refreshed as often as once per day.

Because the sandbox refresh process is a destructive process, Salesforce requires that newly refreshed orgs be activated. In reality, the newly refreshed org is a different org than the sandbox being refreshed. Activating simply deletes the existing sandbox and redirects the sandbox name to the newly created org. Activation thus gives the ability for teams to continue working in an existing sandbox until the refreshed version is available, so that they can save their work and then resume working in the newly activated org immediately.

Salesforce provides the ability to perform setup actions by triggering the execution of an Apex class after a sandbox is created or refreshed. This setup script can perform a variety of actions. Common scenarios include deleting or obfuscating sensitive data in the org, creating or updating users, and so on.

There are a number of AppExchange products such as Odaseva and OwnBackup that provide helpful capabilities such as copying or sanitizing large volumes of data when creating testing environments.

Planning Org Refreshes

Understanding the org refresh process enables you to make an appropriate plan to support your development and testing needs.

The function of org refreshes is to bring metadata and data into sync between environments. Historically, org refreshes have been one of the main ways that teams have attempted to create consistent metadata between orgs. But configuration drift (metadata differences) between orgs is a symptom of lacking governance and continuous delivery. So you should use the mechanisms described in this book to ensure metadata stays in sync and rely on sandbox refreshes mostly for syncing data.

Making small, frequent deployments reduces the risk of any single deployment into production. Building your metadata into unlocked packages reduces differences between orgs and simplifies the deployment process. Locking everybody out from changing metadata in sandboxes and production ensures that orgs behave consistently and that changes are tracked. These are the mechanisms you should rely on to ensure that metadata is consistent. Note that these methods lead to changes being propagated from development through testing to production. The old pattern of refreshing sandbox metadata from production implies a lack of control over the deployment process, with changes in production being back-propagated to development and testing environments instead of the other way around.

But org refreshes still provide a clear and simple way to update testing environments with production-like data. Your final UAT or staging environment should closely resemble your production environment. One reason for this is to ensure that functionality is performant in the face of large data volumes. Many Salesforce solutions have been sent back to developers after testing in a full sandbox showed unacceptably poor performance. Another reason is to capture the full diversity of data, especially data used for configuration. Complex CPQ applications can behave entirely differently depending on how they're configured. Subject matter experts need to be able to validate that your solutions function properly with the data they'll have in production.

If your org relies heavily on data for configuration, and you don't have some other mechanism to synchronize that configuration data, plan on refreshing your full and partial sandboxes relatively frequently. But bear in mind that if these orgs are kept in sync with external systems, you may have to update your org to point to those external systems after refreshing, and you may also need to resynchronize data with those systems or update records' external IDs to match the external systems. Challenges like this can make org refreshes onerous. Continuously seek methods to automate the post-refresh process, and balance the benefits of freshly synchronized data with the cost of performing refreshes.

Planning and Communicating Changes to Org Structure

Having determined your environment strategy, how you will use scratch orgs and how you will maintain and refresh your sandboxes, you need to ensure that anyone who works on those environments is aware of changes that might impact them.

You should establish a clear communication channel with all of the people impacted by changes to particular orgs. In large enterprises, you might identify subsets of stakeholders who work on particular environments. Establishing a shared calendar and repeatedly directing people's attention to it can help build awareness about scheduled changes.

Because refreshes and other org changes can interfere with people's work or even cause them to lose work, you should approach such changes carefully, emphasizing clear and regular communication in advance.

If you are unsure who is using a particular org and are planning to delete or refresh it, you can identify active users by using the Login History page in the Setup UI.

Working with Lightning Dev Pro Sandboxes

Salesforce has recently announced a new type of sandbox called Lightning Dev Pro sandboxes (LDPS). These have the same characteristics as normal Dev Pro sandboxes (1 GB of storage) but are designed to be created and destroyed using Salesforce CLI or API commands, just like scratch orgs. The enterprises that would benefit most from scratch orgs have also had the most difficulty in adopting them because of the challenges of untangling metadata dependencies into coherent packages. Thus most organizations remain focused on building with sandboxes.

Lightning Dev Pro sandboxes enable developers to create a pristine sandbox on demand using the CLI, modify it as needed, and capture their changes for deployment to target orgs. Soon it will also be possible to perform source synchronization for these orgs to make it simple to pull and push changes from these orgs. LDPS address the need for individual developers to have their own development environments that are up to date. The ease of creating and destroying these also helps ensure that developers can regularly restart their work in a clean environment that does not contain any "cruft" left over from previous development.

The Salesforce Upgrade Cycle

Salesforce performs a major version update three times a year. Their biggest update in any given year is their Winter release, which happens in the Autumn, but is named after the upcoming year (e.g., Winter '20 was released in the fall of 2019). This release is timed to coincide with Salesforce's mega-conference Dreamforce, the largest tech conference in the world, and many features are kept secret until they are revealed during Dreamforce keynote speeches, amid much fanfare.

Early in the new year, the Spring release is launched, followed by the Summer release sometime around June. In between these major version updates, minor patches are released to address bugs, performance, and stability issues. The schedule varies each year, but is posted in advance at `https://trust.salesforce.com`.

Each major release is accompanied by a new major version number in the API (e.g., Winter '20 is API v47.0, and Spring '20 is API v48.0). The API versions apply to REST and SOAP APIs, Apex classes, and documentation, among other things. Versioning their APIs allows Salesforce to change functionality between API versions while not breaking existing integrations and customizations.

These major releases are generally seamless and accompanied by a short 5-minute release outage. Most Salesforce users simply awaken to a new logo in the upper left of their org and notice few other changes aside from some new features.

Salesforce emphasizes that trust is their primary corporate value, and they go to great lengths to ensure that these major releases are indeed seamless and do not cause disruption for their customers. One aspect of their preparation for releases is an early access program in which the upcoming version of Salesforce is made available in some environments a month or so before it is released in production.

Getting Early Access to a Release

Prior to each seasonal release, Salesforce offers two methods for customers and partners to get early access to the upcoming release: prereleases and previews. Four to six weeks before a release, Salesforce makes it possible to sign up for prerelease Developer Edition orgs. These orgs provide the earliest access to upcoming functionality, although if issues are discovered, it's possible that features introduced in a prerelease will not be included in the eventual release; it's during this prerelease time that Salesforce runs their "Apex Hammer" regression tests to ensure they didn't break customers' functionality. Then, typically 2-3 weeks later, Salesforce opens up a sandbox preview window during which it's possible to create sandboxes and scratch orgs that use the impending version. Salesforce hosts webinars and publishes an updated blog post prior to each release which explains the details of the preview window for that release.

To get access to prerelease functionality, you can sign up to get a prerelease developer edition org by going to `www.salesforce.com/form/signup/prerelease-spring19/` (changing the URL to match the next impending version). That sign-up form is only available for a few weeks prior to each release, so you have to pounce if you want to get one. The good news is that prerelease org remains available to you just like an ordinary developer edition org, but is always upgraded to the next Salesforce edition before regular developer edition orgs are (I still use a prerelease org created years ago as my main org for learning and experimentation).

Preview sandbox instances require some understanding and planning from Salesforce admins, so you should ensure you are clear on the process. If you are managing your company's sandboxes, I strongly encourage you to read and understand the article called "Salesforce Sandbox Preview Instructions [for the … Release]" to understand the process fully.[8] In brief, every sandbox is on either a preview instance of Salesforce or a nonpreview instance. The instance number of your sandbox determines whether it's a preview or nonpreview instance (e.g., CS21 is a preview instance, whereas CS22 is a nonpreview instance). Preview instances get updated about a month before the nonpreview instances.

As explained in the article mentioned earlier, the date on which you refresh your sandbox determines whether the sandbox is on a preview instance or a nonpreview instance, so the preview window will impact your sandbox refresh plans.

It's now possible to define whether scratch orgs created during the preview window are on the preview release or the previous release. By default, scratch orgs are created using the same release as the Dev Hub from which they're created. You can add the property "release": "Preview" to your scratch org definition file if you want the scratch org to be on the preview release, or "release": "Previous" if your Dev Hub has already been upgraded, but you want to create a scratch org that's on the previous release. These distinctions are only temporary; once the preview window closes, all orgs are upgraded to the latest release.

As mentioned, one thing that Salesforce does behind the scenes during this prerelease window is to run what's known as the Apex Hammer. Apex Hammer is a comprehensive execution of all Apex unit tests across all customer instances to ensure that they behave the same in the new version as they did in the previous version. One reason Salesforce implemented the requirement for customer Apex code to have 75% test coverage was to allow Salesforce themselves to perform regression testing on this code before seasonal releases. If Salesforce detects an inconsistency between your unit tests' output when run on different versions, that triggers an investigation and remediation. Again, this happens behind the scenes, but is a way of ensuring the reliability of the platform.

Deploying Between Environments That Are on Different Releases

Preview instances are very useful for getting early access to Salesforce capabilities and also to ensure that your customizations continue to work. You should take the preview window as an opportunity to revisit some or all of your custom functionality to ensure that it is still behaving as expected.

---

[8]The latest version of this article is always listed at `www.salesforce.com/blog/category/seasonal-release.html`

One challenge when working during the preview window is that it's possible to experience deployment errors if you attempt to deploy functionality from a preview instance (which may have new types of metadata) to a nonpreview instance. The Metadata API is versioned, so you can continue to retrieve metadata using the earlier API version number, even if you're now on the new version. However, sometimes new metadata changes can sneak in.

The most common issue I've seen is with new UserPermissions appearing in profiles. When you download a profile from a prerelease or preview instance, it may contain UserPermissions that don't exist in the current version. These will cause errors when deployed to an older version and so have to be manually removed from the profile for the deployment to succeed. As discussed in the section "Managing Org Differences" in Chapter 9: Deploying, it can be very helpful to have an automated method to strip out problematic tags arising from different org versions.

Sometimes a release will bring major changes to the metadata format. For example, during the transition between v37.0 and v38.0, the field type for all picklists was renamed valueSet, and the structure for managing picklists was changed in record types. Changes like this can require changes across the whole codebase to match the new format.

Prior to Salesforce DX, projects generally stored the API version for their metadata in the src/package.xml file for their project. That provided an explicit statement of the Metadata API version used for that metadata. Although projects can still specify a sourceApiVersion parameter for the project in their sfdx-project.json files, the default behavior is to determine the API version dynamically. It remains to be seen whether the Salesforce CLI handles this smoothly across every release, but it's at least now possible to quickly convert the entire codebase. Simply do an sfdx force:source:push of metadata in an older format, and then do an sfdx force:source:pull from a scratch org that's on a newer version of Salesforce, and you can expect to see the metadata format updated.

A Behind-the-Scenes Look at Orgs

One of the benefits of using Salesforce is that you don't have to know anything about its architecture; all you need to know is that it works and is sufficiently fast. But sometimes it can be helpful to have a bit of insight into the underlying architecture. In addition to impressing your coworkers, you can gain practical insights into topics like security, backups, and large data management.

I'm not an expert on this, and some of this architecture may be subject to change. Salesforce employs fleets of Site Reliability Engineers, sysadmins, database admins, and so on who help make all of this magic happen. They also share some of their insights and challenges publicly in Dreamforce sessions and on blogs like `https://engineering.salesforce.com/`. So look to those original sources for more information if you're curious. As mentioned in Chapter 2: Salesforce, the architecture described here applies only to Salesforce's core products like Sales Cloud and the Lightning Platform. The architecture for products like Heroku, Commerce Cloud, and MuleSoft will be substantially or completely different. As the product grows, there are an increasing number of additional aspects to this architecture, such as the Enterprise Messaging Platform (EMP) that are not explained here.

To make Salesforce core available, the company maintains nine of their own data centers, but also uses AWS to host their instances in some regions.[9] Salesforce announced a plan last year to partner with Google to use Google Cloud infrastructure to support Salesforce's international expansion.[10]

Within these data centers, Salesforce maintains over 100 "Pods" or instances known by names like NA42 and AP28. Each of these pods represents a self-contained set of resources to service a group of customers. Salesforce is a multitenant system which means that all customers use the same underlying database and application servers, but that data is segregated based on an Org ID to prevent the data or metadata for one customer from being accessible to or affecting that of another customer. This kind of multitenancy is at the heart of the cloud; from one point of view, "the cloud" is just mainframes with user partitioning.

Each of these Pods has a backup instance that can be used as a failover in the event that the main instance goes offline. There is even cross-data center data replication in the event that an entire data center goes offline.[11] Within each Pod there is a cluster of application servers and a cluster of database servers. When you first log in to Salesforce at `https://login.salesforce.com`, your request is routed to one of many authentication servers. Salesforce validates your credentials and then based on your username routes you to the appropriate Pod.

---

[9]`https://help.salesforce.com/articleView?id=000257307&language=en_US&type=1`
[10]`https://cloud.google.com/salesforce/`
[11]`https://help.salesforce.com/articleView?id=000231130&type=1`

Your interactions with a Salesforce instance are interactions with the application servers. These application servers provide standard functionality like record detail pages, as well as API access and any custom functionality such as custom apps, Lightning, Apex, or Visualforce pages you've created. To serve your data, these application servers reach out to the database servers to get access to the data for your org.

Importantly, all of your org's metadata including custom code is also stored in the database, in tables for standard and custom metadata. When you upload Apex code, that code is actually stored in the database to be executed as needed. Salesforce compiles page requests on demand, using the standard and custom metadata such as page layout definitions to structure the way that data is displayed in the output. There's a remarkable amount of custom processing that happens with each request to Salesforce, but they have managed to keep page load time relatively fast. This flexible structure is what allows admins to modify metadata and users to modify data simultaneously across thousands of orgs without impacting other tenants on the system.

The Salesforce database uses a generic structure to store all of the various custom fields and custom objects you create. They maintain one database table with records for standard objects. But any custom fields or custom objects you create are actually stored in a separate table. Records from all customers and all objects are stored together in those tables. One field is a globally unique ID (GUID) for that record, one field indicates the Org ID (the customer), and another field indicates which object the record is for (a lookup to the metadata table mentioned earlier). There are standard fields for CreatedBy, CreatedDate, SystemModStamp, LastModifiedBy, and LastModifiedDate, and the remaining fields hold the data for all the fields in that record. One reason why there are strict limits on how many custom fields you can have on an object in Salesforce is that Salesforce has a finite number of fields in the underlying database table. Each custom field you create consumes one of the available fields in that table, until eventually there are none left.

There are historical reasons for this structure: originally Salesforce didn't allow custom fields or objects, and so when those were added, they needed a new table to live in. Undoubtedly, there are good reasons why Salesforce has chosen to retain that structure. Presumably, this allows them to optimize the database performance for standard (known) objects while allowing for the table containing custom fields to favor flexibility over performance.

The net result of this is that Salesforce performs a number of table joins when querying data in your org. This leads to some of the behavior around query performance and opens the door for Salesforce to offer optimizations like skinny tables—a dedicated table that speeds queries on very large data volumes by prejoining standard and custom fields. Salesforce maintains additional indexes for querying and searching this data.

The canonical description of this architecture can be found in this article by Steve Bobrowski, which is kept up to date over time: `https://developer.salesforce.com/page/Multi_Tenant_Architecture`.

Summary

It's important to understand the difference between Salesforce orgs and conventional servers, as well as the different types of Salesforce org. We've looked at how to secure and access orgs, as well as how to determine which environments are needed for your project.

Scratch orgs can be created "from scratch," but sandboxes are always cloned from an existing org. Sandbox cloning has become more versatile, allowing for new development patterns, and scratch org shape and snapshots promise to ease the scratch org creation process as well.

One key benefit of using Salesforce is that orgs are upgraded for you automatically, but it's important for teams to be aware of the timing of these upgrades and the impact on the development process.

Having understood Salesforce environments, the next chapter deals with the linear progression of changes through development, testing, and production: the delivery pipeline.

CHAPTER 7

The Delivery Pipeline

The delivery pipeline, or deployment pipeline, refers to the sequence of automated processes that manage the build, test, and release process for your project. The term was popularized by the book *Continuous Delivery*, which says:

> *A deployment pipeline is, in essence, an automated implementation of your application's build, deploy, test, and release process. ... Every change that is made to an application's configuration, source code, environment, or data, triggers the creation of a new instance of the pipeline. ... The aim of the deployment pipeline is threefold. First, it makes every part of the process of building, deploying, testing, and releasing software visible to everybody involved, aiding collaboration. Second, it improves feedback so that problems are identified, and so resolved, as early in the process as possible. Finally, it enables teams to deploy and release any version of their software to any environment at will through a fully automated process.[1]*

The function of the delivery pipeline is to facilitate the movement of features and fixes from development environments, through a testing process, and to end users. Thus the delivery pipeline connects the different types of Salesforce environments and is the path through which innovation flows.

Salesforce development projects always have a development lifecycle, but they do not necessarily go through a delivery pipeline. A delivery pipeline depends first of all on the presence of version control. On the foundation of version control, you must then have automated testing (to identify flaws and prevent them from being deployed) and automated deployments (to move functionality in a reliable and traceable way). This chapter discusses the basic foundations of version control and CI automation that pertain to any technology, while the later chapters in this section go into detail on testing, deployments, and releases on Salesforce.

---

[1]Jez Humble and David Farley, *Continuous Delivery* (Pearson Education, 2011), 55.

Why You Need Version Control on Salesforce

At 6:45 pm PDT on Friday, May 16, 2019, Salesforce operations deployed a database script that impacted every org that had ever had Pardot installed.[2] This script inadvertently gave Modify All Data permissions to all users in those orgs, enabling every Salesforce user to access (and potentially modify) any data in that org. Such a change constitutes a security breach, and so out of an abundance of caution, Salesforce moved to lock users out of the affected orgs. But Salesforce didn't have an easy mechanism to prevent access to only specific orgs, so they took the "nuclear option" of disabling access to every org that shared a "Pod" (such as NA42) with an affected org. That left 60% of US Salesforce orgs inaccessible. Not only could these orgs not be accessed directly, but integrations that rely on them (including customer-facing web sites) were unable to contact Salesforce.

After 15 hours of downtime, access to these orgs was finally reenabled. But on the orgs which were directly impacted (those with Pardot installed), all non-admin users had their permissions entirely removed. Only admins were given access, along with instructions to restore the missing permissions.[3] Those instructions advised admins to restore permissions from a recently refreshed sandbox, or to restore them manually if they had no sandbox. But deploying profile permissions is notoriously challenging and without care and precision can easily lead to overwriting other metadata.

Salesforce is a remarkably stable and reliable system. But some of the admins affected by this outage will have struggled for days or weeks to restore their users' access. While no Salesforce user could have prevented the outage, the struggle to recover is entirely preventable.

My colleagues at Appirio manage the release process for a large medical device company. They had used version control and continuous delivery for the project from the very beginning, and their work formed an early foundation for Appirio DX. When access to their org was reestablished, they immediately began redeploying correct permissions to all their orgs. Even in the "fog of war," they were able to assess and repair the permission changes in just over 2 hours. Had they known exactly which permissions had been removed, they could have fixed things far more quickly. None of this would have been possible without a robust delivery pipeline being in place.

---

[2] https://status.salesforce.com/incidents/3815

[3] https://success.salesforce.com/issues_view?id=a1p3A000001SHDlQAO&title=s ome-user-profiles-and-permission-sets-were-modified-by-salesforce

Version control provides an extremely reliable backup for such metadata. And having a reliable delivery pipeline that you can use to restore configuration will protect you from extreme situations like this, as well as from a myriad of smaller problems.

Most of the problems that version control averts are not worthy of news headlines. But there is simply no substitute for having visibility into the history of changes on an org. And in large and small ways, that knowledge enables you to restore, diagnose, and experiment with complete confidence.

Version Control

Version control refers to a system for keeping track of different versions of a file and in its modern usage generally refers to software used to track versions of text files like source code. The most basic step that you and your teams can use to reduce risk while coding is to use version control on every single project without exception. Using version control is like keeping your money in the bank as opposed to under your bed. Banks protect your money, track all the inflows and outflows, and make it available anywhere to you and to those you authorize through ATMs and wire transfers. Similarly, version control means you never have an excuse for losing code, and all changes are tracked. That code is also accessible to you from any computer, and you can share it with those you authorize.

There are many types of version control technology, but in this text we'll be discussing Git almost exclusively. There are two reasons for this. First, I'm personally more familiar with Git than with any other type of version control. Second, Git has become overwhelmingly the most popular type of version control today.

It's important to note that Salesforce DX itself works entirely independently of the version control tool you choose to use. Many teams are successfully automating their Salesforce development lifecycle using TFS, Perforce, SVN, and other technologies. Most of the version control concepts shared here remain relevant regardless of the technology that you choose to use.

Git has its detractors and its disadvantages; it's more complicated to use than some competing tools. But it's undisputedly the dominant version control tool in the market, according to numerous developer surveys.[4] The Google Trends graph shown in Figure 7-1 shows that interest in Subversion (SVN) surpassed interest in Concurrent Version System (CVS) in 2005, while interest in Git surpassed SVN in 2011 and has continued to climb.

---

[4]https://rhodecode.com/insights/version-control-systems-2016

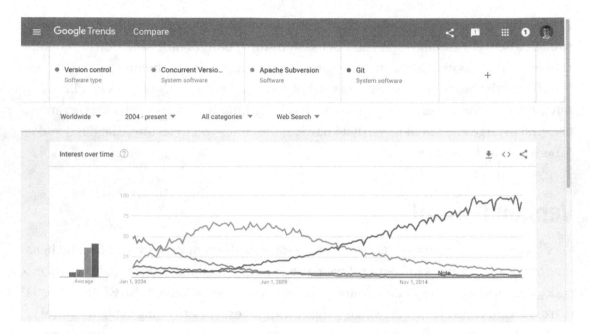

Figure 7-1. *Interest in version control in general, and CVS, SVN, and Git in particular, as measured by Google Trends in early 2019*

Git Basics

If you're not already familiar with Git, there are an amazing number of learning resources available to help you get started. In addition to endless articles, you can find interactive tutorials, videos, learning games, and live instructors. Even Salesforce Trailhead has a module on Git and GitHub.

Git itself is free and open source. It is an open technology that is interchangeable across all the different Git providers. People inevitably get confused, however, between Git and GitHub. GitHub is a commercial platform for hosting Git repositories that has become enormously popular over recent years. It faces competition from companies like Bitbucket and GitLab that also offer Git hosting. All these companies provide a secure, shared platform for teams to collaborate on Git repositories. They may offer a free tier, but they are commercial enterprises that charge for at least some of their hosting services.

Since Git is an open standard, it has also become possible for other version control systems and providers to provide Git-compatibility modes. For example, both Perforce and Microsoft Team Foundation Server (TFS) have their own proprietary version control technologies. But you can enable Git-compatibility mode on those code repositories to allow developers to use TFS or Perforce as version control hosts while using Git commands and Git GUIs on their local machines.

Git is a distributed version control system, which means that every collaborator "clones" their own local copy of the code repository. Technically, every cloned instance of Git is identical to every other instance, and every cloned instance can directly share updates with any other copy of the repo. In practice, however, most teams establish a single central code repository (often hosted on GitHub or another Git hosting provider) and use that as the definitive copy of the repository. This creates a clear and simple client-server relationship between each developer's local repository and the central repository. This makes Git behave more like traditional version control systems like CVS and SVN, with the added benefit that you can easily work offline, since you have a complete copy of the repository on your own machine.

Having a shared, central repository is also the foundation for having a single, shared delivery pipeline. Although all of the automation done in a CI/CD system could also be done on a developer's local laptop, consolidating these processes on a shared service provides visibility and traceability, which are critical to reducing confusion about the state of your environments and builds.

If you haven't gone through a Git tutorial yet, here are the absolute minimum bits of knowledge you need to get started:

- Once you have cloned your project using `git clone <repository>`, you can create branches following the branching strategy of your project:

  ```
  $ git checkout -b <branch name>
  ```

- Once you have created a new branch, you are free to start making changes. To see the changes you have made, run

  ```
  $ git status
  ```

- Before you can commit the changes, you need to move them to a staging area. To stage the files you want to commit, run

  ```
  $ git add <file_name>
  ```

- To commit the staged changes, run

  ```
  $ git commit -m <commit message>
  ```

- Finally, to push the changes to the remote repository, run

  ```
  $ git push
  ```

- If you want to retrieve the latest changes present in the remote
  repository, run

  ```
  $ git pull
  ```

- This will merge the remote changes into your local copy. When you
  pull, your repository should have no uncommitted changes.

- If you and someone else made changes to the same lines in the same
  file, you'll get a merge conflict that you'll need to resolve manually.
  VS Code and other Git GUIs offer built-in support for merge conflict
  resolution, which can make it easier to understand and resolve the
  conflict.

Figure 7-2 summarizes these commands. If you understand this diagram, you have
enough knowledge to get started with Git. But going through a thorough tutorial is well
worth the time.

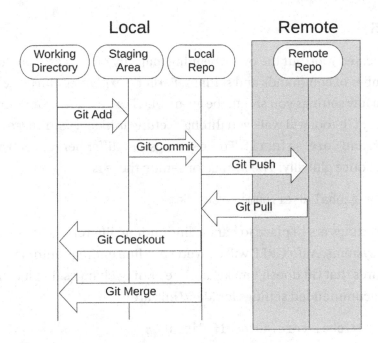

Figure 7-2. *Summary of the basic actions in Git*

Git Tools

There are many different ways of working with Git. The most common are summarized here for your convenience.

The classic way of using Git is to download the tool and run it from the command line as shown earlier. All of the other tools mentioned here actually use the Git command-line interface behind the scenes to work their magic. It's important to have a general understanding of how Git works on the command line, and even GUI users may find they need to perform commands on the command line occasionally.

Most Git tutorials explain using the command line. It's important to know how to run Git commands in that way, but I personally find it easier to use a graphical interface such as VS Code or SourceTree (`www.sourcetreeapp.com/`) for most daily operations. You can perform most Git commands using any of these tools, and you can mix and match these tools. For example, you could clone a repository using the command line, view the history of changes to that repository using SourceTree, make new commits using VS Code, and create a merge request using GitLab. All of these tools use the same underlying mechanism, so they stay in sync with one another naturally. I recommend that you get familiar with all of these tools because they excel at different tasks.

Git Settings

Git is a sophisticated tool, but the overwhelming majority of use cases are handled by a very small number of commands and settings. Earlier, I explained the basic commands. There are just a few settings you should be aware of. There are four common settings that almost every Git tool will walk you through setting initially: `user.name`, `user.email`, `core.autocrlf`, and `core.safecrlf`. These settings can differ per repository, but are typically just set once globally. The format for setting these is

```
git config --global user.name "Your Name"
```

The CRLF settings are in place to handle line ending differences between Windows and Mac/Unix systems. Auto CRLF will convert your line endings automatically, while Safe CRLF ensures that Git doesn't make any line ending changes that it can't reverse. The standard recommended settings for Mac/Unix are

```
git config --global core.autocrlf "input"
git config --global core.safecrlf "true"
```

And for Windows are

```
git config --global core.autocrlf "true"
git config --global core.safecrlf "warn"
```

When Salesforce teams are first migrating to version control, it's not uncommon to encounter line ending errors, especially with static resources which are uploaded from a user's local machine. There's a well-known utility called `dos2unix`[5] that you can use to batch convert the line endings in your project files. This is usually a one-time action when you first add files to the repository. After that Git takes care of the line ending conversions.

There is one Git setting that I've found tremendously helpful in dealing with the large XML files in Salesforce projects. Changing your Diff algorithm to "patience" ensures that Git takes extra care in comparing old and new versions of a file. XML contains lots of repetitive blocks, so this setting makes the actual changes more clear.

```
git config --global diff.algorithm "patience"
```

---

[5]http://dos2unix.sourceforge.net/

Git GUIs

Git GUIs like SourceTree, Tower, GitKraken, or GitHub Desktop excel at showing you a visual overview of the entire repository. You can quickly review changes across commits and branches and see changes to many files at one time. Release Managers and Tech Leads might find these tools particularly helpful since they need to review changes across many developers.

SourceTree is a free desktop application built by Atlassian that provides a UI for managing a local Git repository. It facilitates all of the Git features such as branching, committing, and merging. SourceTree makes it easy for new users to get started with Git, and it provides experienced Git users with a powerful way to manage even the most complex Git repositories.

Even if you're a command-line Ninja who was using computers before GUIs even existed, I'd strongly recommend you get familiar with one of these graphical tools. Especially if you're developing on a shared sandbox, you'll have to sort through metadata changes distributed across tens or hundreds of files, and you may need line-level precision when choosing what to commit and what to omit. Scratch org development makes the process far simpler, but graphical tools allow you to review changes and history with a speed and precision that are hard to match on the command line.

Git Embedded in the IDE

IDE plugins, such as VS Code's native Git support, excel at allowing you to make changes to files and then commit them quickly as you're working.

VS Code has built-in support for version control, which makes it an easy way to integrate the use of Git or other version control technologies into the development process. VS Code features a simple "sync" feature that pulls from the remote repo, merges, and then pushes your changes in just one click. It also has a great editor for resolving merge conflicts.

Git on the Command Line

Some people prefer to use Git on the command line, and it can be useful for everyone if you need to run less common Git commands. But be careful! Make sure you know what you're doing before just running a Git command that you found on the Internet. Some commands can have undesired consequences.

Git Host Web Interface

Working on the repo through the web browser interface of a Git host like GitLab can be useful for making quick changes, creating pull/merge requests (which are not a native Git capability), reviewing and commenting on other's code, or monitoring the progress of continuous integration jobs triggered from that Git host.

Git hosts provide a UI to navigate the Git repository as well as additional features such as merge requests for approving and merging changes. These hosts typically have many features to enrich collaboration, such as being able to add comments and have discussion around particular lines of code or merge requests.

The web interface can be a convenient way to solicit contributions from less technical members of the team. You can invite help from colleagues just by giving them access to GitHub, Bitbucket, or GitLab, without them having to download or learn Git. On the Appirio DX project, we passed documentation updates to an editor who used the web interface for her review.

Naming Conventions

The purpose of using a version control system is to make collaboration, experimentation, and debugging easier by providing a clear history of changes. Since this is a form of communication (across the team and across time), it's important that this communication be clear and done in a consistent way.

Every commit requires a commit message. Ideally, every commit represents a single, meaningful change to fix a bug or add a feature and is accompanied by a clear explanation of the change. In practice, unless a team is very disciplined about this, most commit histories are littered with unhelpful messages. I'm personally guilty of a lot of hasty messages like "fix the build." Similarly, a single commit might contain multiple unrelated changes, or conversely, related changes may be spread across multiple commits. While it's not always necessary for a commit history to be clean and clear, there are several approaches to commit messages and branch names that can help add value.

Commit Messages

Assuming that you're working in a team which is tracking their work in a ticketing system, each commit message should make specific reference to the ticket number that the commit is relevant to. This helps you track code changes back to the requirement (user story, issue, or task) that prompted the change. This "requirements traceability" can also be important for complying with legal regulations. The ticketing system generally indicates who created a particular feature request and who approved it, while tying a commit message to the ticket indicates when that change was implemented in the codebase.

```
$ git commit -m "S-12345 I-67890 Added region to Account trigger"
```

If you are building CI automation around your commit messages (such as updating the external ticketing system based on a job status), be aware that commit messages can be truncated in the CI system. For this reason, it is helpful if the ticket number is placed at the beginning of the commit message. Any story/issue/task numbers used toward the end of a long commit message may be truncated and so not be available to the automation.

As various Git hosts have evolved their feature offerings and competed with each other, many of them have built integrated ticketing systems such as GitLab issues or GitHub issues. Similarly, Bitbucket provides native integration with Jira and Trello, also Atlassian products. These integrations allow for deeper integration between the ticketing systems and Git commits. For example, Atlassian allows you to view all related Bitbucket commits directly inside Jira. GitHub and GitLab allow you to close issues on their boards by referencing issues in commit messages such as "… fixes #113."

Feature Branch Naming

If you're using feature branches, the name of your feature branch is included by default in the commit message when you merge the branch into the master branch. This means that the names of your feature branches impact the commit history and can be used to make the history more meaningful.

Git GUIs such as SourceTree will recognize slashes in feature branch names and show them as a tree. Thus you can give your feature branch a detailed name that is prefixed with `feature/` to have all similarly named branches grouped together. To make it clear to everyone on the team what this branch pertains to, it's a good practice to include the ID of the work it relates to and a brief description. Teams with large numbers of developers each working on individual branches may find it helpful to include the name of the developer in the branch like `feature/sdeep-S-523567-Oppty-mgmt`.

- Using the / in `feature/` allows those branches to be grouped in SourceTree like a "folder."

- If your team has large numbers of branches assigned to individual developers, including your name (e.g., `sdeep`) causes your branches to be sorted together and makes it easier for you and your colleagues to identify your work in progress.

- Including the work ID (e.g., `S-523566`) will uniquely identify that work and allow you to automatically reference commits in that branch from your ticketing system.

- Including a description (e.g., `Oppty-mgmt`) helps humans (like you) identify what that work is about.

Some commercial tools like Appirio DX facilitate quickly adhering to such naming conventions.

Techniques such as Git Flow make use of a variety of branch types, which benefit from following a consistent naming convention such as hotfix/, release/, and so on. As discussed in the following, this is generally a less efficient workflow than trunk-based development.

Squash Commits

Another useful capability if you're developing in feature branches is the ability to squash commits. Squashing commits means to combine the changes from multiple commits into a single commit. This allows developers to make numerous small commits as they iterate through code changes while still creating a public history of commits that is succinct and meaningful. GitHub and GitLab both allow you to merge a branch into a single "squashed" commit, with a more meaningful message.

Semantic Release and Conventional Commits

There are several initiatives to enforce and make use of more rigorous commit message conventions. Probably the best known approach is called "Semantic Release," which uses a commit syntax called "Conventional Commits." There are tools such as Commitizen that can help you to enforce these conventions.

In Conventional Commits,[6] every commit message begins with a keyword indicating what type of change this is. The main keywords are `fix` indicating an issue fix, `feat` indicating a feature, or `BREAKING CHANGE` indicating a change that is not backward compatible. Several other keywords are widely accepted such as `chore`, `docs`, `style`, `refactor`, and `test`.

Following the **type** keyword, you can add an optional scope, indicating which part of the system you're modifying. The type and scope are followed by a colon and then the description of the change, so that the commit message would read like these examples:

```
feat(lang): added Polish language
docs: correkt speling of CHANGELOG
BREAKING CHANGE:extendskey in config file is now used for extending other
config files
```

Semantic Release builds on this convention to enforce the semantic versioning standard. Semantic versioning (semver) is the convention where version numbers are expressed as major.minor.patch numbers (e.g., 2.1.15). According to the semver proposal, if you are releasing a fix, you should increment the patch version number; if you are releasing a new feature, you should increment the minor version number; and you should only increment the major version number if you are implementing a breaking change. So, for example, Gulp 4.0.0 is not backward compatible with Gulp 3.9.1, but Gulp 3.9.1 **is** backward compatible all the way back to Gulp 3.0.0.

Semantic Release aims to enforce this numbering convention by updating version numbers solely based on commit messages. Semantic Release provides plugins that work with different technologies and version control hosts to enable version numbers to be incremented automatically based on commit messages.

To help your team enforce these naming conventions, tools like Commitizen provide interactive prompts as shown in Figure 7-3 which allow you to specify the type of change from a dropdown list before prompting you for the scope, a description, and whether the commit referenced any issues in the ticketing system.

---

[6]`www.conventionalcommits.org/en/v1.0.0-beta.2/`

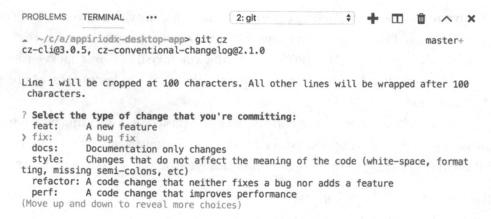

Figure 7-3. Commitizen provides a series of prompts to help you write consistent commit messages

Preserving Git History When Converting to Salesforce DX

When you begin working in Salesforce DX, you will convert your project files from the Metadata API format into the Salesforce DX format. If you have an existing code repository and want to keep your Git history, you can follow this process.

The metadata conversion process copies your metadata into a folder such as `force-app/main/default`. Some types of metadata such as custom objects are then "decomposed" into smaller files.

To retain a history of these files in version control, you should delete your original `src/` files at the same time that you commit the new Salesforce DX files. In most cases, Git will recognize this (deletion of an old file and creation of a corresponding file) as a rename operation and your history will be preserved.

Stage these "rename" changes before making any other changes to the metadata. In some cases, Git will not correctly identify the origin and destination files. In those cases, you can stage and commit "renamed" files in smaller batches. For example, you can stage only the deletion of `src/classes/` and the creation of `force-app/main/default/classes/` and commit them together as a single commit. You can then proceed with committing other metadata types, one batch at a time.

Note that you cannot preserve history on the "decomposed" metadata. Classes and workflow rules are simply moved to a different folder or renamed slightly. But Object files are broken into many smaller files. The complete object file will appear as deleted in version control, and many smaller files will appear in its place. Nevertheless, even after they're deleted, you can go back to the earlier history for those files should the need arise.

After you commit these changes, you will almost certainly want to divide the source code into subdirectories or multiple repositories to enable modular/package-based development. Git recognizes file movements as a rename operation, but relies on the file contents to be relatively unchanged. So if you are simply moving metadata files into a separate folder, you should first save and commit any changes to those files and then move the files into the other folder and commit that change before proceeding with further changes.

If you decide you need to split your codebase into a separate repository, I recommend cloning or forking the existing repository rather than just creating a new repository. This will preserve the history of the files in both repositories. Clone the "parent" repository to create a "child" repository. Then delete from the parent repository any metadata files that should now belong only in the child repository. Finally remove from the child repository any metadata that belongs only in the parent. Commit those changes and you will have divided your codebase while still retaining the history.

Branching Strategy

One beautiful capability of version control systems is that they allow for the creation of branches or alternative versions of the codebase. These branches allow individuals and teams to share a common history, track changes in isolation from one another, and in most cases eventually merge those changes back together. Branches can be useful for experimentation, when one member of the team doesn't want their unproven changes to impact others on the team. And they can be useful for protecting one's codebase from the potential impact of other teams' changes.

Your branching strategy determines to what degree multiple variations of your code can diverge. Since version control drives automation such as CI/CD processes, branches can be used to drive variations in the automated processes that are run.

The use of version control is not controversial among professional programmers. The appropriate way to use (or not use) branches, however, is an almost religious debate.

Trunk, Branches, and Forks

Most code repositories have one main branch, which we can call the trunk. In Git, this is usually called master as shown in Figure 7-4. Other branches may branch off from this trunk, but they'll typically need to be merged back in eventually. This trunk is sometimes also referred to as the mainline.

In Git, even the trunk is just another branch. But in this context, we'll use branches to refer to versions of the code that separate off from trunk. In Git, a branch functions like a complete copy of the codebase, but one that can evolve separately from the trunk and from other branches. A short-lived branch is one that lasts for less than a day. A long-running branch is one that lasts for more than a day. Because Git is a distributed version control system, every time someone edits code on their local copy of master, they are effectively working in a branch. However, as soon as they push their changes to the shared repository, it is merged into `master`, so (assuming that they push daily) they are effectively developing on the trunk. Only when a branch is given a name does it become formally separate from the trunk.

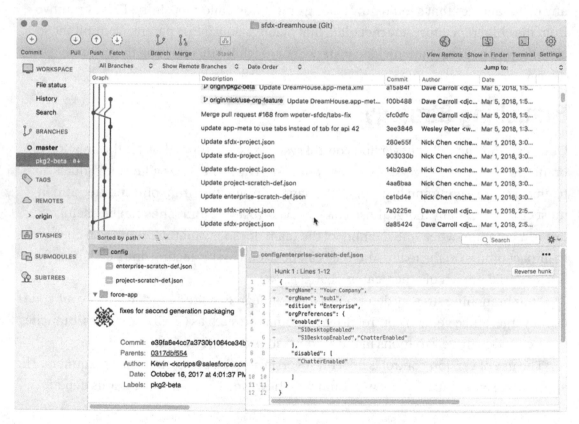

Figure 7-4. *Branching in the Dreamhouse app*

A Fork is a complete copy of a code repository that maintains a connection to the original repository. Whereas a branch begins as a copy of the trunk (or of another branch) but still lives in the same repository, a forked copy of a repository begins as a copy of an entire repository. This new repository is independent of the original repository and can evolve separately from it. But because they share a common history, changes from the forked repository can be merged back into the original repository or vice versa. In essence, a forked repository is like a super-branch: a branch of all the branches.

There are two reasons for forking repositories. One reason is when a team wants to take independent responsibility for their copy of a project. They might want to evolve it in a different direction (like the Jenkins CI server was forked from the original Hudson project), or they might want to use the project internally and customize it to their needs. The other reason for forking a repository is to securely allow for contributions to a project from unknown or untrusted contributors.

For example, Salesforce published their Dreamhouse repository on GitHub. They can allow their own developers direct editing rights on that project. But if a non-Salesforce employee such as myself wanted to contribute a change, they should not automatically trust that change. By forking the project into my own account as shown in Figure 7-5, I have full permission to edit this new copy. I can make changes and contribute a pull request back to the original project even though I have no permissions on the original repository. The team that owns that repository can then review the changes and accept or reject them.

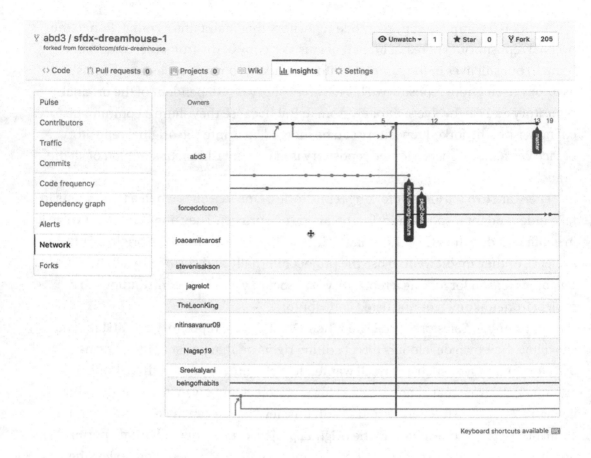

Figure 7-5. *A forked copy of Salesforce's Dreamhouse repository*

Well-Known Branching Strategies

There are many Git branching strategies that have been proposed and used. Table 7-1 lists the best-known strategies, along with my subjective view on them.

Table 7-1. *Brief summary of the best-known Git branching strategies*

Branching Strategy	My View
Centralized Workflow/ Trunk-based Development[7]	Simplest to understand, similar to SVN, a good place to start, the most efficient and proven workflow.
Git**Hub** Flow[8]	Uses feature branches and then merges them into trunk. This allows for systematic code reviews and is well suited to open source development with unknown contributors.
Feature Branch Workflow[9]	Very similar to GitHub Flow, but includes rebasing commits onto master.
Git**Lab** Flow[10]	Useful for versioned software. Generally more complex than needed.
Gitflow[11]	Sophisticated and popular, but tends to leave branches unmerged for too long, making it the antithesis of continuous integration.
Forking Workflow[12]	Useful when contributing to open source projects or highly complex, multi-repo programs. This compounds the risks of long-lived branches.

The Research on Branching Strategies

In the early days of enterprise software development, it was common for teams to work in isolation from one another for months or years at a time and then to have an integration phase involving weeks or months of risky and tedious merges of the codebase. The Extreme Programming[13] movement in the late 1990s popularized the practice of continuous integration, also known as trunk-based development,[14] in which teams performed the integration on an ongoing basis and worked together on a common mainline.

---

[7]www.atlassian.com/git/tutorials/comparing-workflows#centralized-workflow
[8]https://guides.github.com/introduction/flow/
[9]www.atlassian.com/git/tutorials/comparing-workflows/feature-branch-workflow
[10]https://docs.gitlab.com/ee/workflow/gitlab_flow.html
[11]www.atlassian.com/git/tutorials/comparing-workflows/gitflow-workflow
[12]www.atlassian.com/git/tutorials/comparing-workflows/forking-workflow
[13]Kent Beck and Cynthia Andres. 2004. *Extreme Programming Explained: Embrace Change* (2nd Edition). Addison-Wesley Professional.
[14]https://trunkbaseddevelopment.com/

The debate about whether to use feature branches or to develop together on master has been a long-running debate. Over several years, the DevOps Research and Assessment team analyzed the impact of branching strategy on a team's software delivery performance. The *2017 State of DevOps Report* shows their conclusions:

> *While our experience shows that developers in high-performing teams work in small batches and develop off of trunk or master, rather than long-lived feature branches, many practitioners in the industry routinely work in branches or forks. [Our study] results confirmed that the following development practices contribute to higher software delivery performance:*
>
> - *Merging code into trunk on a daily basis.*
>
> - *Having branches or forks with very short lifetimes (less than a day).*
>
> - *Having fewer than three active branches.*
>
> *We also found that teams without code lock periods had higher software delivery performance. (The ability to work without code lock periods is supported by the practices described above.)*
>
> *Additional analysis also showed:*
>
> - *High performers have the shortest integration times and branch lifetimes, with branch life and integration typically lasting hours.*
>
> - *Low performers have the longest integration times and branch lifetimes, with branch life and integration typically lasting days.*
>
> - *These differences are statistically significant.*
>
> *There's clear guidance to offer from these findings: Teams should avoid keeping branches alive more than a day. If it's taking you more than a day to merge and integrate branches, that's a warning sign, and you should take a look at your practices and your architecture.*[15]

Freedom, Control, and Ease

To understand why trunk-based development yields such benefits, and to understand what branching structure is most appropriate for your team, it's helpful to think about freedom, control, and ease.

---

[15]2017 State of DevOps Report https://puppet.com/resources/ whitepaper/2017-state-of-devops-report

In general, there is a tension between freedom and control—the more control, the less freedom; the more freedom, the less control. In an effort to overcome common problems in application development, it is typical for teams to oscillate between freedom and control as they define their processes. Where developers encounter too many obstacles deploying hotfixes to solve production problems, the team may give the freedom for certain changes to be expedited to production. Where individuals are seen to be making changes that break core functionality in production, additional controls may be put in place to prevent any changes directly in production.

What aspects of your version control system are conducive to freedom? Which are conducive to control? How should you best balance your options?

The fundamental idea of continuous delivery is that if you hope to have any control at all over your application and configuration, you need to be using version control, locking everybody out from changing metadata manually, and instead using an automated process for deploying those changes. That control comes at the expense of individuals being able to make ad hoc changes in any environment. But this level of control is a basic foundation that you should never compromise. Without version control and deployment automation, you will never have any real degree of control over your environments.

Once you control your Salesforce environments using version control and CI/CD, they function as a control panel for your development and release process. The guiding principle here is that you tune the freedom and control in your version control and CI system to determine the balance of freedom and control in your applications and environments.

What are the aspects of version control and CI that you can tune?

Your file and folder structure determines the content and structure of your application. If you divide your applications across multiple repositories, each of those repositories can control separate parts of the system. But forked copies of a repository and long-running branches within a repository allow for multiple alternative versions of that application. The major risk that branches and forked repositories present is that if they're all destined to control a single application, you will eventually have to merge them.

Merging can be risky. The more time elapses between a branch being created and merged, the more people forget the reasons why certain changes were made. And the more changes that are made on that branch, the greater the risk that the merge will cause conflicts or errors. These two factors, forgetfulness and the size of merges, are what make continuous integration (trunk-based development) a superior strategy in most cases.

The KISS principle applies (keep it simple and straightforward). Your files and folders should represent the structure of your application. Your commits represent changes to that application over time. CI jobs are used to manage stages of automation done on any given commit. That's three degrees of freedom already.

The advent of SaaS and auto-update technologies increasingly allow teams to only support one latest version of an application. If you have to support multiple versions of an application (imagine the patches to various versions of the Windows operating system), you will need to use multiple branches or repositories. But for modern applications like VS Code or the Salesforce CLI, for example, "only the latest version is supported." That's an enormous simplification and one that we should strive for with our own applications. One reason why Salesforce is able to innovate so quickly is that there are no "old versions" of Salesforce that their teams have to support.

Adding additional branches adds another degree of freedom ... that you will eventually have to bring back under control. Better to do it straightaway, by not allowing the branch to last for more than a few hours. Adding additional forked repos adds yet another degree of freedom. Although I know teams that have taken this approach, and it is one that Atlassian's Salesforce development team used to recommend, in my view this can create an enormous amount of overhead and bring limited benefit. Forking repositories should generally only be used to allow untrusted developers to propose contributions to open source projects.

Merge requests (aka pull requests) are a way of adding control to a system by providing a formal approval process for branches being merged. Again, this is extremely useful for open source projects, but be very careful about adding merge requests as a requirement for your internal developers to submit a change to `master`. In practice, most tech leads do not review those changes carefully, so approving merge requests just delays the merging of feature branches and adds bureaucracy. Developers (and everyone else) definitely need feedback on their work, but real-time peer programming or informal code reviews generally yield higher performance without increasing the number of bugs in the system.

In addition to considering the balance between freedom and control, it's also important to improve the **ease** with which your team can deliver changes. The ease of managing your application's lifecycle depends on several factors:

1. Automating builds and deployments of all configuration eases the release process.

2. Automating tests eases the release process tremendously, in helping to identify bugs before they hit production.

3. And finally, tuning your approach to branching can help to
    ease the development process by not allowing any unnecessary
    variations to exist and addressing conflicts as they arise as
    opposed to allowing them to accumulate on long-running
    branches or forks.

Figure 7-6 summarizes the concepts in version control. Each aspect of this system
represents a "freedom" or variation that can exist. Each aspect also provides an
opportunity for control. You should tune your use of version control to maximize the
ease of delivering changes while providing the appropriate balance of freedom and
control. While branches and forks offer freedom to innovate without sacrificing control
over the trunk, they bring significant inefficiency. Wherever possible, promote trunk-
based development.

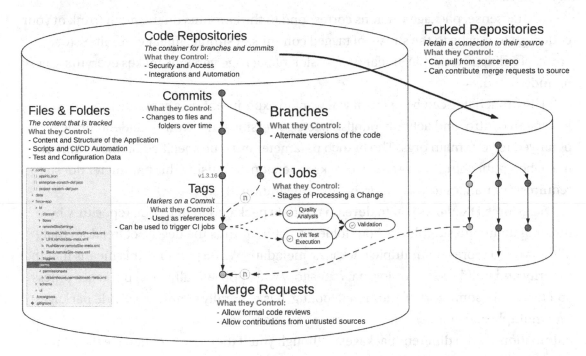

Figure 7-6. *An illustration of core version control concepts*

Branching for Package Publishing

Publishing Salesforce unlocked packages lends itself well to a simple branching strategy. Whereas for org-based development (see later), there are legitimate reasons why you may need to use long-running branches to manage differences across orgs, that's not necessary for managing packages.

Although unlocked packages and managed packages allow for a `branch` parameter to be specified, you'll need to take special care if you want to use that. If you are a managed package developer and need to support old versions of your package or different editions of Salesforce, there may be a need for a more complex process. But for enterprises developing unlocked packages, you should generally just use a single branch for your package's metadata, and allow its versions to reflect the linear history of improvements to the package.

In that sense, package versions correspond to the commits on the main trunk of your codebase or maybe to the subset of tagged commits. A simple, linear commit history corresponding to a simple, linear progression of package versions makes everything easy to understand.

The branch flag can be useful if you want to experiment on a separate branch in version control and actually publish package versions that won't accidentally be deployed to your main orgs. The branch parameter must be specified on the command line when publishing or installing a package version, and using this parameter doesn't require any changes to your underlying configuration files.

Salesforce DX allows you to develop multiple packages in one code repository by dividing them into subfolders. Your folder structure is thus the degree of freedom that allows you to represent multiple packages' metadata. While possible, this means that the security and build processes for that repository will apply equally to all packages unless you have built some sort of additional tooling. It is generally simpler to divide packages into multiple code repositories. That gives you the freedom to have different security and automation for the different packages; although you'll then need to manage their build processes separately and risk those processes getting out of sync.

Using one main trunk branch, you can still use feature branches and formal code reviews if you deem it necessary.

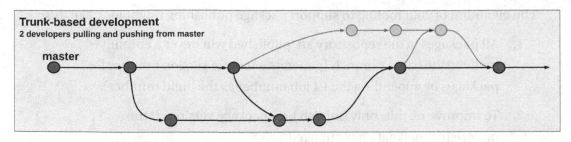

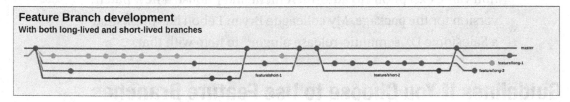

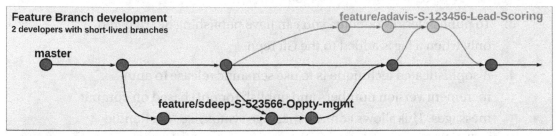

Figure 7-7. *Trunk-based development vs. feature branching*

As you can see in Figure 7-7, trunk-based development in Git is equivalent to using short-lived feature branches, with the difference that those "branches" are just developers' local copies of the `master` branch, so you can't run separate CI processes on those branches, although developers can run automated processes locally. You can also use Git hooks like pre-commit or post-commit hooks to enforce that certain processes are run with each local commit.

You can gradually implement tooling to support a refined CI/CD workflow around this branching structure. Common processes that you may want to run include

1. Static code analysis

2. Unit test execution

3. Manual jobs to allow the creation of review apps on a particular commit

4. Package publishing

5. Package installation in a target environment

The evolution of your tooling to support package publishing might look like this:

1. All packages in the repository are published whenever a commit is made to the `master` branch (generate a unique version number for packages by appending the CI job number as the build number).

2. To improve on this, only publish new package versions if the underlying metadata has changed.

3. To publish less frequently, you can have publishing be triggered only when a tag is added to the Git repo.

4. A sophisticated technique is to use semantic release to auto-increment version numbers and publish (or not) based on commit messages. This allows commit message syntax like "fix: handle null value exception" to auto-increment and publish a new patch version for the package. My colleague Bryan Leboff has published a Salesforce DX semantic-release plugin[16] to help with that.

Guidelines if You Choose to Use Feature Branches

There are several reasons why you might choose to use a feature branch workflow:

1. It allows you to use merge/pull requests to perform formal code reviews. Without the mechanism of merge requests, it is difficult to ensure that changes are reviewed and approved systematically.

2. It allows special CI jobs to be performed only on work in progress before it's merged into the `master` branch. Code in feature branches can be scanned for quality issues and validated to ensure it will deploy successfully before it's ever merged into the `master` branch.

3. It allows for in-progress features to be reviewed using review apps.

---

[16]https://github.com/leboff/semantic-release-sfdx

Although feature branches can be useful for these reasons, it is important to **avoid long-running feature branches**. Continuous integration is a well-established principle of software engineering which demands that code from different developers be merged frequently (at least daily if not within a few hours) so that conflicts can be detected and resolved quickly.

If you use feature branches, it is helpful to enable teams to create review apps based on a particular branch. This allows the branch to be previewed in a live environment for demo, review, or QA purposes. Reviewers can then give feedback before merging that code into the master branch. Changes related to one story are isolated from changes to any other work in progress, and the QA team can begin testing without waiting for a deployment to a QA sandbox.

If you use feature branches, it's helpful to delete them after they've been merged. This only deletes their name, not the history of changes. This reduces clutter, allowing only active branches to be listed in your Git tools.

See also the earlier guidelines on "Feature Branch Naming."

Before merging your work into the master branch, you should *merge the master branch into your feature branch* as shown in Figure 7-8. That forces each developer (who knows their code changes best) to resolve conflicts with the master branch (if any) rather than requiring the reviewer of any merge request to make judgments about how merge conflicts should be handled. When you're developing on the trunk, you have to pull and merge the latest remote version into your local repository before pushing your updates. Merging master into your feature branch is exactly the same concept.

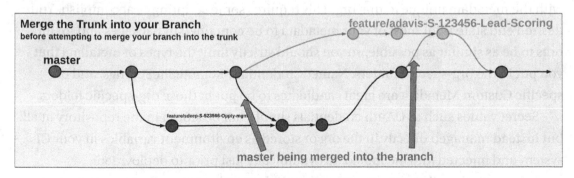

Figure 7-8. Merging the master branch into a feature branch

Branching for Org-Level Configuration

Just as it's important to use an automated process to track and build your packages, it's critical to also track and deploy your org-level configuration from version control. Prior to the development of Salesforce DX, managing configuration at the org level was the only way to implement continuous delivery for Salesforce. Therefore even for teams who are not yet ready to move to scratch orgs and unlocked packages, establishing a proper org-level delivery pipeline is extremely helpful.

Managing org-level configuration requires a different approach from package development. Orgs should generally contain identical metadata, but there are three important exceptions:

1. Some configuration (such as integration endpoints) needs to vary between the orgs.

2. Orgs are populated with metadata at different stages of development.

3. Some metadata in each org (such as most reports) does not need to be tracked.

How can you establish an automated process to keep orgs **identical yet different**?!

One effective approach is to have one folder to store the metadata that is common to all orgs and separate folders for each target org that can store metadata that is unique to that org. Deployments are made to each org by combining the common metadata with the metadata unique to that org. This requires some scripting to accomplish. Your desired end state is for most of your metadata to be contained in packages and for all orgs to be as similar as possible, so you should strictly limit the types of metadata that you put in the org-specific folders. NamedCredentials, RemoteSiteSettings, and org-specific Custom Metadata are great candidates to be put in those org-specific folders.

Secret values such as OAuth credentials should not be stored in the repository at all, but instead managed directly in the org or stored as environment variables in your CI system and injected into the metadata dynamically just prior to deployment.

Folders work well to handle common metadata and org-specific differences. But they are not a good solution for moving metadata through the stages of the development lifecycle. Because branches can be merged into one another, branches are the ideal solution for tracking metadata that should be sent to the testing environment now, but will soon be ready to move to the staging and then production environments. As shown in Figure 7-9, you can use a testing branch to deploy metadata to the testing org; when you're ready, merge the testing branch into the staging branch and have that trigger a deployment to the staging org. Finally, do the same to production.

As a convention, you should use the `master` branch to refer to the metadata in production. The reason for this is that `master` is the default branch in your repository (the one you never delete); and while you may eventually delete or refresh sandboxes, you will never delete your production org.

From `master`, you can create branches that correspond to different sandboxes. You only need branches for sandboxes that are used to **test** features under development. Typically, organizations will have one, two, or three environments that are used to test features that have been released from development but still need to be verified. You only need sufficient branches to manage those variations.

Therefore not every sandbox should have its own branch. You can use a single branch to manage the configuration for multiple sandboxes, as long as you're happy to update those environments at the same time. For example, you can have an automated process that updates your training sandbox from the same branch used to update your staging sandbox. Whenever you deploy updates to the staging org, you can deploy updates to the training sandbox in parallel.

Although it's now possible to clone sandboxes, the default approach is to create and refresh sandboxes from the production org. When you create or refresh an org, this destroys any customizations made in that org. To reflect that, you can simply delete the corresponding branch. If the updated org has been cloned from production, you can then recreate the corresponding branch from `master`, since the sandbox is now in an identical state to `master`.

Bear in mind that the more branches you have, the more chance there is for those branches to get out of sync. Therefore, try to reduce the number of branches if at all possible. One small but important simplification can be made to the branch used to manage your final testing environment. The last environment used for testing should be your most production-like environment. Sometimes this is a full sandbox; sometimes it's called "stage" or "staging" to indicate that it's for configuration that is preparing to be sent to production. To say with confidence that you have tested your configuration before sending it to production, you can use the exact same branch (`master`) to deploy to this staging environment and to production. But whereas every commit made to this `master` branch will be deployed to this staging environment, you can use tags on this branch to selectively trigger deployments to production. These tags also provide a quick reference to your production deployments. Using the same branch to manage both staging and production gives you ample confidence that you have tested your production changes in another environment. To be extra safe, you can use these tags to create a job in your CI system that you must trigger **manually** to actually perform the production deployment.

Finally, there are certain types of metadata that do not need to be tracked in version control. These are metadata like reports that you want to give your users freedom to create and edit directly in production. See "What's Safe to Change Directly in Production" in Chapter 12: Making It Better for a discussion of the types of metadata that do not need to be tracked.

An Illustration of This Branching Strategy

The branching strategy just described is one we have been using at Appirio since long before Salesforce DX appeared. This is not the only possible approach, but is one that is simple to implement with minimal automation. See Figure 7-9.

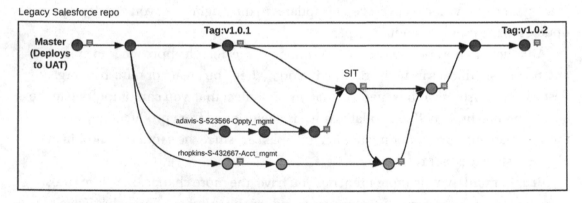

Figure 7-9. *Branching for org-level metadata*

We've found this approach generally works well and provides a balance between simplicity and power. To allow for formal **code reviews** and **branch-level automation**, many of our projects use feature branches while reducing complexity by limiting the number and lifespan of those branches.

The master branch is used to deploy code to the UAT org, and we use tags to deploy selected commits on the master branch to production. Every commit to the master branch triggers a deployment to UAT **followed by** a validation against the production environment. Additionally, if the commit to UAT contains a tag with a format like v1.0.3, this unlocks a manual option to deploy to production. In this way, we ensure that the

UAT and production environments contain the exact same codebase, and we never have to struggle with keeping those in sync.

Whenever a sprint starts, the Tech Lead or Release Manager should create an SIT (system integration testing) branch from the latest commit on master. When developers start their work on a story or issue, they create a feature branch from the latest commit to SIT. Once they commit their changes to their feature branch, a validation against the SIT environment is triggered. The developer can then go to the CI system to view the job status. If the validation job is successful, they then merge any recent changes to the SIT branch into their feature branch and create a merge request from their feature branch into the SIT branch. A dev lead can then view that merge request, see the code changes in the merge request, and approve or reject the merge request. If the merge request is accepted, the changes will be deployed to SIT and validated against UAT.

At the end of each sprint, the Tech Lead or Release Manager merges the SIT branch into master and **deletes** the SIT branch to allow this cycle to start again. Deleting and recreating this branch is very important since it reduces complexity in the repository. If you don't do this, branches will become increasingly hard to synchronize over time.

To sum up the process:

1. A developer makes a feature branch from SIT. As they work, they make commits to that feature branch. When they are ready to submit their work for review, they merge any recent changes from SIT into their feature branch and then push those changes to the repository.

2. The push to the feature branch triggers a validation against the actual SIT org.

3. If the validation to SIT is successful, they then make a merge request from the feature branch to the SIT branch. If there was a problem with the validation, the developer fixes that error and then pushes their changes again.

4. The merge request is reviewed by the tech lead and/or dev lead. They can see the lines edited/added on the merge request itself.

5. When the tech lead or dev lead approves the merge request, that code is merged into the SIT branch. That triggers a deployment of code to the SIT environment and validates it against UAT.

6. When a sprint ends, the SIT branch is merged into master and
    deleted.

7. A merge commit to the master branch triggers a pipeline which

    a. Deploys code to UAT

    b. Validates code against production

    c. Deploys the code to production if a tag with a particular format (e.g.,
        "v1.0.3") is present

Branching Strategy with an Example

This example walks through the stages of this process:

1. The master branch of your project contains the codebase of the
    UAT environment. Let's say the two latest commits are as shown in
    Figure 7-10.

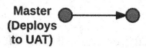

Figure 7-10. Initial commits on the master branch

2. To start any new development, you'll make a feature branch from
    the latest commit on the master or SIT branch. (In this case, we
    are starting with just a master branch). Let's spin up a feature
    branch as shown in Figure 7-11. Feature branches are nothing
    but branches which contain the prefix "feature" before the actual
    branch name. You'll name the branches as follows:

```
feature/[yourBranchName]
```

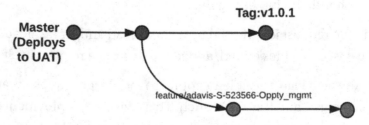

Figure 7-11. Create feature branch from master

3. Each commit you make to your feature branch validates the codebase changes against the SIT environment and displays any errors in the job status page in the CI system. You can access that by going to your CI tool's pipeline view. You'll see something like Figure 7-12 if the job passes.

Figure 7-12. *CI job status*

4. Moving on, let's say you're done making all the changes to your feature branches and your pipelines have succeeded. You're now ready to move your changes to the SIT environment.

5. The Dev Lead or Tech Lead should have merged the `SIT` branch into `master` and deleted it at the end of the previous sprint. They then create it again for the current sprint (this discipline helps ensure that the repo stays simple).

6. To simulate this process, create a branch called `SIT` from `master` as shown in Figure 7-13. Any commit to this branch will deploy the code straight to SIT.

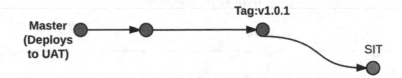

Figure 7-13. *Create an SIT branch from master*

7. Before merging your feature branch into SIT or any other branch it is important to first pull and merge the changes from the target branch into yours, fix any conflicts, and then push the combined changes. This ensures that each developer takes responsibility for bringing in the latest version of the shared code and ensures their changes are compatible with that.

8. Now, go ahead and merge SIT into your feature branch, resolve conflicts (if any), and make a merge request from your feature branch into SIT.

9. Go into your Git host's GUI to review that merge request. You can then approve the merge request to complete the merge into SIT as shown in Figure 7-14.

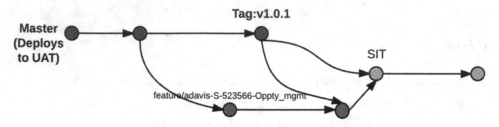

Figure 7-14. *Merging a feature branch into SIT*

10. Let's assume a sprint is over and you want to move changes to UAT. Make a merge request from the SIT branch to the master branch and approve it. This will deploy the code to UAT and validate it against production.

11. Create a tag on your commit to master called **vx.x.x** (where each x is a number between 0 and 9) as shown in Figure 7-15. This will initiate a manual deployment to production.

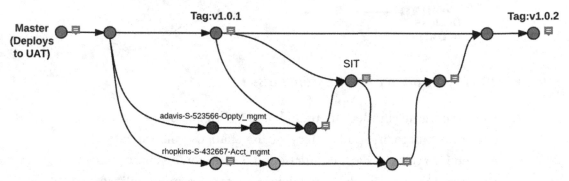

Figure 7-15. *The final branching structure for org-level metadata*

Deploying Individual Features

In pre-Salesforce DX CI processes, it was often difficult to elegantly move discrete changes from one environment to another. The org-level workflow just described (one of the only branching strategies that worked well) is focused on merging the entire content of test environment branches into the branch for the next stage of deployment. This works well as long as you're happy to move **all of the changes** from one environment to the next.

But inevitably some features are more important than others and need to be expedited before all features in that batch can be tested. It's unsafe to move large batches of untested changes into the next environment, just to expedite one of them. This is the fundamental problem with large batch sizes that lean software development strives to avoid.

The best solution to allow features to be deployed independently is to adopt unlocked packages. This allows package development teams to publish and install updates independently and thus allows certain features to be deployed more quickly than others.

Some commercial tools like Copado include powerful, automated branch management that allows feature-level deployment across any environment. If you're handling branching manually, there are two alternative approaches to managing the codebase at a feature level: cherry picking and feature branching. These approaches have been used by many teams prior to the availability of unlocked packages. Either approach may occasionally be useful to expedite certain features, but their disadvantages should also be understood.

Granular Feature Management Using Cherry Picking

One method to manage features independently is by making extensive use of cherry picking. Cherry picking is a native Git capability that allows you to apply a commit from one branch onto another branch without merging the entire branch. Deploying individual features by cherry picking will require significant discipline on the part of the development team. The basic concept is this:

1. Every commit should be explicitly tied to one work item, and the ticket number for that work item should be listed in the commit message.

2. Those commits can be made on a branch that is autodeployed to your first test environment.

3. When you're ready to deploy a feature to the next environment, you cherry pick the related commit(s) into the branch corresponding to the next environment.

4. Since commits depend on their predecessors, you should cherry pick commits in the order they were originally made and periodically merge the full branches to ensure that orgs remain consistent.

Challenges with this approach:

- Since this leads to environments being different, you are not actually testing an integrated production configuration before deploying it.

- It's easy to forget to cherry pick some commits. For this reason, you should still merge the full org branches as often as possible.

- Since commits are not really independent, features may not work properly if they are missing dependencies from other commits.

- This approach makes it easy for work to remain in progress for too long. This is a major warning sign in lean software development.

To enable certain features to be expedited to an environment, this approach can be used occasionally. But the risks in this approach make it inferior to building and deploying packages as a long-term strategy.

Granular Feature Management Using Branches

Another approach that can be used to manage features independently is to use feature branches to deliver features to each testing environment and to production. This is similar to the feature branch workflow described earlier, except that feature branches are merged not just into the first testing environment but also retained and used to merge into all subsequent testing environments and then into production. Although, in general, you will minimize the risk of merge conflicts if you first merge your destination branch into your source branch, if you follow this approach, it is important that you **do not merge the destination branch into the feature branch**.

Unlike cherry picking, merging branches brings the entire history of that branch's parents. Imagine, for example, that others on your team have merged five features into the SIT branch and that you have just completed work on a new feature branch.

As shown in Figure 7-16, if you merge the SIT branch into your feature branch prior to merging your feature branch into SIT, the other five features will then be included in your feature branch. If you later merge this feature into another testing org, you will be deploying both your own feature and those five other features.

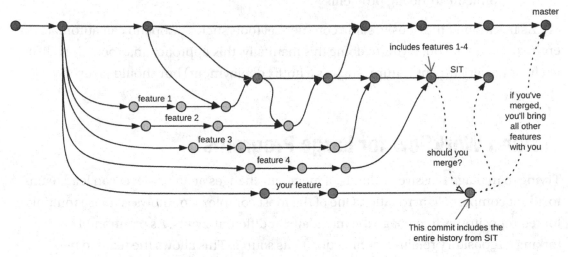

Figure 7-16. *Delivering feature-level granularity requires careful branch management*

Challenges with this approach:

- Since you can't safely merge your target branch into your feature branch, if you combine this approach with using merge requests for approval, this puts the burden of resolving merge conflicts onto the person approving the merge requests.

- This leads to a large number of long-running feature branches, which greatly increases the number of variations of your code. This tends to make every merge into a minor research project, as you assess whether that branch's code is up to date.

- It is harder for teams to understand and reason about the changes that will happen when branches are merged compared to cherry picking. Cherry picking moves just the changes in that commit. Branch merging brings all preceding changes.

- Such complicated merging can lead to subtle problems. If the person doing a merge chooses to ignore or remove some files from a merge, those files may automatically be excluded from future merges as well. This is due to the way Git calculates merges and can lead to very difficult-to-debug problems.

As mentioned previously, some commercial tools such as Copado can automate this entire process for you. If you're doing this manually, this approach may occasionally be useful for a very urgent feature (such as a hotfix deployment) but should be used very sparingly.

Forking Workflow for Large Programs

Trying to manage massive amounts of metadata changes at an org level can lead teams to adopt complex Git acrobatics. One of the most complex workflows is to use multiple forked repositories to manage the metadata for different teams. As mentioned earlier, forking a repository retains a connection to its source. This allows the team to perform merges between repositories. I've seen this pattern used when large numbers of teams each had their own sets of development and testing sandboxes, which were eventually merged into a shared staging environment and eventually into a single production environment. One repository was used to manage the staging and production environments, and separate repositories were used for each team's collection of sandboxes.

This approach allows different repositories to have different security restrictions (you can provide limited access to the repository governing staging and production) and allows each team to have a relatively simpler repository just to manage changes relevant to their team. For a time, this workflow was recommended by Atlassian in a site they had created to provide guidance on the Salesforce development workflow. The cynic in me wondered if their intention was to sell more code repositories although, in their defense, Atlassian Bitbucket does not charge per repository. This site has subsequently been taken down, but a number of Salesforce teams I'm aware of adopted this approach.

The inevitable consequence of this is that each repository drifts further and further apart. Be prepared to have multiple people working full time to handle upstream and downstream merges.

CI/CD and Automation

As mentioned earlier, continuous integration (CI) means that teams work on a common trunk in the codebase and run automation such as builds and tests with every commit to that trunk.

"CI" is often used to refer to tools such as Jenkins that perform automated actions on a schedule or based on code changes. In reality, tools like Jenkins are just tools for running and reporting on automated processes, and their use may be utterly unrelated to CI. These tools can be used to trigger any kind of job, either on a schedule, by a code commit, by an API call, or by some other mechanism. In spite of this, these tools themselves are frequently referred to as "continuous integration tools," and the jobs they run as "continuous integration jobs." The name has stuck and for our purposes is not inaccurate.

The reason for this word association, however, reveals an interesting history. In a situation where disparate teams work on different parts of the codebase and integrate near the end of a project, it is reasonable that the integration phase include extensive manual testing. The extreme programming movement promoted the practice of continuous integration as a more efficient alternative. Instead of having an extensive and error-prone integration phase, teams benefit from being able to integrate in small pieces on an ongoing basis. Conflicts are quicker and easier to resolve, overall code architecture can be more coherent, and teams can immediately benefit from each other's contributions.

But integrating code continuously in this way opens the door for regression failures to happen at any time. Any aspect of the system could potentially be broken at any time, and repeated manual regression testing is impractical. Continuous integration thus drives the need for automated testing. And for compiled languages, automated testing requires automated builds to be performed first.

Build automation is not a new concept, but in the early days, this was typically done on a schedule, such as a "nightly build." But a nightly build and test execution could mean a 23-hour delay in noticing that a developer's change had broken a test. To get that feedback as quickly as possible, teams moved to building and testing "continuously," every time the code changes. "Continuous integration" tools to automate these builds and tests thus became an essential component of the development workflow.

Once an automated system is in place for building and testing code, it's a small step to add deployments to that automated process. Thus the practice of continuous delivery grew naturally out of continuous integration.

241

To actually benefit from this automated test execution, you have to pay attention to the results. Simply putting in place automated builds and testing does not imply that the team is benefitting from this. For this reason, it's critical that teams develop the discipline of paying attention to the build status and fix failing CI jobs immediately as the top priority. A failing CI job, or "broken build," implies that changes have been made that cause builds, tests, or deployments to fail. Human short-term memory is notoriously unreliable, and so with each passing hour the team will find it harder to remember exactly what changes may have caused the failure. Of course version control gives a history that can be used to resolve these problems after the fact, but once a single error arises, all subsequent contributions will also fail. Thus a broken build is a blocking problem for the entire team. Practicing CI/CD implies not only that the team is merging their code continuously but also that they are ensuring the code can be built, tested, and deployed successfully at all times.

It's very common for people to believe they are practicing continuous integration just because their team has set up a CI server like Jenkins. Jez Humble is known for challenging this belief by asking three simple questions[17]:

1. Does your entire team merge their work into a common trunk at least daily?

2. Does every change to that codebase trigger a comprehensive set of tests to run?

3. If the build breaks, is it always fixed in less than 10 minutes?

If you cannot answer yes to those three questions, you are not actually practicing continuous integration.

Early detection and fixes are key to ensuring quality at the earliest possible stage. Developers should focus on setting up a simple CI/CD process as early as possible in the development lifecycle. Continuous delivery is the main technical capability at the heart of DevOps.

---

[17]https://continuousdelivery.com/foundations/continuous-integration/

Automating the Delivery Process

Using version control reduces much of the risk and tedium associated with the development process. But it is only when version control is tied to a CI system that its power to automate the delivery process is really unlocked. What are the elements in creating this automation?

CI Basics

Continuous integration is a process built around version control that allows code to be built, tested, and deployed every time it changes. To make this possible, everyone on the development team needs to be using the same version control system, and you need a CI tool that's configured appropriately for your project. A CI tool has three parts: the actual **CI engine** that orchestrates all the automated jobs, **configuration** that defines the specific jobs to run, and one or more **runners** that execute those jobs.

The role of the CI engine is to allow teams to create projects, give individuals access to those projects, define and configure one or more automated jobs for that project, trigger those jobs, and then monitor the jobs' status. The CI engine is generally the tool that you log into to see the configuration of a CI job or to check the status of that job.

CI job configuration determines what code is used as the basis for the job (e.g., which repository and which branch in that repository), when a job is triggered, what processes are run as part of that job, and what kinds of notification, reports, or artifacts are created as a result. Multiple jobs are often grouped into pipelines, in which the pipeline itself is triggered by some event, and it in turn triggers each job in the appropriate order.

CI runners are where the action happens. A CI runner is an isolated environment in which the CI job runs. The runner might simply be a dedicated folder on the main CI server, it might be a separate server or virtual machine, or it might be a container such as a Docker container. CI runners are typically separated from the main CI engine for three reasons:

1. Runners can be scaled out "horizontally," with one CI engine controlling scores of runners. Even if CI jobs are long running and resource intensive, they will never slow down the CI engine.

2. Runners can have entirely different hardware, OS, and software. iOS or Mac OS software builds usually have to be run on Mac hardware. For example, while most of the CI runners used at Appirio host Docker containers, we have some that run in Mac VMs, on Mac hardware.

3. CI runners provide security isolation, so that one team cannot view content on other runners or hack their way into the main CI engine.

In addition to creating logs, artifacts, deployments, notifications, and any other results, running any CI job always returns a pass/fail status. If jobs are arranged in a pipeline, subsequent jobs will not run if the preceding jobs have failed. This allows teams to, for example, not deploy code if the unit tests did not pass.

Pipeline Configurations

Most CI systems allow jobs to be organized into pipelines which define sequences of jobs. A pipeline is a group of jobs that get executed in stages or batches. All of the jobs in a particular stage are executed in parallel (if there are enough concurrent CI runners), and if they all succeed, the pipeline moves on to the next stage. If one of the jobs fails, the next stage is not executed (unless you've stated that job can "allow failure"). Pipeline configuration thus allows jobs to be organized in series, in parallel, or in some combination of the two. Specifying stages allows us to create flexible, multistage pipelines.

As mentioned earlier, you can specify under what circumstances you want particular pipelines to run. For example, you might want certain tests to run only when a commit is made to the `master` branch, and you might want commits to different branches to deploy to different environments. Making a commit on a particular branch can thus trigger a pipeline appropriate to that branch, which in turn triggers different jobs in a particular sequence.

CI pipelines are thus the mechanism used to manage a continuous delivery pipeline. Each commit triggers a pipeline, which triggers jobs for builds, tests, and deployments.

A pipeline is typically triggered when a commit is made to the repo, but can also be triggered manually, based on tags, based on a schedule, or using the CI engine's API, if it has one.

Multiproject Pipelines

A multiproject pipeline is a more sophisticated version of a pipeline, in which one pipeline may trigger other pipelines on other projects to run. This can be useful in many cases; one example is triggering the rebuild of one project whenever its dependencies are rebuilt. The dependency itself would trigger the parent project to be rebuilt in that case.

GoCD is an open source CI tool that was custom-built by ThoughtWorks, largely to handle the challenge of multiproject pipelines, since not all CI tools have this capability. GoCD itself is built using a multiproject pipeline (in GoCD!) that requires several hours to build and test numerous subprojects before compiling the final tool.

Seeing CI Results in Merge Requests

Merge requests (aka Pull Requests) are requests to pull and merge one branch into another. They create a formal opportunity to review code changes, and can also be used to review CI job results. For example, the CI process can perform automated validations on a feature branch; then a merge request can be created for validated feature branches to allow someone else to review and approve that branch before merging it into the `master` branch. Version control tools like GitHub, GitLab, and Bitbucket Pipelines can all show CI job status alongside the list of code changes in merge requests.

Environments and Deployments

Some CI systems use the concept of "Environments" to represent systems such as Salesforce Orgs that are affected by particular CI jobs. Where available, it's helpful to use these, since it gives a way to cross-reference which CI jobs (such as deployments) have run against particular environments.

CI Servers and Infrastructure

What are the different kinds of CI systems, and how should you choose between them?

Generic CI Systems vs. Salesforce-Specific CI Systems

Because of the historic challenges involved in managing the Salesforce development lifecycle, numerous Salesforce-specific release management tools such as Copado have been created. Increasingly, these tools are supporting and promoting the concepts of version control and continuous integration. These tools are dealt with in more detail in the section on "Commercial Salesforce Tools" in Chapter 9: Deploying.

In most languages and for most applications, the tools used to manage the development lifecycle are generic tools such as Jenkins. Jenkins can be used to automate the development lifecycle for any application in any language. When we refer to a "CI Server," we're generally referring to these generic tools, although the concepts usually translate to Salesforce-specific tools as well.

Although Salesforce-specific tools natively support Salesforce deployment and testing, they are often not as flexible as the generic tools. Using Salesforce-specific tools frees your team from the complex challenge of having to build and manage their own scripts, at the cost of some control and visibility over the complete process, as well as quite a few dollars.

The movement to Salesforce DX increasingly allows generic CI tools to support every aspect of the Salesforce development lifecycle. If your team has the ability to write or gather their own deployment scripts, they can create their own comprehensive process. You can also find some well-developed open source tools like CumulusCI to help.

Although generic CI tools are a viable option, as the person who oversaw the engineering team who built Appirio DX over the course of 2 years; I promise you that there are some unusual challenges involved in building Salesforce release tooling. Unless you have truly unique needs and a skilled developer tooling team, the total cost of buying a prebuilt solution will generally be far lower than the cost of building everything yourself.

Choosing a CI Server

As mentioned before, a CI tool has three parts: the actual **CI engine** that orchestrates all the automated jobs, **configuration** that defines the specific jobs to run, and one or more **runners** that execute those jobs.

Different CI tools handle those three parts differently, but this structure is more or less universal, and CI tools are more or less interchangeable. Most CI tools can handle most CI jobs and scenarios, so you can choose the CI tool that is most effective for your team. Both the *State of DevOps Report*[18] and the book *Accelerate*[19] present research on the importance of teams having autonomy to choose their own tools. Enforcing a single corporate standard for version control and CI can help ensure a company maintains expertise in those tools and can reduce overhead such as server or subscription costs. But it's important for teams to be able to deviate and implement their own tools if the benefits they bring outweigh the long-term costs of maintaining them.

Requiring all teams across a company to use a common CI server commonly leads to a bottleneck where the IT infrastructure team needs to be involved in every change

---

[18]https://devops-research.com/assets/state-of-devops-2017.pdf

[19]Nicole Forsgren, Jez Humble, and Gene Kim. 2018. *Accelerate: The Science of Lean Software and Devops Building and Scaling High Performing Technology Organizations* (1st ed.). IT Revolution Press.

to the CI server configuration. That limits the adoption of CI tools and a team's ability to experiment.

Some CI tools have an architecture that allows for teams to have full autonomy even if there is only a single instance of the CI tool. When selecting a CI tool, look for one that has these three characteristics:

1. The team has autonomy to control access to CI configuration such as job status and logs.

2. You can store CI job configuration as a code file inside your codebase itself.

3. You can run each CI job in an environment that the team controls, typically a Docker container.

It should be clear why the team needs the freedom to access their own job status and logs: DevOps implies that it's the team's responsibility to monitor the status of their own jobs and to use logs to debug failing jobs. As John Vincent famously said, "DevOps means giving a s**t about your job enough to not pass the buck."[20]

The benefits of storing CI configuration as code are discussed in the next section; but why is it so beneficial to use Docker containers to run CI jobs?

Why Use Docker Containers to Execute CI Jobs?

One capability that enables a flexible CI system is the ability for teams to control the environment used to run the CI jobs. CI jobs are simply processes that execute and report back a pass/fail result. To run, these processes need an execution environment that has all of the necessary software installed. In the early days of CI systems, that meant configuring a server and manually installing software in it. As teams' needs evolved, a server admin installed or upgraded supporting tools as needed. Jenkins popularized a plugin model that allowed teams to install common build tools like Ant and Maven from a plugin library. Jenkins still has the richest collection of CI plugins available. But plugins have to be installed and configured in the Jenkins instance itself. In large organizations, the project team may not have permission to install plugins themselves and may have to submit a ticket to IT and go through an approval process.

---

[20]http://blog.lusis.org/blog/2013/06/04/devops-the-title-match/

Recent CI systems have taken the extremely flexible approach of allowing CI pipelines and jobs to be run in Docker containers. Docker is a tool that enables the fast creation of lightweight execution environments ("containers") from images that are defined using simple configuration files ("Dockerfiles"). Dockerfiles always define a Docker image as a starting point. This allows a team to define a custom image that is based on an existing Docker image, removing the need to rediscover all of the software dependencies they might need. Docker images can be stored in a custom Docker repository, but an enormous number of predefined images are available on `https://hub.docker.com`. Most of these also link to the Dockerfile used to create them, making it trivial to recreate these images if you want complete control over how they are defined.

For example, the sample Dockerfile shown in Listing 7-1 is based on the official Docker image for Node.js version 8. On that basis, we use the Node package manager called Yarn to install Salesforce DX and then set a few environment variables. This Dockerfile is then built into a Docker image, which can be used to reproduce any number of execution environments, each of which has Salesforce DX installed and ready to execute.

Listing 7-1. myCompany/salesforceDXimage—a sample Dockerfile for Salesforce DX

```
FROM node:8

#Installing Salesforce DX CLI
RUN yarn global add sfdx-cli
RUN sfdx --version

#SFDX environment
ENV SFDX_AUTOUPDATE_DISABLE true
ENV SFDX_USE_GENERIC_UNIX_KEYCHAIN true
ENV SFDX_DOMAIN_RETRY 300
```

Docker images are almost always based on a Linux variation like Ubuntu. Windows images have recently become supported by Docker, but the OS version in the image must match the OS version of the host. This means that you can now create a Docker image that runs Windows Server 2016, but it can only run on a Windows Server 2016 host. Mac images are not currently supported.

The ability to run CI jobs in Docker containers is extraordinarily powerful. It means that there is no need to load the CI server up with endless manually installed pieces of software or plugins. A CI configuration file can simply specify the name of the Docker image that it wants as its execution environment and what commands it wants to execute in that environment. When the job runs, the CI runner spins up a Docker container *exclusively for that job*, executes those commands, reports a pass/fail value, and then destroys that Docker container.

Any piece of software that you want can be available in that Docker container, and importantly you are guaranteed that the server environment is identical and clean every time the job runs. With Docker containers, there is zero possibility that one job might create a side effect that would change the behavior of subsequent jobs. Such side effects are extremely hard to debug, making Docker containers a simple and low-stress execution environment.

CI systems like Bitbucket Pipelines, GitLab CI, and CircleCI do an excellent job of caching Docker images. This means that although the first time a Docker image is used to run a CI job it might take a minute to download, subsequent containers can be created in (milli)seconds. Container creation is so fast that the uninitiated would never dream that each CI job begins with the creation of a unique new computing environment!

The (slightly contrived) GitLab CI configuration file in Listing 7-2 shows the power and simplicity of using Docker images. At the start of the file, we specify that the Docker image called `salesforceDXimage` (defined in Listing 7-1) should be used as the default image for running each CI job. Two pipeline stages are defined, each of which has one job. The first job, `create_test_org`, uses the default image and executes Salesforce DX commands to create a new scratch org and push source to it. The second job shows how you can override the default Docker image for a specific job. In this case, we run a Ruby script in a container based on the official Ruby image.

Thus this one CI configuration file allows us to make use of two entirely different execution environments. The `salesforceDXimage` defined in Listing 7-1 does not have ruby installed, and the `ruby` image does not have Salesforce DX or Node.js installed. The environments are entirely independent, yet we can make use of both and define the sequence and conditions under which they'll be used. If the first job in this pipeline fails, the entire pipeline fails and `run_tests` will not execute.

Listing 7-2. Sample .gitlab-ci.yml file for running tests

```
image: 'myCompany/salesforceDXimage:latest'

stages:
  - build
  - test

create_test_org:
  stage: build
  script:
    - sfdx force:org:create -a testOrg --setdefaultusername --wait 10
    - sfdx force:source:push
  only:
    - master

run_tests:
  stage: test
  image: ruby:latest
  script:
    - ruby -I test test/path/to/the_test.rb
  only:
    - master
```

Defining servers using Docker images has become the default approach for new IT projects and is the most flexible approach you can take for defining your CI processes as well. If you're using a generic CI tool, choose one that allows you to define and run jobs in Docker images.

Although Appirio DX is a commercial tool, it provides a Docker image `appirio/dx` that contains the Salesforce CLI and many other helpful tools. You can freely use or build off of that image as a starting point for your CI process.

Example: Using GitLab

At Appirio, we chose to use GitLab because of their fast pace of innovation and because a feature-rich CI system is built into the tool. Other version control platforms increasingly bundle CI tools, and CI tools increasingly support the capabilities mentioned earlier.

GitLab is available as a SaaS hosted service on `https://gitlab.com` or as a self-hosted service. Both the SaaS and self-hosted instances have free tiers, as well as paid tiers such as Bronze, Silver, and Gold.

GitLab itself is a version control tool. GitLab CI is the engine that orchestrates all the automation, and it's tightly integrated with the rest of GitLab. The configuration for GitLab CI is all contained in a simple text file called `.gitlab-ci.yml` that lives alongside your project's code in the repository; it's simple enough to be easy to read, but powerful enough to describe almost any CI/CD configuration. To set up CI for your project, you don't need to log in and configure anything; just drop a `.gitlab-ci.yml` file into your project repo and the whole CI system comes to life!

The GitLab **runner** typically hosts Docker containers—super lightweight Linux shells that allow us to run almost any kind of software and code that we want. You can create runners that do not host Docker containers as well. Most runners can be shared across many projects, but you may sometimes need to create special GitLab CI runners for specialized applications like building OS X apps or other Docker images.

Because GitLab CI integrates with GitLab, everyone who makes changes to the code repository is implicitly using GitLab CI. For example, just by creating and pushing a feature branch, a developer triggers the execution of any CI jobs that run on feature branches. Using CI is thus very easy, you just use version control and you're automatically using CI!

User Permission Levels for CI Systems

User permission levels for CI systems are directly or indirectly related to the security of the underlying code repository. This relationship is natural because if you have permission to make a commit on the repository, then in effect you have permission to trigger any jobs based on that repository. Some CI systems such as CircleCI base their access permissions on the permission that users have on the underlying repository. Delegating access control and privileges to GitHub, for example, ensures that the CircleCI security model is simple but robust. Other CI systems such as Jenkins have access controls that are not directly related to the access controls on the repository.

Git itself does not handle access control. Instead, security is enforced by the Git host. And hosts such as GitLab, GitHub, and Bitbucket provide numerous layers of security over the repository itself.

The most basic level of access is simply whether a user can access the repository in any form. Additional layers of security exist to determine whether users can clone repositories, create branches, make commits on particular branches, and so on. On top of that, the CI system has a security model to determine which users can trigger jobs, see job logs, and see secret variables.

Most CI systems provide different security levels you can assign to users. For example, in GitLab, "developer" access is appropriate for most users since it allows them to use GitLab CI, but not to see or change secret values such as credentials.

To enable CI/CD, it's necessary to store credentials for the systems you connect to such as your Salesforce instances. Because your CI system has access to these credentials, it is important to secure the CI system just as you would secure access to the connected systems themselves. Only authorized users should have access to the repository, and you should monitor or periodically audit the list of who has access.

From a practical point of view, it's important to allow developers the ability to make commits on branches that trigger CI jobs. It's also important that they be able to see job logs so they can debug failures. But it's good practice to limit the visibility of the secret variables to just a few members of the team. This restriction does not interfere with the work or effectiveness of the team, but provides a layer of protection for these important credentials.

Creating Integration Users for Deployments

An entire team makes use of a single set of CI jobs, and to ensure consistent behavior, a single set of environment credentials are generally stored in the CI project and used by everyone. For example, if a team configures a job to automatically deploy metadata to a Salesforce org, which user's credentials are used for that deployment? It's often the case that a senior member of the team will configure the CI system and be tempted to use their own credentials for the deployment. That can lead to jobs failing if that person's user account is ever deactivated (think of the rate at which tech workers switch companies!). This can also leave that user's Salesforce credentials vulnerable or allow jobs to impersonate that user.

CI jobs that connect to other systems are integrations. As with any integration, you should consider the security of that integration. It's appropriate to create or use an integration user account for Salesforce deployments and tests and to use those credentials in your CI system. Until recently, deployments required "Modify All Data" privileges, but the new "Modify Metadata through Metadata API Functions" permission provides a more secure alternative. Create a permission set that includes the permissions required to deploy metadata and configuration data to your orgs, and assign that permission set to an integration user. Then use those credentials in your CI process as opposed to the credentials for a specific individual.

Configuring CI/CD

As described earlier, every CI tool has their own way of configuring jobs. Nevertheless, there are certain common features to all CI systems. The main unit of CI configuration is a job. Each job has a name and then defines the source code used for that job, what triggers the job, what actions ("build steps") the job should take, as well as prebuild and postbuild actions and notifications. In other words, "what code are you working on?", "what action should be performed?", "when?", and "who/what should we notify?".

Groups of multiple jobs that have a single trigger but execute in a particular sequence are called a pipeline. Jobs may also be grouped into "projects" or some other kind of grouping for purposes of enabling or disabling access.

Some CI systems require you to log in to that system to configure jobs, but there are many reasons why it's helpful to use a CI system that allows you to store configuration as code.

Why Store CI Configuration As Code?

Storing CI job configuration as a configuration file inside the codebase is an example of "configuration as code." This ensures that any changes to this configuration are versioned and tracked and gives the team who controls the code the power to control their own CI processes without having to go through another group. Travis CI was the first CI tool to popularize this approach, but this approach is now used or supported by most CI tools. Each CI tool varies in the syntax used in this configuration file, but the files are generally short, easy to understand, and written in a human-readable markup language such as YAML or TOML.

Storing configuration in this way makes the configuration visible to everyone on the team, allows you to monitor changes to the configuration, and easily replicates it to other projects. It's even possible to autogenerate CI configuration files as part of project setup.

Storing Secrets and Using Environment Variables in CI Jobs

Environment variables are strings that are stored in memory and used to dynamically configure running applications. The most famous environment variable is PATH. If you type echo $PATH in Mac/Linux or echo %PATH% in Windows, you will see a list of all the paths that your system will check to find executables when you run a command from the command line.

Continuous integration processes are driven from source code stored in version control. But there are some things like passwords and tokens that should never be stored in version control. Environment variables are a perfect way to securely provide a continuous integration engine access to such "secret" configuration. This is also a recommended best practice for 12-factor apps (https://12factor.net/config).

There can be many types of configuration needed for a CI process to run. In general configuration for a CI process is best to be stored in the CI configuration file itself. But there are two main cases for using environment variables to store configuration:

1. Storing secrets like usernames, passwords, and tokens

2. Storing flags that you want to be able to change without changing the underlying config files, such as flags that enable/disable deployments

Environment Variables in the CI System

Most CI systems allow you to set environment variables in their configuration files or as secret variables injected on the fly. These variables are available in the job environment when it executes and can be referenced by all executed commands and scripts. Variables stored in configuration files should only be used to store nonsensitive project configuration.

Credentials and other secrets that are stored in the CI system's secret store are securely passed to the CI runner and made available as environment variables during a pipeline run. These values are not visible as plain text, and most CI systems will autodetect the presence of these secret values and obscure them if they appear in logs. This type of security is not impervious to being exposed, but nevertheless represents an important precaution. This is the recommended method for storing things like passwords, SSH keys, and credentials.

While you can set custom variables for use by your applications, CI systems typically include numerous built-in environment variables that you can also make use of. These CI variables provide information such as the commit message or ID, the URL of the CI system, the name of the branch, and so on. These CI-supplied variables supply useful information to allow you to write scripts that are more dynamic and context-aware.

Project-Specific Variables on Your Local System

If you need to store project-specific secrets as environment variables, you can put them in a local configuration file that is **not** checked into version control. Prior to the Salesforce CLI, it was common to store credentials for Salesforce orgs in a `build.properties` file that could be used by the Ant Migration Tool. The Salesforce CLI now has its own credential store for Salesforce orgs, but your project automation may still need to store some secret variables.

One common convention is to create a file called `.env` in the root of your project that contains any key=value pairs that you want to set. Node.js has a `dotenv` module that can be used to load these values, and tools such as Appirio DX provide out-of-the-box support for `.env` files. To load variables from this file manually on Mac or Unix systems, you can run the command `source .env` in a script.

Group-Level Configuration

Many CI systems allow you to organize multiple projects into groups and to specify configuration at the group level in addition to the project level. Specifying group-level configuration is important for two reasons. First it allows you to specify configuration that can be reused across many projects. If the configuration needs to change, it can be updated in one place to avoid the risk of individual projects getting out of sync. The other benefit of group-level configuration is to protect secrets that should not be visible to members of individual project teams. You might store the credentials for a production salesforce org at the group level and allow projects to make use of those credentials. But for users who don't have permissions at the group level, the credentials are not visible, providing a layer of added security.

Example CI/CD Configuration

Now that you're familiar with the concepts, let's review the automated jobs that you might configure as part of your Salesforce CI/CD workflow.

CI Jobs for Package Publishing

The core component of a Salesforce DX CI/CD workflow is package publishing. The "Branching for Package Publishing" section describes how a simple trunk-based strategy is sufficient for package publishing. Although feature branches can be used, they're not essential, and your initial CI configuration does not need to handle them.

Assuming your trunk branch is called `master`, your delivery pipeline will be triggered on every commit to `master`. First you can perform automated code checks such as static code analysis, then you can trigger unit test execution, then you can publish a new version of the package, and finally you can install it in a testing environment.

Continuous Delivery[21] suggests beginning by creating a "walking skeleton" that includes CI jobs for every step you intend to create, even if you've not yet determined the implementation details. In this case, define a CI pipeline (using whatever configuration your CI tool requires), specify that it should be triggered on `master`, and specify four jobs: "static code analysis," "unit testing," "package publishing," "package installation." The initial scripts for each of those jobs can be simple `echo Hello World` statements. If you're working with this CI tool for the first time, just getting this walking skeleton working may take you a few hours or more. Most CI tools have helpful tutorials to get you started.

Setting up a walking skeleton in this way is a type of agile development; within a short time, you have established a working CI process. You can now begin to refine the details and continue to refine and improve the process over the life of your project.

Salesforce DX jobs need to authorize with a Dev Hub and also with any target orgs. See the section on "Salesforce DX Org Authorizations" in Chapter 6: Environment Management for an explanation on how to use an Auth URL or a JWT token for org authorization. You will store these special strings as secrets in your CI system and use these secret environment variables to authorize the orgs before performing Salesforce DX commands.

---

[21]Jez Humble and David Farley. 2010. *Continuous Delivery: Reliable Software Releases Through Build, Test, and Deployment Automation* (1st ed.). Addison-Wesley Professional.

The most important job to define is the package publishing job, the heart of the workflow. Packages must first be created and their ID specified as an alias in the `sfdx-project.json` file. Then versions of that package can be published as the metadata evolves. See the Salesforce DX Developer Guide for detailed steps, but essentially you will be executing the command `sfdx force:package:version:create --wait 10`. This will create a new version of the default package defined in `sfdx-project.json`. If you are storing multiple packages in one repository, you will need to use the `--package` flag to publish versions of any nondefault package(s). The purpose of the `--wait` command is to force the package creation CI job to not terminate immediately but instead to wait for up to 10 minutes for this job to complete (you can adjust the duration as needed). Package version creation can be time-consuming, especially if you have specified managed package dependencies.

Each newly published package version has an ID. This ID begins with `04t` and is also known as a "subscriber package ID" because it can be used to install that package in another ("subscribing") org. When building this type of automation, it is best to request the output in JSON format by appending `--json` to the Salesforce DX commands. JSON can be read natively in most coding languages, especially JavaScript. You can also use the command-line tool `jq`[22] to allow for simple JSON parsing and reformatting. `jq` is one of several tools that I ensure are present in Docker images intended for use with Salesforce DX. See "Other Scripting Techniques" in Chapter 9: Deploying.

After extracting the subscriber package ID(s) from the results of the package version creation, you'll need a way to pass the ID(s) to the next job. Each job in a CI system is independent, and if you use Docker containers for your CI jobs, they each run in entirely different execution environments. CI tools provide mechanisms, however, for transferring information and files from one job to the next. In GitLab CI, for example, to retain files between jobs, you define "artifacts" containing particular files and folders. I will typically write any JSON outputs I need for other jobs into a file and include that in an artifact, along with the project's `.sfdx` folder.

The next job to configure is the "package installation" job. In this job you will unpack the subscriber package ID from the previous job and install the package you just created in a target org. This allows others on your team to review and test your updated package

---

[22]https://stedolan.github.io/jq/

in a live environment. First, use the `auth:sfdxurl:store` or `auth:jwt:grant` command to authorize the target org based on the Auth URL or JWT token you stored as a CI secret. You will then run a command like `sfdx force:package:install --package 04t...` `--targetusername yourAlias --wait 10`. The package ID is the subscriber package ID, the `targetusername` is the alias of the target org, and the `wait` parameter performs the same function as earlier.

Once those two jobs are in place, you have accomplished the deployment components of your CI system. Now you can define the first two test-related CI jobs based on the tools you're using for testing. You may wonder why I'm suggesting this order of defining the jobs, since it's not the linear order in which they'll eventually run. The purpose in doing this is to establish a functioning, end-to-end deployment process as early as possible, even if it's not perfect. DevOps implies a process of continuous improvement. But you can't improve your delivery pipeline if you don't actually have a delivery pipeline. The philosophy here is the classic approach to refactoring[23]: "make it work; make it right; make it fast." Package publishing and installation make this work. Static analysis and testing help make it right. There will certainly be opportunities to make this process faster once it's created, by being more selective about which tests run, and when packages are published and installed.

Running a static code analysis job depends on your having a static code analysis tool. Chapter 8: Quality and Testing explains the various options for static code analysis. Static analysis is most effective when presented as real-time feedback for developers in the form of "linting" in their IDE. But having a central static analysis job is useful to enforce team standards and to track metrics in a shared tool. Static analysis runs directly on your codebase. Most static analysis tools run locally, which in the case of a CI job means that the code is scanned within the CI job's execution environment. If you are running PMD, then there is no communication with an external static analysis server. You can export reports as downloadable artifacts in your CI system or (better yet) create a mechanism to upload and analyze the results in a central location. Other tools such as SonarQube communicate with a static analysis server to get the rule definitions, then run the scans locally, and report their results back to the static analysis server. This is a common architecture for static analysis tools that scales well even for hundreds of scans being run in parallel. When communicating with a static analysis server, you will need a token of some sort for authentication. You'll store this along with the other CI secrets.

---

[23]`http://wiki.c2.com/?MakeItWorkMakeItRightMakeItFast`

Running unit tests is somewhat trickier, since this requires a Salesforce instance for those tests to run. Ideally developers should run tests on their development scratch org and ensure they pass before pushing changes for publication by the CI system. You can enforce the process of developers executing tests by adding that as a post-commit or pre-push hook in their local Git configuration. But synchronizing Git hooks across developers requires a tool like Husky,[24] and it's useful to have a mechanism to enforce test execution centrally.

Running unit tests requires a Salesforce environment that you can push your latest code to and run tests on. As mentioned earlier, it's important to establish a script that can be used to provision developer environments, review apps, and testing orgs. To create a test environment, simply run this script to create a new scratch org, install packages, and push source as you would when setting up a development environment. Then run your Apex tests (or an Apex Test Suite with a chosen subset of them) and pass or fail the job based on the test results. Typically, if a test fails, the command will return a nonzero status code, which Unix systems use to report failure. You can also set a test coverage threshold, report the test output in JSON, and then parse the coverage results to determine whether to pass or fail.

Once this entire system is set up and you have a working test and deployment pipeline, you've established the basic foundation for delivery automation. There are of course improvements you can make to make the process more effective or more efficient. If your scratch org creation process is time-consuming, you can consider whether you need to create a new testing scratch org each time. If not, you can store the org's access credentials as an artifact and access it repeatedly between jobs. To do this, simply persist the user level `~/.sfdx` folder as an artifact between jobs, and add logic to recreate the environment automatically if the scratch org has expired and can't be opened.

Perhaps you can add UI testing in the scratch org after Apex tests have run; or perhaps you want to run security scans or custom checks, for example, to ensure that custom fields all have descriptions in your XML metadata.

Do you need to publish every package every time? Perhaps you can dynamically determine which packages have changed and need updating by doing a Git diff between publish jobs. You can also use a tool like semantic release or monitor for changes to version numbers in the `sfdx-project.json` file to not publish new versions on every commit.

---

[24]`https://github.com/typicode/husky`

Do you want to enable automated or manual installation of this updated package in other environments? If so, you can enhance the package installation step or install into other environments as needed. A great tool to help with package installations is the Rootstock DX plugin rstk-sfdx-package-utils available on NPM.[25] `sfdx rstk:package:dependencies:install` checks your target org to see which package versions have already been installed and then installs any package versions that may be missing based on the list of package dependencies in sfdx-project.json.

To what degree you improve this workflow will depend on your team's priorities. The overarching goal of this process is to enable your team to be more effective by publishing small updates more frequently and reducing the frequency, severity, and duration of production failures. Use those goals to guide your priorities as you evolve this workflow.

CI/CD is what makes version control come to life and become a truly indispensable part of your workflow.

CI Jobs for Org-Level Management

Just as the package publishing workflow is based on the branching strategy for packages and brings it to life, so the CI process for org-level metadata management builds on the "branching for org-level configuration" described earlier and brings it to life.

As discussed in that section, the goal here is to provide centralized visibility and control over all orgs, allowing for both temporary and long-term differences between the orgs. Orgs have temporary differences due to features and fixes being gradually promoted and tested. Orgs have long-term differences related to integration endpoints, org-wide email addresses, and other org-specific configuration. While the goal of version control is to gain visibility into these similarities and differences, the goal of CI is to enforce control over the orgs.

As mentioned before, your goal should be to move the vast majority of your metadata into packages and use org-level management strictly for org-level configuration. As such, the static analysis and unit testing jobs have less importance in the org-level workflow, although it can be beneficial to add suites of integration tests that can be run on orgs to test the interplay between multiple packages.

As before, begin by creating a walking skeleton of the CI process that you want to enforce. This time, because you'll probably need to use multiple long-running branches

---

[25]www.npmjs.com/package/rstk-sfdx-package-utils

to manage configuration for your sandboxes, you'll be establishing multiple pipelines, each triggered by deployments to a particular branch.

Let's assume that you are managing SIT, Staging, and Production environments, and you are following the branching pattern described previously. You'll use the master branch to deploy to the staging environment, Git tags on the master branch to trigger the deployments to production, and a branch called SIT to manage the metadata in that environment. If you're using GitLab CI, a walking skeleton might look like the one in Listing 7-3.

Listing 7-3. Sample .gitlab-ci.yml file for managing org-level metadata publishing

```
image: myCompany/salesforceDXimage:latest

stages:
  - deploy

deploy_to_SIT:
  stage: deploy
  script:
    - echo Hello World
  only:
    - /^SIT/

deploy_to_staging:
  stage: deploy
  script:
    - echo Hello World
  only:
    - master

deploy_to_production:
  stage: deploy
  script:
    - echo Hello World
  only:
   - tags
   - /^v[0-9.]+$/
  when: manual
```

Because we are managing multiple branches, there are multiple CI pipelines defined even when there's only one job in each pipeline. It is the only property that establishes these three jobs as distinct pipelines. We are indicating that this job will only be triggered when changes are made to a particular branch or tag. In GitLab, pipeline jobs are calculated dynamically based on trigger conditions like only, except, and when. We can add additional jobs to a pipeline by using the same trigger conditions on multiple jobs.

Begin by defining the specific scripts to run to deploy updates to the SIT environment. Once you determine the appropriate pattern for that deployment, you can replicate it in the job configuration for the other environments.

The basic pattern for each org is to install any package updates, build and deploy the metadata specific to that org, build and deploy configuration data specific to that org, and then execute automated acceptance tests. While there are multiple ways to divide jobs, you might group the middle two (closely related) processes and have jobs called update_packages, update_configuration, and acceptance_tests.

Managing the installed package versions at the org level provides central visibility on the differences between orgs. But since package installation can also be done using the delivery pipeline for packages, we can begin by defining the update_configuration job.

The section on "Managing Org Differences" in Chapter 9: Deploying provides more details on a folder structure for tracking metadata differences between each org. But in short, it's helpful to separate the metadata that is common to all orgs from metadata that is unique to particular orgs. When you perform deployments, that metadata will need to be combined in a temporary folder from which you create a single deployment. This takes advantage of Salesforce's transaction processing which allows the entire deployment to be rolled back if any part of the metadata fails to deploy.

Configuration data can be combined in a similar way, giving precedence to org-specific configurations over the default configurations. That configuration data can then be loaded in the target org using the data loading methods provided by the Salesforce CLI.

With these processes, there's obviously room for optimization once they're established. As described earlier, I've typically used Git tags to mark a successful deployment and Git diffs to determine what metadata or data has changed since the last deployment. This information allows us to fill a temporary deployment folder with only the metadata and data that needs to be updated, making for a faster deployment and update.

The acceptance testing process is similar to the unit testing process described earlier, with several differences. First, there is no need to create a testing environment, since these tests will run on sandboxes and production. Second, these acceptance tests should be more comprehensive and wide ranging than the unit tests. While there is no need to repeat the unit tests, these acceptance tests should exercise key user workflows, especially critical business process calculations, to ensure that there are no regression failures.

An acceptance test is not different in nature from a unit test, it simply involves tests across multiple parts of the system and may be longer running as well. See the section on "Automated Functional Testing" in Chapter 8: Quality and Testing.

When defining the scripts to manage package installation at the org level, you'll approach this in three phases. In your first iteration, simply (re)install all the packages for the org each time the job runs. That gives you a way to push out package upgrades from your CI system, but is clearly inefficient unless you have a tiny org. In your second iteration, determine currently installed packages and update only the ones which differ from your configuration. This creates a highly efficient package upgrade process. Finally, build a mechanism to connect the repositories that manage your package publishing with the repository for org-level metadata, such that publishing a new package version triggers a package upgrade process in your org-level repository. That kind of multiproject pipeline allows each repository to be simple and effective while still orchestrating a larger process.

Salesforce DX does not contain explicit guidelines for managing packages at the org level. But the `sfdx-project.json` gives a format for listing package dependencies that can be extended for use in managing org-level package "dependencies." The folders used to hold org-specific metadata can be listed as "packages" in `sfdx-project.json`. The package versions to be installed in that org (both external managed packages and unlocked packages from your own team) can be listed as "dependencies" of that package. Any automated methods to install dependent packages in a scratch org can then be extended to manage package installation/update in a sandbox or production org.

Determining the package versions currently installed in an org is an important way to avoid spending time with redundant installations of packages that are already up to date. Salesforce provides the command `sfdx force:package:installed:list -u yourOrgAlias` as a way to query those packages. By using the `--json` flag, you can export an easy-to-parse list of those packages which you can then compare with the package versions held in version control. Again, the Rootstock package installer[26] can be used to automate this entire process.

Once you establish a reliable method to install packages at the org level, you should remove the capability to install packages from the package publishing workflow. This prevents the risk of the two CI pipelines installing different versions of the packages.

Instead, you should establish a mechanism for package pipelines to generate commits or merge requests onto the org-level pipeline. When a new package version is published, it can push a change to the org-level repository to share the new package version or ID. The most effective mechanism to do this will depend on your CI system and your team's chosen workflow. GitLab has a robust API that can be used to make updates to files and generate commits, branches, and merge requests. If your CI system does not offer such an API, you can trigger a CI job that queries the Dev Hub for the latest versions of particular packages and then writes the latest version back to the repository. Note that CI jobs don't normally write to their own repository so you may need to add a token for your repository as a secret variable and use that to perform a push from the CI job back to the repository.

Any detailed scripts you create should be stored as files in your repository, outside of the CI configuration file, allowing the CI configuration to remain concise and readable. Nevertheless, if you find you're accumulating repetitive blocks of YAML, you can use anchors to indicate blocks of YAML that should be repeated in the configuration. Anchors are a standard part of YAML syntax, but you should confirm whether your CI system supports them.

Instead of a block like the one shown in Listing 7-4, you can use anchors to avoid repetition as shown in Listing 7-5. While the difference here is small, anchors can be a helpful way of keeping your configuration readable as it grows.

Listing 7-4. Sample .gitlab-ci.yml YAML file with repetitive blocks

```
image: myCompany/salesforceDXimage:latest

stages:
  - install
  - deploy
  - test
```

---

[26]www.npmjs.com/package/rstk-sfdx-package-utils

```
update_packages_in_SIT:
  stage: install
  script:
    - ./scripts/getInstalledPackages.sh $TARGET_ORG
    - ./scripts/updatePackages.sh $TARGET_ORG
  variables:
    - TARGET_ORG: SIT
  only:
    - /^SIT/

update_packages_in_staging:
  stage: install
  script:
    - ./scripts/getInstalledPackages.sh $TARGET_ORG
    - ./scripts/updatePackages.sh $TARGET_ORG
  variables:
    - TARGET_ORG: staging
  only:
    - master

update_packages_in_production:
  stage: install
  script:
    - ./scripts/getInstalledPackages.sh $TARGET_ORG
    - ./scripts/updatePackages.sh $TARGET_ORG
  variables:
    - TARGET_ORG: production
  only:
   - tags
   - /^v[0-9.]+$/
  when: manual
```

Listing 7-5. Sample .gitlab-ci.yml file using YAML anchors

```
image: myCompany/salesforceDXimage:latest

stages:
  - install
  - deploy
  - Test

.fake_job:
 <<: **&update_packages**
    stage: install
    script:
      - ./scripts/getInstalledPackages.sh $TARGET_ORG
      - ./scripts/updatePackages.sh $TARGET_ORG

update_packages_in_SIT:
  <<: ***update_packages**
  variables:
    - TARGET_ORG: SIT
  only:
    - /^SIT/

update_packages_in_staging:
  <<: ***update_packages**
  variables:
    - TARGET_ORG: staging
  only:
    - master

update_packages_in_production:
  <<: ***update_packages**
  variables:
    - TARGET_ORG: production
  only:
   - tags
   - /^v[0-9.]+$/
  when: manual
```

Summary

The delivery pipeline is the mechanism to deliver features and fixes safely and quickly from development to production. The foundation for this is version control, and your version control branching strategy is used to balance the needs for freedom, control, and ease in your deployments. CI automation tools are driven from version control, and are the engine that enables deployments, tests, and any metadata transformations that may be needed.

In the next chapter, we'll look in detail at testing, the aspect of the delivery pipeline that fulfills the need for safety and reliability.

CHAPTER 8

Quality and Testing

Quality refers to the degree to which software does what it's supposed to do, and is built in a way that is structurally sound. Testing refers to checking and giving feedback on software quality. Testing can assess functional quality: does it do what it's supposed to do and not do things it shouldn't? Testing can also assess structural quality: is it reliable, secure, maintainable, performant, and appropriately sized?

Some amount of everyone's work and customizations will be thrown away or never used. If your work is lucky enough to be used in production, it will always be tested. Your work will either be tested intentionally prior to release, or it will be tested implicitly when it's used or updated. When end users intentionally review and give feedback on functionality that is pending release, this is called "user acceptance testing." But sometimes unsuspecting end users are exposed to functionality that has not been tested by any other means. In that case, the "testing" is inadvertent, uses real business data, and can lead to confusion, problems, and ill-will.

The purpose of this chapter is to explain key concepts of Salesforce software quality, share the many available testing mechanisms, and encourage practices that increase the reliability of your production systems. Although I frequently reference "code" quality, Salesforce customizations involve an interplay of code and non-code configuration. In this chapter, the term "code" is mostly used as concise shorthand for any Salesforce customization.

Understanding Code Quality

Quality is subjective, but needs to be considered from the perspective of both end users and the technical team that creates and maintains the entire system. End users are concerned mostly with whether code functions as it should, whereas it is the role of the technical team to ensure that the code is maintainable, secure, performant, testable, and

A. Davis, *Mastering Salesforce DevOps*, https://doi.org/10.1007/978-1-4842-5473-8_8

so on. Although end users aren't concerned with the underlying implementation, flaws in the code that lead to slow performance, data loss, and exploits can quickly become massive issues that capture the attention of the business, customers, and even the media.

Quality code can be seen as code that meets the current and *potential* needs of the customer. This is by definition a very challenging problem. Quality is not something you can perfect; but it's often something you can improve.

Functional, Structural, and Process Quality

As shown in Figure 8-1, software quality can be divided into functional quality, structural (or nonfunctional) quality, and process quality.

Functional quality refers to whether the software functions as it should and meets the stated needs of the customer. In agile terms, code that fulfills the purpose of the story and meets the acceptance criteria can be said to have functional quality. One of the benefits of iterative development is that the sooner you can put working software in front of end users, the sooner you can validate that it meets their actual needs. If end users are not satisfied, further development cycles can focus on increasing the functional quality in their eyes.

Structural quality, also known as nonfunctional quality, deals with the quality of the underlying implementation. Well-crafted software will function *reliably*, day in and day out, even as other aspects of the system evolve. The evolution of any IT system is inevitable—it is a living thing—and so the *maintainability* of code is also crucially important. It should be possible to make small changes to the system in a small amount of time, without undue effort spent deciphering the meaning of poorly named, poorly commented, rambling "spaghetti code." And as the user base continues to grow, functionality continues to expand, and data accumulates, the application should *perform* consistently at scale. Software is designed with certain users and use cases in mind. But how will it behave when unintended users do things to the system that were never considered in its design? The IT world exists under the shadow of countless threats. Any system exposed to the Internet will immediately be exposed to thousands of automated attacks from bots built to identify and exploit common vulnerabilities. The *security* of your application is thus a critical hidden factor that must be considered.

In all of this, the *size* of your code, both its scope and the LOC (lines of code) count, has a great impact. For example, a design that served the application well when it was just beginning may be entirely unsuitable once the application has grown to enterprise levels.

Process quality refers to the quality of the development process: whether it supports the development of quality software in an efficient and reliable way. Much of the rest of this book focuses on process quality, such as the use of version control, continuous integration, and automated testing. Process quality also includes the process of gathering and tracking requirements and coordinating the work of the development team.

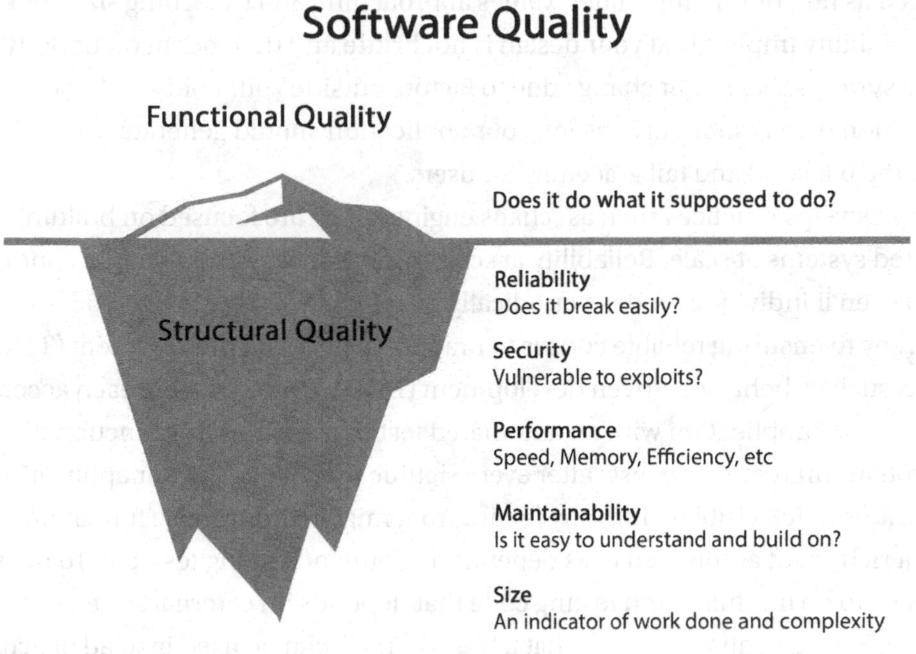

Software Quality

Functional Quality

Does it do what it supposed to do?

Structural Quality

Reliability
Does it break easily?

Security
Vulnerable to exploits?

Performance
Speed, Memory, Efficiency, etc

Maintainability
Is it easy to understand and build on?

Size
An indicator of work done and complexity

Figure 8-1.   *Code quality has many hidden levels*

Understanding Structural Quality

It is important for development teams to understand structural quality in more detail, so they can understand how to improve and ensure it. Different sources use different terms to describe the aspects of software quality, but the following divisions cover most concerns.[1]

---

[1]https://en.wikipedia.org/wiki/Software_quality

Reliability

Reliability refers to the ability of your code to perform consistently, every time it's executed, in spite of variations in inputs, changes to other systems, and ongoing updates to functionality. A reliable system "just works": no 500 errors, unhandled exceptions, and the like. This implies that the system has been tested with inputs including edge cases such as null or missing values, values approaching and exceeding size limits, and so on. Reliability implies that your design is not brittle and dependent on underlying data and systems that might change due to factors outside your control. If a key piece of configuration data is suddenly absent, your application should generate a meaningful error on the backend and fail gracefully for users.

Many DevOps practices such as "chaos engineering" are focused on building reliable distributed systems at scale. Reliability at scale implies that systems should continue to function even if individual nodes periodically go offline.

One key to ensuring reliable code is to practice test-driven development (TDD) or its offshoots such as behavior-driven development (BDD). Underpinning each acceptance criteria for your application with an automated test that ensures this functionality allows you to run regression tests after every significant change to your application. This provides quick visibility into any failures that might compromise functionality. Writing a rich set of automated tests depends on your code being testable. To be testable, code needs to be modular. And testing code that depends on external systems requires there to be a layer of abstraction so that a "test double" can be used instead of actually contacting the external system. In this way, the process of writing tests creates a natural pressure toward good coding practices.

Maintainability

The people who maintain software are rarely the ones who originally wrote it. If a developer revisits code they wrote 6 months ago, it might look as unfamiliar as code written by another person. Maintainability means that software is written in such a way that the purpose of each method is easy to understand and that small changes can be made easily without huge effort and without fear of breaking the application. Clear naming of variables, classes, and methods is critical. If it takes you 5 minutes to figure out what a small method does, take 1 minute to give it a more helpful name that clearly describes its purpose. As Figure 8-2 indicates, naming things is hard. Invest time in choosing self-explanatory names.

Programmers' Hardest Tasks

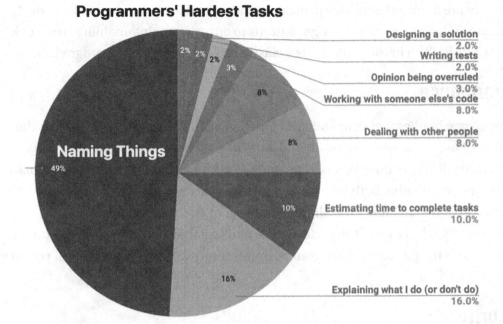

Designing a solution
2.0%
Writing tests
2.0%
Opinion being overruled
3.0%
Working with someone else's code
8.0%
Dealing with other people
8.0%
Estimating time to complete tasks
10.0%
Explaining what I do (or don't do)
16.0%

Naming Things
49%

2% 2% 2% 3% 8% 8% 10% 16%

Figure 8-2. *Naming things is hard[2]*

Another important aspect of maintainability is reducing the "cognitive complexity" of the code by reducing the number of if statements, loops, and other logic in a single block of code. This is also known as "cyclomatic complexity": the number of different logical paths a section of code could follow.

Reducing the sizes of classes and methods is a key way to ensure maintainability. The "single responsibility principle" states that every piece of code should have just one purpose. A method that does two things should be divided into two methods with very clear names. Adding abstraction in this way makes code quick and easy to understand, without requiring maintainers to spend hours deciphering complex logic.

Code comments are very important to explain complex pieces of logic and to otherwise clarify the code. But wherever possible use simple logic, clear names, and short methods instead of writing comments. A standard to strive for is "self-documenting code," where the names are so clearly chosen, and methods are so brief and well structured that even a nonprogrammer could understand its purpose just by reading it.

---

[2]www.itworld.com/article/2833265/don-t-go-into-programming-if-you-don-t-have-a-good-thesaurus.html

There are many other design principles that contribute to maintainable code. Larger codebases require enterprise design patterns to ensuring maintainability. The book *Clean Code* by "Uncle" Bob Martin[3] is a classic recommended for all programmers.

Performance

Performance implies that your code will function at an acceptable level even as the number of users, parallel processes, and data increase. Performance testing in a "production-like" environment is a key stage of software development. And capacity planning—anticipating both best case and worst case rates of growth—is important to ensure you don't encounter a scaling crisis a year or two into production.

Salesforce takes care of the performance and scalability challenges of the underlying platform. But the performance of your customizations is the responsibility of your own team.

Security

Security vulnerabilities are arguably the scariest flaws in software. Nevertheless, security analysis and remediation are among the most neglected aspects of quality analysis. Developers may be oblivious to security threats or simply hopeful that they're not an issue. Security analysis can also be a specialized skill, neglected during developers' basic training. For these reasons, having automated tools that can identify security vulnerabilities and recommend resolutions is key. This is especially important for any system that faces the public Internet or carries sensitive information such as financial data. Web administrators can assure you that the Internet is a hostile place, with new servers receiving automated scans and attacks within minutes of going online.

Size

Size is a consideration in structural quality simply because the larger the application becomes (both in terms of code and functionality), the more challenging the preceding issues become. As the size of an application increases, its *attack surface* increases, meaning that there are more possible vulnerabilities. The principle of *security asymmetry* says that it's always harder to defend than to attack, since an attacker only needs to find one way in, whereas the defender needs to defend all possible points of entry.

---

[3]Robert C. Martin, *Clean Code: A Handbook of Agile Software Craftsmanship* (Prentice Hall, 2008).

Understanding Process Quality

Whereas functional and structural quality relate to *what* is being built, process quality refers to *how* you are building.

There are two main aspects of process quality: does your process lend itself to creating a quality product and is the process itself safe, sustainable, efficient, and so on?

The main focus of this book is to suggest technical processes that lead to higher-quality work as well as a more sustainable and efficient process, so the entire book can be seen as falling into this topic. A comprehensive discussion of process quality would also touch on many business and human aspects and is beyond the scope of this book.

Testing to Ensure Quality

Many factors ensure quality. As the saying goes, "quality is everyone's responsibility." It's also said that quality is far too important to be left to the QA team. Developer training and skill is of course important, as is a manual testing process. But between development and manual testing are automated systems that can be put in place to provide fast feedback to developers, early warning of issues, and reduced burden on manual testers.

Many aspects of this book deal with development process improvements such as the use of version control, continuous integration, and modular architecture. But what processes and systems can be put in place to help enforce and ensure quality in the development process?

Why Test?

The purpose of testing is to protect current and future users from unreliable systems. Another way of expressing this is that testing helps build quality into the work you're delivering.

As shared in Chapter 3: DevOps, there are five metrics you can use as key performance indicators (KPIs) of your software delivery process. While the first two deal with speed, the latter three deal with system reliability: deployment failure rate, mean time to recover, and uptime. Historically, most teams assumed there is a tradeoff between speed and reliability, or between innovation and retaining users' trust. But the *State of DevOps Reports* validate that high-performing DevOps teams excel in both speed and reliability.

The only way to deliver innovation to production more quickly without sacrificing reliability is to build quality into your delivery process. W. Edwards Deming, widely credited with transforming industry in Japan and later the United States, offered a 14-point synopsis of how businesses can improve their operations.

> *Cease dependence on inspection to achieve quality. Eliminate the need for inspection on a mass basis by building quality into the product in the first place.*[4]

—Point 3 of Deming's 14 points

Deming's work is credited with instigating the Total Quality Management movement in business. The basic idea is simple: as shown in Figure 8-3, the earlier issues are caught, the less expensive they are to resolve. Finding bugs through manual QA is time-consuming and expensive compared to using automated methods. But that cost is far less than the cost of end users finding and reporting these bugs in a system they assumed was reliable.

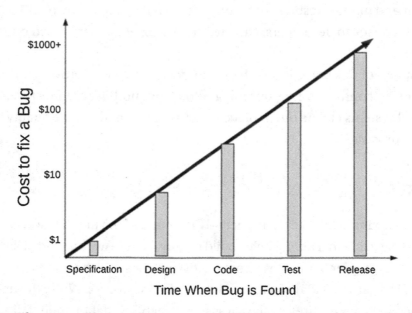

Figure 8-3. *The cost of fixing bugs increases the later in the process they are found*

---

[4]Deming, W E. Out of the Crisis. Cambridge, Mass: Massachusetts Institute of Technology, Center for Advanced Engineering Study, 1986. Print.

This also gives rise to the exhortation to "shift left." As shown in Figure 8-4, this means to put increasing emphasis into ensuring that the original design, architecture, and coding are of high quality, rather than attempting to catch most bugs in a manual testing phase. Manual QA will never be 100% reliable. In addition to the high costs of manual testing, if nothing is done to address the quality of the inputs (the original development), quality issues will continue to slip through no matter how much you adjust your manual testing methods. Deming often used the "Red Bead Experiment"[5] to provide a visual demonstration of this concept. If an incoming collection of white beads is contaminated by some amount of red beads, those red beads will continue to pollute downstream processes despite the best efforts of workers and management. The only way to ensure that the final product is reliable is to ensure that the inputs are reliable, which points to the importance of giving developers fast, high-quality feedback.

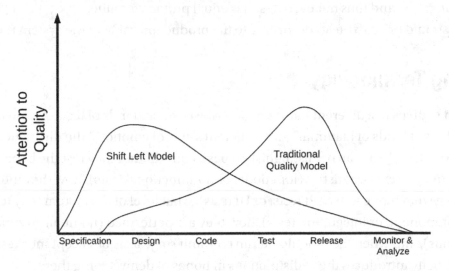

Figure 8-4. *"Shifting left" reduces overall costs by addressing quality issues earlier in the development lifecycle*

---

[5]www.youtube.com/watch?v=geiC4UgpDyw

What to Test?

In general, you need to test the business-critical customizations you make on the Salesforce platform. With extremely rare exceptions, you don't need to test Salesforce itself; and you don't need to test trivial customizations like page layouts. But you can and should test any places you use complex logic (including complex validation rules and workflow rules) to ensure that your own logic is correct. And you should have automated regression tests in place to ensure that critical business functionality remains correct, especially around the systems that help your company to make money.

If your employee idea board goes down for 8 hours, it may be an annoyance to employees, but it's not likely to cost your company any money. If your sales people are unable to work for 8 hours, or your eCommerce site goes offline for that period, you will have sacrificed a portion of your annual sales. In short, not every system has equal value to the company, and thus not every test has equal protective value.

You should prioritize tests according to the production value of the system under test.

Testing Terminology

Different sources use different names to describe different kinds of tests. And just as with "different kinds of mammal" and "different kinds of emotion," the distinctions are not always clear. Tests can be distinguished based on whether they test the behavior of the system or its characteristics (functional or nonfunctional tests), how they interact with the system (code tests, API tests, or UI tests), what level of the system they test (unit, component, or integration tests), how they are performed (manual, automated, or continuous), and when they should be run (commit stage tests or acceptance tests). This section briefly introduces those distinctions in hopes of demystifying them.

Don't waste time feeling bad if you're confused about testing terminology. The software testing community has created an amazing variety of terms to describe types of tests. Perhaps this is because they have been forced to do so much tedious, manual testing that their creativity needed to find an outlet. I'd be complicit in this linguistic crime if I shared them all, but I refer you to `www.softwaretestinghelp.com` if you want to satisfy your curiosity about how monkey testing differs from gorilla testing.[6]

---

[6]`www.softwaretestinghelp.com/types-of-software-testing/`

Functional and Nonfunctional Tests

There are different ways to look at a system: what it does, and what it's made of. Functional tests judge what something does. For example, if a bit of logic is supposed to apply price discounts for customers with an annual contract value above 1 million dollars, you can write functional tests to ensure that logic is correct. Nonfunctional tests look at other aspects of the system, like how long it takes to run, whether it suffers from security or coding style flaws, and so on. This is discussed in detail in the section "Functional, Structural, and Process Quality."

Code, API, and UI Tests

The only built-in testing tool that Salesforce provides is the ability to run tests written in Apex. For this reason, when people refer to "Salesforce testing," they are often referring to tests written in Apex that test the behavior of other Apex classes or triggers. It's helpful to take a broader view of this though and distinguish that there are three ways that a test might be run: via code, via an API, or via UI tests.

Code-based tests include Apex tests as well as JavaScript tests of Lightning Components and the JavaScript used in VisualForce. API-based tests are those that use Salesforce's APIs to test behavior. API tests become quite important when exercising integrations with other systems. MuleSoft's MUnit capabilities[7] are integration tests that can be used to validate behavior using an API. There's a gray area between code and API in cases where tests are written in languages such as Ruby or Python to test the behavior of Salesforce, since those tests generally use the Salesforce API to test.

UI tests are what you do when you log in to Salesforce to observe and check its behavior. Manual QA and UAT are almost always done in this way. UI testing can also be done in an automated way, using tools such as Selenium, Puppeteer, Provar, or Tosca.

Unit, Component, and Integration Tests

It's very common to use a threefold distinction between unit, component, and integration tests. Unit tests are those that exercise only one unit of code, such as a single method. Component tests are those that exercise multiple units of code or configuration, such as a test on a Trigger that also executes Trigger handler classes, or other business logic. Integration tests are those that exercise an entire integrated system, cutting across

---

[7]www.mulesoft.com/platform/munit-integration-testing

multiple Salesforce components or maybe even across other systems. Apex can be used to write unit tests or component tests that also test workflow rules, processes, and flows. But it can't make HTTP callouts and has CPU, memory, and execution time limits that limit your ability to write true integration tests in Apex.

This threefold distinction is also the most common source of terminology confusion. "Integration test" can be used to mean different things. Salesforce developers often refer to any Apex-based test as a "unit test" even if it cuts across many components. I use the term "unit test" exclusively for code-based tests, but I've (unfortunately) heard people refer to narrowly scoped manual tests as unit tests. Google did a nice job of cutting through such confusion by dividing tests simply into small, medium, and large.[8]

Manual, Automated, and Continuous Testing

Central to the points made in this book is this threefold distinction in terms of how tests are performed. Manual tests are those where humans perform actions and check the output. Manual testing is the default behavior for traditional quality testers, for user acceptance tests, and even for programmers and tech leads wishing to validate a system. I've heard it said that you can't automate something that you can't do manually, so manual testing may also be a precursor to other kinds of automated testing.

The benefit of manual testing is that much of it can be done by relatively low-skilled workers, it doesn't require any specialized tools, and it doesn't require much planning or architectural consideration. The challenges with manual testing are that it's relatively slow (minutes or hours instead of seconds), it's error-prone, it's tedious (if you have to perform regression tests repeatedly), it requires people to be available (which may cause delays), and it's expensive (even offshore resources get paid more than computers). The challenges with manual testing should drive you to reduce reliance on it and to upskill your manual testers to help write automated tests.

Automated tests are those that can be done by computers. The benefits of automated tests are in speed, reliability, and cost. Those benefits change the economics of testing and open the door to performing automated tests far more frequently and across a diversity of platforms. Platforms like SauceLabs and BrowserStack revolutionized web testing by allowing companies to test their web sites or applications across a myriad of devices and browsers in parallel, uncovering issues in minutes that might otherwise have taken weeks to discover.

---

[8]https://testing.googleblog.com/2010/12/test-sizes.html

Continuous testing refers to running automated tests every time code is changed on a particular branch in version control. Continuous testing is in fact an aspect of continuous integration/delivery, since it provides a way to ensure the reliability of a system that is undergoing rapid change. Not all automated testing tools support continuous testing. For example, Tricentis Tosca provides a nice set of tools to build UI tests for Salesforce. But it can only run on Windows-based systems, and so it can be a struggle to use it for initiating automated tests from a Linux-based CI system.

Commit-Stage Tests and Acceptance Tests

Finally, tests can also be distinguished in terms of the point in the development lifecycle when they are run. This distinction is made in the *Continuous Delivery* book and is relevant when planning your approach to testing.

The basic idea is that some tests should run every time you make a commit in version control (continuous testing), but that it's important that those tests can complete in 5 minutes or less. The reason is that unless developers get fast feedback from those tests, they are likely to ignore them. It also makes it harder to recognize if a test failure is associated with a particular change if several hours have elapsed since the change was made.

In addition to this fast-running subset of tests, you need a robust and comprehensive set of tests that can be run before code is finally released. Acceptance tests refer to the broader set of tests designed to ensure that your work meets requirements before it's released. These tests are generally functional tests that ensure your code functions properly. They're often accompanied by different nonfunctional tests that also help ensure quality.

Thus commit-stage tests represent a small and fast-running subset of acceptance tests. Commit-stage tests rarely include UI tests, since those tend to take longer to run. In the Apex world, it's beneficial to create one or more test suites that contain certain critical test classes you want your developers to run regularly. The point of these commit-stage tests is to provide an early warning to developers if they break something and to provide it immediately to minimize time spent diagnosing the cause.

The remainder of this chapter is divided into two sections: "Fast Tests for Developers" and "Comprehensive Tests." "Fast tests" is the simplest term I could think of to describe commit-stage testing, and hopefully the meaning is unambiguous. "Comprehensive tests" is the simplest term I could think of to describe acceptance tests, which will accumulate over time to represent the widest range of test cases, with much less regard for how long they take to run.

Yes, I just added two new names to the overflowing lexicon of testing.

Test Engines

The different types of test discussed later require different "test engines." For Apex tests, the Apex test runner is a native capability of Salesforce. For manual tests, the "test engine" is the person performing that test. For other types of test, you'll typically need a tool to help with this process.

In each of the following test types, you'll find discussion about which tools can help support that process. Some tools like JMeter are specific to one type of testing, in this case performance testing. Other tools, like static analysis tools, can help across different stages of the test lifecycle.

Test Environments

Different types of testing bring different demands for test environments. The general strategy to support these demands is to "shift left" as much as possible and to try to batch multiple different demands into a small number of environments as illustrated in Figure 8-4. Details about the environments needed for the various types of tests are shared along with the description of those tests later.

As described in the following, some kinds of testing require long-lived, fully integrated sandboxes, whereas other types can be performed in scratch orgs or disposable developer sandboxes. Long-lived sandboxes that need to be integrated with external systems and require manual setup are probably best to be created manually from the **Environments ➤ Sandboxes** screen in your production org. If you find yourself regularly needing to refresh them, however, you may consider investing in automating their creation.

Short-lived testing environments should be created and destroyed automatically as part of your CI process, using the Salesforce CLI and the same set of scripts you use to provision developer environments. The Salesforce CLI now also allows you to create and log in to sandboxes, so this process can be used to automate the refresh of testing sandboxes.

Test Data Management

The vast majority of test types require data. "Given certain input data, do we receive the correct outputs?" Some types of test require minimal data, others require massive amounts of data. Managing test data is an integral part of your test setup. Details on providing appropriate data are integrated with the following descriptions of each test type.

Fast Tests for Developers

This section and the following "Comprehensive Tests" section constitute a twofold division of all the different types of tests. Fast tests refer to tests that should be run before and/or after every commit. The formal name for this is commit-stage testing, which consists of code analysis and unit tests.

Coding is hard. Managing a team of distributed programmers, enforcing style guidelines, and performing code reviews are even harder. Fortunately, there are automated tools that can help enforce and remind developers of standards and best practices for each language.

Code quality analysis is an automated system for providing code feedback and a helpful mechanism to improve code quality. It's like spelling and grammar check for your code. Code quality maintenance and improvement requires attention and focus throughout a project's lifecycle. Issues with code quality, such as poorly designed or poorly documented code, will accumulate easily if left unchecked. These issues are known as **technical debt**, and if left to grow, they make software maintenance increasingly difficult, time-consuming, and risky. In the same way that one might deal with financial debt, the key to mitigating technical debt is to acknowledge and address quality risks or concerns as early as possible in the development process—not to let them accumulate.

Throughout the remainder of the chapter, we introduce several types of test and how you can run them. In each case, we address the following questions:

- What is this test? Why do you need it?

- When are these tests triggered?

- What environment(s) does the test run in?

- What data do you need to run this test?

- How do you create these tests?

- What else should you consider regarding these tests?

- What happens with the results of these tests?

Hopefully this will provide a consistent guide as you gradually layer in different types of testing.

Static Analysis—Linting

Static analysis is an automated analysis of the source code to identify possible structural faults in performance, style, or security. A simple example is measuring the length of each class or method and marking long classes or methods as possible maintainability problems. The benefit of static analysis is that it can be run quickly and inexpensively, as often as needed, and so can provide feedback faster than any other type of test.

Static analysis can be performed as one stage in a CI process, but is most effective when it's done in real time in the developer's code editor. This kind of immediate feedback is called *linting* and is similar to spell checking or grammar checking. This provides real-time feedback on code right inside the code editor ... there's no better method to ensure developers see and act on feedback.

Linting is a great example of shifting left, since it's done during the coding process itself as opposed to waiting for the CI/CD server. Whereas unit tests are used to confirm the specific behavior of your code, static analysis checks to ensure that it complies with general rules such as "methods should not have too many parameters."

How to Run Linting

By definition, linting runs in the developer's code editor in real time. Linting is language-specific. For JavaScript there are many linting tools available, but ESLint has come to be the dominant choice. ESLint provides general feedback on JavaScript style. It offers a set of recommended rules, but can also be configured to enable or disable additional rules.[9] Additional ESLint rules have been written for both (Aura) Lightning Components[10] and Lightning Web Components,[11] making ESLint the clear choice for JavaScript linting in Salesforce.

I am aware of two linting solutions for Apex code: ApexPMD and SonarLint. PMD is the most popular static analysis tool for Apex (partly because it's free). Chuck Jonas wrote a well-maintained PMD extension for VS Code.[12] PMD is also integrated into the commercial IDEs, Illuminated Cloud and The Welkin Suite.

---

[9]https://eslint.org/docs/rules/

[10]https://github.com/forcedotcom/eslint-plugin-aura

[11]https://github.com/salesforce/eslint-plugin-lwc

[12]https://marketplace.visualstudio.com/items?itemName=chuckjonas.apex-pmd

SonarLint is the linting component of SonarQube, a very popular static analysis tool. SonarLint can be run "online" or "offline." When run "offline" it just uses a standard set of built-in rules. When run "online" it actually connects to a SonarQube instance to download a customized ruleset for your company or project and so ensures that the linting engine runs the same rules as the static analysis you run on the entire codebase. The largest set of static analysis rules for Apex can be found in CodeScan, a variant of SonarQube focused just on Salesforce.[13] SonarQube Enterprise Edition now also supports static analysis rules for Apex and is working to make them increasingly robust.

When Does Linting Run?

As described, linting runs continually in the IDE as the developer works, similar to spell checkers or grammar checkers (Figure 8-5). Linters typically deal with just one code file at a time (see Figures 8-6 and 8-7), although most linting tools also allow developers to run those rules systematically across their local codebase.

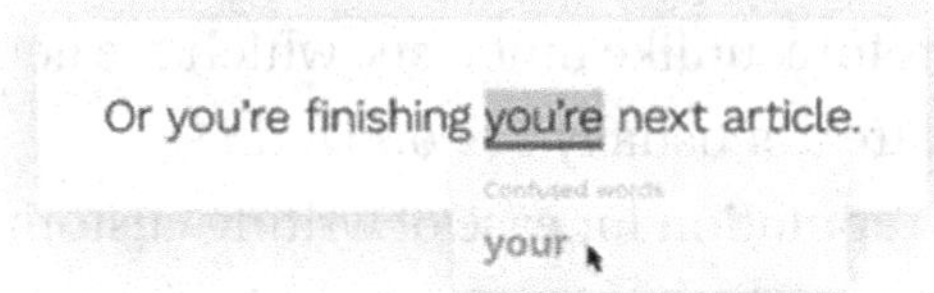

Or you're finishing you're next article.

Confused words

your

Figure 8-5. *Grammar checking using Grammarly*

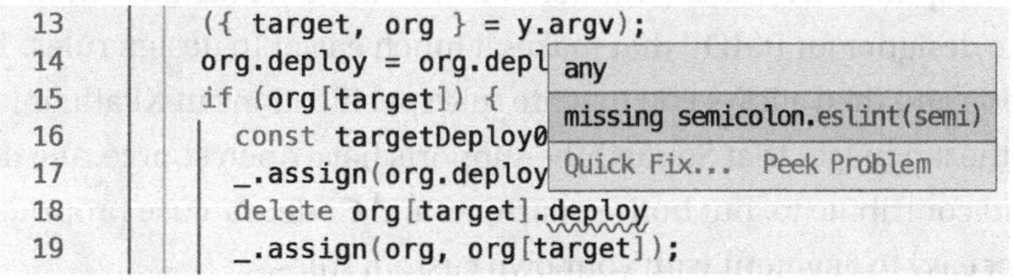

```
13      ({ target, org } = y.argv);
14      org.deploy = org.depl  any
15      if (org[target]) {
16        const targetDeploy0   missing semicolon.eslint(semi)
17        _.assign(org.deploy   Quick Fix...   Peek Problem
18        delete org[target].deploy
19        _.assign(org, org[target]);
```

Figure 8-6. *Instant feedback on JavaScript from ESLint*

---

[13]www.codescan.io/

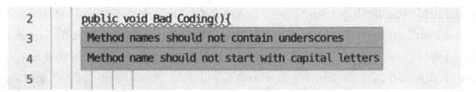

Figure 8-7. Instant feedback on Apex from ApexPMD

Where Does Linting Run?

Linting is performed in the IDE, directly on the codebase, and so does not require a Salesforce environment.

Data Needed for Linting

Linting analyzes the code itself and does not require any test data.

Linting Rules

Linting applies generic rules to the codebase, as opposed to testing for specific business scenarios or use cases. Therefore, unlike unit tests, which are generally unique to each Salesforce org, linting rules are not usually customized.

ESLint has an excellent reputation for ease of writing custom rules. So it's certainly possible for you to write ESLint rules for your team, although with the same effort you could benefit all Salesforce teams by contributing those rules to the open source ESLint projects.

PMD has a reputation for being harder to write rules for. Fortunately, there is a graphical rule designer for PMD[14] that makes it much easier to design rules. The designer parses the code and then allows you to write rule specifications in XPath or Java.

Some of the languages that SonarQube supports have open source rule definitions that you could contribute to, but both SonarApex and CodeScan use proprietary rules and so are not easy to augment with your own custom rules.

Again, while it's possible to write custom rules, it's rare that you would need or want to do that. What's more common is simply to define a specific subset of rules that you want to run for your projects. All of these linting tools provide mechanisms to do this.

---

[14]https://github.com/pmd/pmd-designer

Considerations for Linting

Linting provides extremely fast, helpful feedback to address common malpractices in coding. The spread of ESLint, for example, has had a very beneficial impact for JavaScript developers. Don't expect linting to catch every issue, but it can hopefully help provide guidelines for both new and experienced developers. Just as being free from speling errors doesn't imply good writing, being free from linting errors doesn't imply good code. But linting can still help you identify and remove certain faults.

How to Act on Feedback from Linting

Just as with spell check and grammar check, this real-time feedback can either be acted on or ignored by developers. The intention is to provide developers with high-quality suggestions but not to force them to make changes. If you find that certain types of rules are not helpful and just add noise to the workspace, you should remove those rules.

Developers are under no obligation to act on the feedback from linting. If, however, you want to ensure that most or all such rules are obeyed, you can use the quality gate feature of many static analysis tools to enforce them.

Static Analysis—Quality Gates

Static analysis tools apply a standard set of automated analyses to code. There are three levels at which this analysis can be done: to provide real-time feedback (linting), to pass or fail a specific set of changes (quality gates), or to provide an assessment of the entire codebase. The rules may be the same at every level, the difference is in the scope of what's assessed. Linting is done "on the ground," as developers are working on a small block of code. Quality gates are typically applied at the level of a commit or a pull request and take a "1,000 foot view" of changes that might span many files. And a full codebase assessment gives a "30,000 foot view" of the state of the overall project.

As mentioned before, linting is not meant to enforce these analysis rules. By contrast, quality gates provide a pass/warn/fail assessment of a group of changes.

How to Establish Quality Gates

Any tool that gives you the ability to assess a specific set of changes, generate a pass/warn/fail status, and prevent those changes from being merged or deployed can be used as a quality gate.

Most static analysis tools such as SonarQube, Clayton, Codacy, or CodeClimate give you this ability, when used in conjunction with pull requests and a CI/CD tool. Those tools are discussed in more detail later.

Some of the commercial Salesforce release management tools also provide this as a native capability, with integrated PMD scans.

Copado Compliance Hub provides a similar capability that is targeted specifically at security-related changes to Salesforce. Compliance Hub works with metadata like profiles, permission sets, Settings, and Custom Objects to ensure that there are no unintentional or malicious changes that could impact the org's security. For example, changing the Org-wide default sharing for an object from private to public could constitute a security breach. This is a very Salesforce-specific form of analysis.

When Do Quality Gates Run?

By definition, a quality gate either runs when a developer makes a commit in a shared version control system or when they make a pull request. Applying these rules to pull requests is the most common scenario. Pull requests aggregate information from static analysis, unit test execution, and check-only deployments and facilitate a formal code review armed with this additional insight.

Where Do Quality Gates Run?

Quality gates are run by the static analysis engine, typically as part of a CI process. As such, they don't require a Salesforce environment for execution. As shown in Figure 8-8, this analysis can be applied as code comments, which are visible in pull requests. More importantly, an overall pass/fail status can also be shown in the pull request itself as shown in Figure 8-9.

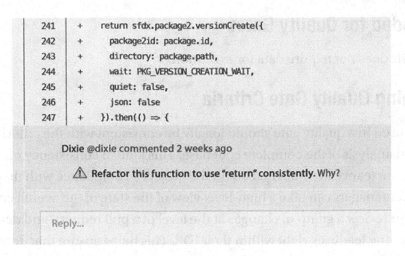

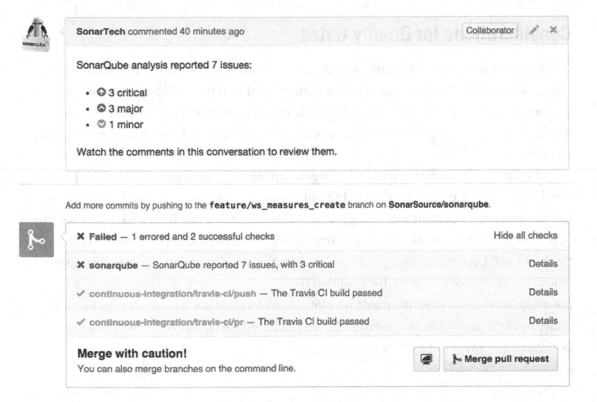

Figure 8-8. *SonarQube can be enabled to write back to a code repository with its feedback*

Figure 8-9. *SonarQube quality gate results shown in a pull request*

Data Needed for Quality Gates

Static analysis does not require data for execution.

Determining Quality Gate Criteria

The criteria used in a quality gate should ideally be consistent with the criteria used in linting and in analysis of the complete codebase. This kind of consistency means that everyone on the team can be aligned about the project's compliance with these standard rules. Project managers can take a high-level view of the state of the overall codebase, tech leads can review a group of changes at the level of a pull request, and developers can review linting feedback right within their IDE. This helps ensure that developers take linting feedback seriously and that unhelpful rules are removed. It gives the tech lead confidence that developers are not ignoring feedback from linters. And it gives a project manager a way to see upward or downward trends in technical debt and other issues.

Considerations for Quality Gates

Quality gates are not a substitute for other forms of quality analysis, but they can help ensure that certain kinds of faults are not introduced into the codebase. A passing quality gate does not guarantee that the code is free from any quality issues; static analysis doesn't even guarantee that code will execute successfully. But it can be a useful indication.

The first project where I used quality gates involved extensive use of JavaScript inside Visualforce pages. We decided to implement JavaScript unit tests for this code, but the existing codebase had negligible code coverage. We implemented a quality gate in SonarQube that assessed the code coverage of recently changed JavaScript code (the "leak period"). Any time we added code or refactored existing code, the quality gate would assess the coverage of the modified lines and prevent us from deploying if the coverage was below 80%. We made no effort to systematically write coverage for old code; nevertheless, over several months we ratcheted up coverage across the entire codebase as shown in Figure 8-10.

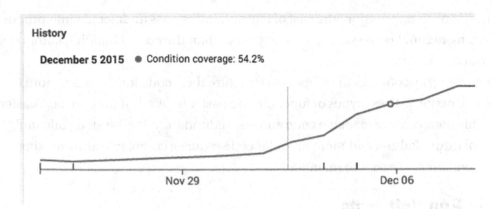

Figure 8-10. *Increase in code coverage after using quality gates to enforce coverage on any modified code*

How to Act on Quality Gate Results

By definition, a passing quality gate allows you to proceed with subsequent steps in an automated process, typically a deployment. By contrast, a failing quality gate will cause your build to fail or your pull request to be rejected. Systems that provide a "warn" status may allow the build to proceed while nevertheless showing you that there may be issues that require attention.

Unit Testing

Unit tests are the best known type of automated test. Because the Apex test runner is part of Salesforce, and because Salesforce requires 75% test coverage on Apex classes and triggers, every Salesforce developer is familiar with Apex unit testing.

Technically, a unit test is a small, fast-running test to evaluate a particular unit of code. I've divided the discussion of Apex tests between this section and the later section "Code-Based Acceptance Tests" to indicate that not all tests written in Apex are truly "unit tests."

While they are developing, your team needs to be able to quickly run a small number of tests to give them feedback whether their functionality is working and that they haven't broken other code.

Whereas static analysis helps to enforce general good practices (coding standards), automated testing checks the specific behavior of the system to ensure it's correct. Creating automated tests is an investment, so skill and thought are required to discern when to use automated tests, what type of test to employ, and how to write the test. But over the life of an application, the cost of letting failures pass undetected into production or repeating manual regression tests is far greater than the cost of building automated tests from the outset.

Unit testing encourages developers to structure their code into smaller, more modular functions. These types of functions are easier to test, but they are also easier to reuse. This means more readable code and less redundancy. Well-tested code mitigates the risk of future failure, and more modular code reduces complexity thus making code safer to refactor and easier to maintain.

How to Run Unit Tests

There are four coding technologies used on the Salesforce platform, and so there are differences in the test engines needed for each. The good news is that three of these technologies are built on top of JavaScript, and Salesforce is increasingly converging on Jest as a recommended test engine for JavaScript.

Apex

As mentioned, the Apex test runner is built into the platform. This test runner is proprietary, and you can't run Apex or Apex tests outside of Salesforce.

JavaScript in VisualForce

VisualForce has long allowed embedded JavaScript as a way to provide more dynamic on-page functionality. My first introduction to unit testing JavaScript involved building business-critical JavaScript that was hosted in Visualforce pages. I have never seen a test framework that actually runs tests inside of a Visualforce page. Instead, we established a strict separation of our JavaScript code into static resources, leaving very little JavaScript in the Visualforce page itself.

We used Visualforce Remoting, and the only JavaScript we embedded into Visualforce was to assign controller-binding variable values to local JavaScript variables. That left us free to treat the code inside of the static resources as separate, independent functions.

You can use any JavaScript testing framework to test code that's stored in static resources. If you don't already have a strong opinion, I would recommend Jest as a very usable test engine.

(Aura) Lightning Components

The original Lightning Components are written in a JavaScript framework called Aura. Some teams within Salesforce created a Lightning Testing Service[15] to allow these Aura components to be unit tested. The Lightning Testing Service supports Jasmine and Mocha, two JavaScript test engines. It's possible that someone will port this over to Jest, but that has not happened so far. All of these JavaScript test frameworks are very similar, but they use slightly different syntaxes to define and run tests.

Unlike testing JavaScript in static resources or Lightning Web Components, these Aura tests have to run inside a Salesforce org, and so the Lightning Testing Service is installed as an unmanaged package in your org.

Lightning Web Components

Lightning Web Components bring many benefits such as being open source, standards-compliant, fast to execute, and executable outside of Salesforce. In addition, they have the first officially supported JavaScript testing framework for Salesforce.[16] This testing framework uses Jest as the engine.

Just as with the convergence on ESLint as the JavaScript static analysis tool of choice, the JavaScript community seems to be converging around Jest as its preferred testing engine. Whereas other test engines require you to use different tools to support aspects of testing such as mocking, Jest bundles everything you need—the test engine, test syntax, mocking frameworks, and more—into one package.

When Do Unit Tests Run?

Unit tests have two purposes: to verify the code currently under development and to verify that current development hasn't broken existing code. Each piece of code generally has a small number of unit tests that directly pertain to it. These should be run throughout the development process to ensure the code itself is functioning.

It's also very helpful to identify any preexisting tests that pertain to related functionality. You can also run those throughout your development to ensure you haven't broken someone else's work.

---

[15]https://forcedotcom.github.io/LightningTestingService/
[16]https://developer.salesforce.com/docs/component-library/documentation/lwc/lwc. testing

Because Apex tests run more slowly than comparable Java or JavaScript tests, if teams are practicing continuous delivery it may not be practical to rerun every Apex test before every release. At a minimum, a subset of Apex unit tests should be rerun before each release. Tools like ApexUnit[17] or the Developer Console query the ApexCodeCoverage table via the Tooling API to dynamically determine which test classes cover which pieces of code. The FlowTestCoverage object provides comparable information when testing processes and autolaunched flows. This information can be used to dynamically determine which tests to run based on which Apex code was changed. Running the full suite of tests as often as possible is still necessary to identify regression failures due to unintended side effects of a change.

One very helpful recent addition to the Salesforce extensions for VS Code was the ability to trigger and monitor Apex unit tests from inside the IDE. Tests can run in the sidebar of your IDE while you work on other changes to the codebase.

As mentioned later in the section on "Code-Based Acceptance Testing," prior to releasing, the entire set of unit tests should be rerun to ensure that new development didn't cause unexpected regression failures in other parts of the codebase.

Unit Testing Environments

Apex code and Apex unit tests can only run in a Salesforce org. Apex tests can also be used to test other kinds of business process automation such as complex process builder processes and autolaunched flows. During the development process, developers should use their development scratch orgs to run tests related to the work they're developing. Scratch orgs can also be created dynamically by the CI/CD system and used to run unit tests as part of the delivery pipeline.

JavaScript code in a Salesforce org (including Lightning Components) can be tested using a JavaScript test framework. JavaScript code that runs on Visualforce pages might be testable directly on a developer's workstation if it can be extracted into a separate static resource. In this case, those tests should be run locally as part of a pre-push hook or using a CI/CD process that runs those JavaScript unit tests. Lightning Components can be tested using the Lightning Testing Service,[18] although these require a Salesforce org to run. As with Apex unit tests, when developers are working on a particular piece

---

[17]https://github.com/forcedotcom/ApexUnit

[18]https://developer.salesforce.com/docs/atlas.en-us.lightning.meta/lightning/lightning_testing_intro.htm

of functionality, they should repeatedly run the relevant tests in their development org. To identify any regression failures, the complete set of Lightning tests should be rerun in the same scratch org created for running all Apex unit tests. Another reason for running these in scratch orgs is that unlike Apex tests, JavaScript tests have no transaction management so they actually change data in the org, and those changes are not automatically rolled back.

One very nice characteristic of the new Lightning Web Components is that they can be tested outside of a browser, which allows those tests to be run very quickly.[19] LWC testing uses Jest, which is arguably the easiest to use JavaScript testing framework.

Data Needed for Unit Tests

The purpose of unit tests is to test the underlying logic of the code. Therefore tests should create their own test data so that their success or failure is determined by the code being tested rather than the underlying data in the org.

When Apex tests were first introduced, they defaulted to being able to see all of the data in the org. This behavior was reversed in the Spring '12 edition of Salesforce, so that tests no longer have access to org data unless they use the `@isTest(SeeAllData=true)` annotation. There remain some rare exceptions where it may be necessary to allow a test to access data in the org, but this should generally be avoided. Tests that do not require access to org data are called "data silo tests," and they help avoid many problems. Relying on data in the underlying org means that tests might pass in some orgs and not pass in others. It also means that a user in that org can inadvertently break tests if they change or delete data used by the test. Data silo tests also make it easier for Salesforce to detect and resolve problems in upcoming releases, since Apex tests are run as part of a regression testing process called the Apex Hammer.

As mentioned later in the section "Code-Based Acceptance Testing," it's possible to specify test data using CSV files or using frameworks such as the open source Apex Domain Builder.[20]

Apex tests run inside a Salesforce database transaction. This means that they can create, modify, and query data, but that data is not persisted after the test finishes.

---

[19]https://developer.salesforce.com/docs/component-library/documentation/lwc/lwc. testing

[20]https://github.com/rootstockmfg/domainbuilderframework

JavaScript tests don't run in a transaction, which means that any data they create or modify in an org will remain in that org after the test completes. Lightning Web Components and JavaScript in static resources can be tested outside of a Salesforce org, using a framework like Jest to specify inputs and check outputs. These tests don't use a database, so data is held in memory and not persisted after the tests finish. But when using the Lightning Testing Service to test (Aura) Lightning Components, you need to be very careful to segregate test data from any other data.

There are three ways to segregate test data used by the Lightning Testing Service from other data. First, you should not use the Lightning Testing Service in a production org; instead run it in scratch orgs or testing sandboxes. Second, each test should create its own data as described earlier and should ideally delete that data after finishing. Finally, any data that's created should be clearly named to distinguish it from any other data.

Creating Unit Tests

Salesforce has prepared helpful guides for creating Apex,[21] LWC,[22] and Aura component tests.[23] And you can find various third-party resources that explain how to test JavaScript in static resources such as the Dreamforce '14 talk I gave entitled "JavaScript-heavy Salesforce Applications."[24]

Considerations for Unit Testing

Salesforce establishes some minimum guidelines for automated testing. Apex classes and triggers must have 75% of their lines covered by automated tests before they can be deployed to production. If you deploy Flows and Processes to a production org as part of a CI/CD process, they also require code coverage if they are deployed as active. You may also enforce your own code coverage thresholds for JavaScript code using external quality gates like SonarQube.

There is a law of diminishing returns on test coverage. The Pareto principle dictates that for many kinds of system, 80% of the progress will require 20% of the effort, while the remaining 20% of the progress will require 80% of the effort. That remaining 20% will not

---

[21]https://developer.salesforce.com/docs/atlas.en-us.apexcode.meta/apexcode/ apex_testing.htm

[22]https://developer.salesforce.com/docs/component-library/documentation/lwc/lwc. testing

[23]https://github.com/forcedotcom/LightningTestingService

[24]www.salesforce.com/video/192779/

necessarily bring much value, so you should never push hard for 100% test coverage. I have personally been guilty of doing code acrobatics to try to achieve 100% test coverage. As soon as you start noticing your Apex code becoming more complex and more difficult to read or filling up with `Test.isRunningTest()` checks, you have started to go too far.

How to Act on Unit Test Results

When you're practicing test-driven development (TDD), you'll generally iterate quickly, running tests every few minutes until you get your code to succeed. In those cases, test success or failure provides you feedback on the functionality of your code. In general, test failures provide a useful indication if you've broken some underlying functionality.

If you notice tests failing because of some harmless change that doesn't impact non-test code, you should consider whether your tests are architected in a flexible way—for example, if you add a new required field to an object that can cause all the tests that create those objects to fail. Using a central test factory to create objects allows you to add such required fields in a single place. Your tests can call the test factory to define the base objects and then modify their data as appropriate before creating them.

Comprehensive Tests

Although there are many types of automated testing, and many names used to describe them, the book *Continuous Delivery* simplifies the various types of testing down into "commit-stage testing" and "acceptance testing." The previous section discussed the use of static analysis and unit testing as commit-stage testing to provide fast feedback to developers. This section addresses acceptance testing: running comprehensive checks on the code prior to release.

Acceptance testing means checking to ensure that functional and nonfunctional requirements are being met. In effect, testers are asking "Does this do what it's supposed to do?" or "Will end users accept what has been built?". The agile convention is to write specifications in the form of user stories, each of which has associated acceptance criteria. Acceptance testing confirms that the acceptance criteria (and sometimes other expectations) are being met.

Acceptance testing can be done manually or in an automated way. Commit-stage tests should run quickly and frequently and can run in a simplified testing environment like a scratch org. Automated acceptance tests are intended to test end-to-end functionality, sometimes including external integrations. To provide realistic results, automated acceptance tests should run in a production-like environment and will generally take far longer to run. They are therefore run less frequently.

This section discusses both functional and nonfunctional testing. Functional tests, whether automated or manual, are intended to check that code and configuration functions as it should and doesn't break other things. Nonfunctional tests look at other aspects of the system such as security, maintainability, reliability, and performance.

As it says in *Continuous Delivery*, "The majority of tests running during the acceptance test stage are functional acceptance tests, but not all. The goal of the acceptance test stage is to assert that the system delivers the value the customer is expecting and that it meets the acceptance criteria. The acceptance test stage also serves as a regression test suite, verifying that no bugs are introduced into existing behavior by new changes."

We first discuss automated functional testing and nonfunctional testing, which both typically make use of automated tools. We conclude with a discussion on manual QA and user acceptance testing.

Automated Functional Testing

Automated functional testing builds on the unit tests described earlier, but may go further to include long-running code-based tests, as well as UI tests that simulate user interactions through a web browser.

Code-Based Acceptance Testing

There is no technological difference between code-based unit tests described earlier and code-based acceptance tests. I've divided this discussion between these two sections to emphasize that the same technologies can be used for two purposes. Whereas unit tests should run quickly and be narrowly focused on giving feedback to the developer, acceptance tests may take hours to run and function as confirmation that code continues to meet specifications and does not suffer from regression failures.

How to Run Acceptance Tests

Because the technology is the same, the same test engines described earlier in "How to Run Unit Tests" can be used to run acceptance tests.

When Do Acceptance Tests Run?

There are typically three occasions when code-based tests are run: during development, during deployments, and triggered by some external process. The preceding section discussed executing these tests during the development process, as unit tests. The same unit tests that help developers ensure their code's logic is reliable gradually accumulate to become the acceptance test suite for the entire org.

Each test can be viewed as an executable specification for how the code should function: given certain inputs, when a particular action occurs, then assert "do we get the correct result?" If a test is written in this way, once added to the acceptance test suite, it provides an ongoing indicator that the specified behavior is still intact. For this reason, code-based acceptance tests provide a powerful built-in mechanism to protect the integrity of your org's customizations.

Salesforce generally has an extremely enthusiastic developer and admin community. But this enthusiasm has been slow to spread to automated testing. Whereas some languages such as Ruby have cultivated a passionate testing community, 42% of the Salesforce orgs scanned by the Clayton analysis tool show a pattern of just using tests to achieve coverage.[25] Appirio's own CMC Metrics tool found an average of one assert for every 222 lines of code across the more than 6,000 orgs we've scanned.

This anemic approach to testing indicates that a large portion of Salesforce developers see code-based testing as an inconvenience and apply minimal effort beyond what's required to get a deployment to succeed.

Salesforce provides the ability to run Apex tests during a deployment. This behavior is enforced when deploying to a production org, along with a 75% minimum code coverage threshold. Tests run during a deployment execute in the target org after the metadata has been successfully deployed to that org, and so can provide a very good indication of whether the related Apex code will run successfully. If one of these tests fail, or if you are deploying in check-only mode, Salesforce rolls back that deployment, thus preventing the deployment from completing. The ability to manage deployments and test execution as an atomic transaction (it either all succeeds or all fails) is one of the excellent capabilities of the platform.

JavaScript tests on Salesforce can't run inside a Salesforce deployment transaction. This means that you can run tests on (Aura) Lightning Components in a target org, for example, but they can only run after the deployment has completed.

---

[25]https://medium.com/@lofrattini/what-we-learnt-scanning-10-2-billion-lines-of-salesforce-code-131af7c5995

In addition to running tests as part of a deployment, you can trigger this test execution at any time. The Salesforce CLI provides an `sfdx force:apex:test:run` command, which you can run as part of a CI process or on a schedule. This command provides the ability to specify one or more test suites if you want to run a predefined set of tests. If desired, it's also possible to use the Salesforce scheduler to run one or more tests. You can create a small block of scheduled Apex that queries a group of test IDs and then executes them on a schedule. See the section "Running Tests Using ApexTestQueueItem" in the Apex Developer Guide.[26]

Acceptance Testing Environments

Code-based acceptance tests can generally be run in scratch orgs or testing sandboxes. This is especially important for JavaScript and UI tests, since these make actual changes to the data in an org which are not rolled back after tests complete. Scratch orgs allow you to create an org and to specify test data for that org. You can then ensure that the testing environment starts clean every time.

Despite the fact that these tests *can* be run in scratch orgs, it is important to have a comprehensive set of checks run in a production-like environment, and thus if there are concerns that your scratch orgs may not fully resemble your sandboxes or production orgs, automated acceptance tests *should* be run in a partial or full-data sandbox. This can be the same sandbox used for manual testing, as long as the data used for automated tests is clearly segregated from the data used for manual tests. You will also need a mechanism for resetting this test data in the sandbox.

Data Needed for Acceptance Testing

As with code-based unit tests, the data used for code-based acceptance tests should generally be stored within the test itself. Tests that rely on data in the org are necessarily brittle, behave inconsistently if that data is changed, and represent a form of tight coupling which makes it hard to refactor your codebase or make it modular.

Apex tests allow for larger volumes of data to be stored as static resources in CSV format. That data can be loaded when a test class first begins to execute using the `@TestSetup` annotation. Each test method has to query that data to access it, but

---

[26]https://developer.salesforce.com/docs/atlas.en-us.apexcode.meta/apexcode/apex_testing_unit_tests_running.htm

the DML operation to load the data only runs once per test class. This reduces test execution time and governor limit usage.

A new open source framework called the Apex Domain Builder (https://github.com/rootstockmfg/domainbuilderframework) offers a very performant and readable way of creating test data. Since Apex-based tests should run in isolation, it's important that each test class create the data that it will need for its test methods. This can easily lead to lots of repetitive code and slower test execution and tends to clutter the test methods with data setup steps that are irrelevant to the test itself. Domain Builder uses a "fluent" syntax similar to that used in the FFLib modules mentioned in Chapter 5: Application Architecture and in fact uses some of the same underlying code. Listing 8-1 shows the elegance of such an approach. Required and boilerplate field values can be defined centrally in the Account_t class, so that inside the tests themselves you only need to define the field values that should be specific to that test.

Listing 8-1. The Apex Domain Builder syntax for creating test data

```
@IsTest
private static void easyTestDataCreation() {

    // Given
    Contact_t jack = new Contact_t().first('Jack').last('Harris');

    new Account_t()
        .name('Acme Corp')
        .add( new Opportunity_t()
                    .amount(1000)
                    .closes(2019, 12)
                    .contact(jack))
        .persist();
    // When
    ...
    // Then
    ...
}
```

Creating Acceptance Tests

As mentioned before, you should write unit tests with the idea that they will each become part of the acceptance test suite for the application.

Unit tests are typically written just to test the behavior of a specific unit of code such as a method or to achieve code coverage so you can deploy. Seeing unit tests as contributing to the integrity of the entire package or org helps you approach them in a broader light, as acceptance tests.

To bridge these two goals, I've found it helpful to adopt the test-writing approach known as behavior-driven development (BDD) introduced by Dan North,[27] sometimes also called acceptance test–driven development (ATDD).

The basic idea of BDD is simple: write each test as a specification of the behavior of the system under test. Sometimes these tests are even called "specs." Each test method name should be a sentence describing the expected behavior, and each test should follow a consistent given-when-then format.

Listing 8-2. A sample BDD-style test in Apex

```
@isTest
static void itShouldUpdateReservedSpotsOnInsert() {
  System.runAs(TestUtil.careerPlanner()) {
  // Given
  Workshop__c thisEvent = TestFactory.aWorkshopWithFreeSpaces();
  Integer initialAttendance = TestUtil.currentAttendance(thisEvent);
  final Integer PRIMARY_ATTENDEES = 3;
  final Integer NUMBER_EACH = 4;

  // When
  Test.startTest();
  TestFactory.insertAdditionalRegistrations(thisEvent, PRIMARY_ATTENDEES,
  NUMBER_EACH);
  Test.stopTest();
```

---

[27]https://dannorth.net/introducing-bdd/

```
// Then
Integer expectedAttendance = initialAttendance + PRIMARY_ATTENDEES *
NUMBER_EACH;
system.assertEquals(expectedAttendance, TestUtil.
currentAttendance(thisEvent),
  'The attendance was not updated correctly after an insert');
  }
}
```

Listing 8-2 shows a method named itShouldUpdateReservedSpotsOnInsert() which clearly states the intended behavior of the class being tested. The BDD convention is for each test to begin with itShould.... The body of the test is grouped into three sections, indicated by the comments // Given, // When, and // Then. This threefold division provides a clear syntax and structure, and is equivalent to the older AAA (Arrange-Act-Assert) division. I advise everyone to use this same structure to write their tests.

In all other respects, this is a normal Apex test. Some languages provide test frameworks such as Cucumber that allow for a human-readable domain-specific test language (DSL) with inputs and expected outputs separated from the actual code. That's not easy to achieve in Apex, but simply structuring your tests in this way provides many of the same benefits.

Considerations for Acceptance Testing

In addition to focusing on acceptance criteria, acceptance tests may also cover a broader scope than unit tests, testing multiple components. Because Apex tests are subject to the same governor limit restrictions as other Apex code, there's a limit to how comprehensive these tests can be. Complex, multistep procedures, especially those involving multiple Triggers, Processes, or Flows, can easily time out or exceed CPU, DML, SOQL, or Heap size governor limits. UI tests might be a better choice for simulating complex test scenarios.

Acceptance test suites focus on thoroughness over speed. But speed is still important. One of the most important ways to speed up your tests is to run them in parallel. Jest runs JavaScript tests in parallel, but JavaScript tests are generally extremely fast anyway. The Apex test engine runs up to five tests in parallel by default, but there's a checkbox in **Setup ➤ Custom Code ➤ Apex Test Execution ➤ Options** to "Disable Parallel Apex Testing." Some teams have disabled parallel execution because they encounter UNABLE_TO_LOCK_ROW errors when Apex tests access the same records.

But this can make test execution extremely slow. As an alternative, mark all of your Apex tests with the `@IsTest(isParallel=true)` annotation, but disable that annotation for those which are not parallel safe.

You will never succeed in testing every aspect of a system, nor should you try. Even with extensive collections of tests, failures will still sneak through your delivery pipeline. Production failures are expensive, at least in terms of stress, and sometimes monetarily. Production failures provide a valuable opportunity to do postmortems and to see whether systems or tests could be put in place to prevent such failures from happening again.

Consider your acceptance tests an investment in the overall reliability of your org. As mentioned earlier, you should prioritize the most business-critical aspects of your processes. By doing this, your investments in testing will be practical and deliver a return on investment by continually blocking deployments that trigger known failures.

How to Act on Acceptance Test Results

Apex tests that run as part of deployments will automatically cause the deployment to fail if any Apex test fails. Deployments to production will also fail if any Apex class or trigger has 0% coverage, or if the overall coverage for that deployment is less than 75%. This coverage gateway is well known and much dreaded by those deploying Apex to production. There's no feeling quite like battling through hundreds of deployment errors, only to have your deployment fail with the error: `Code coverage is insufficient. Current coverage is 74.92840025717459% but it must be at least 75% to deploy.`

JavaScript test results are not built into deployments in the way Apex is, but can still be used to pass or fail a build, by using your CI system. If you have any JavaScript testing in your delivery process, you should run that as one stage in your delivery pipeline. Failing tests should block later stages of the pipeline.

Tracking Code Coverage

Code coverage reports provide some indication of whether you have written thorough tests. High code coverage doesn't guarantee that you've written good tests; but low code coverage guarantees that you have not.

The Salesforce Developer Console and some IDEs can show your Apex code coverage including which lines are covered or not covered. Some code quality tools like SonarQube also allow you to ingest unit test code coverage reports. This allows you to track coverage over time, as shown in Figure 8-11, and to view coverage in a single UI alongside code quality feedback as shown in Figure 8-12. One benefit of such tools is that they can track coverage information for both Apex and JavaScript tests. Enabling this capability may take a bit of experimentation.

Figure 8-11. *A snippet of the code coverage graph from SonarQube*

```
230  dan...         private void saveIssues(InputFile sona
231                     Collection<CheckMessage> messages
232  dan...             messages.forEach(message -> {
233  dan...    Not covered by tests.  y ruleKey = checks.rulek
234                     Issuable issuable = resourcePe
235
236                     if (issuable != null) {
237                         Issue issue = issuable.nev
238                             .ruleKey(ruleKey)
239                             .line(message.getl
240                             .message(message.c
241                             .build();
242                         issuable.addIssue(issue);
243                     }
244  dan...         });
245  dan...     }
246
```

Figure 8-12. *Many static analysis tools like SonarQube also show line-level coverage results*

Both CodeScan and SonarQube allow you to ingest Apex code coverage results generated from the Salesforce CLI. To do this, you first run your Apex tests using `sfdx force:apex:test:run -c -d test-results -r json` to generate the coverage results in a file called `test-results/test-result-codecoverage.json`. This file can then be uploaded at the same time you run your static analysis jobs. In CodeScan you add the parameter `sf.testfile=test-results/test-result-codecoverage.json` to your static analysis job, and in SonarQube you add the parameter `sonar.apex.coverage.`

`reportPath=test-results/test-result-codecoverage.json`. Other quality analysis tools may offer similar capabilities with different syntax.

If you are using Jest to test your JavaScript, you can output coverage files that can then be ingested by SonarQube. Running `npx jest --ci --coverage` will create coverage files in a `coverage/` directory and summarize it in `config/lcov.info` as shown in Figure 8-13. You can then specify that directory when running your static analysis job by adding the parameter `sonar.javascript.lcov.reportPaths=coverage/lcov.info`. This property will ensure that coverage information is uploaded and tracked in the SonarQube user interface.

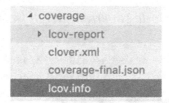

Figure 8-13. *Code coverage results output from Jest*

UI Testing

Automated acceptance tests can also be done using UI automation tools. The most common UI testing technology is Selenium, although commercial testing tools like Provar and Tricentis Tosca are also available.

There are several benefits to using UI tests on Salesforce. First, they can be used to test complex sequences of actions that would otherwise exceed Salesforce governor limits if run using Apex. Second, they require significantly less expertise to create and understand, since they use the Salesforce user interface which is already familiar to manual testers and business users. Finally, they can be used to test things that can't be tested just with Apex or JavaScript, including things that happen in the web browser but not directly inside of Salesforce.

Although they are easy to create, UI tests are generally significantly slower than Apex tests, which in turn are slower than JavaScript tests. UI tests are also notoriously brittle, since even small changes to the UI can cause these tests to break if they are not written carefully. *Continuous Delivery* makes the case for avoiding UI tests whenever alternatives exist, but on the Salesforce platform, there are few alternatives. Creating robust tests is likely to require careful thought, including involvement from developers and architects to ensure that the tests remain reliable and performant.

How to Run UI Tests

As their name implies, UI tests automate actions that are normally performed through a user interface, and can verify the output that would appear in that user interface. Salesforce does not provide a built-in engine for running UI tests. Therefore you'll need to provide your own mechanism for running these tests.

UI tests can be run programmatically like other code-based tests, using either Selenium or Puppeteer. There are also several click-based tools that provide graphical interfaces for building these UI tests.

Selenium is the most popular framework for building UI-based tests. It's free and allows you to use a wide range of programming languages such as JavaScript, Ruby, Java, and Scala to drive interaction with a web browser. Selenium runs on any web browser, on any platform. This capability allows companies like BrowserStack and SauceLabs to offer UI testing as a service, so that you can test your web applications across a wide range of browsers and desktop or mobile platforms.

Puppeteer is a new offering from the team who builds Google Chrome that allows you to build UI tests using JavaScript and to run them in a "headless" Chrome browser. Many UI tests actually run in a headless browser, which means that they interact with web pages through the underlying DOM rather than actually rendering a user interface. Puppeteer only supports JavaScript and Chrome. But it is quickly growing in popularity due to its speed and simplicity. It won't help you catch browser-specific edge cases, but it handles 80% of the UI testing needs, with less overhead to manage than Selenium.

Be advised that building Salesforce UI tests programmatically is not for the faint of heart and brings significant challenges compared to testing home-grown web applications. The Salesforce user interface is subject to change at least three times per year, and the HTML underpinning it is dynamically generated, so you can't rely on IDs or other elements to remain consistent. Repetitive actions like logging in and data entry will need to be put into centralized modules, so you don't need to maintain many repetitive blocks of code.

For this reason, it's almost certainly more cost-effective to use a prebuilt Salesforce UI testing solution. Both Copado and AutoRABIT offer the built-in ability to record user interactions as Selenium scripts and to replay those as tests. They have invested time and energy in handling repetitive tasks and can keep that up to date for all their customers as the Salesforce UI evolves.

There are two other commercial options for UI testing. Provar is a Salesforce-specific UI testing tool that allows you to set up and tear down test data, record and replay user interactions, and run tests interchangeably across Lightning and Classic. The entire company is focused on supporting Salesforce, so they stay up to speed on the latest releases and are able to handle complex Salesforce UIs such as the Service Console.

Another commercial UI testing tool that supports Salesforce is Tricentis Tosca. Tosca has a good reputation and strong capabilities. They may be a good fit if you want to test non-Salesforce user interfaces as well. But if your only concern is testing Salesforce, Provar is likely to be more robust.

When Do UI Tests Run?

Because UI tests typically take longer to run than unit tests, they're not usually run by developers as part of the development process. They are best suited to be run as part of regression tests to confirm that deployments have not broken anything. Because they can take so long to run, you should parallelize them if possible.

UI Testing Environments

Unlike Apex or JavaScript tests, UI tests depend on a fully rendered Salesforce user interface to run. You have to actually deploy your customizations into a Salesforce environment and then point your test engine to that environment. If you're able to supply a full set of test data and keep it up to date, you can run these UI tests in a scratch org. This is ideal since the tests modify data during the course of execution and so may make undesirable changes to long-running test sandboxes. Test sandboxes can be used, as long as your UI tests don't make undesired changes to data that's needed for manual testers.

Data Needed for UI Tests

One of the biggest challenges in maintaining automated UI tests is that test data needs to be maintained along with the tests themselves. As your Salesforce org evolves, you're likely to need to add new kinds of configuration data, specify new fields on existing objects, and adjust to ongoing changes to things like user roles.

If possible, it's ideal if your automated UI tests can use the same test data you use for your manual testers. Even code-based tests may depend on large groups of records stored in CSV files, and you can reuse this same data in your UI tests. Maintaining a single consistent set of test data that can be loaded into scratch orgs for manual testers or fed into the UI test engine will help ease the overall maintenance burden. Test data updates then only need to be done once.

As with code-based tests, you should be sure to supply each UI test with the data it needs and never make assumptions that underlying data will remain unchanged.

A possible exception to this rule is when your tests depend on configuration that is stored as data in sandboxes. Sandbox refreshes let you benefit from cloning underlying configuration data (like CPQ data) from a production org, so that it remains up to date. As mentioned earlier, UI tests actually change data in the underlying org so take steps to ensure that you are never changing data used by manual testers.

Creating UI Tests

There are three ways of creating UI tests: programmatically, by using a test recorder, or by specifying a test data model. Programmatic tests work similarly to other code-based tests, but rely on libraries (either Selenium or Puppeteer) that allow them to navigate to URLs, modify input fields, check output, and so forth.

As mentioned earlier, the Salesforce UI is subject to change at least three times a year and is autogenerated with each page load. Standard HTML tags are dynamically generated, CSS classes are subject to change, and the underlying DOM is basically far more dynamic than a home-grown web app.

At Appirio, our QA team invested substantial time building a dynamic, Selenium-based testing engine. They wrote standard modules to handle login, data load, record page and list view navigation, and so forth. Unless you're prepared to invest substantial time building and maintaining your own Salesforce testing architecture, I'd advise you to use a prebuilt tool for your UI testing. Whereas there are ample online resources about doing Salesforce deployments, you'll find almost no assistance on the Internet if you decide to venture into automated testing of the Salesforce UI.

Provar and Tosca provide test recorders to record user interactions and supplement that with the ability to use a test data model to load and query test data using the API. That combination provides an excellent balance of reliability, speed, and usability. Just as code-based tests shouldn't bother to test standard Salesforce functionality, your UI tests shouldn't take time to input test data into standard Salesforce record detail pages. Test data should be loaded using the API, which is fast and reliable. Your tests can then focus on validating complex, custom aspects of the UI or multistep processes.

Copado and AutoRABIT both use variations on the open source Selenium test recorder to record user interactions.

The most important guideline when create custom pages that can be tested more easily is to add Id attributes to all page elements. UI tests typically use HTML DOM Ids to uniquely identify the elements in any page. Salesforce will either not generate Ids or autogenerate them if none are specified. These autogenerated Ids can easily break

Selenium scripts that were written to search for an Id that isn't always present on the page. If defining an Id is not feasible, you can use the class or other data attributes to uniquely identify DOM elements.

It can be helpful to use a naming convention to name the Id attributes. This leads to more readable and maintainable UI scripts. Appirio typically recommends **PageName_ FieldName_FieldType.** For example, if you have a custom Case Summary page that has a dropdown selector for owner, you can give that the Id **CaseSummary_Owner_Picklist.** Both tests and code need to be clear to be maintainable.

UI Testing Considerations

If you've used a test recorder to build your initial test, you have access to modify the steps and the criteria used to select elements on the page. It's this step that requires care and sophistication. Any user can turn on a test recorder, make a few clicks, and enter a bit of data. But for your tests to be stable, you should think about what field elements are most likely to remain stable as your org evolves.

This is one of the reasons that the UI testing architecture needs to be robust and flexible. If a new required field is added to the Account object, you want to be able to update all of your UI tests at the same time. If your tests are simply recorded sets of clicks, you may be forced to rerecord them, unless you are comfortable editing the underlying scripts or have built a modular testing architecture.

With the arrival of the tools mentioned earlier, Salesforce UI testing is a more achievable goal than it was in 2016. UI testing provides unique opportunities for ensuring your delivery pipeline is reliable. But adoption is still in its early phases, and you should reserve this form of testing only for critical or complex processes that cannot be tested by any other method.

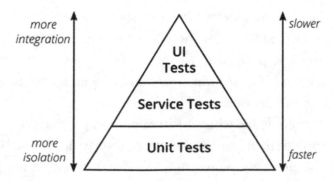

Figure 8-14. *The test pyramid, introduced by Mike Cohn*

Figure 8-14 is known as the test pyramid, an often-cited recommendation for how many tests of different types to create.[28] The diagram indicates that the foundation of your test strategy should be code-based unit tests, which run quickly and test isolated parts of your codebase. There should be more of these than any other test. At the top of the test pyramid are UI tests, which test the entire integrated system but are slower to run. You should have far fewer of these tests than unit tests. The middle layer refers to acceptance tests which cover larger chunks of functionality, but don't require a fully rendered UI. You should have a middling number of these. As mentioned, such tests go by various names, such as "integration tests," "component tests," and "service tests."

There are several reasons you should have fewer UI tests than other types of test. A single UI test can cover many underlying pieces of functionality, and thus fewer tests suffice. UI tests also require more time and care to maintain, since a change to one underlying piece of functionality can require a change to many UI tests, and so more tests are more expensive. Since UI tests cover broad segments of the org's behavior, they have vastly more permutations of inputs and possible outputs, and so it might be tempting to use them to cover every edge case. The test pyramid advises restraint from such temptations. You should test the critical path and fragile scenarios that are frequent causes of regressions, but never try to cover every test case with UI tests.

How to Act on UI Test Results

As with other types of tests, UI tests should be integrated into your delivery pipeline so that you can run at least a subset of them every time you deploy code. UI tests can only run after a deployment is completed, but if a UI test fails after deployment to one org, your CI system can prevent that code from proceeding to subsequent orgs.

Perhaps more than other types of tests, UI tests can be brittle and subject to false positives. UI tests that are "flappers," alternating unpredictably between success and failure, should be removed or fixed. Like the proverbial "boy who cried wolf," tests that generate frequent false positives will lead your team to ignore test results altogether, thus undermining their effectiveness.

---

[28]https://martinfowler.com/articles/practical-test-pyramid.html

Nonfunctional Testing

Nonfunctional testing examines the structural characteristics of the code. As mentioned, there are five structural characteristics to software quality: reliability, maintainability, security, performance, and size.

There are different ways to evaluate those structural characteristics, both manual and automated. In this section, we again look at static code analysis, this time in the context of assessing the entire codebase, followed by discussions of security analysis, performance analysis, and code reviews.

Static Analysis—Full Codebase

Static analysis provides fast, automated feedback on code quality with no risks and little or no effort. For that reason, it's now appearing for the third time in this chapter, in hopes that you will hear this message loudly and clearly. I might be accused of repeating the previous sections on linting and quality gates, but this section is introducing a third distinct use of static analysis: assessing the entire codebase and evaluating trends over time.

There are many tools which can help give insight into code quality by scanning code and flagging vulnerabilities. Tools such as PMD, SonarQube, and CheckMarx can identify many issues and track trends over time. This allows project teams to view the current and historic code health of their project.

When the main focus is simply getting code to work, code quality may not be a developer's first priority (`https://xkcd.com/844/` provides a lighthearted depiction of this challenge). However, as professionals, improved code quality and efficiency should be one of the main concerns for the project team (and consequently the developer).

Code quality maintenance and improvement requires attention and focus throughout a project's lifecycle. Issues with code quality, such as poorly designed or difficult to understand code, will accumulate easily if left unchecked. These issues are known as **technical debt**, and if left to grow they will make software maintenance increasingly difficult, time-consuming, and risky. In the same way that one might deal with financial debt, the key to mitigating technical debt is to acknowledge and address quality risks or concerns as early as possible in the development process and not to let them accumulate.

This section reviews recommended components and tools that project teams can use to monitor and improve code quality across the entire codebase.

How to Run Static Analysis

As indicated previously, static analysis tools can be used to give feedback on the code currently being edited (linting), on a collection of changes being staged for deployment (quality gates), or on the entire codebase. In some cases, the same engine can be used for all three of these purposes. For example, SonarLint is able to connect to a SonarQube instance to synchronize the ruleset between the two.

There are six well-established tools for performing static analysis on a Salesforce codebase: Clayton, SonarQube, CodeScan, PMD, Codacy, and CodeClimate. We'll look at each of these in turn before discussing how to integrate static analysis with your workflow.

Clayton

Among these static analysis tools, Clayton is the only one designed exclusively for Salesforce. Clayton can connect directly to a Salesforce org, or more commonly to a code repository stored in GitHub, GitLab, or Bitbucket. Clayton provides a library of rules to select from, based on the experience and insights of Salesforce Certified Technical Architects, principally its founder, Lorenzo Frattini. Clayton analyzes your metadata based on the rules you select to identify security, maintainability, and performance flaws.

When used as a quality gate, Clayton can add code comments to a pull request or block that pull request until issues are addressed. When run on the entire codebase, Clayton generates a report that you can view through its user interface or export as a CSV.

In addition to offering a carefully thought-through set of rules, Clayton provides references to training materials on Trailhead and clear suggestions for remedying any errors that are detected.

SonarQube

SonarQube is an open-core product used to track quality metrics across multiple languages and projects. SonarQube scans are typically run as part of continuous integration jobs whenever changes are made to a codebase.

These scans identify issues ranging from excessive complexity to security flaws. It can also track unit test coverage and code duplication. SonarQube tracks issues over time, ranks them by severity, and attributes them to the developer who last touched that line of code. This allows your project team to see quality trends, take action on particular issues, and prevent code from proceeding through the continuous deployment process if it shows significant quality issues.

SonarQube examines and evaluates different aspects of your source code: from minor styling details, potential bugs, and code defects to lack of test code coverage and excessive complexity. SonarQube produces metrics and statistics that can reveal problematic source code that's a candidate for inspection or improvement.

Appirio made extensive use of the free Enforce plugin for SonarQube[29] to provide support for Salesforce Apex code analysis. That plugin only works for SonarQube version 6 and below and struggles to parse some kinds of Apex. Since 2019, SonarQube enterprise edition offers native Apex support. Appirio technical architect Pratz Joshi collaborated with SonarSource to write specifications for many of the Apex rules.

It's also possible to use SonarCloud.io for a fully SaaS-based code analysis solution. SonarCloud now has feature parity with SonarQube, supporting more than 25 languages without requiring you to install your own server.

CodeScan

CodeScan is a static analysis tool for Salesforce that is based on SonarQube. They use SonarQube community edition as their underlying engine and user interface and have written a very extensive set of rules for Apex, Lightning, and Visualforce. CodeScan offers both a Cloud/SaaS edition and a self-hosted option.

Since it's based on SonarQube, it has the same underlying capabilities, but has a completely separate set of rules from the ones provided by SonarSource or Enforce. CodeScan was among the first to market for Salesforce static analysis and offers the largest number of quality rules among its competitors.

ApexPMD

Because it's open source, PMD (`https://pmd.github.io/`) forms the underlying analysis engine for many other products and is thus the most widely used static analysis engine for Apex. Robert Sösemann did most of the foundational work for ApexPMD and remains its biggest and most popular champion. PMD itself does not provide a graphical UI. But tools such as Codacy or CodeClimate add a UI layer on top of the PMD engine. Many of the commercial Salesforce release management tools such as AutoRABIT also include a built-in PMD scanner.

---

[29]`https://github.com/fundacionjala/enforce-sonarqube-plugin`

PMD can be run from the command line, or from within the ApexPMD extension for VS Code, and its results output in multiple formats such as CSV and HTML.

PMD finds common programming flaws like unused variables, empty catch blocks, unnecessary object creation, and so forth. It comes with a rich and highly configurable set of rules that developers can quickly set up, straight out of the box. It also includes CPD, the copy-paste-detector, to help identify duplicate code.

After installing the PMD extension for VS Code, you can use it to scan all the files in your current workspace by running Apex Static Analysis: Current Workspace in the VS Code Command Palette. Problems will appear in the **Problems** panel, as shown in Figure 8-15, and be indicated on the files themselves.

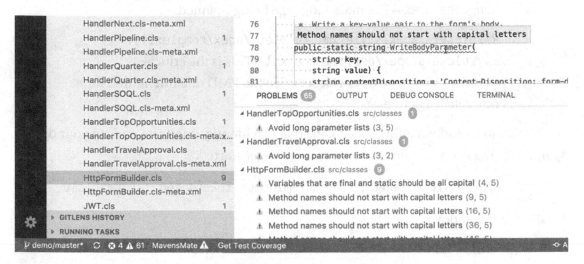

Figure 8-15. *A full code analysis using Chuck Jonas' VS Code PMD extension*

People often struggle to get started with using PMD on the command line. You can run this sample command inside a Salesforce project directory as an example to help you get started:

```
$ pmd -d src -failOnViolation false -f text -language apex -R rulesets/
apex/style.xml,rulesets/apex/complexity.xml,rulesets/apex/performance.xml
```

Breaking that down:

- `-d src`—Which subdirectory do you want to scan? This assumes you're running the scan in a directory that has a subdirectory called "src".

- `-failOnViolation false`—When running on the command line, set this to `false`. If you want to run this as part of a CI job and you want the scan to FAIL if PMD generates errors, you can set this flag to `true`.

- `-f text`—The file output format. Other formats include `csv`, `xml`, and `json`.

- `-language apex`—The main language being scanned.

- `-R rulesets/apex/style.xml,rulesets/apex/complexity.xml,rulesets/apex/performance.xml`—This is the critical parameter, the three Apex rulesets. See the PMD documentation for a complete list of rulesets.

PMD also includes a utility called CPD that can identify duplicate code in your org. Again, here is a sample command you can use to get started:

```
$ cpd --files src --language apex --minimum-tokens 100 --format csv
```

Breaking that down:

- `--files src`—The subdirectory, same as earlier.

- `--language apex`—The code language, same as earlier.

- `--minimum-tokens 100`—The minimum number of "tokens" that need to match for two sections to be considered duplicates. Smaller values will find more matches, but more of them will be "false positives" or insignificant duplication.

- `--format csv`—The output file format, same as earlier. Other options include `text`, `xml`, and `json`.

Codacy

Codacy provides a SaaS-based static analysis tool that connects to your codebase in GitHub or Bitbucket and provides static analysis across many languages. Codacy uses well-established analysis engines such as ESLint and PMD but provides a user interface, authentication, and other capabilities on top of that.

Codacy also offers an Enterprise Edition that companies can host themselves. The Enterprise Edition also supports GitLab.

CodeClimate

CodeClimate is similar to Codacy in using PMD and ESLint as its underlying analysis engines for Apex and Lightning, respectively. CodeClimate provides a user interface to allow you to track quality trends in your codebase over time.

CodeClimate offers two products: Velocity and Quality. CodeClimate Quality is the actual static analysis tool. CodeClimate Velocity analyzes developer activity to help you track DevOps metrics such as cycle time, as well as metrics of interest to engineering managers such as what activities are consuming most of the team's time.

When Does Static Analysis Run?

Some of the analysis tools mentioned earlier, such as Clayton, connect directly to your code repository and run analysis when commits are pushed. Others such as SonarQube or CodeScan require you to run the analysis as part of a CI job, which is then uploaded to the tool.

Running regular scans builds a history that allows you to track trends over time.

Where Does Static Analysis Run?

Static analysis runs either in a CI job or in the backend of one of the SaaS analysis tools, and never inside of your Salesforce org.

Data Needed for Static Analysis

As mentioned earlier, static analysis does not require test data to run.

Creating Static Analysis Rules

Rather than creating static analysis rules, your focus is typically on selecting or deselecting which rules will run from among the options provided by each tool. It is very important to monitor your team's response to various rules when you first roll them out, so you can ensure they are providing value and not just noise.

Creating static analysis rules is generally outside the skillset of most developers. One exception is configurable rules such as class naming conventions. Tools such as SonarQube allow you to use regular expressions to specify acceptable patterns for your class and method names.

Considerations for Static Analysis

There are two common reactions to scan results from those new to static analysis. One reaction is cognitive overload, since these scans can expose thousands of issues in need of remediation. It was SonarQube that first introduced me to the term "kilodays" when describing the estimated time required to address issues on one codebase. The other reaction is exaggerated optimism in the tools' ability to identify quality issues. Just because Clayton doesn't find any issues with your code doesn't mean that you've written good code. It's entirely possible to write buggy and incoherent code that passes static analysis. Other forms of testing such as code reviews and unit tests are important complements to these scans.

How to Act on Static Analysis Results

Tracking trends provides a way to identify whether issues are accumulating over time and to see hotspots in your codebase. Figure 8-16 shows the analysis of a large codebase in SonarQube. One particular Apex class, `MetadataService.cls`, is five times larger than the next largest class and represents one quarter of the total issues in the codebase. Understanding or updating this class is likely to be a nightmare for future developers, so it should be prioritized for refactoring while the developers responsible for this abomination are still around.

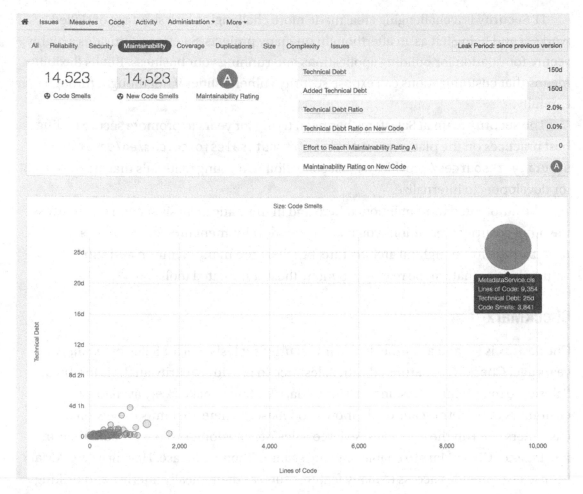

Figure 8-16. *A bubble chart from SonarQube revealing that one Apex class is vastly more complex than anything else in the codebase*

Security Analysis

Having thoroughly discussed static analysis, we can look at tools focused on security. There is some overlap between static analysis tools and security analysis tools. All of the static analysis tools discussed in the last section also include some security-focused rules, but there are other tools that explicitly focus on security testing for Salesforce. The points made in the static analysis section about how and when scans run generally apply here as well. The two tools introduced here, CheckMarx and Fortify, can scan and identify security vulnerabilities in Apex code. Salesforce also has a tool called Chimera available for ISV partners to perform security scans on non-Salesforce web sites.

IT Security is a challenging area, made more challenging by a shortage of skilled workers and being left as an afterthought on many projects. Salesforce provides a highly secure foundation for building applications and running your business. But its flexibility means that customizations can expose security vulnerabilities if not thought through carefully.

The security team at Salesforce has been trying for years to promote secure coding best practices on the platform. And `https://trust.salesforce.com/en/security/security-resources/` provides a great collection of training materials that are important for developers to internalize.

The automated tools mentioned here and in the static analysis section can buttress the other security precautions you take in your development processes. There's no substitute for thoughtful architecture, but there are many common and subtle vulnerabilities that can be readily caught by these automated tools.

CheckMarx

CheckMarx is far and away the dominant security analysis tool for Salesforce. Many years ago, CheckMarx partnered with Salesforce to provide security analysis for Apex. Salesforce maintains an instance of CheckMarx that they make freely available to customers to perform scans on their own codebase.[30] There are limits to how often customers can run the free scans, so large Salesforce customers often procure their own instances of CheckMarx to enable ongoing scans of their codebase. Having a CheckMarx license also provides access to many features such as dynamically filtering and drilling into results, marking some as false positives, and so on.

Unlike the static analysis tools mentioned earlier, CheckMarx provides the ability to identify security issues that cross file boundaries. One of the most commonly surfaced issues is SOQL injection vulnerability, in which input from a text field could find its way, unfiltered, into a SOQL query and potentially expose private information. For example, CheckMarx can identify when text field input is passed unsanitized from Visualforce to an Apex controller to an Apex service class and finally into a query. In the same way, CheckMarx can detect stored XSS attacks in which unsanitized script data might be written into the database and possibly rendered in users' browsers.

---

[30]`https://security.secure.force.com/security/tools/forcecom/scanner`

Micro Focus Fortify also provides Apex scanning capabilities, but CheckMarx is almost unchallenged because of the sophistication of their tool and their partnership with Salesforce. Their tool is expensive, and so not in the toolkit of most small or medium enterprises, but it provides an important complement to developer training, especially if you are building highly secure or Internet-facing applications.

The basic CheckMarx application can connect to a code repository to retrieve your metadata, or you can manually upload it as a ZIP file. If you purchase the add-on integration package, you can also use their command-line tool CxSAST or plugins for CI tools like Jenkins, Bamboo, or VSTS to run security analysis as part of your build process.

Micro Focus Fortify

Fortify is a security analysis tool originally developed by HP. It is much less well known in the Salesforce world, but does support scanning Apex. One benefit over CheckMarx is that Fortify also provides an on-demand SaaS-based scanner. CheckMarx must be installed on a server, whereas Fortify provides either cloud or on-premise options.

Performance Testing

Performance testing is very different from either static analysis or security analysis. It is an aspect of nonfunctional testing that evaluates how well your applications will perform under normal or higher-than-normal load. This is generally used to evaluate response time (delay) and throughput (how many transactions per second the system can handle). It also provides useful information on side effects, such as whether the response time changes for other applications during the tests.

Salesforce handles performance tuning for the underlying platform for you, and provides load balancing and many other mechanisms to ensure that your applications scale and remain performant. In general you don't need to worry about how well Salesforce will handle large volumes of transactions as long as you're using built-in capabilities of the platform.

But as you begin to create complex custom applications on the platform, you may encounter scalability issues that don't surface until you are receiving large numbers of requests. Two of the most common scalability issues are large data volume (LDV) issues and large traffic issues.

LDV issues relate to the amount of data stored in the org, rather than current usage. They usually begin to arise when you are dealing with tens of millions of records on a single object or are making reports or SOQL queries that are unusually expensive. If a query or report is inefficient, that issue will arise whether you are receiving 1 request or 1 million requests. Thus LDV issues can be investigated relatively easily by developers and architects as long as there is an org with sufficient data. LDV issues are dealt with at length in Salesforce's documentation.

Large traffic issues are much harder to monitor and assess, since they happen in real time and may not be visible to every user. For normal IT systems, monitoring traffic is a large focus of the operations teams. Salesforce orgs are mostly accessed by employees with user accounts, and so the number of users is typically predictable. But as you start to expose your org to customers through Sites or Communities, you may be exposed to more unpredictable levels of traffic.

This is just a superficial review of the topic, largely to introduce high-level performance testing concepts that might be useful to help with LDV or traffic issues. The following tools can be used to generate large volumes of randomized sample data in a testing org prior to go-live. They can also be used for actual performance testing: simulating real-time traffic to help determine whether performance issues begin to appear when the system is under load.

How to Run Performance Tests

A simple subset of performance testing can be done just using Chrome Dev Tools or Firebug from a developer's machine. If your concern is simply with page load time, this may be sufficient. When Lightning Components were first launched, they were slow and buggy, and the Salesforce Lightning Inspector[31] was extremely helpful to identify performance bottlenecks. The Developer Console also remains a helpful way to identify performance issues on the Salesforce backend. But none of these tools allow you to test the system under large loads, which is the true meaning of performance testing.

To run performance tests, you will need a commercial tool such as Micro Focus LoadRunner, an open source tool such as Apache JMeter, or a cloud-based testing tool like SendGrid's Loader.io. JMeter is popular and open source, but will require a bit more scripting and experimentation to get working. Loader.io offers a free tier and a simple SaaS-based user interface and may be sufficient to help you get started. LoadRunner is the most well established of these but will require installation and high license fees. There are now many other options as well.

---

[31]https://chrome.google.com/webstore/detail/salesforce-lightning-insp/pcpmcffcomlcj
gpcheokdfcjipanjdpc?hl=en

If your only goal is to generate large volumes of sample data, you may be able to use a data-focused tool such as Odaseva or OwnBackup which provide tools for loading large volumes of data.

Performance testing is normally divided into load testing and stress testing. Load testing means simulating expected volumes of transactions and possibly varying that load across the normal range. Stress testing simulates higher-than-normal numbers of transactions to determine how the system behaves as loads increase. Stress testing can either take the form of soak testing or spike testing. Soak testing applies a stable or steadily increasing load over an extended period of time; in traditional applications that's useful to determine memory leaks, whereas in Salesforce it can give you an indication of how data or asynchronous jobs accumulate over time, and whether you see changes in the performance of the underlying Salesforce Pod. Spike testing applies sudden bursts of traffic to assess what happens in extreme circumstances.

Performance testing tools have several main capabilities. First, they allow you to design tests that can send data to Salesforce's API or user interface. You can specify what data you'll send, how often, in what volumes, and so on. Second, they include tools to actually orchestrate and generate that load. Like UI testing tools, they can record and replay user interactions in a browser, but in parallel at an extremely high rate; they can also apply large numbers of API requests in parallel. Finally, these tools record response times and error rates, summarizing this in time series graphs that allow you to monitor throughput and correlate load with response time. Those time series graphs can also reveal side effects like increasing response times on unrelated parts of Salesforce as your main test load increases.

When Do Performance Tests Run?

Unlike the other types of testing discussed in this chapter, performance tests should **not** be run on an ongoing basis as part of your development lifecycle. Salesforce prohibits large-scale performance testing in sandboxes except by prior authorization. Salesforce provides specific guidance on performance testing at `https://help.salesforce.com/articleView?id=000335652&type=1`. Such tests need to be planned and scheduled at least 2 weeks in advance and must be done in conjunction with Salesforce support staff so that they can abort the tests if they cause adverse effects on other customers.

Performance Testing Environments

Salesforce is a multitenant system, and the "pods" that host sandboxes generally have lower spare processing capacity than production systems. The good news is that if something performs well in a sandbox, it will generally perform even better in a production org. Because this testing must be scheduled in advance and involves creating and changing large volumes of data, performance testing should be done in a full sandbox. It can also be done in a partial copy sandbox, but you'll need to ensure you have enough space available to perform the tests.

Data Needed for Performance Tests

One of the main capabilities of performance testing tools is their ability to generate large volumes of randomized data. This requires time to set up and configure, since the data must be appropriate to the objects and fields under test. If your goal is to diagnose actual performance issues seen in production, then you will definitely want a freshly cloned full sandbox or at least a partial copy sandbox that includes data from all of the relevant objects.

Creating Performance Tests

As with any kind of testing, it's important to start small and build your tests up gradually. How exactly each test is created is highly dependent on the tool. An older Dreamforce talk on performance testing by Raj Advani and Randy Case[32] offered a generalized four-step process for building your performance tests: build a test plan, run a baseline test, identify your target load, and scale up your tests gradually.

After selecting and setting up your performance testing engine, your first step is to build your test plan. This is an essential preparation and is also something you'll need to submit to Salesforce before you can schedule your test. Your test plan must identify the key business transactions you want to test. Your focus should be on testing your custom code and processes, not on testing Salesforce itself. Even if you discover some performance bottlenecks coming from Salesforce, you won't be able to fix those, so focus your tests on areas under your own control like Apex code and Processes. Your test plan should assess what data will be needed, what data volumes and rates, and what APIs or UI endpoints you'll be testing. The Salesforce help article at `https://help.salesforce.com/articleView?id=000335652&type=1` can be your guide.

---

[32]`www.slideshare.net/developerforce/df121279-patterson-randy-changes`

You can and should run multiple baseline tests before actually beginning performance testing. Baseline tests use your performance testing tools to execute small groups of transactions. This lets you validate your scripts and establish baseline expectations for performance.

Based on that initial information, and your expectations about the loads you need to test, you can then identify your target load. Your target number should be realistic. For example, if you estimate you may encounter 200 parallel requests, you do not need to test against 10,000 parallel transactions.

Once you've identified your target load, when it comes time to coordinate your load test with Salesforce, you should scale the test up gradually. Begin with half your estimated load, then move to 75%, before finally running the full load.

Performance Testing Considerations

Again, performance testing is prohibited on Salesforce except by prior arrangement and at a scheduled time. You can develop your performance tests by using these tools to load small amounts of data, but if you start generating unusually high volumes of data, you will violate Salesforce's terms of use.

How to Act on Performance Test Results

The main purpose of performance testing is to gain confidence that your applications will be able to handle normal traffic and some level of surge traffic. If issues are identified, they become the starting point for analysis and remediation. Next steps depend on the issue being uncovered. As mentioned, Salesforce provides excellent resources for addressing large data volume issues, from indexing fields and checking query plans to creating skinny tables and looking at archiving solutions.

Salesforce's multitenant platform means that the performance of your org is not entirely under your control. And their governor limits mean that you can hit hard limits if you have not designed your applications in an efficient way. But performance testing can give early insights into these issues and make the difference between going live with confidence and experiencing unanticipated failures.

If your baseline tests indicate that a particular process takes 5 seconds to complete, you may be looking to see the variability in that response time. The testing tools can help you determine which stages in each transaction take the most time or are subject to the most variance or errors. Identifying and remedying a small number of performance hotspots can make a huge difference in the eventual performance.

Code Reviews

Having extensively discussed various forms of automated tests, we now look at code reviews, a manual form of nonfunctional testing. Code reviews are one of the most powerful methods of ensuring consistent high-quality code, providing training to developers, and ensuring that more than one person is familiar with every line of code in the system. Code reviews can be performed by one or more senior members of the development team, or they can be peer reviews done by other members of the development team. An Extreme Programming (XP) version of the code review is "pair programming" where developers always work in pairs, taking turns having "hands on the keyboard," but applying both of their minds to the problem at hand.

Coding standards are sets of rules adopted by development teams based on collective experience and wisdom. These standards are typically adopted by an organization, but may vary slightly from project to project. These standards may also differ for each programming language (Apex, Visualforce, JavaScript, Python, etc.) but typically concern metadata organization, indentation, commenting, declarations, statements, white space, naming conventions, programming practices, and the like. The main advantage of defining and holding true to standards is that every piece of code looks and feels familiar. Consistent organization makes code more readable and helps programmers understand code written by others more quickly.

If coding standards are followed consistently throughout a project and across an organization, code can be more easily extended, refactored, and debugged.

Using coding standards in the development process is important to programmers for a number of reasons:

- Software is almost never maintained for its whole life by its original author.

- Enforcing collective standards reduces the time and cost required for software maintenance.

- Code conventions improve the readability of software, allowing programmers to understand unfamiliar code more quickly.

One easy way to ensure that code adheres to coding standards is to include (and effectively use) a code review step in the development process. This ensures that you always have at least two sets of experienced eyes on all of the code on your project.

How to Perform Code Reviews

Often, code reviews are the responsibility of a project's Tech Lead or Dev Lead, but that may vary by project. Through the code review process, reviewers are able to coach developers, provide feedback on code quality, and ensure the delivery of high-quality code. Everyone learns and improves along the way.

Consider the following suggestions to improve code quality:

- Follow the programming language style guide for the language(s) being developed in.

- Give descriptive names for methods and variables.

- Do not overdesign.

- Use efficient data structures and algorithms.

- Create proper test classes and modularize code.

- Document any complex manual steps, provide scripts to simplify them if possible, and try to make your code self-documenting as much as possible.

- Keep all elements of your project in a version control system.

By sticking to these points and using the code quality analysis tools suggested earlier, project teams can create more readable, reliable, and manageable code. Improved code quality helps development teams work quickly and safely, which benefits them and the businesses they support.

When Are Code Reviews Performed

As mentioned, code reviews can either be done at the same time as development using pair programming, informally after the fact through peer review, or as part of a formal code review process, possibly using a pull request.

One of the most important recommendations to come out of the *State of DevOps Reports* was based on analyzing the relationship between team performance and how they managed code reviews and change approvals. As summarized in the book *Accelerate*:

[The State of DevOps Survey] asked about four possible scenarios:

1. All production changes must be approved by an external body (such as a manager or change advisory board).

2. Only high-risk changes, such as database changes, require approval.

3. We rely on peer review to manage changes.

4. We have no change approval process.

The results were surprising. We found that approval only for high-risk changes was not correlated with software delivery performance. Teams that reported no approval process or used peer review achieved higher software delivery performance. Finally, teams that required approval by an external body achieved lower performance.

We investigated further the case of approval by an external body to see if this practice correlated with stability. We found that external approvals were negatively correlated with lead time, deployment frequency, and restore time, and had no correlation with change fail rate.[33]

Based on that analysis, they recommend using a lightweight change approval process. Furthermore, while pull requests are an ideal approach for reviewing untrusted contributions to open source projects, using them for code reviews within a team implies the use of feature branches instead of trunk-based development and thus can interfere with a team's velocity and ability to refactor.

Such recommendations contrast sharply with the practices and expectations of many teams, especially those subject to regulatory compliance. If you're in doubt, I strongly recommend you read the three-page discussion on this topic in the book *Accelerate*. In brief, it is logical that external reviewers with limited understanding or time to evaluate changes will add little or no benefit compared with the teams who have spent days creating and testing a feature. By contrast, pair programming or intrateam reviews bring a more educated review.

---

[33]Nicole Forsgren, Jez Humble, and Gene Kim, *Accelerate: The Science of Lean Software and Devops Building and Scaling High Performing Technology Organizations* (IT Revolution Press, 2018): p. 79

Peer review together with ensuring that all changes are tracked and deployed through the delivery pipeline will satisfy both the letter and the spirit of "segregation of duties." Review processes cannot guarantee that a change won't lead to a failure, but being able to quickly deploy small changes reduces the risk of such deployments. It also allows for easier debugging, faster rollback, and an efficient feedback loop to the developers who most need to learn from any failures.

Code Review Environments

Code reviews are based directly on the source code and so don't require a test environment. They are most effective when done as peer reviews or pair programming, but can also be done by reviewing pull requests in a version control system like GitHub.

Data Needed for Code Reviews

Code reviews are based directly on the source code and so don't require any test data.

Performing Code Reviews

Code reviews provide an opportunity to give feedback on coding style, the efficiency of the logic, naming conventions, and many other aspects of coding. Importantly, code reviews also transform development from an isolated activity into a social and collaborative activity.

Part of the mythos surrounding programming casts it as a solitary activity done by socially awkward individuals who are more comfortable interacting with machines than with humans. In the United States, that stereotype layers in images of young, white males binging on junk food and working mostly at night. Those stereotypes are so strong that they have affected university enrollment in computer science programs for decades, leading to gender and racial imbalances across the IT industry.

In reality, programming never happens in isolation from the business or social needs it's serving, and there are many social networks (in the original, human sense) that support people in building code and making wise decisions.

Code reviews provide a way to transfer knowledge organically throughout a team and so avoid knowledge getting overconcentrated in one person. They lead to standardization and improved code quality, as well as deep camaraderie between those involved.

It was W. Edwards Deming, the father of industrial modernization, who debunked the myth that domineering and judgmental managers help ensure a quality product. Deming's 14 points for management emphasize the importance of driving out fear, breaking down barriers, eliminating performance reviews, and focusing on pride in workmanship and achieving a common goal.

Although this book is full of exhortations to automate processes, it's in the spirit of freeing teams to focus on productive, valuable work. Software is a codification of shared knowledge and so must necessarily be a shared activity. Code reviews provide a perfect opportunity to carry that out.

Manual QA and Acceptance Testing

Having discussed both functional and nonfunctional testing, we finally look at manual testing. Whereas code reviews are part of structural analysis, looking "under the hood" at how applications are built, manual testing involves manually checking whether the application functions as it should. This can be done by specialized members of the QA team, or developers can take turns performing QA for one another's work.

Manual testing is mentioned last, only after extensive discussion of many automated test methods, not because it is not important, but because the time and skills of testers will be far more valuable when used to supplement and extend the kinds of automated testing described earlier. Where automated tests are available, they are cheaper, faster, and easier to run than manual tests. Wherever possible, QA resources should focus on exploratory testing and testing one-off scenarios that don't justify automation.

Manual testing is a critical aspect of the development process. But one of the highest value activities that testers can do is discern when a test should be automated and help to implement effective automated tests. By automating critical aspects of the system, and aspects that are brittle or require repeated testing, the skill and energy of testers can remain focused on exploratory testing and high-value analysis that cannot be automated.

There are typically two phases of manual acceptance testing. The first stage is performed by members of the development or QA team themselves, prior to making functionality available to potential users. The second stage involves user acceptance testing (UAT), getting feedback from actual subject matter experts.

Prior to UAT, the development or QA team should perform a round of manual exploratory testing as a sanity check to confirm that functionality seems to be working as specified. Catching issues at this stage is far preferable to exposing UAT testers to obvious bugs. Not only does this allow bugs to be caught earlier, but UAT testers are often performing this testing part-time, alongside their regular responsibilities, and will quickly grow weary of sending obviously defective work back to development teams.

How to Do Manual QA and UAT

There is a distinct difference between the skills and attitude of a developer and the skills and attitude of a tester. Developers focus on building things and moving on as quickly as possible; testers focus on breaking things and not moving on until they are confident something won't break.

With increased emphasis on automated testing, test-driven development, and other methods of building in quality, the role of manual QA sometimes comes into question. Teams are still experimenting with variations on the role of traditional testers, to see what works best. Understandably there are tradeoffs with all approaches.

The leanest approach is to simply rely on developers to test their own work. While developers should certainly test as much as possible, this doesn't tend to work well. Development takes a massive amount of mental energy and is sometimes done under significant time pressure. Exhaustion and wishful thinking can combine to make developers overoptimistic that they can quickly move on to their next task. Excessive familiarity causes developers to make assumptions about how users will behave and makes them stay close to the "happy path" of using the application the way it was designed.

Salesforce's own IT teams are among the groups who have experimented with a variation on this, which is to have developers alternate between doing their own work and testing the work of others. Like peer reviews, this is a fantastic way of knowledge sharing and encouraging dialog around solutions. But even when testing the work of others, developers still display a bias toward moving things along rather than trying hard to break them.

Good testing is indeed a specialized skill, and although the role of QA testers is evolving quickly, it's not going away any time soon. Testers require patience, a tolerance for repetitive behavior, and an eye for how applications might break when used in unanticipated ways. QA testers hold institutional memory of the most common failures that occur and can remain watchful to ensure developers don't introduce regressions.

QA testers engage with developers in a dialectical way, representing the realistic viewpoint that whatever can break will break. I've underrepresented the role of QA, since I come from the development side, but it suffices to say that realism lies somewhere in between the optimism of developers and the pessimism of testers. Therefore they should continue to work together to deliver the best results.

When to Do Manual QA and UAT

As mentioned, manual testing should be done on work that has passed all automated tests and can thus be considered a candidate for release. This allows testers to use their time more effectively to focus on exploratory testing.

User acceptance testing (UAT) is done once a team's internal testers are satisfied that work meets specifications and may be ready for use. User acceptance testers are generally subject matter experts (SMEs) from the business team that has requested or will use the application. On large transformation projects, there will typically be a UAT phase of the project when SMEs work full or part-time to evaluate the systems that have been built to ensure that they behave correctly under realistic conditions and represent an improvement over what's currently in use.

QA and UAT Environments

QA testing is a great candidate for shifting left and being done in a scratch org. This can allow for very fast feedback, since QA can provide feedback in the same scratch org that the developer is using or in a "Review App"—a scratch org spun up directly from the CI system. This requires that you have test data stored in your code repository that is sufficient to support the testing needs of the QA team. Although maintaining test data in a code repository may be a new process for QA teams who are accustomed to testing in a long-lived sandbox, it provides a powerful method to curate and improve a reasonable set of test data that is seen by both developers and testers and which is regularly reset.

A key concept in Lean software development is to enable every worker to **pull** raw materials to do their job whenever they have capacity. For QA testers, their raw materials are features or fixes under development. In the absence of automated deployments, QA teams are left waiting for deployments to happen, which is a massive source of waste. Automating deployments reduces this waste, and allowing QA testers to create their own scratch orgs to evaluate work in progress is an excellent example of workers being able to pull raw materials in.

UAT testing should be done in a production-like environment, a partial or full sandbox. This allows UAT testers to experiment with familiar data, including complex scenarios that they have to handle during their daily work. This also ensures that they are testing in an environment that is fully integrated with external systems. If functionality is automatically deployed to this production-like environment, and behaves properly in the face of realistic data and live integrations, then the same results can be expected in production.

Data Needed for QA and UAT

QA teams typically spend significant time creating, cloning, and updating collections of manual testing data that they can use in their tests. Traditionally, teams use a single QA sandbox, since this allows them to establish that testing data and share it across the testing team. There's usually opportunity to make the process of creating test data more efficient.

Data management tools like OwnBackup and Odaseva allow you to anonymize and import collections of data from production that can be used by testers. Salesforce DX also includes mechanisms like `data:tree:export` to export collections of data into version control so that it can then be loaded into scratch orgs for testing.

Effective practices for managing test data are still evolving, but wherever possible it's important to export test data in a form that can be reused, so that QA teams are not shackled to a single org that never gets refreshed for fear of losing manually curated testing data.

UAT data should match the data from the actual production org, which is why partial and full copy sandboxes are the right place to perform such testing. Data management tools give you the flexibility to selectively migrate data into developer sandboxes, but it's almost certainly more efficient to just use a sandbox that includes a copy of production data.

The most important data for UAT is actually the configuration data that determines business logic and essential information such as Products and Pricebooks. After that, it's critical that key Accounts, Opportunities, and so forth are created that match the production system. UAT testers are uniquely able to exercise edge cases that might be likely to fail. But to do this, they need to have familiar data from production.

QA and UAT Test Cases

For formal testing, it's common to create test cases, which are sequences of steps needed to perform certain transactions. This is particularly important for QA testers since they may be unfamiliar with business needs. But even UAT testers can benefit from having explicit test cases generated by a senior member of their team so they can ensure they are testing all the features that are under development.

QA and UAT Considerations

There's much more that can be said about these areas, and there are people who devote their careers to managing teams of testers and facilitating user acceptance testing. The reason for initiating this discussion here is to show where it fits in an increasingly automated process of delivery and testing.

How to Act on QA and UAT Feedback

The final result of testing is either approval and release or sending the work back to developers. In either case, the more time elapses from when features are first developed, the less efficiently developers will be able to implement any feedback. Passing UAT does not mean that features will actually be accepted and bug-free in the hands of large groups of users. Users always have the last word in testing, and they too need feedback mechanisms to express approval or to log issues.

Developers genuinely want to build the right things, and to build things right. There's an enormous amount of creativity and effort that goes into building things, and developers are generally excited to share the results with users or to improve applications based on their feedback. But just as when giving feedback to pets or children, the more time elapses the less effective that feedback becomes.

I confessed earlier that developers just want to get work out the door. And this entire book focuses on helping teams get their work out the door more quickly. But that doesn't mean that anyone benefits from shipping unreliable, half-baked functionality to production. The point of automating delivery is to get features to QA, UAT, and end users with the highest quality in the shortest time. Feedback from testers is the critical end result of expediting delivery and is the most effective way to improve the product and developers' understanding of the real needs.

In the words of Jez Humble, "A key goal of continuous delivery is to change the economics of the software delivery process to make it economically viable to work in small batches. ... Working in small batches ... reduces the time it takes to get feedback on our work, makes it easier to triage and remediate problems, [and] increases efficiency and motivation."[34]

---

[34]https://continuousdelivery.com/principles/

Summary

Quality can be a moving target, challenging to define, and impossible to perfect. But by considering these various aspects of quality—functional, structural, and process—teams are enabled to be more effective in achieving a design that will meet both present and future needs. By keeping a focus on quality and adopting a discipline of continuous improvement, the goal of long-term user satisfaction becomes far easier to achieve.

Table 8-1 summarizes the different types of test described in this chapter.

Table 8-1. *A summary of different types of test and their characteristics*

	Automated	Environment	Speed	Purpose	Technology
Fast Tests for Developers					
Linting	Yes	IDE	Real time	Coding style, common faults	PMD, SonarLint, ESLint
Quality gates	Yes	Desktop, CI engine, web application	Fast	Code issue overview, duplicate detection, trends	PMD, SonarQube, Clayton, Copado
Unit tests	Yes	Scratch org, Dev sandbox, or locally	< 5 min total	Fast feedback for developers	Apex, Jest/Mocha
Comprehensive Tests					
Code-based acceptance tests	Yes	Scratch org, test sandbox, CI job	Minutes to hours (run in parallel)	Comprehensive regression tests	Apex, Jest/Mocha
UI tests	Yes	Scratch org, test sandbox	Minutes to hours (run in parallel)	Regression testing critical parts of complex applications	Selenium, Provar, Puppeteer, Tosca

(continued)

Table 8-1. (*continued*)

	Automated	Environment	Speed	Purpose	Technology
Static analysis	Yes	CI job, static analysis tool	Fast	Tracking trends and identifying quality hotspots	SonarQube, Clayton, CodeScan, PMD, Codacy, CodeClimate
Security analysis	Yes	Security analysis tool	Minutes	Sophisticated identification of security flaws	CheckMarx, Fortify
Performance testing	Yes	Full or partial sandbox	Minutes to hours (run in parallel)	Occasional and targeted performance analysis	JMeter, LoadRunner, Loader.io
Code reviews	No	In-person or using pull requests	Real time or later	Code quality analysis, shared learning, collaboration	Fellow developers
Manual QA and acceptance tests	No	Testing sandbox	Indefinite	Exploratory testing and getting feedback from users	Mouse, keyboard, monitor, human

The purpose of testing is to ensure quality, and the process of testing is facilitated by promoting features and fixes to progressively higher environments for progressively more sophisticated testing. This process of promoting features is called deployment and is the heart of continuous delivery. In the next chapter, we discuss mechanisms and techniques to make your deployments as fast and painless as possible, thus allowing your testing and release process to proceed as smoothly as possible.

CHAPTER 9

Deploying

Deploying means moving software and configuration between environments. Deployment allows software to be built in a development environment, tested in one or more test environment, and then released to one or more production environments.

In the case of traditional software, deployments send that software to a server such as an EC2 host on AWS. In the case of Salesforce, deployments are changes to the configuration of a Salesforce instance. In both cases, deployments have a reputation for being painful and challenging, and have been one of the driving reasons behind the development of DevOps approaches.

Why are deployments so challenging? First of all, any nontrivial piece of software is complex, includes extensive logic, and varies its behavior based on user input, changing data and other conditions. Second, it's very hard to fully encapsulate software, since it depends on the server and network infrastructure on which it runs, and typically interacts with other applications.

The complexity of the application itself is understandable and somewhat unavoidable. But deployment problems related to variations in server and network infrastructure are enormously frustrating for developers. A difference in a proxy setting, database configuration, environment variable, or version of a piece of server software can make the difference between an application running fine and an application which fails to run. Even worse, the application may run but experience strange behavior for some users or occasional performance issues. Replicating such problems can require hours or days of developer time, and resolving the behavior may depend on server-wide changes that cause impacts for other applications as well. If there's a deep divide between development and operations teams, developers might even adopt a glib attitude that "it worked in dev," even when the operation team is struggling.

© Andrew Davis 2019
A. Davis, *Mastering Salesforce DevOps*, https://doi.org/10.1007/978-1-4842-5473-8_9

The immense frustration of attempting to debug an application that "worked fine in dev" but doesn't work in a test or production environment has been a driving force behind the rising use of containers (principally Docker containers) as the execution environment for applications. Containers are lightweight execution environments that can be created quickly, are identical every time they are created, and are isolated from their surrounding environment. Containers guarantee a consistent execution environment, which makes them extremely attractive platforms for deploying and running applications. The ability to define (and update) containers using simple configuration files that can be stored and modified as source code makes them even more valuable.

Because Salesforce abstracts away the underlying server, database, and networking infrastructure, Salesforce developers don't experience the same infrastructure problems that plague developers creating traditional applications. (The Salesforce employees who actually build Salesforce may experience these pains, however!) Nevertheless, there is an analogous problem faced by Salesforce developers in that they are deploying their application into an Org which has its own customizations and competing applications. It is equally possible for Salesforce developers to experience mysterious problems with their production application that simply never appear in the development environment. It is for these reasons that DevOps, and in particular continuous delivery, is so important for the Salesforce world as well—and why it's important to gradually bring your entire org and all its applications into a well-defined delivery pipeline that provides you precise visibility into what's in each org and the differences between them.

At the heart of continuous delivery is automating deployments. People have been doing deployments between Salesforce environments since the platform was created, but there has been a tendency to do ad hoc deployments or manually modify target environments. This chapter introduces the deployment technologies available, including commercial tools, the process of resolving deployment errors, how to set up continuous delivery, and how to manage org differences and multi-org scenarios. We conclude with a discussion on how to analyze dependencies and the risks associated with deployments.

Deployment Technologies

What are the different techniques or technologies available to deploy to a Salesforce instance?

The Underlying Options

There are only four underlying ways of deploying Salesforce metadata: using change sets, using the Metadata API, using packages, and manually recreating the configuration of one environment in another environment.

The change set UI is built into Salesforce and provides a simple graphical interface that can be used to deploy metadata between a production org and its related sandboxes.

The Metadata API provides API-based access to read and update most Salesforce configuration. This API is the tool that is most relevant to the task of continuous delivery. This is also the foundation for all of the third-party release management tools. The Metadata API also includes some limited capabilities for working with change sets.

Using packages as a mechanism for deployment has long been the approach for ISVs to make applications available to customers. There are now several varieties of packaging available on the Salesforce platform, and the use of unlocked packages is a core part of the Salesforce DX workflow, described in detail later.

Manually recreating changes is a fallback that is still surprisingly common. As of this writing, there are still many types of metadata that can't be deployed in any automated way. Fortunately, most of this "undeployable" metadata relates to minor aspects of configuration that don't need to change often. Almost all aspects of an org's configuration can be deployed automatically, but the gaps requiring manual configuration are persistent and frustrating.

Another reason that manually recreating changes across environments is common is lack of developer education on how to automate deployments. Fortunately, this gap is easier for companies to address by themselves, and hopefully this book can help.

A surprising number of Salesforce developers are uneducated about the capabilities of change sets and the Metadata API and may rely on manually recreating configuration to "deploy" functionality that could easily be automated. Even very senior Salesforce developers may be hanging on to the outdated view that "much" or "most" configuration can't be automatically deployed. The growing number of customers successfully implementing continuous delivery is a proof that automated deployments are achievable.

Manual Changes

The Metadata Coverage Report[1] and the Unsupported Metadata Types page[2] describe the limitations of what Salesforce metadata can be deployed. Salesforce developers should bookmark these pages and use these as the definitive reference for what can and cannot be automatically deployed.

Salesforce has championed an "API first" approach for many years. For example, the Salesforce Lightning Experience that began rolling out in 2015 was built on updates to the Tooling API that allowed Salesforce to query its own APIs from the web browser to retrieve information like lists of picklist values. Those responsible for doing Salesforce deployments, however, have often felt that the promise of "complete metadata coverage" was a mirage that never got any closer.

Despite annual improvements to the Metadata API, the pace of Salesforce development meant that new features were regularly rolling out that could not be automatically deployed. With each release, some of the Metadata API's backlog would be retired, but new Salesforce capabilities keep being released, and so the backlog has been growing almost as fast as it was being retired.

As mentioned in the introduction, this entire book deals with the "Salesforce Core" product, and those parts of Salesforce such as Marketing Cloud and Commerce Cloud that were the result of acquisitions require entirely separate processes to manage deployments. Even on the core platform, there have been some notable and massive gaps in the Metadata API. Community Cloud is built on the Core platform and has been a major focus for Salesforce in recent years. Metadata API support for Community customizations is still limited, as of this writing, but that is scheduled to be addressed with the ExperienceBundle metadata type in the Winter '20 release.

Fortunately, there are now processes in place to ensure that any new capabilities on the Salesforce core platform must be supported by the Metadata API. The Metadata Coverage Report mentioned earlier is generated automatically by the build process that builds Salesforce. And a quality check now ensures that any new capabilities created by product teams at Salesforce must be accessible through this API.

---

[1]https://developer.salesforce.com/docs/metadata-coverage/
[2]https://developer.salesforce.com/docs/atlas.en-us.api_meta.meta/api_meta/meta_
unsupported_types.htm

The moral of this is that teams should continually strive to reduce their reliance on manual "deployments," but that certain edge cases will need to be handled manually for the foreseeable future. For this reason, teams should maintain notes on necessary manual steps in whatever system they use to track work items.

One workaround for automating these manual steps is the use of UI automation to change configuration. Both AutoRABIT and Copado enable users to configure pre- and postdeployment steps using Selenium. In fact, any UI test automation tools that work on Salesforce can be scripted to perform this process. For example, to automate the configuration of Account Teams, your script can navigate to the appropriate place in the Setup UI and confirm that all of the appropriate Account Team Roles are configured, and if any are missing, the script can add them. This kind of scripting requires significantly more work to set up and maintain than automating this behavior declaratively using the Metadata API. In particular, you need to ensure those scripts are idempotent (don't unintentionally create duplicate functionality if they are run more than once) and guard against unintended behavior. Your scripts are also vulnerable to breaking if Salesforce updates parts of the UI.

Change Sets

Change sets are the only "clicks-not-code" deployment option built into Salesforce. This is the default approach to deployment for most Salesforce admins and many Salesforce developers. Nevertheless, change sets suffer from many limitations and have not been improved much since they were initially introduced.

Change sets are specifically for managing deployments between a production org and its related sandboxes. Change sets require that you first create inbound and outbound deployment connections between the orgs that will be the sources and destinations for each change. For security, these connections need to be configured in each org, so that a particular "Dev" org might have an outbound connection to a "QA" org and that "QA" org might have an inbound connection from "Dev" and outbound connections to "UAT" and "Prod" orgs.

Once these deployment connections have been made, you can build a change set in a source org by selecting the metadata items that you want to be included in that deployment. Change sets provide a very helpful capability to "view dependent metadata." This means that you can, for example, select a single Lightning Application and then view its dependencies to pull in the related Apex controller and any custom fields that controller might reference. Once built, the change set can be uploaded to its target org.

Once a change set has been uploaded to the target org, you need to log in to that target org to perform a validation of that change set. The validation ensures that there is no missing metadata or other conflicts that would prevent a successful deployment. Once validated, the change set can be deployed into the target org.

It is significant that the change sets are not directly deployed to the target org, rather they are simply uploaded and made available in the target org. The actual deployment needs to be performed by an administrator from inside that target org. This helps to fulfill a compliance requirement of laws such as Sarbanes Oxley (SOX) that the people responsible for developing applications should not directly have the power to deploy those applications to the target org. This separation of duties is important in theory, but problematic with change sets in that the person deploying them can only see the names of the metadata items contained, and not their details. With both Salesforce and traditional IT applications, approving admins generally lack the time and knowledge necessary for detailed review of what they are installing in the target system. A change set is more or less a black box, and admin approval is more or less a rubber stamp. Compliance requirements are better met by using version control and continuous delivery.

One benefit of requiring admins to trigger the final installation, however, is that the target org can receive many change sets from different developers and install them all at an allotted time after first notifying affected users. This still creates a bottleneck where the developers need to handoff installation responsibilities to a busy admin. If that admin is maintaining multiple sandboxes, this can cause delays when the development teams and end users (or testers) need something installed but that admin is not available.

The main limitation of change sets is that they are tedious to build if you are managing large volumes of changes. Tools like Gearset and Copado provide very nice metadata pickers that allow users to sort and filter metadata by type, name, last modified date, and last modified by. But the change set UI requires you to navigate to each metadata type one by one and select the metadata items to be deployed. If you happen to navigate to the next page without clicking "Add," your selections are lost. There is no indication in that UI of who last modified an item or when it was last modified, which makes selecting changes a painstaking and error-prone process.

Some companies do not allow change sets to be uploaded to production directly from development, which means the change set must first be uploaded to a testing environment and then *manually recreated* in that testing environment and uploaded to the production org.

Another limitation of change sets is that they don't cover many types of metadata. Of the 240 types of Salesforce metadata, change sets support only 53% of them, whereas the Metadata API supports 93% of them. Change sets also don't support *removing* metadata from the target org, only adding or updating it.

Finally, change sets can only facilitate deployments between a single production org and its related sandboxes. You cannot use change sets to deploy to multiple production orgs.

These limitations of change sets have been a boon for the creators of commercial deployment tools. The various commercial tools listed in the following provide vastly more functionality than change sets, and most of them have far better user interfaces. ClickDeploy's marketing pitch emphasizes the superiority of their tool to change sets: "Deploy Salesforce 10x faster than change sets. … Deploy metadata types beyond the ones supported by change set. … Know exactly what you are deploying via instant line-by-line diff viewer. … No more tedious, manual rebuild of inbound change sets. Clone & reuse inbound change list in a single click."[3]

ClickDeploy has built an easy-to-use alternative to change sets. But at least some of the benefits that they offer—deployment speed, supported metadata types, and line-by-line visibility—are equally true of any tool that is based on the Metadata API.

The Metadata API

The Metadata API performs deployments many times faster than Change sets do and also supports a far larger set of metadata. Every tool that supports Salesforce release management is built on the Metadata API, so in theory all of these tools can claim to be faster than change sets and to support more types of metadata. The speed of the Metadata API (how fast metadata can be retrieved and deployed) is the upper limit for all Salesforce release management tools; no tool can operate faster than the Metadata API allows, although some of them are definitely far slower.

The Metadata API also defines the upper limit of which types of metadata a tool can support. If something is not supported by the Metadata API, it is not deployable on Salesforce. But not all third-party tools support all of the metadata types supported by the Metadata API. For example, the now deprecated Force.com IDE based on Eclipse supported only a limited subset of metadata. The most flexible tools use the Metadata API's "describe" calls to dynamically query a Salesforce org to determine which types of

---

[3]https://clickdeploy.io/ accessed 2019-02-17

metadata are supported, and then permit all of those types. Tools that have not built in such dynamic logic are likely to always lag behind the Metadata API and to support only a limited subset of metadata.

Org configuration that is not deployable using the Metadata API can only be set manually. However some tools such as Copado and AutoRABIT have a clever capability whereby they use Selenium automation to dynamically log in and check or change org configuration. Selenium is normally only used for UI testing, but this kind of automation allows org setting changes to be propagated in an automated way.

With Salesforce DX, several new capabilities have been released or are in Pilot that allow changes that otherwise wouldn't be possible through the Metadata API. Sandbox cloning is a new capability that allows all of the configuration (and data) in a sandbox to be replicated to another sandbox. Scratch org definition files allow developers to define scratch org features that are beyond the scope of the Metadata API. And the forthcoming Org Shape and Scratch Org Snapshots provide capabilities similar to sandbox cloning whereby characteristics of scratch orgs can be defined that are beyond the scope of the Metadata API. All of these capabilities are in the context of *provisioning new orgs* however, so they are not actually deployments.

The Metadata API remains the defining mechanism that both provides and limits the capabilities of all other tools. All of the following tools simply provide different user interfaces and different types of metadata storage and processing on top of the Metadata API. Importantly, the Metadata API also allows retrieving and deploying metadata from and to any Salesforce org, as long as you have authorization on that org. This makes it a far more versatile tool than change sets, especially for companies with multiple production orgs.

Deploying Using Packages

Packaging means making discrete collections of code and configuration into a single bundle or package.

Salesforce enables several different types of packages, but they all function in a similar way. Packages allow a developer to specify various metadata items and take a snapshot of them which is uploaded to Salesforce and made available for installation in other Salesforce orgs using a package installation URL such as `https://login.salesforce.com/packaging/installPackage.apexp?p0=04tB000000000Ad`.

There are currently four types of Salesforce packages: classic unmanaged packages, classic managed packages, second-generation managed packages, and unlocked packages. Of these, this book deals mostly with unlocked packages. Although there are differences in how these package types are created and their characteristics, they all allow you to create package versions with an ID beginning with 04t that allow that version to be installed in a target org using a package installation URL like the one earlier.

Deploying Using an IDE

All the various Salesforce IDEs use the Metadata API in the background to make metadata available to be created, read, updated, and deleted. Salesforce was originally a clicks-not-code system, with no IDEs available or required for development. With the introduction of Salesforce domain–specific languages such as Apex, Visualforce, Aura, and Lightning Web Components, it became necessary to have a rich development environment.

The Dev Console created by Salesforce only allows for editing code files. But most other IDEs give access to every type of XML-based metadata available in the Metadata API. Because these tools already enable retrieving and deploying this metadata to the development environment, many of them also allow this metadata to be deployed to other environments as well.

One challenge with deployments is that they typically involve many interrelated pieces of metadata. For example, an Apex class may depend on a particular field, and that field may depend in turn on another field or object. IDEs typically work on one code file at a time, so for an IDE to truly support deployments, it needs to provide a metadata picker with which you can select multiple related pieces of metadata and then specify an environment to deploy them to. For this reason, not all IDEs have built useful tools for doing deployments.

Even when IDEs do allow for developers to do deployments directly, there are risks in allowing them to do so. First and foremost, in the absence of version control, it is difficult for an individual developer to ensure that they have the latest version of all affected metadata, and that their deployment won't overwrite customizations in the target org and cause unintended consequences. Moreover, this behavior does not provide any traceability about what a developer deployed, when, or why. This may violate compliance requirements and certainly makes changes difficult to trace or roll back.

While the mechanism used to deploy from a developer's IDE is essentially the same as that used by the following scripted methods, this approach is increasingly problematic as teams scale and as the sensitivity of the production environment increases. A last minute deployment from a developer leaving for a camping trip far out of cellphone coverage can lead to an enormously stressful and expensive production outage. The team struggling to understand and recover from this disaster will have no visibility into what exactly changed, making their cleanup process far more painful than it has to be.

Command-Line Scripts

Every operating system makes available a command line—a text-based interface for interacting with the machine and its applications. Generally, everyone finds graphical user interfaces (GUIs) to be easier to understand and interact with than command-line interfaces (CLIs), but nevertheless the use and importance of CLIs persist and have continued to grow. Why is this?

While GUIs provide simplicity and clarity, and allow complex phenomena to be visualized and acted upon, there are tradeoffs in that approach. A CLI allows infinite flexibility in what commands are used, with which parameters, and in which order. Importantly, they also allow commands to be tied together in sophisticated ways using programming languages to define loops, modules, variables, and more. And once written, these commands can be shared and run in an automated fashion. Creating GUIs requires a development team to make decisions about what options to give users and what information to show or hide. CLIs allow individuals and teams to choose what information to access, what actions to take, and what logic should tie these interactions together. In short, they allow the same flexibility as natural languages or programming languages, but can be used to orchestrate processes across multiple applications and multiple systems, making them immensely powerful.

Even if you're not accustomed to working on the command line, it's important to recognize that command-line scripts are the go-to tool for classic system administrators and for developers looking to build automation into their workflow. Importantly, CLIs are also the foundation used by DevOps tools for automating testing, analysis, builds, deployments, and reporting.

Introduction to Scripting

If you have rarely used the command line and never written command-line scripts, this process can seem daunting at first. As with anything, the initial steps you take are the hardest. But if you follow clear guides, it's easy to create a "Hello World" script. From there you can gradually improve that script and build confidence. Before long you can have a robust set of tools to help in all aspects of the software development and delivery process.

What's a script? The term script generally refers to small pieces of code where the source code is readily visible and modifiable by its users. It's a common simplification to divide high-level programming languages into three categories: compiled languages like C++ are compiled into machine code that can be executed directly; interpreted languages like JavaScript, Ruby, Python, and Perl are executed using an interpreter; and scripting languages like Bash and PowerShell are executed using a shell. Most scripts are based on the latter two types of language so that they can be modified and executed on the fly, without having to be compiled.

Windows has two built-in scripting languages: Batch files and PowerShell. Unix and Mac environments typically have many available shells, but the most common is Bash. Even if you and your team are Windows users, it's important to be aware of what kinds of scripts can run on Linux environments. This is because the world's servers are predominantly Unix-based,[4] and it is increasingly common for CI/CD systems to use Docker containers based on Linux. One reason that Macs have historically been attractive to developers is that they allow the use of Unix commands and scripts. Fortunately, Windows 10 and Server 2019 recently introduced the Windows Subsystem for Linux which finally allows Linux shell scripts to run on Windows machines without installing third-party tools.[5]

For these reasons, if you're just starting out on the command line, I would recommend learning to use the Unix-style commands and shells. If you're on a Windows machine, you'll first need to install the Windows Subsystem for Linux or use tools like Cygwin or GitBash. But once you've done that, you can navigate any other computer in the universe: Windows, Mac, or *nix. Unix command-line syntax and shells provide an enormous array of tools for working with your filesystem and automating your workflow. PowerShell will only ever be useful when working on Windows machines.

---

[4]For example, 70% of web servers are Unix-based https://w3techs.com/technologies/overview/operating_system/all

[5]https://docs.microsoft.com/en-us/windows/wsl/about

To avoid these kinds of platform incompatibilities altogether, and to get the benefit of more sophisticated programming languages, many teams use JavaScript, Python, Perl, or Ruby to write their scripts. These languages each provide interpreters to ensure consistent cross-platform execution.

One beauty of Unix-compatible systems is that you can quickly and easily combine and use scripts written in a variety of different languages. By convention, the first line in Unix scripts specifies which interpreter should be used for that script. For example, I wrote this book in Scrivener and used a set of scripts called Scrivomatic to automatically process the raw files and convert those to DOCX and PDF. The scripts were contributed by different users over time and are written in a mix of Python, Bash, and Ruby. I can run and modify any of those scripts with equal ease, without having to recompile them.

Listing 9-1 shows a sample Ruby script, while Listing 9-2 shows a simple Bash script. Assuming Ruby is installed, both of these scripts are executable as is on any Unix or Mac environment.

Listing 9-1. A simple Ruby script

```
#!/usr/bin/env ruby
input = $stdin.read
puts input.gsub(/Alpha/, 'Beta')
```

Listing 9-2. A simple Bash script

```
#!/bin/bash
cd "$( cd "$( dirname "${BASH_SOURCE[0]}" )" && pwd )"
```

The first line in these files starts with a "shebang" (the "sharp" character # and the "bang" character !) followed by the shell or interpreter that should be used to interpret the remaining lines. These scripts can both be executed from the command line in the same way, but they will use the appropriate shell or interpreter to run.

Shell scripts are typically just lists of commands, just as you might type on a command line, with the possible addition of some simple variables, loops, conditions, and functions. They are most useful when you are simply combining multiple command-line instructions, with a bit of added logic.

Interpreted languages allow for more sophisticated logic, such as importing modules, using data structures like objects and arrays, and using object-oriented principles.

Old School Salesforce Scripting

Salesforce itself is written in Java, which was the most promising up-and-coming programming language when Salesforce began in 1999. These Java roots explain why Salesforce metadata is expressed in XML, and the tools to support the development lifecycle have traditionally been written in Java.

There are two command-line tools that have traditionally been key for the Salesforce development lifecycle: the Ant Migration Tool (aka "Force.com Migration Tool") and the Salesforce Data Loader.

The Ant Migration Tool allows users to interact with the Metadata API using Ant. Ant is the original Java build tool, released in 2001. At the time, Ant was state of the art and used XML to define "targets" or actions that could be run in a particular order. The Ant Migration Tool is written in Java and allows users to define Ant targets to retrieve or deploy metadata, run tests, and so on. To use this, you first need to install Java, Ant, and the Ant Migration Tool on your local machine and then define a build.xml file that defines the commands you want to run.

Listing 9-3 shows a simple Ant build configuration that defines an Ant target that you can run by executing ant retrieveDev. It depends on the Ant Migration Tool being present in the local directory as lib/ant-salesforce_46.jar and the credentials for the org being stored as a file called build.properties. Storing the Migration Tool (and any other scripts you depend on) in version control is an important way to ensure that those tools are available to everyone on your team and can be upgraded for everyone simultaneously. By contrast, storing credentials in the separate build.properties file allows these to be **excluded** from version control and instead live only on developers' machines or be injected by a CI/CD tool.

Listing 9-3. A simple Ant build.xml configuration file using the Ant Migration Tool

```
<project name="AntClassProject" basedir="." xmlns:sf="antlib:com.
salesforce">
    <!-- this taskdef helps locate the ant-salesforce jar in the project -->
    <taskdef
      resource="com/salesforce/antlib.xml"
      classPath="lib/ant-salesforce_46.jar"
      uri="antlib:com.salesforce"/>
```

```xml
<property file="build.properties" />

<tstamp>
  <format property="date" pattern="yyyy-MM-dd" />
  <format property="dateTime" pattern="yyyy-MM-dd_kk-mm-ss" />
</tstamp>
<property name="projectSource" value='../src' />
<property name="entireProject" value="${projectSource}/package.xml" />
<property name="sourceDev" value='${basedir}/source/dev' />
<property name="logFile" value="${basedir}/log/${dateTime}.txt" />

<target name="retrieveDev">
  <mkdir dir="log" />
  <record name="${logFile}" action="start"/>
  <echo>Retrieving from Dev...</echo>
  <delete dir="${sourceDev}" />
  <mkdir dir="${sourceDev}" />
  <sf:retrieve username="${dev.username}"
               password="${dev.password}"
               serverurl="${dev.serverurl}"
               retrieveTarget="${sourceDev}"
               unpackaged="${entireProject}"
               pollWaitMillis="10000"
               maxPoll="5000" />
  <record name="${logFile}" action="stop"/>
</target>
</project>
```

Ant scripts constitute "Old School Salesforce Scripting." If you aren't using these already, don't start. First of all, Ant is not the build tool of choice for modern Java developers. Ant was replaced by Maven and now by Gradle as the Java build tool of choice. Maven made it easy to include external modules to help with common tasks, and Gradle made it easy to write very readable build scripts. If you want to do anything outside of executing basic commands, XML is an absolutely terrible language to write in. And it's generally not very readable.

If you are inheriting existing Ant scripts, you can easily import them into Gradle and then benefit from Gradle's rich and readable syntax. For example, Listing 9-4 shows a brief Gradle snippet that imports an existing Ant script but then defines dependent tasks in a very readable way. Executing `gradle deploy2QA` will trigger the Ant targets `deployAndDestroyQA` and then `deployProjectToQA`. Before the release of the Salesforce CLI, Gradle was the main language I used for build scripts.

Listing 9-4. A simple Gradle script that imports existing Ant targets

```
logging.level = LogLevel.INFO
ant.importBuild 'ant/build.xml'

task deploy2QA (dependsOn: ['deployAndDestroyQA', 'deployProjectToQA'])

task deploy2Full (dependsOn: ['deployAndDestroyFull', 'deployProjectToFull'])

task deploy2Training (dependsOn: ['deployAndDestroyTraining',
'deployProjectToTraining'])

task deploy2Prod (dependsOn: ['deployAndDestroyProd', 'deployProjectToProd'])
```

The Salesforce Data Loader is a frontend for the Bulk API, used to retrieve and load large volumes of Salesforce records. There is a GUI for the Data Loader, but it can also be executed from the command line if you're on Windows, making it an excellent companion to the Ant Migration Tool.

There are some other tools that have been written to support the Salesforce development lifecycle such as Solenopsis[6] and Force-Dev-Tool,[7] but they are not as commonly used as the tools mentioned earlier.

If you're inheriting existing scripts, expect to see these ones I've mentioned. If you're getting started from scratch, focus on the following tools.

---

[6]https://github.com/solenopsis/Solenopsis
[7]https://github.com/amtrack/force-dev-tool

Salesforce CLI

The Salesforce CLI is one of the flagship innovations of Salesforce DX. The Salesforce CLI is a unified wrapper around the Salesforce APIs that adds sophisticated capabilities for managing the Salesforce software development lifecycle. Its capabilities are extensive and growing, but here is a subset of some of the most notable:

- All the new capabilities of Salesforce DX are available through this tool; no new capabilities are being added to the Ant Migration Tool, which is scheduled for deprecation this year.

- It securely manages credentials for all the orgs you need to access.

- It provides concise commands for creating and managing scratch orgs, packages, and projects.

- It automatically converts metadata from the native Metadata API format to the more usable "Source format."

- It tracks the metadata in target orgs to allow quick synchronization of changes between source and the org.

- It provides convenient commands to execute queries, anonymous Apex, data loads, and more.

- It provides access to the Bulk API for data retrieval and loading.

- It supports the development of plugins.

- It allows for command output to be formatted as JSON which makes it easier to parse and chain commands.

The Salesforce CLI is now based on a generic CLI engine called OCLIF, the Open CLI Framework, which itself is based on the Heroku CLI. OCLIF is still relatively new, but it provides a mechanism to build custom CLI tools in Node.js that can support plugins and auto-updating, among other capabilities.

There are many reasons why Node.js makes a compelling foundation for writing the Salesforce CLI. First, JavaScript is now the dominant language used by both professional and amateur developers[8]; Node.js allows you to write backend code such as web servers and CLIs using JavaScript. Second, the Node package manager (NPM)

---

[8]https://insights.stackoverflow.com/survey/2018/#technology

provides the world's largest collection of reusable software modules. Finally, JavaScript is already familiar to Salesforce developers who build Lightning Components or client-side JavaScript. VS Code and its extensions are also written in JavaScript (technically, TypeScript), which allows developers to use the same tools and libraries for both.

Creating Salesforce CLI Plugins

The Salesforce CLI allows you to build or install plugins that contribute new functionalities and take advantage of the many capabilities that the CLI offers. As Salesforce did in so many other areas, they have made the CLI into a platform that allows teams to build custom tools and lets ISVs and open source contributors build and share powerful add-on capabilities.

From the beginning, the Salesforce CLI was designed with plugins in mind. The standard Salesforce commands all exist in the force:... namespace to ensure that plugins could offer commands like sfdx acme:org:list without interfering with standard commands like sfdx force:org:list.

Salesforce now offers an official Salesforce CLI Plug-In Developer Guide[9] that provides instructions on how to build plugins. OCLIF, mentioned earlier, provides a generic foundation for building CLI tools that handles much of the complexity associated with building a command-line toolbelt. OCLIF enabled capabilities like accepting parameters, auto-updating, and more. Salesforce CLI plugins go further by giving developers access to many of the same libraries, parameters, and data used in the Salesforce CLI itself.

Plugins are developed in JavaScript or TypeScript and can make use of NPM libraries like @salesforce/core and @salesforce/command to handle org authentication and other actions. The Salesforce CLI handles parameters, logging, JSON output, and most of the other "boilerplate" activities, so you can focus on building the commands you need.

This is a growing area of development. One of the most promising capabilities is the possibility of creating "hooks"[10] into standard Salesforce commands. While not possible as of this writing, hooks would allow a plugin to execute code before or after standard Salesforce CLI commands are run. Imagine running a command sfdx force:org:create to create a scratch org and having a plugin automatically notify your project management

---

[9]https://developer.salesforce.com/docs/atlas.en-us.sfdx_cli_plugins.meta/sfdx_cli_
plugins/cli_plugins.htm
[10]https://developer.salesforce.com/blogs/2018/04/developing-plugins-for-the-
salesforce-cli.html

tool that you now have a new environment. The possibilities are vast, and Salesforce is working on the foundation to enable secure, signed plugins that can be distributed and executed in a trusted fashion.

Free Salesforce Tools

The Salesforce CLI is an officially supported command-line tool managed by the Salesforce DX team. There are also many free scripts or CLI tools that you might find helpful. Some, like force-dev-tool, have been around for many years. Some like SFDX-falcon are much newer. And some like CumulusCI are actually supported by teams within Salesforce.

This is an ever-changing field, and I don't have deep familiarity with most of these tools, but some of the best known are listed here for your benefit.

CumulusCI[11] is probably the best developed of these tools, but is unfortunately not very well known. This project is managed by the Salesforce.org team who produces the nonprofit success pack and other nonprofit resources. Over the course of several years, they have built a highly sophisticated set of tools in Python to automate many aspects of release management. They've even built tools based on the Robot Framework to make it easier to perform Selenium UI testing on Salesforce.

SFDX-Falcon[12] has become well known from the Salesforce DX Trailblazer Community as one of the first full project templates for Salesforce DX. The tool is optimized to help ISVs build managed packages and has evolved from simple Bash scripts to being a full Salesforce CLI plugin.

Force-dev-tool[13] was one of the earlier CLI tools to help with Salesforce development. It's now in "reduced maintenance" mode, since the Salesforce CLI was launched, but still receives updates occasionally. Appirio DX makes use of this project behind the scenes to aid with parsing and managing Salesforce's XML metadata.

The Salesforce Toolkit[14] created by Ben Edwards is a nicely designed group of tools to help with common Salesforce challenges such as comparing org permissions. The project is no longer maintained, but the apps are still fully functional and run on Heroku. The source code is available so that they can also be forked and a private and trusted instance can be created within your own company.

---

[11]https://github.com/SFDO-Tooling/CumulusCI
[12]https://sfdx-isv.github.io/sfdx-falcon/
[13]https://github.com/amtrack/force-dev-tool#readme
[14]https://cloudtoolkit.co/

These community-contributed tools are all works of love from their developers and maintainers. Some now suffer from neglect, and I'm sure I've overlooked many others, but many of these free tools provide powerful and effective solutions to development and release management challenges.

Using package.json to Store Command Snippets

Despite my droning on about the benefits of command-line tools, no one actually likes to remember complex sequences of commands and parameters. Command-line instructions allow for infinite flexibility and combinations and are a lifesaver in solving complex challenges. But once you've invested 5 minutes (or 5 hours) getting a sequence of commands just right, you should **save that somewhere** so you and others can reuse it.

If you don't already have strong opinions about where to save such commands, do the following:

1. Install Node.js (which comes with npm).

2. In your project folder, run `npm init` to initialize a new project.

3. Unless you have ambitious plans to actually write code in Node.js, just accept the defaults. This will create a file called `package.json` in your project directory.

4. Edit that file, ignoring everything except for the `scripts` section. Begin to curate the `scripts` section so that it contains a helpful collection of common commands.

For example, the Trailhead Sample App `lwc-recipes`[15] contains a `package.json` file with the `scripts` block shown in Listing 9-5. The five "scripts" shown here are actually just command-line sequences. To run any of them, just execute `npm run scriptname` (e.g., `npm run lint`) from a terminal prompt anywhere inside that project folder. There are numerous benefits of defining scripts in a `package.json` in this way:

1. They are stored in version control and shared with the team.

2. They can be run easily using `npm run ...`

3. They always run from within the project root folder, no matter which folder you have navigated to in the terminal.

---

[15]https://github.com/trailheadapps/lwc-recipes

4. You can chain these commands, for example, the `lint` script in turn calls `lint:lwc` and `lint:aura`.

5. You can pass parameters to these commands. After the name of the script, append `--` followed by any parameters you want to pass through. For example, running `npm run test:unit -- --watch` will pass `--watch` as a parameter, which is equivalent to `lwc-jest --watch`.

Listing 9-5. The scripts section from a package.json file, showing some common script commands

```
"scripts": {
    "lint": "npm run lint:lwc && npm run lint:aura",
    "lint:lwc": "eslint */lwc/**",
    "lint:aura": "sfdx force:lightning:lint force-app/main/default/
    aura --exit",
    "test": "npm run lint && npm run test:unit",
    "test:unit": "lwc-jest",
    ...
},
```

Other Scripting Techniques

When writing scripts, it is important to have a way to parse the outputs from each command, so that they can be passed as inputs to subsequent commands. The most straightforward way to start scripting using the Salesforce CLI is to pass the `--json` parameter to each command and then to parse their output using the lightweight JSON parsing utility `jq`.[16] JQ allows you to read, query, and transform JSON output.

Andrew Fawcett wrote a helpful blog post of the different methods to build scripting around Salesforce DX.[17] Restating some of the points he shared there, piping the output of a Salesforce DX command into jq provides a formatted output as shown in Listing 9-6, which you can then refine further with queries and filters as shown in Listings 9-7 and 9-8.

---

[16]`https://stedolan.github.io/jq/`
[17]`https://andyinthecloud.com/2019/02/10/salesforce-dx-integration-strategies/`

Listing 9-6. Simply piping sfdx JSON output into jq provides a nicely formatted output

```
$ sfdx force:config:list --json | jq
{
  "status": 0,
  "result": [
    {
      "key": "defaultdevhubusername",
      "location": "Local",
      "value": "MyDevHub"
    },
    {
      "key": "defaultusername",
      "location": "Local",
      "value": "test-v1asf98g72x5@example.com"
    }
  ]
}
```

Listing 9-7. JQ allows you to go further by querying the results

```
$ sfdx force:config:list --json | jq '.result[0]'
{
  "key": "defaultdevhubusername",
  "location": "Local",
  "value": "MyDevHub"
}
```

Listing 9-8. JQ provides many sophisticated filtering options

```
$ sfdx force:config:list --json |
    jq '.result[] | select(.key == "defaultdevhubusername").value'

"MyDevHub"
```

You can then stitch together complex sequences of commands using Bash scripts and variables. Listing 9-9 shows us querying the alias of our default Dev Hub and saving the result in a variable DEFAULT_DEVHUB. We then use this variable as the targetusername for a SOQL query that simply lists the top ten creators of scratch orgs in that Dev Hub.

Listing 9-9. This runs a simple query to show which users have created the most scratch orgs on our default Dev Hub. Bash allows commands to be strung together easily. Note the use of \ to allow commands to span multiple lines

```bash
#!/bin/bash
DEFAULT_DEVHUB=$(sfdx force:config:list --json | \
    jq --raw-output '.result[] | select(.key == "defaultdevhubusername").
    value')

sfdx force:data:soql:query --query \
  'SELECT CreatedBy.Name, Count(Id) FROM ScratchOrgInfo
   GROUP BY CreatedBy.Name
   ORDER BY Count(Id) DESC
   LIMIT 10' \
  --targetusername $DEFAULT_DEVHUB
```

Bash scripts and JQ can take you a long way down the path of custom scripting. But for full control over the process, you may want to move to using Node.js or another programming language. Node.js is particularly convenient for scripting Salesforce DX, since you can more easily dig into the Salesforce DX internals if needed.

If you're using Node.js, you can also take advantage of the Salesforce Core API (https://forcedotcom.github.io/sfdx-core/). The Salesforce Core API is not a standard REST or SOAP API. Rather it's a public API for accessing Salesforce DX functionality programmatically from your local system. It contains a wide variety of commands, but we've most commonly used it to access and run commands against the Salesforce orgs that have been authorized by the user. This means that users can securely authorize orgs one time, and then your scripts can make calls to Salesforce Core to access and perform commands against those orgs.

Salesforce Core is helpful, but doesn't make all of the Salesforce CLI commands available in Node. My colleague, Bryan Leboff, wrote an NPM module sfdx-node[18] as a wrapper around the Salesforce CLI. You can use this command to access Salesforce CLI commands directly from your Node.js code. In Listing 9-10, we pass a configuration object into sfdx.auth.webLogin({...}). This is the equivalent of running sfdx force:auth:web:login --setdefaultdevhubusername ... from the command line to authorize a new org.

Listing 9-10. This Node.js code snippet makes use of both the official salesforce/core module and the unofficial sfdx-node module to authorize an org

```
const { SfdxProjectJson, Org } = require('@salesforce/core');
const sfdx = require('sfdx-node');

const authWeb = async (destination, isDevHub) => {
  if (!isDevHub) {
    try {
      const orgObj = await Org.create(destination);
      return orgObj;
    } catch (e) {
      // Do nothing
    }
  }
  return sfdx.auth.webLogin({
    setdefaultdevhubusername: isDevHub,
    setalias: destination,
  });
};

module.exports = {
  authWeb,
};
```

---

[18]www.npmjs.com/package/sfdx-node

Writing scripts in this way is very powerful since you can use the rich, expressive syntax of JavaScript, choose from any of the 800,000 NPM modules that might assist with common challenges, and mix in Salesforce DX commands to accomplish any build process you might require. Such scripting takes time and experimentation to build, but it can be created and refined gradually as your processes evolve.

Commercial Salesforce Tools

Build vs. buy is a classic decision. Salesforce DX has been made freely available "as a downpayment on our debt to developers" in the words of Jim Wunderlich from Salesforce.[19] However the Salesforce DX team is focused on building the underlying capabilities rather than solving every common use case. For example, they have not thus far released an admin-friendly user interface for managing the development lifecycle.

There are many commercial vendors who have built tools to help with the Salesforce release management process. Most of these tools were built before Salesforce DX was released, however, and so still emphasize the org-based workflow of selecting, retrieving, and deploying individual pieces of metadata. They also emphasize a click-based workflow, similar to Salesforce's declarative tools.

These tools greatly reduce the pain of org-based deployments and may provide benefit for your team. But the movement to Salesforce DX is a deep shift, so I would encourage you to focus on achieving the goal of real source-based development and use these tools to help your adoption of Salesforce DX, rather than just reducing the pain of org-based development.

One caveat for using any of these commercial tools. I've seen numerous companies adopt these tools, but attempt to limit costs by limiting the number of users who are given licenses. The goal of your DevOps processes should be to empower developers and remove bottlenecks in your process while at the same time establishing traceability and automated testing. Having a small number of users use a commercial tool to deploy the work of a larger development team will save license costs, but at the expense of making the entire process less efficient. If you choose to use a commercial tool, be generous in equipping all of your developers and admins to make use of it.

---

[19]www.salesforce.com/video/317311/

Appirio DX

Full disclosure: I'm the original architect and product manager for Appirio DX, and DiXie (Figure 9-1) was drawn by my wife :-)

Figure 9-1. *Appirio DX's mascot, DiXie*

Appirio DX is a suite of tools that Appirio developed to help their consultants and customers develop and deliver Salesforce more effectively. Appirio has been one of the top Salesforce consulting partners since its inception in 2006. In 2019, Appirio DX was made available as a commercial product.

Appirio DX aims to make CI/CD and Salesforce DX easier to adopt. It is similar to Salesforce DX in that it includes a CLI that can be run locally or as part of an automated job. It removes or reduces the need for teams to write custom Salesforce DX scripts, by providing commands and project templates for scenarios like initializing scratch orgs and publishing package versions.

Appirio DX includes a desktop app that allows click-based developers to work with Git branches, create scratch orgs, and synchronize changes from those orgs back into version control. The desktop app also eases the installation and configuration of developer-focused tools like Git and VS Code and provides capabilities like setting and toggling proxy settings across these tools.

Appirio DX provides an instance of GitLab and SonarQube that customers can use if they don't want to provide their own DevOps stack. But the tools will run on any CI platform, and you can supplement the workflow with your own command-line tools.

Appirio DX's CI/CD process is defined using whatever config files are standard for that CI platform, such as `.gitlab-ci.yml` or `bitbucket-pipelines.yml` files. As a result, the process is set up and managed in the same way that a pure-code solution would be, and is not obscured behind a GUI. For those who are comfortable with developer tooling, this gives them visibility and the flexibility to bring their own tools. But those more accustomed to click-based GUIs may find this daunting.

For teams using GitLab as their CI engine, Appirio DX can set up and configure the complete CI/CD pipeline for you in minutes. As of this writing, other CI engines have to be set up manually, but the process is straightforward. Appirio DX offers a Docker image `appirio/dx` that provides a consistent, predefined execution environment in any of the CI tools that support running jobs in Docker.

For teams wanting the control and visibility that other DevOps tools provide, Appirio DX provides a readymade solution that allows you to get started quickly with Salesforce DX.

Released: 2018

Architecture: Node.js and Docker, bring your own CI servers, or use Appirio DX's GitLab

Benefits:

- Similar to CI/CD tools on other technologies

- GitLab provided, but works with any Git-based version control host

- GitLab CI provided, but works with any CI server

- SonarQube static analysis provided, but allows the use of any third-party tools

- Three development modes:

  - CI/CD using the pre-SFDX Metadata API format

  - SFDX package development process

  - SFDX Org development process

- Includes an admin-friendly UI for syncing scratch org changes to Git

- A good fit for professional developers or DevOps specialists

Disadvantages:

- Click-friendly capabilities are limited.

- Feature set is limited compared to some of the more mature Salesforce RM tools.

- Not a SaaS product (like Salesforce DX, some parts of Appirio DX run on the desktop). Software can be installed and configured automatically, but IT security restrictions might limit what tools can be installed.

AutoRABIT

AutoRABIT provides a SaaS-based suite of tools that allows companies to manage the complexities of the Salesforce release management process. One of their biggest customers is Schneider Electric, which is one of the world's largest Salesforce tenants. AutoRABIT claims over 40 *Fortune* 500 customers, including 20 in the highly regulated finance and healthcare industries. If needed, AutoRABIT can be deployed behind corporate firewalls as an on-premise solution to satisfy corporate security and compliance policies.

AutoRABIT allows users to connect multiple orgs, capture metadata differences, and deploy those differences between orgs. They also support Salesforce DX capabilities like creating scratch orgs. They have a powerful data loader that can be used to deploy large volumes of data between orgs while preserving relationships. They have built-in Selenium integration, including the ability to use Selenium to change org settings as part of a deployment process. AutoRABIT acts as the CI engine that allows teams to customize and orchestrate these processes according to their specific needs.

AutoRABIT has recently added a data backup and recovery solution, Vault, to their product suite. Vault automates the capabilities of AutoRABIT's Data Loader Pro to make ongoing incremental backups of production orgs and sandboxes and to allow data recovery that preserves references across objects. Vault backs up both data and metadata, including Chatter messages and attachments, and provides unlimited storage. This backup data can also be used to seed test environments, using a data masking capability to maintain the security and privacy of user data.

AutoRABIT has a large range of capabilities, and their professional services team can integrate with most other third-party tools (such as Jira, CheckMarx, and test automation tools). They also offer a managed services option for ongoing support.

Common user complaints are that the UI is slow and inflexible. Their metadata picker doesn't have the sorting and filtering capabilities of Copado or Gearset, which makes manually selecting metadata a more tedious process.

AutoRABIT implementations take more time to provision (typically a month) and also require their professional services team to be involved (professional services hours are bundled with the up-front installation costs). Contrast this with Copado or Flosum, which are downloadable from the AppExchange, or with ClickDeploy, which provides easy OAuth-based single sign-on from your Salesforce org. This implies more lead time and commitment from customers wishing to implement AutoRABIT, although the learning curve on the tool is not necessarily steeper than most of the other commercial tools.

Released: 2014

Architecture: Built on OpenStack using Java

Benefits:

- SaaS-based, on public or private clouds. They also offer an on-premise option.

- Hierarchical data migration (DataLoader Pro).

- Several prebuilt integrations into common tools (Jira, CheckMarx, test automation tools, etc.).

Disadvantages:

- Takes a long time to install and train users.

- Clumsy metadata picker.

- UI can't be customized.

Blue Canvas

Blue Canvas is another newer release management tool for Salesforce. Blue Canvas uses Git and Salesforce DX behind the scenes while providing a simple user interface for authenticating to orgs and managing deployments between them.

At the heart of Blue Canvas is a system to take regular metadata snapshots of connected orgs and record changes in Git, along with the user who made that change. This allows you to use Git as a type of setup audit trail that provides more detail on the nature of each change compared to Salesforce's built-in audit trail. This is what my colleague, Kyle Bowerman, referred to as "defensive version control": passively tracking changes made through the admin interface. Blue Canvas also supports "offensive version control," where changes tracked in version control are automatically deployed to further environments.

Based on this underlying Git tracking, Blue Canvas allows you to compare the metadata in any two orgs. Once the comparison has been made, you can select metadata in your source org that you want to deploy to the target org. Blue Canvas will check for merge conflicts and run a validation to ensure that changes can be deployed. These deployment requests can then be grouped into a larger release and be released at once.

Blue Canvas also allows you to connect external Git repositories like GitHub so that you can mirror the Blue Canvas repository into those.

Blue Canvas is still relatively early in their development. They recently added the capability to run Provar tests after deployments. Provar is a Salesforce-specific tool for doing UI testing that allows you to perform regression testing to ensure that your deployment has not broken functionality. They plan to allow for a wider variety of postdeploy actions to be run.

Released: 2016

Architecture: AWS, Auth0, Go, Git, Salesforce DX

Benefits:

- Git is built in to the tool, providing fast metadata comparisons and deployments.

- Changes are tracked in Git in near real time and specify who made the change.

Disadvantages:

- Blue Canvas doesn't currently track profiles or permission sets in their main tool, although they provide a very nice free tool to compare and deploy permissions.

- No support for data migrations or Selenium-driven manual setup steps.

ClickDeploy

ClickDeploy is one of the newest of the commercial release management tools and one of the easiest to get started with. ClickDeploy is truly SaaS hosted in that there are no downloadable tools and no managed packages to install in your org. They also offer a free tier that allows up to 15 deploys per month, enough to serve a small customer or do a POC. You can use your existing Salesforce credentials to sign in to ClickDeploy and use OAuth to connect to any number of Salesforce orgs.

For those with simpler release management needs, ClickDeploy provides an easy and superior alternative to change sets. You can connect to your source org, easily sort, filter, and select metadata, and then deploy it to one or more target orgs. ClickDeploy can be used to support multiple production orgs, something that is not possible with change sets.

As teams mature, they can upgrade to the Pro version which provides unlimited deployments and the ability to collaborate as a team. Team collaboration is fairly basic as of this writing. Every user associated with the same production org is grouped together into a team. Members of a team can collaborate around deployments, viewing, cloning, modifying, validating, or executing a deployment. This provides team-level visibility into the history of deployments.

ClickDeploy's Enterprise version allows teams to collaborate using version control. You can connect to all the common Git hosting providers to track the evolution of metadata across your orgs. ClickDeploy provides a Salesforce-aware frontend for Git to allow users to select metadata and commit it to a repository. You can compare metadata between Git and a Salesforce org, and you can deploy metadata directly from the code repository. Deployments can be based on the complete metadata in a branch, differences between two branches, or an arbitrary subset of metadata from that branch.

Git support enables several capabilities. First, ClickDeploy allows you to build a scheduled backup of your orgs to a Git repository. Importantly, you can customize the metadata that is included in this backup. Incremental metadata changes will then be recorded as Git commits each time the backup job runs. The other capability this enables is to automate deployments from Git based on a schedule, or each time a commit is pushed to the repository. This allows for continuous delivery without the need for a separate CI tool.

ClickDeploy supports the Salesforce DX source format and can retrieve or deploy metadata from or to scratch orgs. As of this writing, they do not support the creation of scratch orgs or package versions.

The user interface is simple to understand and use and provides the essential tools needed to manage deployments.

Released: 2017

Architecture: AWS

Benefits:

- Easy to get started with
- Free tier
- Nice metadata selection capabilities
- Metadata comparisons (org-to-org, org-to-Git, Git-to-org, Git branch-to-branch)
- Git integration, including an admin-friendly UI to make commits, and automated deployments from version control

Disadvantages:

- Doesn't automate scratch org or package creation.
- No data migration tools.
- No support for Selenium testing or UI automation.
- Team access controls are somewhat limited.

Copado

Full disclosure: I'm currently a product manager for Copado.

Copado was founded in 2013 by two European Salesforce release managers based in Madrid, Spain, to ease the pain, complexity, and risk of the Salesforce deployment process. Since then they have retained growth capital from Salesforce Ventures and Insight Ventures, attracted over 150 global customers, and brought on a seasoned US senior leadership team to build their US business.

Copado uses Salesforce as its user interface, for authentication, and to store data on orgs, metadata, and deployments. But (unlike Flosum) it delegates backend processing to Heroku. That allows Copado to leverage Heroku's power and speed to handle metadata retrieval, processing, and deployments. This architecture allows customers to customize aspects of the Copado frontend and tap into its data and business logic in Salesforce.

Interestingly, Copado doesn't store any data on Heroku; instead Heroku dynos are created on an as-needed basis to perform metadata operations. Information about that metadata (is that called "meta-metadata"?) is then stored in Salesforce. While Copado boasts that this eases security reviews since dynos are never persisted, it also has a startup cost. If Heroku is being used to deploy metadata from a code repository, it has to clone that metadata first. If a deployment is being made based on org metadata, the metadata is never cached in Heroku; it has to be retrieved each time. This leads to some performance cost for each job. Copado claims to have optimized this process, fetching only the minimal amount of history to enable the merge.

Unlike most competing tools, Copado includes its own Salesforce-based ALM (Application Lifecycle Management) tools for creating stories, bugs, and so on. This allows metadata changes to be associated with particular features or bugs in the ALM tool and for deployments to be made at a feature-level granularity. This is somewhat similar to GitHub issues, GitLab issues, or Jira-Bitbucket integration, where each Jira issue can show which commits made reference to it. Copado includes native integration with Jira, Azure Devops, VersionOne, and Rally to sync stories from existing ALM tools and update their status.

Copado offers a Selenium recorder that simplifies the creation of UI tests. It hosts the Selenium tool in Heroku and can orchestrate functional testing as part of their quality gates. The Selenium scripts can even be used to automate "manual" setup steps in an org. Copado also offers a compliance tool to ensure that excessive permissions are not deployed as part of the release process. Companies can write their own rules to match their policies.

Copado is priced on a per user per month basis with two levels of licensing: one for developers and the other for release managers. Additional CI functionality is currently tied to a Branch Management license. The Selenium Test and Compliance Hub products are also licensed separately. Copado uses a credit system, similar to Salesforce governor limits, to enforce a "fair usage" policy. Copado claims that in practice customers never hit these limits, but these ensure that usage remains proportional to the number of licenses purchased.

Released: 2013

Architecture: Salesforce with Heroku as a processing engine

Benefits:

- Nice metadata picker

- A good choice for those already using Salesforce itself to manage their Salesforce development

- Rich suite of tools, including ALM, data migrations, and Selenium testing

Disadvantages:

- All logs and other files are stored as attachments in the Salesforce package, making them hard to read.

- The UI is built on Salesforce and looks slightly awkward. For example, notifications about job results are not very obvious.

- Jobs are run on Heroku but not stored on Heroku. This means that each job takes a nontrivial amount of time to start (such as cloning the repository).

Flosum

Flosum is a release management app for Salesforce that is built entirely on the Salesforce core platform. They have the highest number of positive reviews among release management tools on the AppExchange.

One benefit that Flosum derives from being built on Salesforce is that no additional security reviews are required in companies that take a long time to whitelist new software.

Flosum claims that their tool allows people to add custom automation such as approval processes using familiar Salesforce tools. But since Flosum doesn't live in your main production org, it won't have access to integrate with your users and data. So any automation you build on top of Flosum will be disconnected from the rest of your business processes.

Based on increasing demands from customers to support version control and CI/CD, Flosum has built basic version control and CI/CD capabilities into their tool. They've also built an integration with Git. But because all of these capabilities are built using native Apex, they are very slow compared to other tools.

Flosum has done an impressive job of building version control, metadata management, and CI/CD capabilities on the Salesforce platform. Their choice of architecture greatly limits their speed and ability to integrate third-party tools, but they have many satisfied customers and provide a vastly superior alternative to change sets.

Released: 2014

Architecture: Built on Salesforce

Benefits:

- Business logic can be customized using Salesforce mechanisms.

- Built on Salesforce, so no additional platforms to pass through security review.

Disadvantages:

- Large operations are very slow.

- Expensive.

- Can't integrate standard DevOps tools.

Gearset

Gearset is a UK-based company founded by Redgate Software. Their Salesforce release management product is based on Redgate's experience building release management tools for SQL Server, .NET, and Oracle.[20] Their aim has been to emphasize ease of use to allow users of all technical backgrounds to adopt modern DevOps best practices.

Gearset is a SaaS tool that provides a full array of release management and DevOps capabilities. Their enterprise customers include McKesson, IBM, and even Salesforce themselves. They have a fast and easy-to-navigate user interface, allowing quick selection of the metadata to deploy and making it easy to build up more complex deployments including changes to things like profiles and permission sets.

Gearset has built intelligence into their comparison engine to automatically fix common deployment issues like missing dependencies or obsolete flows, before pushing your changes to Salesforce. This means deployments with Gearset are more likely to work the first time, avoiding the time-consuming iteration cycle of fixing failed deployments.

This intelligent comparison engine is used for manual deployments, as well as automated deployments triggered from CI jobs. This means a higher deployment success rate and less time spent iterating and fixing repetitive deployment failures.

Gearset's Pro tier offers a drop-in replacement for change sets and is ideal for admins and low-code developers. Connect any number and type of orgs, compare them to see a detailed breakdown of their differences, explore dependencies between metadata components and automatically include them in your deployment, and finally push your

---

[20]https://gearset.com/about

changes between orgs. Gearset integrates with all of the major Git hosting providers and allows you to connect to any Git repo, making it easy to run comparisons and deployments with Git branches, just as you would with orgs.

For larger teams, the Enterprise tier includes a variety of automation features, including org monitoring to alert you to any changes made to your orgs, and scheduled metadata backup. Gearset also comes with built-in continuous integration to monitor Git branches and push any detected changes to your orgs. Finally, Gearset offers a data deployment feature, making it easy to deploy hierarchical data between orgs, preserving any relationships.

Gearset's pricing is per user, allowing you to connect as many orgs as you like and run unlimited comparisons and deployments. Support is included in the price. Interestingly, Gearset doesn't have a distinct support team, so questions and issues are managed by the Gearset development team itself, likely yielding higher-quality initial responses.

Released: 2016

Architecture: .NET and C# on AWS

Benefits:

- Nice UI.

- Quick navigation of metadata.

- Metadata comparisons (org-to-org, org-to-git, git-to-org, git branch-to-branch).

- Comparison engine automatically fixes common deployment errors.

- SaaS-based.

- Git integration with an admin-friendly UI, allowing admins and developers to all work from version control together.

- Full Salesforce DX support, including scratch org creation.

- Hierarchical data migration.

Disadvantages:

- No support for Selenium testing or UI automation.

- UI can't be customized.

- Can't mix in third-party DevOps tools.

Metazoa Snapshot

Snapshot is a desktop-based change and release management tool for Salesforce. It was first launched by DreamFactory in 2006, but the makers of Snapshot spun it off under a separate company, Metazoa, in 2018.

Snapshot is written in Visual C++ and runs as a desktop app. The user interface looks extremely dated, but it runs on Mac or Windows and has been updated recently to include some Salesforce DX capabilities.

Snapshot is built around the concept of visual workspaces. Each workspace allows the user to arrange snapshots (metadata retrieved from an org) and projects (local folders containing metadata) graphically. Those snapshots and projects can then be connected to build out a pipeline view that flows from development to testing to production. This pipeline automatically batches metadata retrieval and deployment, allowing it to bypass the 10,000 metadata item limits of the Metadata API.

Each snapshot or project allows you to perform actions on it by right-clicking and selecting from the menu. Actions typically involve running reports on that org, and Snapshot boasts over 40 reports that can be run, such as "generate a data dictionary."

The connections between snapshots/projects enable actions such as doing comparisons, deployments, or rollbacks. Chaining together snapshot connections from development to production allows for continuous delivery, where changes can be deployed from org to org in an automated way. Snapshot also provides support for connecting to code repositories including Git, SVN, and TFS.

Snapshot runs on the user's desktop, but allows users to synchronize workspaces with other team members. For security purposes, org credentials are not stored online or shared between team members. Admins can enforce controls on the activities of other Metazoa users, for example, enforcing code quality gateways on deployments.

Snapshot also supports extracting and loading data while keeping complex data relationships intact. It can scramble data fields, making it useful for seeding new sandboxes while scrubbing sensitive data.

In short, Snapshot provides a versatile, admin-friendly toolkit with many commands and reports that are not present in competing tools. Despite the "retro" user interface, the underlying capabilities are robust and powerful.

Released: 2006

Architecture: Desktop app written in Visual C++

Benefits:

- Quick to download, install, and experiment with

- Allows management of multiple orgs

- Contains many reports that are not present in competing products

- Supports Salesforce DX metadata format

- Works relatively quickly (limited by the speed of your local machine and the Salesforce APIs)

Disadvantages:

- Old-looking UI

- Doesn't automate the scratch org or package creation process

- Not cloud-based, but configuration can be synced across teams

Packaging

Modular architecture is an important software architecture pattern that helps make applications more manageable and easier to understand. Packaging is a form of modular architecture that allows you to develop and deploy code and configuration in discrete bundles. That makes software development and delivery far easier. As mentioned earlier, packaging is a critical part of Salesforce DX and provides a superior method to manage deployments.

Classic Packaging

For completeness, we'll briefly discuss classic packaging. But if you're looking for a quick recommendation on how to build Salesforce packages, skip to "Second-Generation Packaging" section.

Although Developer Edition orgs have no sandboxes and thus can't make use of change sets, all orgs are able to create packages. Until the recent release of unlocked packages, the main audience for package-based deployments were ISVs producing apps for the AppExchange. The Salesforce AppExchange is a business "app store" which provides over 5,000 Salesforce apps, 40% of which are free.[21] The vast majority of these apps are actually managed or unmanaged packages.

Unmanaged packages and classic managed packages are actually based on the same technology as change sets and have a similar user interface for building them. You begin by giving a name and description for the package and then proceed to creating your first version of the package by adding metadata to it. Package versions are named and numbered, and you can set a password to prevent unauthorized individuals from installing this metadata. In the case of unmanaged packages, you can optionally link release notes and post-installation instructions and specify required dependencies in the target org such as enabled features and object-level configuration like record types.

Once a package version is uploaded, it is given a unique 04t ID and is thus available for installation into any org. If the package is published on the AppExchange, you can then make this package version available using the AppExchange publisher tools.

One significant limitation of unmanaged packages compared to the other three types of packaging is that once an unmanaged package is installed, its metadata is no longer associated with that package. It is as if the unmanaged package is a cardboard shipping container that is discarded after opening. This makes them useful for deployment, but not at all useful for modularizing your code architecture.

Classic managed packages are similar to unmanaged packages in most ways, but require the use of a namespace which is prepended onto metadata names like myMgdPkg__ packageContents__c. Partly for this reason, managed packages must be developed and published from a Developer Edition org. The major benefits of managed packages are that

- Package components such as custom code cannot be inspected in the org in which they're installed, which helps to protect the intellectual property of the publisher.

- Managed packages are upgradeable.

- Package components remain associated with the source package.

- Components are distinguished by their namespace.

- Package metadata has its own set of governor limits above and beyond those in the installation org.

---

[21]https://appexchange.salesforce.com/appxContentListingDetail?listingId=aON3A00000F HBPkUAP

For these reasons, commercial AppExchange apps are almost always managed packages, while free AppExchange apps are almost always unmanaged packages. Unmanaged packages are far easier to create, but don't obscure their contents or allow for upgrading. That makes them far simpler to maintain, but also harder to build a business around.

Managed package development requires an additional layer of sophistication, one which I'm not well qualified to comment on. In my view, managed package development is a dark art, but there are many thriving ISVs who have successfully navigated the challenges in building, upgrading, and supporting managed packages. See the Salesforce developer documentation on managed packages and Andrew Fawcett's excellent Force. com *Enterprise Architecture*[22] for more detailed discussion on their development.

Unlike change sets, which give you the *option* to include dependencies, unmanaged and classic managed packages *automatically* add dependencies to the package metadata. This is because packages by definition need to be self-contained so they can be installed in any org. Change sets, by contrast, can only be installed in related sandboxes which necessarily share similar metadata. Excluding dependent metadata from a change set limits the scope of changes (the blast radius) and means that change sets don't automatically upload the latest version of all dependencies from the development sandbox.

Second-Generation Packaging

Salesforce DX brought a new type of packages, sometimes called second-generation packages. Whereas unmanaged packages and classic managed packages are artifacts created from org-based development, this new type of packaging is designed for source-driven development. Unlocked packages are a type of second-generation package that are well suited to enterprise development (building and migrating functionality for use within a single enterprise). Second-generation managed packages are intended to be the successor to classic managed packages and are intended to simplify the development process for managed packages.

Second-generation package publishing is a key part of the Salesforce DX workflow, and we've already discussed "Branching for Package Publishing" and "CI Jobs for Package Publishing" in Chapter 7: The Delivery Pipeline. The concepts are similar to

---

[22]Andrew Fawcett. 2014. *Force.Com Enterprise Architecture*. Packt Publishing.

the concepts for managed and unmanaged packages, but second-generation packages are defined using configuration files, published using the Salesforce CLI, and can easily express dependencies on other packages as well as org-level features and settings.

Unlocked packages are discussed implicitly and explicitly throughout this book, since our main focus is Salesforce DX development for the enterprise. A major improvement over unmanaged packages is that metadata remains associated with the unlocked package that included it, and that package deployments cannot overwrite metadata that is included in another package.

One of the trickiest aspects of classic managed package development is the use of namespaces, since each namespace is tightly bound to one and only one Developer Edition org. Salesforce DX now allows a single Dev Hub to be associated with multiple namespaces so that scratch orgs can be created that use any of those namespaces. Second-generation managed packages can now also be published to the AppExchange. It is a great relief that the enterprise workflow can now be united with the ISV workflow and Salesforce DX technology can be used similarly for both.

Unlocked Packages

Change sets, the Metadata API, and most of the commercial Salesforce release management tools are built around the concept of hand-selecting individual pieces of metadata and deploying them between different environments. Deploying unpackaged metadata in this way has many disadvantages. First, it puts the burden on the person doing the deployment to ensure that they are not including too much or too little metadata. Second, combining metadata from multiple developers requires some Salesforce-specific XML processing. Third, the process is error-prone, and it's hard to ensure that metadata is being deployed consistently across environments. The use of version control helps tremendously in this process, but still requires developers to pick through metadata changes to determine which changes to commit.

Imagine if deploying your Salesforce customizations were as easy as installing a new package from the AppExchange. Unlocked packages make this possible. These allow you to bundle customizations into one or more packages and install them automatically or manually.

Unlocked packages are stored on the Dev Hub. Thus a team building unlocked packages should collaborate on the same Dev Hub so that they can contribute to the same packages.

To build and publish unlocked packages:

1. First ensure that packaging is enabled in the Dev Hub.

2. Packages are basically a container for metadata. The `sfdx-project.json` file has a "packageDirectories" section that contains the configuration for each folder that will hold your package metadata. When you first create a Salesforce DX project using `sfdx force:project:create`, this file is initialized for you and contains a single `force-app` folder. Update this file if needed so that it points to the folder that holds your metadata.

3. Then create the package on your Dev Hub, specifying the name and definition of your package by executing `sfdx force:package:create` along with appropriate options. This step defines the package and gives it an ID that begins with 0Ho, but does not actually add any metadata to the package.

4. When this command completes, the `packageAliases` section is given a new alias pertaining to the newly created package, and the `packageDirectories` section is given a new object corresponding to the newly created package.

5. Having created the package, you can then begin creating package versions using `sfdx force:package:version:create` along with the appropriate options. These package versions encapsulate the metadata in the package folder so that it can then be installed in another org. The result of running this command is that the `packageAliases` section will be given a new entry containing the `04t` ID for the package version. That is the same ID that can be used to publish the package.

Initial package creation is a one-time process, but the package *version* publishing should be scripted as part of your CI process so that it will run every time the code in the master branch for that package is updated. If you're building branch versions of your package using the --branch flag, it's a good practice to automatically set that parameter based on the Git branch you're publishing from and to automatically add a Git tag to the repository when a new version is published, as described in Chapter 7: The Delivery Pipeline. This makes your Git repository a comprehensive reference to the version and change history of your packages. You can add other automation such as only publishing versions when a particular keyword such as "#publish" is included in the commit message.

Although there is a little bit of setup required, once built, this simultaneously makes your code architecture cleaner and deployments easier. By dividing your metadata into subfolders, the application's structure is made clear. By publishing package versions, you can then deploy updated versions to any org using a single ID, instead of trying to deal with hundreds or thousands of metadata files. There is no chance of including too much or too little metadata, and the results are identical with every installation.

Package Dependencies

Salesforce DX allows you to specify package dependencies on other packages (unlocked or managed) and on particular org configuration. Specifying such dependencies is one of the most important aspects of packaging. Refactoring metadata so that it can be built into unlocked packages is the single most challenging aspect of adopting Salesforce DX, but it is also the most beneficial. This topic is addressed in more detail in the section on "Packaging Code" in Chapter 5: Application Architecture.

Adding and Removing Metadata from Packages

Unlocked packages have a number of helpful characteristics that make it easier to adopt packaging gradually. First, these packages can take ownership of existing metadata. For example, imagine you have a custom object called MyObject__c in a particular org, and you then build a package version that contains MyObject__c. When you install that package in your org, it will take ownership of that custom object. The custom object will then display a notice (shown in Figure 9-2) that it is part of an unlocked package and that changes to it will be overwritten if the package is updated.

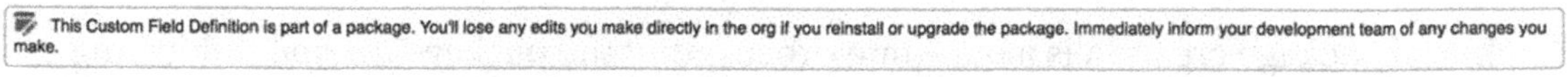

Figure 9-2. *When viewing metadata that is part of an unlocked package, users see an indication that the metadata is part of a package*

This behavior allows you to create small unlocked packages that can gradually subsume existing metadata and make it part of the package. There is no data loss or interruption to business logic when doing this. Although you can add a namespace to unlocked packages, doing so would prevent your package from taking ownership of existing metadata, since the API name of the packaged metadata would actually be myNamespace__MyObject__c and so wouldn't match the existing metadata.

Unfortunately, if you attempt to update that metadata using the Metadata API, you will not receive such a warning, so teams should put some additional automated checks in place to ensure that there is no overlap between the metadata in their various packages and their unpackaged metadata.

Similarly, it's also possible to remove metadata from unlocked packages, either because it's no longer needed or to move it to another package. Propagating metadata deletions has long been challenging in Salesforce. Deletions are not supported at all in change sets, and with the Metadata API, deletions need to be explicitly listed in a `destructivechanges.xml` file, which requires separate logic be built if tools want to automate the deletion process.

Metadata that is deleted from an unlocked package will be removed from the target org or marked as deprecated. In particular, metadata that contains data like custom fields or custom objects is not deleted, since that could cause data loss. Instead, this metadata is flagged as deprecated. This is a best practice recommended in the classic book *Refactoring Databases*.[23] This allows data to be preserved and copied over to new data structures. Care is needed however to update any integrations that point to the old data structures and to ensure that data is replicated between the old and new structures during that transition.

If you want to migrate metadata from one unlocked package to another, you can simply move the metadata files from one package to the other. Publish new versions of both packages. Then install the new version of the package that previously contained the metadata in your target org using the command `sfdx force:package:version:install --upgradetype DeprecateOnly` .... The `DeprecateOnly` flag ensures that metadata which is removed from one package will be deprecated rather than removed. You can then install the new version of the package which now contains that metadata, and it will assume ownership and undeprecate that metadata without causing any change to the data model, business logic, or UI.

---

[23]Scott W. Ambler and Pramodkumar J. Sadalage. 2006. *Refactoring Databases: Evolutionary Database Design*. Addison-Wesley Professional.

Resolving Deployment Errors

Deployment errors are extremely common when using CI/CD in legacy Salesforce projects since it is very easy for the metadata tracked in version control to become inconsistent. By enabling source synchronization, Salesforce DX greatly reduces the frequency of deployment errors, although they are still a fact of life for Salesforce development teams.

One very attractive capability of Gearset is their problem analyzers, which automatically identify and fix problems like missing dependencies before the deployment is performed. Copado includes a version of this which addresses the common challenge of profile deployment errors by automatically modifying and redeploying profiles.

General Approach to Debugging Deployment Errors

Resolving deployment errors is actually what consumes most of the time during deployments. Resolving these errors quickly depends on an understanding of Salesforce, its different types of metadata, and how they interdepend. I probably could have written an entire book on how to tackle the various kinds of deployment errors, but I'm grateful that you've even gotten to this point in this book, and I don't want to press my luck. What follows is a concise set of suggestions:

1. **Don't panic**. On large deployments, it's not uncommon to get hundreds of deployment errors. In many cases, these errors are closely related to one another and resolving one issue can resolve dozens of related issues.

2. If there are a large number of deployment errors, and you're not using a tool that organizes them for you, I recommend you **copy the list into a spreadsheet** to make it easier to manage and work through the list.

3. Deployment errors can cascade to cause other errors; this means that errors later in the list can be caused by errors earlier in the list. Therefore the order of the errors is an important clue to resolving them. For example, if a new field can't be deployed, that can cause a class that uses that field to fail. That class failure can

cause the failure of other classes. That in turn can cause the failure of Visualforce pages, which can themselves cause other errors. All of those errors will be resolved once that field is deployed.

4. Begin by identifying and **deleting any duplicate errors** from your list. They will all be resolved in the same way.

5. Then identify and **delete any dependent errors** that are actually caused by earlier errors.

6. Then work through the errors **from the top down**. Take note of any clues such as files, metadata names, or line numbers that are mentioned in the message.

7. Being able to view the metadata line by line allows you to take steps like temporarily commenting out lines of metadata that are causing deployment errors so that you can get the main body of the deployment to succeed.

8. In the case of large deployments, it can help to temporarily remove pieces of metadata that give persistent errors, so that the main deployment can go through. After deploying the main body of the metadata, you can quickly iterate on the small number of problematic metadata items you've isolated. This allows for faster trial-and-error deployments as you work toward a resolution.

9. The type of error that is most challenging to debug is in the form "An unexpected error occurred. Please include this ErrorId if you contact support: 94477506-8488 (-1165391008)" This error reflects an internal "gack" or unhandled exception in Salesforce itself. The error number shown is a number from Salesforce's internal logs, so to get any insight into it, you'll need to file a case with Salesforce and request their Customer-Centered Engineering team to look that up in Splunk. In the meantime, you'll need to do some sleuthing to figure out what caused this error. This debugging is far easier if you're doing frequent small deployments, since that immediately narrows down the cause. Rather than getting stuck for days, follow the recommendation in point 8 and deploy your metadata in subgroups until you have isolated the source of the problem.

Getting Help

I highly recommend the Salesforce Stack Exchange group (`https://salesforce.`
`stackexchange.com/questions/tagged/deployment`) for finding and resolving more
obscure deployment errors.

General Tips for Reducing Deployment Errors

To reduce the frequency of deployment errors, focus on deploying small batches of
changes frequently. In the case of org-based development, ensure that developers are
making use of feature branches that run validations of the metadata in their branch
against the next higher org (e.g., QA). If the metadata in a feature branch validates
successfully, it is likely to also deploy successfully when merged with the main branches
and deployed to higher orgs.

As mentioned earlier, using Salesforce DX scratch orgs for development greatly
simplifies the development process since it removes the need to handpick metadata
items from a source org, a very error-prone process. Instead, Salesforce DX works
through pushing and pulling metadata to and from a scratch org in its entirety. In most
cases, this ensures that the metadata is coherent.

Continuous Delivery

According to Jez Humble,

> *Continuous Delivery is the ability to get changes of all types—including
> new features, configuration changes, bug fixes and experiments—into pro-
> duction, or into the hands of users, safely and quickly in a sustainable way.*

> *Our goal is to make deployments—whether of a large-scale distributed sys-
> tem, a complex production environment, an embedded system, or an app—
> predictable, routine affairs that can be performed on demand.*

> *We achieve all this by ensuring our code is always in a deployable state, even
> in the face of teams of thousands of developers making changes on a daily
> basis. We thus completely eliminate the integration, testing and hardening
> phases that traditionally followed 'dev complete,' as well as code freezes.*[24]

---

[24]`https://continuousdelivery.com`

Continuous delivery is thus a maturation from the practice of making ad hoc deployments to a state where deployments are happening on an ongoing basis. Separating deployments from releases, as described later, allows you to practice continuous delivery even if features should not be immediately released to users.

Why Continuous Delivery?

Continuous delivery builds on the practice of continuous integration, adding the additional layer of ensuring that code is actually deployable from trunk at any time. In Salesforce, the best way of doing this is to validate or deploy metadata to a target environment whenever code changes on trunk. Your exact process may vary depending on your needs, but assuming that you have two testing environments (QA and UAT) prior to your production environment, a good default is to automatically deploy metadata from your main branch to QA and then (if that succeeds) to immediately trigger a validation (a deployment with the check-only flag set) of that metadata against UAT. This ensures that there is no delay in your QA testers getting access to the latest functionality from developers (or giving feedback if developers have broken something). It also helps ensure that code is also deployable to UAT and that no one has made any "out of band" changes to that environment that would interfere with your eventual releases.

Why perform deployments continually in this way? Consider the alternative, batching deployments at the end of each week or each sprint. Such infrequent releases mean that testers and users are continually waiting, and deployments are massive and accompanied by massive numbers of deployment errors. In a typical team, one person might be delegated to do the release, meaning that they have to lose half a day of work to resolve errors, and have to make imprecise judgment calls, adding or removing metadata from the deployment to get it to go through. They're also typically under stress and time pressure to complete the deployment within a particular window or outside normal working hours. You might call this alternative approach "continuous waiting" or "periodic stress."

Continuous delivery distributes deployments into small batches across time and across the development team. This ensures that deployment challenges can be addressed in small chunks, and distributes expertise in resolving deployment errors over the entire team, which helps them to prevent these errors in the first place. If everyone on your team did a perfect job of ensuring the metadata they commit to version control was accurate and comprehensive, there would be no deployment errors. The best way to give members of the team feedback on how well they're doing that is if they are actually shown deployment results from each change they make.

Automating Deployments

Implicit in continuous delivery is the use of automated scripts or tools to perform deployments. Most of the commercial Salesforce release management tools offer continuous delivery capabilities in the sense that they can perform ongoing automated deployments from version control. That's also something that can be accomplished through scripts run in traditional CI tools, which is the approach that Appirio DX takes.

Reducing the Size of Deployments

When automating deployments, one key is to be able to make deployments small and fast while still having visibility into the state of the metadata in each org. Making deployments small is important in reducing the risk and impact of each deployment. It also helps to not change the lastModifiedDates of Salesforce metadata that has not actually changed. Making deployments fast is important so that fixes and updates can be released and tested quickly. It's also important in case there are deployment errors, since debugging and resolving those requires rerunning deployments repeatedly. The time required to resolve all errors is proportional to the time required for a single deployment.

If you're building your own CI/CD process, one technique I've used with great success for org-based deployments is to use Git tags to mark the points in time when deployments were made successfully, and then to use Git diffs to determine what has changed since that time. Tags are labels or "refs" which are used to mark a particular point in a chain of Git commits. You may have more than one of these tags on the same commit.

The branching for org-level configuration shows how to manage multiple orgs from one repository. In this case, we use tags based on the org name and a timestamp. Figure 9-3 shows an example of this with tags indicating that particular commits were successfully deployed to int, uat, and prod environments.

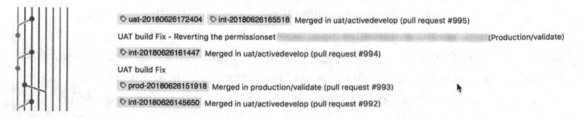

Figure 9-3. *This diagram shows the use of tags to track successful deployments. In this case, there are tags pertaining to uat, int, and prod environments*

Tagging a commit with the org name after a deployment succeeds allows us to determine what metadata has changed since the last deployment. The basic approach is as follows.

Different branches have different rules that apply to them. When a commit is made on a branch that governs the UAT environment, for example, we first use `git describe` as shown in Listing 9-11 to determine the last successful deployment to the UAT environment.

Listing 9-11. A Git describe command to find a tag that matches "uat-"

```
$ git describe --tags --match "uat-*" HEAD
```

Having found that tag, we then use that as the input into a git diff command as shown in Listing 9-12 to determine what files have changed since that time.

Listing 9-12. A Git diff command to find files that have changed since a particular point in time

```
$ git diff --name-only --ignore-all-space [name of the tag found above]
```

This command gives a list of changed files that you can then copy into a new directory and use as the basis for your "differential deployment." If you're using the Metadata API format and not doing any further XML processing, you'll be limited to deploying entire `.object` files, which can be massive. Even short of adopting other Salesforce DX practices, using the "Source" format for metadata makes it easier to deploy smaller subsets of metadata such as particular fields instead of complete objects.

If this subset of changed files deploys successfully, you can then tag the repository with `uat-[timestamp]` to mark this commit as the new state of the repository.

Deploying Configuration Data

As explained in the section "Configuration Data Management" in Chapter 4: Developing on Salesforce, using data to store configuration requires a thoughtful approach to ensure that configuration can be easily migrated.

Wherever possible, you should use Custom Metadata instead of using Custom Settings or Custom Objects to store configuration data. One main reason for this is that Custom Metadata is deployable using the Metadata API along with the rest of your configuration, so it does not require any special management process.

Deploying configuration that is stored as data (either in Custom Settings or in Custom Objects) requires that data to be extracted from one org and loaded into another org. You should store this configuration in version control, along with the scripts used for extracting and loading it. You may also need to transform that data if it includes IDs or other data that are org-specific. Some of the commercial release management tools like AutoRABIT, Copado, Gearset, and Metazoa have built-in capabilities for doing this. If you want to build this capability yourself, you'll be relying on Salesforce's REST API (or Bulk API if the configuration data is massive).

Some AppExchange apps like CPQ solutions and FinancialForce involve extremely detailed configuration data. Vlocity built a sophisticated tool specifically to help their customers extract and load their data packs[25] as part of a CI/CD process.

Continuous Delivery Rituals

The term "continuous delivery" is often used to refer simply to automating deployments. But there are several additional behaviors that truly characterize this practice. I've referred to these as "rituals" here, to emphasize that these behaviors need to be internalized to the point that they become automatic and need to be reinforced as "sacred" to fully achieve the benefits of continuous delivery.

Continuous delivery evolved out of continuous integration and is based on the same behavioral rituals. Those rituals are

- Code is developed on a single trunk, with feature branches not persisting more than a day.

- Every commit to that trunk triggers a set of automated tests.

- If the build breaks, the team's highest priority is to fix the build within 10 minutes (either by making a fix or reverting the changes).

In particular, paying attention to the build status and regarding it as critical to the team's operations is a learned behavior that needs to be reinforced by team leadership and by the individual members of the team.

Examples of malpractices that contradict this ethic are committing on top of a broken build. If the build is broken, everyone else should refrain from pushing their commits to the trunk and if necessary swarm to help resolve the broken build.

---

[25]https://github.com/vlocityinc/vlocity_build

Continuous delivery takes this process further by automatically performing deployments or validations from trunk to one or more target environments with every change. This allows for an additional layer of automated tests: unit tests that accompany the deployment and postdeployment UI tests.

The DevOps literature is filled with references to teams enacting elaborate release processes and automation, but failing to pay attention to the build status over time. The second law of thermodynamics in physics states that the entropy of any isolated system can never decrease. In other words, things fall apart unless you continually apply effort. The rituals of continuous delivery treat a green build as sacred, meaning that it is the top priority of the team to ensure that they always have a clear path for any member of the team to make a next deployment. Such behaviors are learned, but become entirely natural once ingrained.

Deploying Across Multiple Production Orgs

Sandboxes, whether for development, testing, or training, are all related to a production org. The implication is that the metadata in that production org and its related sandboxes should always remain relatively similar, and any differences are meant to be temporary. Thus deploying across sandboxes to a single production org is actually a process of making those orgs more consistent with one another and resolving any metadata differences that interfere with deployments.

It is an entirely different challenge when deploying across multiple production orgs, where the metadata is generally meant to be different. Salesforce provides methods to segregate data access within a single production org, so data isolation is not normally a reason to have more than one production org. Companies who adopt multiple production orgs generally do so because they need to serve independent and incompatible needs across different business units within their organization. See "Multiple Production Orgs" in Chapter 6: Environment Management for more information.

Nevertheless, it's common for teams with multiple production orgs to want to share certain functionality across orgs. If that functionality is available in a managed package created by a third-party ISV, the problem is mostly solved. Managed packages ensure consistent metadata across each installation. All that remains is ensuring that the package is configured consistently and upgraded simultaneously across those orgs.

Prior to the arrival of unlocked packages, there was no easy way for enterprises to syndicate metadata across multiple production orgs and still keep it in sync. "Configuration drift" is a risk for any IT system, and since Salesforce customizations are basically 100% configuration, Salesforce orgs are often the ultimate nightmare in terms of configuration drift. A team might start by introducing a set of code and configuration from one org into another org, but differences arise and increase continually as time wears on.

Building and maintaining unlocked packages (or finding an alternative managed package solution) is the only option I would recommend for organizations who need to maintain similar functionality across more than one production org. Needless to say, they also help maintain consistency across sandboxes.

Managing Org Differences

Perhaps a corollary of the second law of thermodynamics is that the differences between any two Salesforce orgs will always increase unless you apply energy to keep them in sync. User and API interactions with a Salesforce org generally lead to data changes, and some activities such as creating or modifying reports or list views also lead to metadata changes. Some of these org differences don't matter from the point of view of the development lifecycle; see "What's Safe to Change Directly in Production?" in Chapter 12: Making It Better for examples.

Significant metadata differences between a related set of orgs can be divided into intentional and unintentional differences. The role of governance is to eliminate significant unintentional differences between orgs. Within the intentional differences, some are temporary while others are meant to be long-term differences.

The earlier section on "CI Jobs for Org-Level Management" in Chapter 7: The Delivery Pipeline provides an overview of how to practically manage both types of intentional difference.

To summarize, temporary differences between orgs are due to features and fixes being gradually promoted and tested. When using packages, temporary differences simply mean that there are different versions of a package installed in different orgs. The expectation is that the testing orgs will contain the latest version of a package, while the production org may lag a few versions behind while testing is in progress.

When using org-based development, temporary differences are best managed by the Git branching process, with the branches corresponding to the testing orgs carrying metadata differences that have not yet been merged into the master branch, corresponding to the production org. There is of course a contradiction between using such a branching model and following true continuous integration or trunk-based development, which is why it's so important to gradually refactor your metadata into packages, each of which can be developed on a single trunk.

Orgs have long-term differences related to integration endpoints, org-wide email addresses, and other org-specific configuration. While the goal of version control is to gain visibility into these similarities and differences, the goal of CI/CD is to enforce control over the orgs.

Even within unlocked packages, it's possible to accommodate org-specific differences to some degree. The most effective approaches I've seen use custom metadata records that cross-reference the org ID to look up org-specific data. In Apex, you can call UserInfo.getOrganizationId, and in formula fields such as workflow rules, you can reference {!$Organization.Id}. You can then perform dynamic lookups such as the one shown in Listing 9-13 to determine integration endpoints (for example).

Listing 9-13. An example of looking up Custom Metadata records based on an Org ID

```
public static String getEndpoint(String serviceName) {
  String orgId = UserInfo.getOrganizationId();

  API_Endpoint__mdt endpoint = [
    SELECT URL__c
    FROM API_Endpoint__mdt
    WHERE OrgId__c = :orgId
      AND ServiceName__c = :serviceName
      AND isActive__c=true
    LIMIT 1];

  return endpoint;
}
```

When managing org-level metadata, you can use that same custom metadata approach. In addition, you can dynamically filter and replace values as part of the deployment process.

XSLT is the most common syntax for searching and replacing across XML documents. See Listing 9-14 for an example of the XML from a Salesforce Approval Process and Listing 9-15 for an example of an XSLT transform. XSLT is a fairly obscure and challenging syntax and requires dealing with XML namespaces (xmlns). Parsing the XML using higher-level languages such as Node, Java, Python, or Perl may make this task easier. It's also possible to use standard Unix tools such as sed for this purpose, although they are less precise.

The good news is that once you've figured out the initial syntax for your replacements, subsequent replacements are easy. Listing 9-15 is not indicating that you should maintain extensive collections of XSLT. If you choose to use XSLT, it is more maintainable to autogenerate repetitive XSLT on the fly using simpler config files to define your search terms and the replacement values.

Listing 9-14. An excerpt of the XML for an Approval Process referencing the user **wrongUser@yourOrg.com.sandbox**

```xml
<?xml version="1.0" encoding="UTF-8"?>
<ApprovalProcess xmlns="http://soap.sforce.com/2006/04/metadata">
    <!-- ... -->
    <approvalStep>
        <allowDelegate>false</allowDelegate>
        <assignedApprover>
            <approver>
                <name>wrongUser@yourOrg.com.sandbox</name>
                <type>user</type>
            </approver>
            <whenMultipleApprovers>FirstResponse</whenMultipleApprovers>
        </assignedApprover>
        <label>Step 1</label>
        <name>Step_1</name>
    </approvalStep>
    <!-- ... -->
</ApprovalProcess>
```

Listing 9-15. An example XSLT transformation to replace the user **wrongUser@yourOrg.com.sandbox** with **correctUser@yourOrg.com** in an approval process

```xml
<?xml version="1.0" encoding="UTF-8"?>
<xsl:stylesheet xmlns:xsl="http://www.w3.org/1999/XSL/Transform"
    version="2.0"
    xmlns:sf="http://soap.sforce.com/2006/04/metadata"
    exclude-result-prefixes="sf">

    <xsl:template match="sf:approvalStep/sf:assignedApprover/sf:approver/
    sf:name/text()">
        <xsl:value-of select="replace(., '(wrongUser@yourOrg.com.
        sandbox)', 'correctUser@yourOrg.com')"/>
    </xsl:template>

    <!-- By default, leave everything else as it is -->
    <xsl:output exclude-result-prefixes="#all"  omit-xml-
    declaration="yes" indent="yes"/>
    <xsl:template match="@*|node()">
        <xsl:copy>
            <xsl:apply-templates select="@*|node()"/>
        </xsl:copy>
    </xsl:template>

</xsl:stylesheet>
```

The example in Listings 9-14 and 9-15 is a bit contrived, since Salesforce has built-in logic to translate sandbox usernames into production usernames for most metadata types. For example, if you deploy metadata containing references to myuser@myOrg.com.dev to a sandbox called "qa," Salesforce will automatically look for a user named myuser@myOrg.com.qa and update the metadata appropriately. But you will encounter errors if there is no such user, and this automatic replacement does not happen in references to org-wide email addresses or for certain metadata references like reports shared to particular users. Salesforce is working on a resolution by allowing "Aliases" in metadata that can vary on a per-org basis, but that is not available as of this writing.

The need to replace email addresses is the most common and most tedious replacement you're likely to encounter, but there are a variety of situations where having automatic replacements is beneficial. Another example is during the transition between Salesforce versions, when it's possible to download metadata that has tags which are not yet supported in your production org. Being able to strip those out on the fly is extremely helpful.

Dependency and Risk Analysis

As your process matures, one area that you might consider exploring is dynamically assessing the risk that may be posed by particular changes. Some changes pose a bigger risk to your org than others and might warrant careful review before they are made.

Some tooling providers such as Panaya[26] and Strongpoint[27] have released tools for Salesforce based on similar tools for other languages. Their tool assesses metadata dependencies and rates proposed metadata changes based on their potential risk to the org. For example, adding a validation rule on a heavily used field could interfere with peoples' work or automated process if it's not well tested.

It's worth noting the research from the *2018 State of DevOps Report* that change approval processes have not been shown to increase org stability and definitely decrease deployment velocity. This holds true even for selective change approval processes that only apply to high-risk changes.

In my opinion, the most useful step you can take to limit the risk of deployments is to track each change in version control and make frequent small deployments from version control so that the impact of any single deployment is minimized, and any resulting problems can easily be diagnosed and remedied. On this basis, your critical business processes should be validated by automated tests tied to every deployment to ensure they are never compromised.

Summary

Deployment is the heart of innovation delivery. I often liken the deployment process to the shipping logistics managed by companies like UPS and FedEx. Whereas there's a lot of variation in the amount of time required to develop features and resolve bugs, the process of deployment can be made into a fast and predictable process. The irony of release management is that it's not a high-value process; it doesn't add much value

---

[26]www.panaya.com/product/rdx-for-salesforce/
[27]https://strongpoint.io/salesforce

compared to other aspects of software development. It's thus important that your team minimizes the time, effort, and pain involved in deployments by automating that process and developing a steady cadence.

This chapter has outlined a variety of techniques you can use to build your own release automation. And we've also introduced many of the excellent tools that have been built to help with this process. In the next chapter, we'll discuss releasing as a separate activity from deploying. This distinction is extremely helpful since it allows you to make the innovation delivery process as fast and fluid as possible, without exposing your end users to ongoing unexpected changes.

CHAPTER 10

Releasing to Users

Deploying and releasing are different. Deploying refers to moving code and configuration from one environment to another. Releasing means making that code and configuration available to users. Releasing depends on deploying: if capabilities are not moved to the environment that users are working in, they have no way to use them. But it's possible to deploy without releasing, by simply "hiding" those capabilities from users until they're ready to use them.

As an analogy, when I was a child my parents would buy presents for my brother and me in the weeks and months leading up to Christmas. But they would hide the presents in the house until Christmas morning to surprise us. Their buying the presents and bringing them to our house is like deploying. Their giving them to us on Christmas morning is like releasing.

This practice of "decoupling" deployments from releases is also known as "dark deploying" and is a highly recommended practice. The influential software consultancy ThoughtWorks has recommended this practice[1] for many years. This is closely related to the concepts of Canary Deployments and of Feature Flags.

There are several reasons why this practice is so useful. First, it reduces the stress and risk associated with deployments. Deployments are often complicated affairs and can involve careful timing, monitoring, and coordination between different teams. When deployments also imply releasing to users, that simply adds to the stress and risk of the process. When features can be deployed to an environment without having any risk or impact on users, it allows those deployments to be done during normal business hours (as opposed to on weekends or evenings) since there's not the concern of interfering with people's work.

Second, this makes releasing far simpler. Even if a deployment is complex, if releasing to users is simply a matter of changing a flag or permission, it can be done at any time, perhaps by an Admin, in coordination with announcements to users or customers. If something doesn't work, the feature can be disabled just as easily as it was enabled.

---

[1] `www.thoughtworks.com/radar/techniques/decoupling-deployment-from-release`

A. Davis, *Mastering Salesforce DevOps*, https://doi.org/10.1007/978-1-4842-5473-8_10

Third, this allows for real *in situ* testing. You can enable the feature first for administrators, then perhaps for a few testers or power users. Even if you've tested extensively in a staging environment with full data, there's no better confirmation that your features will work in production than actually seeing them working in production!

Fourth, this allows you to deploy functionality that isn't finished yet. This "benefit" will seem shocking to most teams, but is actually a requirement for practicing continuous deployment. For your team to be able to regularly check their code into a common trunk, there has to be a mechanism for them to hide work that is not yet ready for release. Rather than working in a feature branch or delaying deployment, it is perfectly safe to deploy that functionality, as long as you're confident it is disabled.

This also allows for Canary Deployments. Canary Deployments refer to releasing capabilities to a subset of users before releasing to all users. These early users act as testers (sometimes without realizing they're doing so) to reduce the risk of a major change simultaneously affecting all users. The analogy comes from the old practice of bringing canaries into coal mines to warn miners if natural gas was released into the mine. The canaries died quickly if natural gas filled the mine. Their death would alert the miners, hopefully giving them time to escape. Please never expose your users to anything quite that dramatic.

Finally, although it's important to get feedback from real production users as early as possible, it's more common that releases to users are made only periodically. Even when sophisticated techniques are available so that functionality *could* be released more often, it's important not to confuse or overwhelm users with continuous changes to the user interface or functionality. Releasing, for example, on a monthly schedule allows for an orderly announcement of the features to be made, which your users are more likely to greet and read with enthusiasm.

Having explained the extensive benefits of separating releases from deployments, it's important to determine whether that's the right approach for each particular situation. In some cases, it's overkill. The point is to know what you're doing, and why.

Releasing by Deploying

The default approach to releasing functionality is to release by deploying. This means that prior to a deployment, certain functionality isn't available to users, and once the deployment completes successfully, the feature is immediately available to users.

A great example of when this is the correct approach is deploying bug fixes. Once they've been tested, there is no reason to delay the release of a bug fix in any way. It should be deployed and made available to users as early as possible.

Another case where functionality can and should be released immediately with a deployment is for the minor tweaks to UIs or the creation of new database fields that would traditionally be done by admins directly in production. As we discuss in the section "Locking Everybody Out" in Chapter 12: Making It Better, it is critically important that even Salesforce sysadmins not be allowed to modify the database, business logic, or UI directly in production. The reason is that even seemingly small and safe changes (like adding a new field to a page layout) mean that production becomes out of sync with version control. When production gets out of sync with version control, those changes do not get propagated to development or testing environments and will be overwritten the next time developers deploy updates to that functionality in production.

The key is to recognize that "Salesforce admin" actually has a dual meaning: the traditional meaning of "someone who manages a production org" and the distinctively Salesforce meaning of someone who builds and modifies applications using clicks not code. Those in the latter role are more correctly termed "App Builders." And they should not be allowed anywhere close to your production org, except as users.

The alternative is to involve App Builders in the same process used by code-based developers to deploy changes, namely, the Delivery Pipeline. That means that App Builders should be making their changes in scratch orgs or development sandboxes, tracking them in version control, and letting the delivery pipeline do what it does best: deliver those changes to production. Read more about how to do this in the section "An Admin's Guide to Doing DevOps" in Chapter 12: Making It Better.

Revoking your admins "System Administrator" privileges in production forces them to make even minor application updates using version control. But that doesn't mean that there should have to be a long lead time to releasing those features. On the contrary, reducing lead time is one of our key goals. We don't want to burden admins unnecessarily, we just want them to track their changes and keep them in sync with developers. So minor updates (minor layout changes, creating new report types, adding fields to an object, etc.) can all be released immediately with a deployment without requiring an additional layer of hiding and releasing.

Separating Deployments from Releases

But what about bigger changes? If there's any chance that a new feature might negatively impact users, cause confusion that requires training or announcements, or modify business logic in a way that requires coordination with other groups, you should hide or disable that feature when you deploy it. One important consequence of hiding features is that you can then deploy continuously to production. Continuous deployment refers to deploying features to production as soon as they're built and tested. The benefit of this is that you can make each deployment very small.

Small "batch" sizes are a key concept of lean manufacturing, and small deployments are the lean software development equivalent. Small, frequent deployments minimize the risk of each individual deployment and allow bug fixes and high-priority deployments to be expedited.

The opposite, large infrequent deployments, implies that even bug fixes and high-value features have to wait in line with every other change to the system. That delays the delivery of value to end users. It also means that if a large deployment causes a problem, it's far more challenging to discern which part of that deployment caused the problem. When a critical problem occurs as a result of a large deployment, you may have to roll back the entire deployment until the team is able to identify the root of the failure. And depending on the nature of the deployment, it may not be easy to roll back.

Separating deployments from releases is a key capability to enable DevOps for your team. The reason is that it forces the team to think about how features can be deployed without impacting the system. This forces good design, designing in such a way that changes are reversible and that the impact of changes can be controlled. As people in the DevOps community describe it, you're "reducing the blast radius" of each change.

Let's look at how this can be implemented.

Permissions

One of the oldest and simplest mechanisms to separate deployments from releases is simply to not assign users the permission to see functionality until it's ready. As mentioned before, you should emphasize the use of Permission Sets rather than Profiles. And this is an area where Permission Sets really shine.

Each package you're developing should have at least one Permission Set associated with it that gives access to the capabilities in that package. When you first install that package in your target org, the Permission Set is included, but it is not automatically assigned to any users. This means that the Permission Set will need to be assigned to users for them to get access to those capabilities. Voila! You've separated the deployment from the release.

When an Admin decides that it's time to release the feature, they simply assign the Permission Set to the appropriate users. Want to do a Canary Deployment? Assign the Permission Set to just a subset of your users. How easy was that??

But imagine if the Permission Set associated with your package has already been assigned to all the appropriate production users. And you're now rolling out new functionality that you don't immediately want to expose to all users. You have several options.

If the changes you're making might never be appropriate for some of the existing users of your package, you should create a new Permission Set. For example, if your package provides capabilities to customer support representatives, but you're adding some features that would only be used by Live Agent chat users, you might create a new Permission Set that is specifically for chat users. That allows Admins to assign the Chat User Permission Set only when they're ready to release those capabilities.

There is some risk, however, that in doing that your permission landscape becomes unnecessarily complex. Complex permissions create a security and maintenance burden for admins, so you should be sure that there's a legitimate use case for a new Permission Set before you create one.

It is of course possible to simply not add your new permissions to the Permission Set and to then add those permissions manually in each environment. While that accomplishes the goal of separating deployments from releases, it means that you're reverting to a manual workflow that can lead to errors and which isn't being tracked in version control. Plus, as discussed in the section "Locking Everybody Out" in Chapter 12: Making It Better, a wise team won't even permit this kind of manual modification. Therefore you need to consider one of the other options in the following.

Layouts

Another time-honored method for revealing features selectively to some users and not to others is the use of Layouts. Salesforce's page layouts allow a single object to have multiple alternative layouts for the View and Edit screens. Which layout a user sees is determined dynamically at runtime based on the user's Profile and on the record type of that record.

Each Layout defines not only which fields of an object are shown but also which fields are read-only and which Quick Actions, Related Lists, and other embedded functionality are shown. This allows a capability such as a new Quick Action for an object to be hidden from users simply by being excluded from the Layout those users are assigned.

Similar to the Chat User Permission Set case earlier, if you are rolling out capabilities for a new team, you might want to create a new Layout to serve the needs of that team. But the same caveats mentioned earlier apply. Be extremely careful about creating a layout (or anything else) that you don't think has a long-term purpose for the org. Everything you create adds complexity, and capabilities built for short-term use have a nasty habit of making their way into production and remaining for a very long time.

Dynamic Lightning Pages

One very nice capability that is now available in the Lightning App Builder is the ability to have Dynamic Lightning Pages. These dynamic pages allow certain components to be shown or not shown based on filters. Filters use formulas that can reference information on a particular record (*show this component when the value is greater than 100*) or based on attributes of the User viewing the data (*show this component when the User has the "BetaUser__c" flag enabled*).

On Salesforce's roadmap is the ability to add much more flexibility into App Builder, including the ability to show and hide specific fields or layout sections in the same way. App Builder's capabilities provide a rich way to hide functionality until it's ready.

Feature Flags

While modifying Layouts or using Dynamic Lightning Pages allows releases to be controlled at the UI level, it's also possible to enable/disable functionality at the level of business logic. Feature Flags (aka Feature Toggles) are another practice recommended by Martin Fowler[2] at ThoughtWorks. Although "Feature Flags" may be new to you, they've actually been around since time immemorial (time began in 1970 in the Unix universe) in the form of "settings."

Yes, settings. You can make your own settings.

---

[2]https://martinfowler.com/bliki/FeatureToggle.html

Why not. Salesforce does it. The Salesforce Setup UI contains thousands of settings that are in effect Feature Toggles that just turn certain capabilities on and off. When Salesforce wants to roll out a prerelease feature to a select group of Pilot users, they simply have their provisioning team enable a hidden feature flag in the Pilot users' org which makes new capabilities available. Voila! Similar hidden capabilities (like enabling Person Accounts) are known as "black tab" settings that Salesforce support agents can enable at administrators' request.

As Martin Fowler mentions, the use of Feature Flags should be a last resort, since it requires some design and adds a bit of complexity. But it's vastly preferable to releasing by deploying if there's any chance that a feature could cause risk or impact to users.

So how do you enable a Feature Flag? There are many possibilities.

A feature flag is simply a Boolean on/off setting that is checked at some point in your logic and that might be enabled or disabled for different users or on different orgs.

First determine where you want this Feature Flag to be checked. If the feature should be enabled or disabled in a Formula (such as selectively rolling out a new Approval Process), you can only use Custom Metadata, Custom Settings, or Custom Permissions. Features that will be checked from Flows or Process Builders can also use logic defined in Apex Invocable Methods and REST External Services. If the feature will be enabled/disabled inside code, you have even more options for how to implement the check.

Custom Metadata, Custom Settings, and Custom Permissions have the benefit that they are stored in Salesforce's Platform Cache and so can be accessed quickly and without risking exceeding governor limits. They are also available in the formulas used in Formula Fields, Validation Rules, Approval Process conditions, and elsewhere.

It's worth mentioning that originally, none of these three capabilities were available, and application configuration was stored as data in Custom Objects. That's still the case with some kinds of applications like CPQ where "configuration data" is far more complex and extensive than can be accommodated by those mechanisms. If you're responsible for architecting an older application that is still using Custom Objects for simple configuration, you should consider migrating to using Custom Metadata instead. Otherwise, in addition to managing metadata in version control, you will need a mechanism for tracking and deploying configuration data. See "Configuration Data Management" in Chapter 4: Developing on Salesforce for more.

Flows and Processes can also call Apex Invocable Methods to calculate the value of a flag and can even use External REST Services. For example, they could reach out to an External Service defined using an OpenAPI-compliant REST service. This kind of capability can be used to create a cross-system feature flag that can enable capabilities both in Salesforce and in other integrated systems such as SAP or Oracle.

Feature Flags that will be checked by code such as Apex can use any conceivable mechanism or calculation to determine whether to enable or disable a feature. Again, Feature Flags are meant for short-term use so you should avoid over-engineering. But code does allow for a wider variety of mechanisms, even in frontend code. For example, a Lightning Component or a Visualforce page could set a cookie in a user's browser to determine whether to display a particular feature. This could even be a user-selectable option, such as "enable compact display" that allows you to solicit user feedback.

One of the most important qualities of Custom Metadata is that their values can be deployed between orgs, just like other Metadata. This means that developers can define these values and push them out as part of a package. But Custom Metadata values can also be overridden in a target org (unless they are marked as "Protected" and deployed as part of a managed package). This means that a Custom Metadata record can be used to enable a feature but can be turned off by default. It can then be selectively enabled in an org to release that feature.

However, in general Custom Metadata should always be used instead of Custom Settings. One exception is in the use of Hierarchical Custom Settings. Hierarchical Custom Settings are ideal for use with feature flags, since they dynamically change their value based on the environment, Profile, or user. For example, a setting can be turned off at the org level, but enabled for all users with a particular Profile. Hierarchical custom settings can even be overridden at the level of an individual user to allow that user to test a feature.

One final note about Feature Flags is that they generally should be removed once they've served their purpose. One of the risks of using Feature Flags is that their designers forget to remove them when they're no longer needed. They then just become a useless if statement in your logic and a type of technical debt. Remove Feature Flags once the feature is stable.

Remember, as John Byrd once said, "Good programmers write good code. Great programmers write no code. Zen programmers delete code."[3]

---

[3]www.quora.com/What-are-some-things-that-only-someone-who-has-been-programming-20-50-years-would-know

Branching by Abstraction

There's no problem in Computer Science that can't be solved by adding another layer of abstraction to it (except for the problem of too many layers of abstraction).

—Fundamental Theorem of Software Engineering
(frequently attributed to John Wheeler)

The basic idea of separating deployments from releases is to hide work from end users, either because it's not ready for them or because they're not ready for it.

So far, we've discussed multiple increasingly sophisticated ways to hide functionality from users. Branching by abstraction has the fanciest name of any of these, but is conceptually simple to understand. This approach was promoted in the book *Continuous Delivery,* but, as indicated by the preceding quote, the concept dates back to the earliest days of computer science.

Branching by abstraction provides a way to gradually transition from an old version of a component to a new version of a component by adding an abstraction layer in between. This technique is useful when that transition is risky or might take some time to implement, since it allows you to make the transition gradually without branching in version control or delaying deployments. This technique can be used in any technology where one component can delegate processing to another component. In Salesforce this means you can use it inside code, Flows, or Processes.

Figure 10-1 illustrates how this works. If you decide that a certain component needs to be replaced, you create an abstraction layer that can be called instead of referencing the component directly. Initially, that abstraction layer simply passes all requests on to the component, making the initial implementation trivial and safe. As you then begin work on a new version of the component, you can add some decision criteria into that abstraction layer that allows you to delegate processing either to the old component or to the new component.

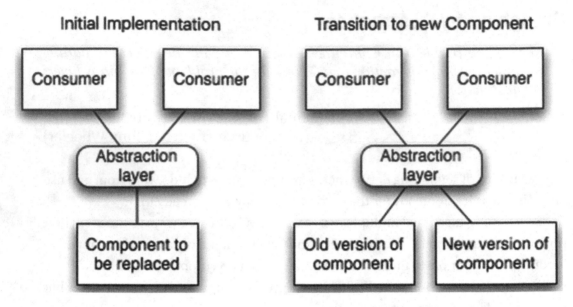

Figure 10-1. *Branching by abstraction*

A practical example of how this works is if you want to transition from using a Custom Object to store configuration data to using Custom Metadata. Let's say your current code includes many SOQL queries that look up values in the Custom Object to determine the appropriate behavior. You've determined that you'll benefit from using Custom Metadata to keep that configuration consistent across environments. This simple example shows how you could branch by abstraction and gradually refactor your codebase to support the new approach.

1.   Listing 10-1 shows the initial version of `CallingCode.cls` that directly makes a SOQL lookup to your configuration object. You might have similar blocks of code scattered throughout your codebase.

2.   Create a class called `ConfigurationService.cls` as shown in Listing 10-2 with a method called `isFeatureEnabled()`. This is your abstraction layer.

3.   Have `isFeatureEnabled` call another method called `theOldWay()` in that class that performs your original SOQL query to access the configuration data in the original configuration object.

4. Refactor `CallingCode.cls` as shown in Listing 10-3 to call ConfigService instead of directly querying your configuration object. You have now added a layer of abstraction without changing the underlying logic.

5. Now add a method to `ConfigService` called `theNewWay()` that implements your new way of getting that configuration information, in this case by querying Custom Metadata instead.

6. You can now develop and test the new way of accessing that configuration and gradually implement that change across the entire codebase. You can use any logic you want to selectively implement the new way. You have now branched by abstraction.

Listing 10-1. The original state of CallingCode.cls, which directly performs SOQL queries of a configuration object

```
public with sharing class CallingCode {
  public CallingCode() {
    String product = 'myProduct';
    Boolean enabled = [SELECT feature_enabled__c
                       FROM Configuration_Object__c
                       WHERE product__c = :product][0]
      .feature_enabled__c;
  }
}
```

Listing 10-2. ConfigService.cls, an abstraction layer that contains both the old and the new ways of accessing configuration data

```
public with sharing abstract class ConfigService {
  public static Boolean isFeatureEnabled(String product) {
    // return theOldWay(product);
    return theNewWay(product);
  }
}
```

```
    private static Boolean theOldWay(String product) {
      return [SELECT feature_enabled__c
              FROM Configuration_Object__c
              WHERE product__c = :product][0]
        .feature_enabled__c;
    }

    private static Boolean theNewWay(String product) {
      return [SELECT feature_enabled__c
              FROM Configuration_Metadata__mdt
              WHERE product__c = :product][0]
        .feature_enabled__c;
    }
}
```

Listing 10-3. CallingCode.cls after adding the abstraction layer instead of directly accessing configuration data

```
public with sharing class CallingCode {
  public CallingCode() {
    String product = 'myProduct';
    Boolean enabled = ConfigService.isFeatureEnabled(product);
  }
}
```

In most cases, branching by abstraction should be a temporary solution, and the abstraction layer can be removed after the change has been completely tested. In this simple example, ConfigService is a useful way of avoiding repetitive SOQL queries and so is beneficial to keep in place.

Summary

Releasing is often confused with deploying. The purpose of this chapter is to highlight the differences between them and to outline techniques for deploying without immediately releasing. In many cases, this means building your customizations so they can be hidden or exposed dynamically. There is some cost in terms of time and complexity in adding such a layer, but in many cases there are enormous benefits in doing so. Such practices allow you to control the risk of deploying changes by enabling you to turn functionality on or off as needed. Fast rollbacks, selective rollouts, A/B testing, and more become possible once you've implemented this practice.

This concludes the main body of this book, the practice of Innovation Delivery. Nestled in between development and operations, the software delivery phase has historically been a viper's nest of risk, pain, inefficiency, and confusion. The Salesforce platform and those who build on it have evolved to the level of sophistication that it is now critical to tame the delivery process.

The logistics companies who handle global and local trade (from container ships to drone delivery) are unsung heroes in our modern economy. From hand-carried parcels, to the Pony Express, to modern expedited delivery, the practice of shipping and delivering physical goods has become steadily more reliable over hundreds of years.

At the heart of the DevOps movement is applying similar process improvements to software delivery, enabling it to become steadily faster, safer, and more predictable. By implementing the processes described here, and leveraging the many excellent Salesforce deployment, tracking, and testing tools, your team can begin to free up more and more of their time for creative, high-value work. It's my sincere wish that all Salesforce development teams can eventually learn to "run the tightest ship in the shipping business."

PART IV

Salesforce Ops (Administration)

The term DevOps has gained enormous traction over the last decade, and is a useful catch-all to describe processes that allow for a high pace of innovation without compromising stability. To emphasize the meaning of that term, I've divided this book into sections on Dev, Ops, and the critical Delivery piece that connects them.

But the term "Ops" or "Operations" is almost never used in the Salesforce world to refer to a team that runs or administers a Salesforce org. Why is that? Because Salesforce is doing that job for you. Very few Salesforce admins "wear a pager" to alert them to outages in the middle of the night. By contrast, Salesforce themselves employs fleets of support staff, application developers, networking experts, database admins, and security specialists to provide ongoing operational monitoring of their service.

By contrast, Salesforce Admins tend to focus on far more creative processes such as building click-based capabilities for the benefit of their users, alongside some traditional operational tasks like creating new user accounts.

Salesforce's Awesome Admins, with their *esprit de corps*, Trailhead badges, podcasts, and dance competitions,[1] are vastly cheerier and more passionate about their platform than the stereotypical sysadmin, holed up in a server room in the basement of their

---

[1]https://admin.salesforce.com/get-your-dancing-shoes-on-and-take-the-awesome-admin-challenge

organization. Classic sysadmins have been the basis of comical and self-deprecating caricatures such as the BOFH (Bastard Operator From Hell).[2] The problems inherent in their being saddled with maintaining systems that they didn't understand and didn't develop were a major basis for the birth of the DevOps movement.

Having already discussed "Click-Based Development on Salesforce," in this final section, we'll focus on the truly operational responsibilities that Salesforce admins take on: keeping the lights on, and making things better.

---

[2]http://bofharchive.com/

CHAPTER 11

Keeping the Lights On

Keeping the lights on in your Salesforce org is generally just a matter of paying your Salesforce bill. They do most of the hard work for you. Nevertheless, in this chapter we'll look briefly at the different ways in which "Dev" and "Ops" can work together in the Salesforce world, as well as how some of the other truly operational aspects of managing a Salesforce org are relevant and can be understood as an extension as the broader development lifecycle.

Salesforce Does the Hard Work for You

I decided to focus my career on the Salesforce platform in part because I enjoyed the simplicity with which businesses and nonprofits could build on the platform. When I first started looking at jobs in this field, I naturally looked at the job openings at Salesforce themselves. I was a bit daunted to see the depth and sophistication of the skills they seek in their employees: Oracle database administration, site reliability engineering, offensive security engineering, network analysis, data science, cryptography, the list goes on.

If you think that the content presented in this book is sophisticated, it's nothing compared to the level of product engineering happening under the hood to allow Salesforce to scale globally, deliver features aggressively, and maintain industry-leading uptime.

Fortunately, that's all someone else's job.

That's the reason we (or our employers) pay Salesforce, and the reason that SaaS makes sense. Let someone else do the performance tuning on the databases. Let someone else understand load balancers, cache invalidation, compilers, and performance optimization. From our point of view, Salesforce basically just works.

© Andrew Davis 2019

A. Davis, *Mastering Salesforce DevOps*, https://doi.org/10.1007/978-1-4842-5473-8_11

If there's an outage or performance impairment in a Salesforce instance, we can check `https://trust.salesforce.com`. It happens sometimes, but it's rare, generally short-lived, and followed by a root cause analysis and improvements to prevent it from happening again.

We can also file support tickets with them, which generally get handled promptly. You can pay for various tiers of support up to and including 24x7 Mission-Critical Applications (MCA) phone support.

So from an operations point of view, keeping Salesforce in operation is enormously complex—but fortunately not for admins.

What Does Dev and Ops Cooperation Mean?

The term DevOps originates from a talk by John Allspaw and Paul Hammond at the 2009 Velocity conference called "10 deploys a day: Dev and ops cooperation at Flickr."[1] That talk was significant for many reasons, but largely because it showed the benefits of cooperation between two teams who had traditionally worked in isolation.

There are several reasons why this isolation had evolved. First, there is a fundamental tension between the goals of development and operations. Developers' job is to continually innovate to better meet the evolving needs of the business. The goal of admin/operations teams is to maintain a trusted system by keeping everything running smoothly without downtime. For operations, innovation and change implies the risk of breaking things. There is thus a tension between innovation and trust. These teams often reported to different managers (e.g., CTO vs. CIO) and had competing goals and incentives, which further deepened the separation.

Another reason for the separation was to enforce separation of duties, a compliance requirement that dictates that those who develop a system should be different from those who put it into production. Separation of duties is a long-standing principle in financial accounting, and organizations subject to audits and regulatory oversight extend that to their IT systems. Access controls are often used to actually prevent developers from releasing code into production environments.

---

[1] `www.slideshare.net/jallspaw/10-deploys-per-day-dev-and-ops-cooperation-at-flickr`

The basic reason why this separation became dysfunctional can be explained by Conway's Law:

> *Organizations which design systems are constrained to produce systems which are copies of the communication structures of these organizations.*[2]

Melvin Conway was a programmer, but Conway's Law is a sociological statement that basically says that your organizational communication structure will affect and limit your architecture. The challenge that the Dev vs. Ops separation introduced was that getting software running in production depends on both the software and the underlying infrastructure, and the two cannot be optimized independently. So if the teams responsible for these areas are not communicating well, naturally the overall system will suffer.

Matthew Skelton and Manuel Pais maintain a web site (`https://web.devopstopologies.com`), documenting some of the many patterns and antipatterns for Devs and Ops to work together effectively. The examples are thought-provoking, and in practice our projects and teams may shift between different patterns and antipatterns over time.

Since the term DevOps was introduced, it's been observed that there are frequently many other communication gaps in the software value chain. Wherever there are role boundaries, such gaps may exist, for example, between business analysts and architects, between developers and QA testers, and between security specialists and everyone else. Terms such as TestOps, DevTestOps, and DevSecOps have come into use, but the underlying concept is the same: creating silos between teams increases inefficiency and generally doesn't succeed in reducing risk. The lesson here is that "DevOps" is not really about "Dev" vs. "Ops" but rather about ensuring that there is strong cooperation between all of the teams who participate in producing the final system.

The remedy for this dysfunction has been described as an "Inverse Conway Maneuver."[3] This sounds like a surgical technique, but basically means that you should organize your teams (and their communication) in a way that is most conducive to your desired architecture.

Bringing all of this academic discussion back down to earth, what does "Dev and ops cooperation" look like on the Salesforce platform?

Since the actual "operations" of Salesforce is mostly handled by Salesforce themselves, the cooperation challenges on the Salesforce platform tend to look different than they might on other platforms. But the core idea remains the same: silos between

---

[2] www.melconway.com/Home/Conways_Law.html

[3] www.thoughtworks.com/de/radar/techniques/inverse-conway-maneuver

teams can negatively impact the organization's effectiveness and the effectiveness of individual teams. Cooperation and communication across teams are critical if they are all collaborating around a single org.

If your Salesforce team is small, any cooperation problems are more likely due to personalities rather than organization structure. If your team fits Amazon's two pizza rule (you can feed them all with two pizzas), your communication will hopefully be pretty smooth, and confusion can be quickly resolved.

As teams scale and grow however, communication can be more challenging. Jez Humble has often made the point[4] that enterprises are complex adaptive systems. By definition this means that individuals, including the CEO, don't have perfect knowledge of the entire company and are not able to fully predict the effects of any action. Your Salesforce org is also a complex adaptive system once it reaches a certain scale.

If you're the sole admin for a new, small org at a small company, you might be familiar with every single customization and interaction in that org. But as your company grows, the dev and admin team grows, and time passes, the complexity grows beyond what one person can hold in their mind. Even a solo admin is likely to forget the details of customizations they implemented several months or years ago.

The basic point is that developers need to be aware of how their applications are behaving in production so that they can debug or improve them if needed. And admins need confidence that development has been well tested before they inherit it in their production org. They also need applications to provide clear information about what they're doing and why, so problems can be resolved easily. The two groups need a way to collaborate with each other easily should problems arise.

Version control can go a long way toward providing shared visibility and answers to "what changed?" even across large and distributed teams. It's also important to establish lines of communication between those who initially built functionality, the users of that functionality, and the admins who support those users.

Multiple development teams can be more easily supported when they can develop their work as packages, with clear boundaries between them. Package boundaries reduce the risk and uncertainty of merging large and complex metadata. Packages also establish clarity about the original authors of certain functionality, making it easy for admins to know who to talk to if questions or side effects arise.

---

[4]`www.youtube.com/watch?v=TcbmRRy-vno`

You can think of your Salesforce "Operations" as being 80% handled by Salesforce themselves and 20% by your own production admins. You can then consider the other roles (or potential roles) you have in your team, such as business analysts, admins (the app-building kind), code-based developers, testers, security specialists, and so on. If you are all collaborating around a single production org, then there absolutely needs to be good and clear cooperation between all of these teams, since that production org is a single interrelated system.

Since these disparate teams are (whether they like it or not) collaborating on a single interrelated system, what are the possible ways in which silos might interfere with effective cooperation? In the words of Skelton and Pais, "There is no 'right' team topology, but several 'bad' topologies for any one organization." Common failure modes include

- Not providing developers access to a Salesforce DX Dev Hub (you can safely give them the "free limited access" production license).

- Long-running parallel development projects not developing in an integrated environment.

- Developers having no access to test in a production-like environment.

- Developers being unable to submit Salesforce support tickets.

- Infrequent release windows.

- Developers neglecting to establish production logging.

- Inefficient release paths or handoffs from development through to production.

- Parallel consulting partner-led projects competing with one another. Development teams from different vendors can easily introduce silos.

This list is not comprehensive, and challenges may change over time.

If you are maintaining multiple independent production orgs, then the need for collaboration across the teams maintaining those orgs is reduced. But companies with multiple orgs invariably have some common standards, processes, and applications across those orgs, and it will be in everyone's best interest if you establish a Center of Excellence to allow for knowledge sharing across these teams.

Salesforce Admin Activities

It's well beyond the scope of this book to share every aspect of activities an admin might need to undertake. The focus in this section is to share tips that can make the overall development lifecycle smoother.

User Management

User management is a fundamental aspect of a Salesforce admin's responsibility. By definition, an admin is delegated by the company to maintain the Salesforce org for the users. It's their responsibility to ensure that people who should have access to the org promptly get the right level of access. It's also their responsibility to ensure that people who should not have access do not get that access.

The most reliable way to ensure correct access is for your company to maintain a single sign-on (SSO) system that acts as the single source of truth for current employees and to use that SSO for accessing Salesforce. Generally, password access to Salesforce should be prevented, except for admins to use in case there's a problem with the SSO.

There are two extremes of access that can interfere with the overall flow of development. One extreme is having too many system administrators in production—this brings a serious risk of untracked and conflicting changes. The other extreme is not allowing developers any kind of access to a production org.

In some cases, your developers may not need or should not have access to Salesforce production data or capabilities. For developers to effectively debug production issues, they need to see debug logs, but seeing those logs requires "View All Data" permission which may again be inappropriate.

The Salesforce DX Dev Hub is necessarily a production org, and for developers to use Salesforce DX scratch orgs or packaging, they need a user account on that production org. Salesforce offers a "Free Limited Access License" that allows use of a Dev Hub on production without the ability to view data or change metadata in that org. If security concerns bar you from even offering such safe and restricted licenses, you will need to establish a separate production org that the developers can use collectively as their Dev Hub.

You will also need to establish one or more integration users that can be used by integrated systems. Ideally, each integrated system (including your CI system) should have its own integration user for security and logging purposes, but since integration user licenses cost as much as regular user licenses, most companies opt to combine multiple integrations under a smaller number of integration users.

Security

Salesforce security follows a layered model, where different security mechanisms such as Profiles, permission sets, and roles can provide increasing levels of access to users. By default, no one can do or access anything, but each of these layers can add permissions; these layers never *remove* privileges, permissions are additive.

Every Salesforce user is assigned a single Profile, which establishes their basic security privileges. Salesforce provides some standard profiles, notably "Standard User," "System Administrator," and "Integration User." These profiles can be cloned and customized as needed. You can also create Permission Sets, which work similar to profiles except that users can have more than one Permission Set.

It's in the best interest of security as well as org governance for there to be a very limited number of people holding System Administrator privileges. Salesforce provides very granular access controls that allow you to add admin-like privileges to a permission set, which you can then apply as needed to users.

Use Permission Sets Instead of Profiles

Because of an early design decision in the Metadata API, Profiles are notorious for being the single biggest pain in the butt for Salesforce release managers. When you retrieve a profile using the Metadata API, the profile definition you receive varies depending on what other metadata you have requested. Managing profiles in a CI tool thus requires sophisticated tooling, and Salesforce release management is plagued by missing profile permissions or deployment errors from permissions for metadata that is not present in the target org. Even groups with sophisticated CI/CD processes sometimes choose to manage profile permissions manually.

Salesforce is working on improvements, but in the meantime I would strongly suggest you avoid using Profiles to provide permissions and use permission sets instead. Since API version 40.0, Permission Sets are always retrieved and deployed in a consistent way, making them a better candidate for CI/CD.

Permission sets can be used for every type of user characteristic except for the following:

- Page layout assignments (which page layout a user sees for a record)

- Login hours

- Login IP ranges

- Session settings

417

- Password policies

- Delegated authentication

- Two-factor authentication with single sign-on

- Desktop client access

- Organization-wide email addresses allowed in the From field when sending emails

I would thus suggest that you use this list to determine what profiles you actually need in your organization. For example, if you maintain a call center and for security you want to lock call center users to a particular login IP range, whereas your salespeople need access to Salesforce from any location, that's perfect justification for having a "Call Center" profile. Don't create different profiles for every category of user in your organization. In fact, even the need for different page layout assignments is small, since you can simply restrict access to certain fields to prevent those fields from cluttering a record layout for users.

Managing Scheduled Jobs

Salesforce provides a system for scheduling jobs that can run periodically in an org. Scheduled jobs are typically used to manage batch processing for activities that would be too slow or too computationally expensive to run on the fly.

One large nonprofit organization I worked with prepared many layers of elaborate reports on daily, monthly, quarterly, and annual cycles. The reports aggregated and summarized data across millions of opportunities, far too much to be handled using standard Salesforce reports. They opted to use Salesforce for this task instead of a separate BI tool, and so our team wrote extensive batch Apex code to summarize all of this data and then created scheduled jobs to run the appropriate batch jobs at the appropriate times.

Such scheduled jobs can represent critically important aspects of your Salesforce configuration. Therefore (you probably know where I'm going with this) they should ideally also be stored in version control and an automated process used to ensure that they are in place. Such a system becomes extremely helpful when promoting such customizations between environments. If scheduled job definitions are stored in version control, they can be promoted and tested gradually between environments and deployed to production when the team is confident in them.

Such a system needs to be idempotent, meaning that you need to ensure you can run the job scheduling task repeatedly without it creating multiple jobs. In practice, I haven't seen many teams doing this, but it's worth considering if scheduled jobs are critical for you, and you want this level of reliability.

Probably the smoothest way to manage this is to write the scheduling system in Apex itself, running queries to check existing schedule jobs and using the `system.schedule()` methods to schedule any that are missing. You can then run this code as anonymous Apex as a postdeployment step. Listing 11-1 shows the syntax for scheduling new jobs and aborting all existing scheduled jobs. Production-ready code should include further checks, such as validating existing jobs and ensuring that jobs are not running before canceling them.

Listing 11-1. Starter code for scheduling and aborting jobs

```
public with sharing class JobScheduler {
  public static void scheduleAll(){
    System.schedule('scheduledJob1','0 0 2 ? * SAT', new
    ScheduledJob1());
    System.schedule('ScheduledJob2','0 1 * * * ?', new ScheduledJob1());
  }

  public static void abortAll(){
    for(CronTrigger ct : getScheduledJobs()){
      system.abortJob(ct.Id);
    }
  }

  private static CronTrigger[] getScheduledJobs() {
    final string SCHEDULED_JOB = '7';
    return [
        SELECT Id, CronJobDetail.Name, CronExpression, State
        FROM CronTrigger
        WHERE CronJobDetail.JobType = :SCHEDULED_JOB];
  }
}
```

One challenge related to scheduled jobs is that you can encounter a deployment error if you update an Apex class that is referenced in a scheduled job. If your classes are written such that changing a class definition midway through a scheduled job being processed won't cause problems, you can enable the Apex Setting "Allow deployments of components when corresponding Apex jobs are pending or in progress."

Monitoring and Observability

Monitoring and observability are two concepts related to gaining insight into the behavior of production systems to become aware of and diagnose any problems that arise. Figure 11-1 helps explain the relationship between these concepts. Observability refers to the degree to which you are able to get information about a particular behavior or system, especially if you need to debug it. For example, debug logs provide one form of observability, but only if those who can make sense of the logs have access to them. Monitoring takes a broader, high-level view of the system, typically tracking trends over time. Monitoring depends on observability because if the behavior of a system can't be observed, it can't be monitored. Finally, analysis is the activity of using monitoring to gain actionable insights into a system. This can be manual analysis, for example, debugging, or automated analysis, for example, raising alerts if exceptions are encountered or thresholds exceeded.

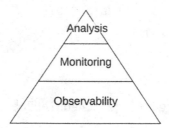

Figure 11-1. *Analysis depends on monitoring, which in turn depends on observability*

The reason this topic is relevant in the context of DevOps is that if production systems are not observable, it's far more difficult to improve the system, and we're left to rely on anecdotal feedback such as users submitting cases. A production system has zero observability if there is no way to inspect that system to see how it's behaving. Conversely, providing access to debug logs, event notifications, and performance metrics means there's a high degree of observability. For observability, more is better, but there are legitimate security concerns that might cause teams to limit who has access to that information.

In terms of monitoring, just because a system **can** be inspected deeply, doesn't mean that you **should** be monitoring every aspect of that system. Google's *Site Reliability Engineering* book advises:

> *Your monitoring system should address two questions: what's broken, and why? The "what's broken" indicates the symptom; the "why" indicates a (possibly intermediate) cause. ... "What" versus "why" is one of the most important distinctions in writing good monitoring with maximum signal and minimum noise.*[5]

The *Site Reliability Engineering* book advises that there are four golden signals of monitoring that you should focus on:

1. Latency (the time it takes to request a service)

2. Traffic (how much demand there is on your system)

3. Errors

4. Saturation (resource utilization).

Salesforce monitors and helps ensure low latency for their services. But you might be interested to observe and monitor the page load time for a complex VisualForce page you built, for example. Traffic is normally fairly predictable for your internal users, but if you are hosting a Community, you might want to monitor that traffic, especially if it's subject to surges due to marketing campaigns and so on. Error reporting is an important topic that we'll deal with later, as is saturation, which mostly equates to governor limits for Salesforce.

Salesforce provides greatly simplified monitoring and observability tools compared to what a traditional sysadmin might deal with when managing a server. This is because Salesforce itself is handling the monitoring of things like uptime, CPU load, network latency, and so on. Nevertheless, as users of Salesforce, we build business-critical capabilities on that platform and so may need our own levels of monitoring and observability. It's worth looking at the existing options and ways they can best be exploited.

---

[5]https://landing.google.com/sre/sre-book/chapters/monitoring-distributed-systems/

Built-In Monitoring and Observability Tools

Salesforce continues to expand the different kinds of monitoring available to users. These different tools are spread across the Setup UI, but many of them are in the **Environments ➤ Jobs**, **Environments ➤ Logs**, and **Environments ➤ Monitoring** sections. Debug logs are typically the most useful for developers. The limits on debug logs and the capabilities for parsing them have been greatly improved by the Salesforce DX team, so that it's finally possible to set your log levels to "Finest" without exceeding log size limits, step through Apex code using the Apex Replay Debugger in Visual Studio Code, and see how the values of your variables evolve as your code executes. Frontend developers working with JavaScript and Lightning Components have had such capabilities (e.g., via Chrome Dev Tools) for many years, so it's a relief to now have such visibility for Apex.

One challenge with debug logs is that you require the "Modify Users" and "View All Data" permissions to see them, which may not be an acceptable level of access to give developers in production. The simplest solution to this is to create a Permission Set called (for example) "Debug and View All Data" that you can assign to developers temporarily if they are struggling to debug a production issue. That's similar to the approach used to get hands-on support from Salesforce or an ISV in your org: an admin "Grants Account Login Access" to the support agent for a period of time.

A workaround that my colleagues at Appirio use regularly is to create a custom object to store error messages and an Apex class that writes the error details (including a stack trace) to that object. That class can then be invoked inside try-catch blocks on code that you want to monitor for errors. Once stored in a custom object, those error messages are persisted across time and no longer require elevated permissions to access. You can use Workflow Email Alerts to provide notifications and Dashboards for monitoring. You can now also use Change Data Capture on that object or fire dedicated platform events to make that information immediately available external monitoring tools.

There are other monitoring capabilities for different aspects of Salesforce. For example, inbound and outbound email logs, data and file storage limits, daily API limits, and background jobs pages.

One of the simplest automated alerts you can establish is to "Set Up Governor Limit Email Warnings" which send email warnings when Apex code uses more than 50% of governor limits.[6] You may want to combine that with email filters to automatically ignore certain kinds of notifications. But this provides basic insight into whether any of your custom code might be at risk of exceeding governor limits.

Add-On Monitoring and Observability Tools

Salesforce Shield is the best-known add-on to aid observability. Shield provides three capabilities: platform encryption, field audit trail, and event monitoring. The event monitoring capability of Shield aids observability by providing real-time access to performance, security, and usage data from across Salesforce. This information can then be ingested into third-party monitoring tools like Splunk. To whet your appetite for this, Salesforce provides user login and logout information for free.

Salesforce also now provides Proactive Monitoring as an add-on service. Salesforce customers who subscribe to mission-critical support or other premier support options have historically been able to contact Salesforce to get access to similar monitoring information to diagnose problems like page load times or transient errors. Proactive Monitoring provides these capabilities as a standard bundle.

There are also a number of third-party solutions that can aid in monitoring. ThousandEyes provides an enterprise-wide view of availability and page load times, including details on which Salesforce data center is being accessed, and the performance of each intermediate section of the Internet between your users and Salesforce. This can be used to monitor uptime or to diagnose network issues that might affect certain branches in a global organization, but it can also be used to monitor page load times if you have concerns about particular applications.

AppNeta is similar to ThousandEyes in monitoring availability and load times, but focuses more on analyzing and categorizing your internal network traffic with an eye toward prioritizing higher-value traffic.

Opsview is an open-core product that provides visibility of system performance across on-premise, private, and public cloud. Their Salesforce connector uses the Salesforce REST API to monitor organizational limits. If you only need to monitor

---

[6]https://developer.salesforce.com/docs/atlas.en-us.apexcode.meta/apexcode/apex_gov_limits_emails.htm

Salesforce, it may be simpler to just periodically query those limits yourself using the Salesforce Limits API.[7]

If you are hosting a Salesforce Community, Google Analytics remains one of the best tools to aggregate and analyze user behavior like page views, click-through rate, and time spent on each page. Because of its applicability to any web site, Google Analytics is probably one of the best-known monitoring tools. For a time at Appirio, we used it to get insight into employee usage of our internal Salesforce instance.

What to Monitor

As mentioned previously, the point of monitoring and observability is to help you identify when something is going wrong, what it is, and why it's happening. The goal is to maintain a high signal-to-noise ratio, by only monitoring things that have real benefit and minimizing distracting information. With observability, more is generally better. But with monitoring, you should aim to be very targeted about what you want to monitor.

An occasion that often warrants monitoring is when rolling out a new business-critical feature. These should be debugged and performance tested in a staging environment, but it's important to have a way to monitor their performance and usage once they've actually rolled out. It's common for development teams to be exhausted from the final push to take a new production application live. If your teams are oriented around doing **projects**, they will be tempted to think of release day as the **last day** that they have to think about that application. But if you think of each application as a **product**, then release day is the **first day** that information becomes available on whether the application is reliable and serving user needs.

There are two main things to monitor when it comes to new services: are they working? And are they helping? To determine whether your applications are working, it is important to gather error messages (e.g., into a custom object as described earlier) and also to look at page load times if performance is a concern. For ad hoc analysis of page load times, the Salesforce Developer Console is still the best tool in my opinion. The Developer Console is a bit buggy, but hidden inside it are excellent tools for analyzing performance. Salesforce wrote a blog post on how to make use of these capabilities.[8]

---

[7]https://developer.salesforce.com/docs/atlas.en-us.api_rest.meta/api_rest/dome_limits.htm

[8]https://developer.salesforce.com/page/A_Guide_to_Application_Performance_Profiling_in_Force.com

Apex itself allows you to monitor limits using the Limits Class.[9] So you could also monitor and log metrics such as heap size and CPU execution time on your newly released applications if there's a concern about a particular metric. Storing such performance metrics in a custom object creates a Salesforce-native way to monitor application performance. You can then build reports and dashboards around those if that helps.

Finally, one of the most important things you can do with monitoring systems is to quiet, disable, or delete them once an application has proven to be stable and the monitoring data no longer identifies any issues worthy of analysis. As the *Site Reliability Engineering* book states:

> *Like all software systems, monitoring can become so complex that it's fragile, complicated to change, and a maintenance burden. Therefore, design your monitoring system with an eye toward simplicity. … Data collection, aggregation, and alerting configuration that is rarely exercised … should be up for removal.*

Other Duties As Assigned

Salesforce admins claimed the title "Awesome Admin" for themselves, and it's well deserved. They are often the main point of escalation for huge groups of users when they encounter challenges or confusion. This chapter just scratches the surface of the potential activities that admins might undertake or the issues that might arise in the service of production users.

Summary

Whereas with traditional IT systems, it is the role of admins to optimize and keep those systems running and patched, Salesforce does most of this hard work for you. Salesforce Admins generally play a dual role: part actual administrator and part App Builder. That dual role entrusts them with the responsibility of ensuring the production org is stable and accessible while also giving them the opportunity to use their creativity to make the org better. Having spoken about the administrative tasks of managing users, tuning security, and ensuring monitoring, we now turn to the more creative work of improving the org for the benefit of users.

---

[9]https://developer.salesforce.com/docs/atlas.en-us.apexcode.meta/apexcode/apex_
methods_system_limits.htm#apex_methods_system_limits

CHAPTER 12

Making It Better

As mentioned before, the term "Admin" in Salesforce is overloaded. It can refer to the traditional role of monitoring a production system to ensure it is stable and available to users, but it is just as likely to refer to a user who makes click-based changes to build or improve Salesforce. That latter role is better described as an "App Builder," but that term hasn't gotten much traction beyond being the name of a Salesforce certification. For example, the Admin Zone at Salesforce conferences or the Awesome Admin community[1] online spends most of its energy explaining the click-based Builders and techniques for innovating on the platform without code.

It's the ease of doing click-based ("declarative") development that has caused so many people to fall in love with the Salesforce platform. But even click-based innovation implies risk, and unmanaged changes quickly devolve into chaos. Thus it's important to manage click-based development in the same way as code-based development: promoting it systematically through development and testing environments, rather than doing it directly in production.

The goal of ensuring Admins follow this systematic process is not to tamp down on their creativity or slow their pace of innovation. In fact adopting a DevOps workflow gives Admins even more power and control, since it ensures that their changes are propagated to all environments, not just done in production. And it also gives the same peace of mind that developers enjoy, knowing that changes can be tracked and rolled back with ease should the need arise.

DevOps balances innovation with stability and security. And is thus equally important for Salesforce App Builders as it is for coders.

---

[1] https://admin.salesforce.com/

A. Davis, *Mastering Salesforce DevOps*, https://doi.org/10.1007/978-1-4842-5473-8_12

An Admin's Guide to Doing DevOps

If your company has invested in a click-friendly release management tool like Copado, consider yourself lucky. You can become a DevOps superstar with clicks not code. If your company is taking a more traditional approach of directly using version control and general-purpose CI tools like Jenkins, don't worry. You have an opportunity to learn powerful and flexible tools, and you can reuse those skills for as long as you work in IT.

A common adage is that DevOps tools are far less important than the culture shift involved. What matters is that everyone whose work impacts your production org is able to collaborate on common systems and that there is a shared sense of responsibility for enabling innovation and reducing risk and confusion.

DevOps implies a process (moving from Dev to production), so it's important to appreciate the benefits of not making changes directly in production. Your work then is to get access to a development environment, make and capture your changes from that environment so that they can be sent through the deployment and testing process, and participate in progressively improving that process.

Getting access to a development environment might mean using a shared Dev sandbox or running commands to clone a short-lived sandbox or scratch org. As soon as you begin working in a development environment, you will understand why developers make such a fuss when those environments are out of sync with production.

Making your own changes (creating fields, using App Builder, etc.) is the part you're already good at. This is the creative part of your job, and it's natural if you initially resent all of the overhead involved in capturing your changes to version control. But if you've not spent much (or any) time writing code, it's extremely empowering to begin tapping into the process of seeing your configuration represented as XML and to track and compare your work in version control alongside developers.

There's an enormous mystique surrounding programming. Popular culture perpetuates this, as do developers, who enjoy the air of mystery and exclusivity of doing work that seems so alien to other people. But writing code is just writing. Code editors are mostly just text editors. And the gap between coders and noncoders is just the gap between those who are literate in a particular language and those who are not. Think of getting comfortable with code as developing basic code literacy. Just as illiteracy rates are falling globally (see Figure 12-1), so too code literacy will serve you well in the modern world.

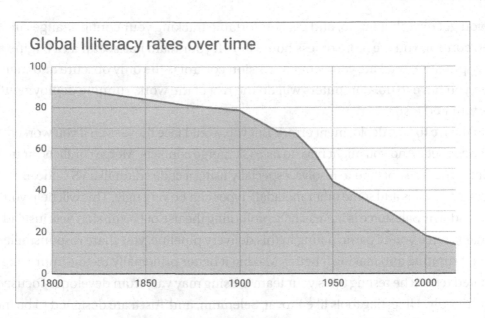

Figure 12-1. *World illiteracy has diminished at a remarkable pace[2]*

Amazingly, code functions as a universal language. But it's one where computers give you feedback about whether you've written it correctly or not. This makes it well suited to introverts who are happy to learn without human interaction. But even experienced coders struggle and fail like tiny children when first learning a new programming language or technique. Their peers may think they have superhuman skills, but, in private, even the most brilliant developers use "Hello World" examples and painstakingly pore through code snippets to get started with new technologies.

In my view, what distinguishes programmers is only that they have the patience, confidence, and motivation to work through this learning process again, and again, and again. Even a little experience using Git and running command-line scripts can give you the confidence that code is not a strange and inaccessible world. The best Salesforce admins I know have taken delight and pride in getting a little experience with code and the command line. Such experience unlocks the possibility of diving deeper into coding, even if you choose not to.

---

[2]https://ourworldindata.org/literacy

If you get over that hump, and get comfortable tracking your config changes in version control, you are more or less home free. If your team has set up a CI engine and delivery pipeline, tracking your work in version control is the only obscure and manual process you have to do. Computers will do the rest of the work, running deployments and automated testing.

You'll have to face deployment errors. But you would face those even if you worked with change sets. And you might have to face Git merge conflicts. Merge conflicts for most metadata types are not hard to resolve, especially using a code editor like VS Code. But merge conflicts for Profiles and some other metadata types can be very ugly. This will help you understand why Salesforce is increasingly promoting the use of Permission Sets instead.

Finally, once you're participating in this delivery pipeline, you share responsibility for keeping it running and making it better. Making it better principally means improving the automated tests. The testing tools your team is using may vary from developer-focused to admin-friendly. UI testing tools like Provar, Selenium, and Tosca are designed to be more accessible than code-based tests. If you have the opportunity to help build or specify those tests, you are helping ensure that the changes you make will be protected over time.

The logic you embed in a Process or Flow may be every bit as complex as the logic in a piece of code. Salesforce has begun to enforce code coverage requirements even on Flows and Processes, which is an interesting decision that affirms Salesforce's view that automated testing is essential. Encourage your developers to write their unit tests in a flexible way so that the expected inputs and outputs can be tuned easily. Behavior Driven Development (BDD) style tests are meant to have human readable inputs and outputs that make it easy to create multiple variations of a test to examine business logic against different edge cases. If developers write tests in a modular way, you can easily copy and paste a single test and adjust the inputs and expected outputs to help validate the logic of your Processes, Flows, Workflows, or Validation Rules. Dabbling in unit tests is one of the easiest and lowest-risk ways to start to code, since they have no impact on the org's behavior.

The point of adopting this approach is to bring admins and developers together in a common system that lets them experiment with less risk of impacting production users. Even Salesforce experts will occasionally screw up. If you're not familiar with working in a development org, it means that every experiment you do puts your data, your users, and their affection for you at risk. Working on a common delivery pipeline is an investment in collaboration and governance that gives you more reason to talk to the development teams, and ensures you can build together with speed and deliver to production with confidence.

Locking Everybody Out

My favorite story about the adoption of DevOps for Salesforce comes from Lex Williams, formerly a lead member of technical staff on Salesforce's own internal IT team. In the spirit of "dogfooding," Salesforce makes extensive use of their own product to run their business. Salesforce's production org is known as Org62. When Lex first joined Salesforce's IT team, there was no automated process in place to deploy customizations to Org62. There was an automated build process based on Ant that was used to build the multi-gigabyte JAR file that is Salesforce itself, but there was not a mechanism to manage or track the customizations made to Org62.

Lex and team set about adapting some existing Perl scripts and setting up a Jenkins instance that could be used to deploy code-based customizations. Of particular interest was building and deploying the tool known as GUS, Salesforce's *Grand Unified System* for tracking features and bugs for their product team.[3] At the time (prior to the rise of StackExchange), there were not many resources available for debugging issues with Jenkins or other aspects of their automation, but Lex and team managed to pioneer an automated workflow that allowed them to deploy GUS and other innovations to Org62.

Nevertheless, the customizations deployed by the IT team were only a fraction of the total customizations being made by users in production. Salesforce grew to market domination on the promise of quick and easy customization. So it is not surprising that a massive number of Salesforce employees using Org62 expected to be able to make their changes directly in production. Salesforce actually had hundreds of people with System Administrator privileges in their org. And they were all making legitimate, valuable customizations to serve the needs of thousands of other Salesforce employees.

Despite the expertise of these Salesforce admins, some small percentage of their changes caused unexpected issues, small and large. Lex and the IT team regularly found themselves having to tackle critical production issues with often mysterious origins. Hours of debugging would frequently yield the conclusion that an ad hoc change made by one of these admins had unintended consequences. Naturally, the IT team began advocating for more control over changes being made in production.

---

[3]The core of GUS was made available on the App Exchange as Agile Accelerator:
`https://appexchange.salesforce.com/listingDetail?listingId=a0N30000000ps3jEAA`

Perhaps more than they would have at any other company, the IT team experienced resistance. "What part of clicks not code don't you understand?" Why should teams be forced to route quick and simple changes through a regimented release schedule that would cause weeks of delay to a valuable improvement? The most strident resistance came from business users who depended on their admin colleagues to make quick changes.

After **years** of back and forth debate, the IT team finally began to compile statistics on the cost of responding to incidents caused by unplanned production changes. The incident response itself (scuttling a team of several developers to debug an incident, often outside of work hours) cost many thousands of dollars' worth of productive time. They showed how changes such as a field being removed from a layout could prevent hundreds of users from doing their jobs; or a validation rule being added could break critical integrations with the payment processing system. It was clear that the cost of each incident was easily tens of thousands of dollars, if not more. It was clearly more costly to allow uncontrolled innovation than it was to restrict it.

And thus Salesforce themselves locked all the sysadmins out of production, at least in the sense of not allowing application changes to be made. Since roughly 2013, the most "admin-friendly" company in the world has forced all admins to go through a DevOps workflow to deploy their updates. With the result that every change is tracked, changes are propagated to every development and testing org in the same way they're propagated to production, and incidents are far less common and far easier to debug than they were before.

If that's the way Salesforce manages their own org, why should we treat our orgs with any less care?

So what does it mean to "lock people out of production"?

First identify which permissions can lead to changes that could break functionality or cause the org to deviate unacceptably from the development and testing environments. The minimum set of restricted permissions are

- Author Apex

- Customize Application

To prevent unnecessary restriction, I recommend you begin by only restricting those two permissions. Making restrictions that inhibit people's ability to do their work is a very bad business strategy, so make sure you solicit input into the impact of any such changes. But review the complete list of "Admin" permissions,[4] and decide if there are any others you need to restrict. You should be extremely careful with giving the following two permissions and remain aware of who is assigned those:

- Modify All Data

- View All Data

Having identified permissions of concern, here is a recommended sequence of steps:

1. Make sure you can clearly understand and articulate the reasons this has to be done. If possible, provide business and financial justification.

2. Check your motivation. You should not be doing this out of distrust for users. Your focus should be on *increasing* the company's overall efficiency. There is some loss of efficiency by restricting permissions; you have to be confident you can make up for that loss through delivering capabilities from dev with more speed and reliability.

3. Make sure that you have established a Delivery Pipeline and that it uses Integration User accounts to do the deployments (see Chapter 7: The Delivery Pipeline). Ensure those Integration User accounts use secure credentials.

4. Ensure that all of your developers and App Builder admins are comfortable making their changes in scratch orgs or developer sandboxes and using the Delivery Pipeline to deploy those changes to production, and that the process is reasonably fast and reliable.

5. Identify which profiles and permission sets give users any of the restricted permissions mentioned earlier and which users are assigned those.

6. Consider whether the sensitive permissions can be removed or separated into a new permission set that can be applied to a smaller number of users.

---

[4]https://help.salesforce.com/articleView?id=000198725&language=en_US&type=1

7. Identify a strictly limited number of people who can be relied upon to retain real sysadmin access but who won't be tempted to make unauthorized changes.

8. Everyone other than the integration users and these few sysadmins needs to be "locked out." Anticipate the complaints and the complainers, make sure you have firm executive backing for this change, find a nice way to explain this to the affected users, decide on a timeline, and then communicate the change.

9. It's best to roll these changes out in waves, spread across several weeks, to minimize business impact and ensure that you and any support teams can manage any issues reported by users.

10. As you implement the changes, reiterate to the executive team what's happened, and why. Put on a helmet, hunker down, wait for the complaints to pour in, find a nice way of deflecting the complaints, and stand your ground.

11. Wait for the grumbling to die down, and then proceed with administering a powerful and stable DevOps workflow for your team. In the short term, you may be a villain. In the long run, you're definitely a hero.

12. By the end of the process, you should have "locked out" everyone other than the integration users and these few sysadmins, either by removing the risky permissions from their Profiles/Permission Sets or by changing which Profile/Permission Sets are assigned to those users.

It is very helpful to have only one or two profiles or permission sets that grant admin-level privileges and to label them clearly as having elevated privileges. As a security precaution, it can also be helpful to add a dynamic step to your build process that enforces this. You can write a script that reviews all profiles and permission sets other than the ones with elevated privileges and either fails the build if restricted permissions are detected or explicitly disables those permissions by setting the XML permission to `false`. Actually setting permissions to `false` ensures that elevated permissions are removed from profiles, even if they happen to be added manually in production. Copado's Compliance Hub is designed to help with concerns such as this.

What's Safe to Change Directly in Production?

The beauty of Salesforce is the ease of making small changes quickly, without having to involve programmers. It's thus very important to draw a clear distinction between which changes can safely be made in production and which changes need to go through the delivery pipeline. This distinction depends on your company's needs and may evolve over time.

There are two types of changes that must go through the delivery pipeline:

1. Changes that could break things

2. Changes that should immediately be made available in all development and testing environments

If these two reasons don't apply, it's safe to make the change directly in production. But the overwhelming majority of configuration changes actually fall into one of those categories.

The vast majority of metadata changes should go through the delivery pipeline. The vast majority of data changes do not need to go through the delivery pipeline. Metadata that can be safely changed in production includes

- Most Reports and Dashboards

- Most Documents

- Most Email Templates

- Most List Views

- Most Queues and Groups

The exceptions to this are when other metadata depend on these things, such as reports whose values are used as part of Visualforce pages.

Apart from metadata, there are also data changes that are very risky if done directly in production. For example:

- Configuration data that is used as part of business logic

- Complex configuration data (such as Products in CPQ systems) that could break data integrations or business logic

Migrating such configuration data through your delivery pipeline requires a different set of tools from metadata migrations. Commercial tools such as Copado, AutoRABIT, and Gearset include hierarchical data migration as a native capability. There are also dedicated tools that specialize in data migration such as Prodly Moover.

Tracking Issues and Feature Requests

Here we come full circle.

The DevOps continuum is often depicted as a loop (either a circle or an infinity loop), because unlike linear production processes, software development is an ongoing iterative process. New features are requested, developed, tested, and released. Users identify defects (often from hard-to-foresee edge cases) and make new requests for the software to further improve their lives. Those defects and feature requests then begin their journey around this loop, as they are developed, tested, and delivered, only to yield to the next round of requests.

Requests often begin their lives as support cases. Admins (as distinct from app builders) are often directly beholden to end users, who might submit support tickets when they encounter issues. Support cases have a different lifecycle from agile user stories, in that support requests are definitely tied to the user(s) who submitted them, and there may be SLAs that dictate a response be sent promptly. It falls to the admin to triage those tickets and respond with instructions on how to do something or actions such as password resets.

It is only when there is not an immediate solution to a support case that it graduates into an issue/defect report or a feature request and then demands a different approach. At Appirio, our IT helpdesk used Salesforce cases to track support requests and a homegrown, Salesforce-based agile project management tool called CMC to manage Issues and User Stories. Our cases had a button that allowed them to be converted into an Issue (for bugs) or a Story (for feature requests).

How to distinguish between these two types of request? The distinction is the same as explained earlier in "What's Safe to Change Directly in Production?" Things that are safe to change directly in production can be attended to quickly by admins. All other changes become requests for features or issue fixes.

Such a distinction is important for several reasons. First, it sets clear expectations for users that their request can't be completed immediately. Second, it allows issues and features to be handled and prioritized alongside other work that the app builder admins and developers need to tackle.

Issues and feature requests imply changes that might affect the behavior of the org, or have side effects, and thus need a clear justification and need to be tracked and tested like other configuration changes. Having a continuous delivery pipeline in place opens up the possibility of expediting changes that are low risk and/or high priority.

Tracking a request as a feature or defect should not imply an indefinite lead time though. Being able to release simple, low-risk changes quickly is a key benefit of an automated deployment pipeline.

Summary

Salesforce admins are the frontline workers making the Salesforce org better for users. Salesforce empowers them to do this through its ease of customization, and we shouldn't remove that ability without replacing it with something better. A smooth running delivery pipeline that provides version control, automated deployments across all environments, and robust automated testing is a superior system. But it is necessarily more complex and will require admins to grow comfortable with the changed approach and slight delay.

Reducing Lead Time (from committing a change to seeing it in production) is a key DevOps metric. And no one is more sensitive to long lead times than admins, who are accustomed to making instantaneous changes in production. Even most Salesforce developers lack familiarity with continuous delivery; so this is definitely an unfamiliar territory for most admins. But there's joy and efficiency in admins being able to collaborate with developers in a development environment. And there's relaxation and confidence in being able to roll back changes or investigate their origin. And fundamentally, a situation where orgs are out of sync for no discernible reason is a massive time waster for everyone involved.

Getting your admins participating happily in a delivery pipeline is the ultimate accomplishment in Salesforce release management. Don't expect to get there immediately, and remember that some people will be slower to change than others. But take note of your successes and build on them. Share internally when version control "saves your butts." And keep tracking and working to improve the key DevOps success metrics: lead time, deployment frequency, change failure rate, recovery time, and uptime.

CHAPTER 13

Conclusion

Salesforce began as an effort to simplify the enormous complexity of setting up an application such as CRM. One of its overwhelming benefits has been the ease of creating and updating functionality using click-based tools. Even Salesforce's programming languages provide rich prebuilt frameworks for interacting with data and the user interface.

Through skillful sales and marketing, ambitious product engineering, and the audacious success of building a community of 6 million click-based developers, Salesforce has grown into a vast platform. Over 150,000 businesses have customized the platform to meet their unique needs, in many cases creating tens of thousands of components, both code and config. Salesforce now supports an entire world of technologies and customizations, from blockchain, to AI, to social media, to user communities, and beyond, most of which can be configured by citizen developers.

The growth of these capabilities has outpaced the sophistication of the methods most Salesforce teams use to manage the development lifecycle. But fortunately the challenge of taming the dev lifecycle is not unique to Salesforce, and there has been an explosion of innovation and experience cultivated on this topic within the broader IT world over the last decades. The DevOps movement has become a gathering place for teams across all technologies to exchange ideas and improve tooling in support of those efforts. And so the Salesforce community is increasingly looking to the DevOps community to understand how to effectively manage such complex configuration at scale.

Throughout this book I've used the word "should" a lot. It's natural for most of us, certainly me, to hear the word "should" and feel inadequate, like we're not doing enough. This book has attempted to introduce opportunities to improve our processes, and I've shared encouragement, sometimes strongly, about practices we should adopt or abandon (see, there's that word again). But fundamentally, what we "should" do is to make life easier and better for ourselves, our coworkers, and the people around us who depend on our work.

© Andrew Davis 2019
A. Davis, *Mastering Salesforce DevOps*, https://doi.org/10.1007/978-1-4842-5473-8_13

We "should" spend more time with our families, and not have to work weekends and evenings doing deployments, or cleaning up in their aftermath. We "should" be able to make small improvements quickly without making other people wait. We "should" be able to exercise our creativity at work instead of being stuck doing monotonous tasks. And we "should" be solving problems once, in an automated way, so that we or our coworkers don't have to face them again.

My motivation in writing this has been to share what I've learned in the process of trying to make work more fun for myself, and more effective for the teams I've worked with. Take every suggestion in this book as optional, and as something you can experiment with, or not, depending on the needs of your team.

My other motivation in writing this has been to introduce Salesforce workers to the world of DevOps, which has become an active and brilliant community filled with life wisdom and technical excellence. Just as Salesforce solves many problems that bedevil people who are struggling to set up and manage their own infrastructure, these DevOps processes can solve many of the problems that Salesforce teams have historically struggled with. My hope is that this book contributes to that conversation and helps build another bridge between these communities of practice.

When we're customizing Salesforce to the needs of our organizations, our goal is to deliver innovation and value. In working together—dev and ops, developer and admin, business and IT, customer and company—we are building trust in each other and increasingly building trusted processes. The goal of innovation is to create value; and the goal of building trust is to reduce risk. Doing these two together, at high velocity and large scale, is the essence of DevOps.

In closing, I'll quote Gary Gruver, who led a dramatic transformation of the HP LaserJet Firmware division's software delivery process, beginning in 2008. At that time, the word "DevOps" had not yet been coined, and the book *Continuous Delivery* had not yet been published. Nevertheless, the HP teams uncovered those same principles as they worked to improve their processes in service of their overarching business needs.

> *At HP we never set out to do Agile. Our focus was simply on improving productivity. … We set off on a multiyear journey to transform the way we did development with the business objective of freeing up capacity for innovation and ensuring that, after the transformation, firmware would not be the bottleneck for shipping new products. This clear objective really helped guide our journey and prioritize the work along the way. …*

We see many companies that embark on a "do Agile" journey. They plan a big investment. They go to conferences to benchmark how well they are "doing DevOps or Agile." They see and feel improvements, but the management teams struggle to show bottom-line business results to the CFO. Not having clear business objectives is a key source of the problem. If they started out by focusing on the business and just using DevOps ideas or implementing some Agile methods that would provide the biggest improvements, they would find it much easier to show bottom-line financial results. This worked at HP. When we started, firmware had been the bottleneck in the business for a couple of decades and we had no capacity for innovation. At the end of a three-plus -year journey, … We had dramatically reduced costs from $100M to $55M per year and increased our capacity for innovation by eight times.

To be clear, achieving these results was a huge team effort. … Without the collaboration with our partners throughout the business we could not have achieved these results. Having a set of high-level business objectives that the entire organization is focused on is the only way to get this type of cross-organizational cooperation and partnership. These types of results will not happen when you "do Agile." It takes a laser-like focus on business objectives, a process for identifying inefficiencies in the current process, and implementing an ongoing, continuous improvement process.[1]

This story of the HP LaserJet Firmware division has been celebrated extensively in the DevOps community, in part because it shows how agility and radical transformation is possible even with a decades-old technology that's rooted in hardware. With a complex topic like DevOps, it's easy to get entranced with the technological changes involved. It's equally easy for business people to feel that things like continuous delivery are irrelevant to their mission. But you can and should drive such process improvements to gain business benefit. When the business case for DevOps is clear to everyone involved, there's never a problem sustaining long-term support for these initiatives.

I hope this book has provided guidance to help you begin or continue your Salesforce DevOps journey. May your process of building trust while delivering innovation become as simple and fun as the act of creating on Salesforce.

---

[1]Gary Gruver and Tommy Mouser, *Leading the Transformation, Applying Agile and DevOps Principles at Scale* (IT Revolution, 2015), 25.

Bibliography

Ambler, Scott W. and Sadalage, Pramodkumar J. *Refactoring Databases: Evolutionary Database Design*. Addison-Wesley Professional, 2006.

Benioff, Marc. *Behind the Cloud*. Wiley-Blackwell, 2009.

Beyer, Betsy, Chris Jones, Jennifer Petoff, and Niall Richard Murphy. *Site Reliability Engineering: How Google Runs Production Systems*. O'Reilly Media, Inc., 2016.

Deming, W E. *Out of the Crisis*. Massachusetts Institute of Technology, Center for Advanced Engineering Study, 1986.

Fawcett, Andrew. *Force.Com Enterprise Architecture*. Packt Publishing, 2014.

Forsgren, Nicole, Jez Humble, and Gene Kim. *Accelerate: The Science of Lean Software and Devops Building and Scaling High Performing Technology Organizations*. IT Revolution Press, 2018.

Gladwell, Malcolm. *The Tipping Point: How Little Things Can Make a Big Difference*. Back Bay Books, 2002.

Goldratt, Eliyahu M. and Jeff Cox. *The Goal: A Process of Ongoing Improvement*. North River Press, 2004.

Gruver, Gary and Mouser, Tommy. *Leading the Transformation, Applying Agile and DevOps Principles at Scale*. IT Revolution, 2015.

Humble, Jez and David Farley. *Continuous Delivery: Reliable Software Releases Through Build, Test, and Deployment Automation)*. Addison-Wesley Professional, 2010.

Humble, Jez, Joanne Molesky, and Barry O'Reilly. *Lean Enterprise: How High Performance Organizations Innovate at Scale*. O'Reilly Media, Inc, 2015.

Kim, Gene, Kevin Behr, and George Spafford. *The Phoenix Project*. IT Revolution Press, 2013.

Kim, Gene, Patrick Debois, John Willis, and Jez Humble. *The DevOps Handbook*. IT Revolution Press, 2016.

Kotter, John P. *Leading Change*. Harvard Business Review Press, 2012.

© Andrew Davis 2019
A. Davis, *Mastering Salesforce DevOps*, https://doi.org/10.1007/978-1-4842-5473-8

BIBLIOGRAPHY

Martin, Karen and Osterling, Mike. *Value Stream Mapping: How to Visualize Work and Align Leadership for Organizational Transformation*. McGraw-Hill, 2013.

Martin, Robert C. *Clean Code: A Handbook of Agile Software Craftsmanship*. Prentice Hall PTR, 2008.

Moore, G. A. *Crossing the Chasm: Marketing and selling technology products to mainstream customers*. HarperBusiness, 1991.

Rogers, Everett. *Diffusion of Innovations*, 5th Edition. Simon and Schuster, 2003.

Index

A

Acceptance test–driven development (ATDD), 302
Access token, 156
Ant Migration tool, 349, 350
Apex classes, 167
API first approach, 340
AppExchange, 374, 375
Appirio DX, 361–363
auth:jwt:grant, 160
Automated acceptance tests, 171
Automated functional testing
  code-based acceptance testing, 298
    CMC metrics tool, 299
    code coverage, 304–306
    creation, 302, 303
    data, 300, 301
    scratch orgs/testing sandboxes, 300
  UI testing, 306
    creation, 309–310
    environment, 308
    Puppeteer, 307
    Selenium, 307
    test pyramid, 310
Automated tests, 280
AutoRABIT, 341, 363–364

B

Bastard operator from hell (BOFH), 410
Behavior-driven development (BDD), 272, 302, 430
Blue Canvas, 364–365
Branching strategy
  best-known strategies, 220–221
  in Dreamhouse app, 218
  feature branch
    merging master, 229
    workflow, 228
  forking workflow, 240
  granular feature management
    branches, 238–239
    cherry picking, 237–238
  illlustration, 225
  org-level configuration
    example, 234, 236
    exceptions, 230
    metadata production, 230–233
  publishing packages, 226, 227
  repositories
    ease of managing application, 224
    fork, 219, 220
    freedom and control, 223
    KISS principle, 224
    trunk, 218
  research, 221

© Andrew Davis 2019
A. Davis, *Mastering Salesforce DevOps*, https://doi.org/10.1007/978-1-4842-5473-8

Branching strategy (*cont.*)
    trunk-based development *vs* feature
        branching, 227
Business process standardization, 163

C

Canary deployments, 396
CI/CD
    automating delivery process
        environments, 245
        merge requests, 245
        multiproject pipeline, 244
        pipelines, 244
        tool, 243
    build automation, 241
    organization level management
        metadata publishing, 261–264
        YAML syntax, 264–266
    package publishing
        creating walking skeleton, 256
        ID(s), 257
        running unit tests, 259
        trunk branch, 256
    servers
        configuration, 246
        configuring jobs, 253
        creating integration users, 252–253
        environmental variables, 254–255
        group-level configuration, 255
        store project-specific secrets, 255
        storing CI job configuration, 253
        systems, 245, 246
        user permission levels, 251
        using Docker containers, 247–250
Click-based development, Salesforce, 410
    data management (*See* Data
        management)

declarative tools (*See* Declarative tools)
no-code, low-code, or pro-code, 84, 85
security model, 99 (*See* Security model)
ClickDeploy, 343, 365–367
Client-side programming
    API access, 108
    aura components, 107
    lightning web components, 106–107
    S-controls, 107
    visualforce remote objects, 107
Code-based tests, 279
Code reviews, 171
Command-line interface (CLI), 25
Command-line scripts, 346
    other techniques
        Bash scripts, 358
        JQ, 356–358
        Node.js, 358, 359
        Salesforce DX, 356, 357
    package.json, 355, 356
    Salesforce CLI, 352, 353
        plugins, 353, 354
    scripting
        Ant Migration Tool, 349, 350
        defined, 347
        ruby script, 348
        Salesforce data loader, 349, 351
        Unix-compatible systems, 348
        Windows, 347
Commit-stage tests, 281
Community Cloud, 340
Component tests, 279
Comprehensive tests
    Automated functional (*See* Automated
        functional testing)
    manual QA and UAT, 330–331
    nonfunctional testing (*See*
        Nonfunctional testing)

Concurrent version system (CVS), 205

Containers, 338

Continuous Delivery, 297, 338, 382

    automated deployments, 384, 385

    automated tests, 387

    behavioral rituals, 386

    continuous integration, 383

    deploying configuration

        data, 385–386

    deployment errors, 383

Continuous integration (CI), 241

Continuous testing, 281

Copado, 168, 341, 367–369

CPQ solutions, 386

Create, read, update, or

        delete (CRUD), 101

Cross-Org Adapter, 166

CumulusCI, 354

Customer relationship

        management (CRM), 2

Custom metadata, 119

D

Dark deploying, 395

Data management

    bulk database operations, 94

    changing the schema, 90

        developer names, 91

        field types, 91, 93

    configuration data, 95–98

    redundant backup systems, 95

    schema, 89, 90

Data migrations, 172

Declarative tools

    community builder, 86

    lightning app builder, 86

    process/flow builder, 87, 88

Default Organization Template (DOT), 165

Delivery pipeline

    branches (*See* Branching strategy)

    CI/CD and automation (*See* CI/CD)

    function, 203

    version control

        Git, 205

        salesforce, 204, 205

Dependencies

    AWS, 112

    loose coupling, 111, 113

    tight coupling, 111

Dependency injection (DI)

    FedExService, 119

    MyClass, 118

    OrderingService, 119–121

    OtherClass, 118

Deployment errors, debug, 382–383

Deployment technologies

    changes sets

        ClickDeploy, 343

        limitation, 342, 343

        managing deployments, 341

        target org, 342

    Command-line (*See* Command-line

        scripts)

    IDEs, 345, 346

    manual changes, 340–341

    Metadata API, 343–344

    packages, 344–345

    risk analysis, 392

    traditional software, 337

DeprecateOnly flag, 379

Developer Console, 424

Developer Edition orgs, 145

Development tools

    console, 72

    IDE, 71

Development tools (*cont.*)
  Salesforce CLI, 71
  VS Code, 73–75
  Web IDE, 72
  Welkin Suite, 75
DevOps, 140, 409, 412–415
  agile manifesto, 32
  better value, faster, safer,
    happier, 42, 43
  blameless postmortems, 38, 39
  business impact, 40, 41
  click-friendly release management
    tool, 428
  concepts, 29
  continuous delivery, 6, 33, 34
  continuous feedback, 34
  continuous improvement, 35
  cycle time, 28
  enabling change, 53–57
  generative culture, 37
  infinity loop, 8, 30
  lean management, 35, 36
  measuring performance, 43–47
  merge conflicts, 430
  process/flow, 430
  research, 8, 9
  Salesforce DX, 7
  tools, 6
  version control, 6
DevOps Research and Assessment
    (DORA), 8
Dev *vs.* Ops, 30, 31
Domain layer, 128
Domain pattern, 132
Domain-specific test
    language (DSL), 303
doSomething method, 118

E

Einstein Analytics tool, 166
Enhancing performance, 47
  theory of constraints, 50–52
  value stream mapping, 48–50
Enterprise design patterns
  domain layer, 128
  selector layer, 129–130
  separation of concerns, 125
  service layer, 126–127
  unit of work concept, 127
Enterprise messaging
    platform (EMP), 123, 199
Enterprise Service Buses (ESBs), 123
Event-driven architecture, 122–124
Extreme programming (XP), 326

F

Factory method/application factory
    pattern, 130
Fast tests
  linting, static analysis (*See* Linting,
    static analysis)
  quality gates, static analysis, 287
  technical debt, 283
  unit (*See* Unit testing)
FinancialForce, 386
Flosum, 369, 370
force:auth:sfdxurl:web, 158
Force-dev-tool, 354
Force-DI package, 119
Full codebase, static analysis
  ApexPMD, 314, 316
  Clayton, 313
  Codacy, 317
  CodeClimate, 317

CodeScan, 314

MetadataService.cls, 318

SonarQube, 313, 314

G, H

Gearset, 168, 370, 371

Generative cultures, 37

Git

    actions, 208, 209

    central repository, 207

    definition, 207

    naming conventions

        commit messages, 212

        conventional commits, 214, 216

        feature branches, 213

        Squashing commits, 214

    preserving history of files, 216, 217

    tools

        command line, 211

        CRLF settings, 210

        GUIs, 211

        host web interface, 212

        IDE plugins, 211

Globally unique ID (GUID), 200

Grand Unified System (GUS), 431

Graphical user interfaces (GUIs), 346

I, J

Identity and Access Management (IAM), 99

Infrastructure as a Service (IaaS), 6

Integration test, 171, 280

K

Keep it simple and straightforward (KISS)

    principle, 224

Key performance indicators (KPIs), 275

L

Language Server Protocol (LSP), 75

Law of diffusion of innovation, 53, 54

Leading effective change,

    DevOps

    build on the change, 63

    communicate the vision, 60

    corporate culture, 63

    encounter obstacles, 61

    powerful coalition, 58

    short term, creation, 62

    urgency creation, 57, 58

    vision for change, 59, 60

Lean management, 35, 36, 139

Lightning Dev Pro

    Sandboxes (LDPS), 146, 195

Lines of code (LOC), 270

Linting, static analysis

    Apex code, 284

    ESLint rules, 286

    feedback, 287

M

Manual acceptance tests, 171

Mean Time to Restore (MTTR), 45

Measuring performance, 43

    change fail percentage, 45

    deployment frequency, 44

    lead time, 44

    MTTR, 45

Metadata

    API, 77, 78, 339, 343–345

    CI/CD process, 80, 81

    configuration changes, 82

    Coverage Report, 340

    convertion between Salesforce DX

        and API, 79

Metadata (*cont.*)
manual changes, 83
retrieving changes, 81
Metazoa Snapshot, 372, 373
Modular development techniques
DI (*See* Dependency Injection (DI))
event-driven architecture, 122–124
naming conventions, 117
object-oriented programming, 117, 118
Monitoring and observability
add-on tools, 423
analysis, 420
built-in tools, 422, 423
signals, 421
Multifactor authentication (MFA), 99
Multiple production orgs, 387, 388
architecture, 162, 164
coordinate, 166, 167
merge, 165
mergers/acquisitions, 164
purchases, 164
splitting, 165, 166

N

Node package manager (NPM), 352
Nonfunctional testing
code reviews, 326–330
full codebase, static analysis (*See* Full codebase, static analysis)
performance, 321–325
security analysis, 319
CheckMarx, 320, 321
Fortify, 321

O

Object-oriented programming, 117
Open CLI Framework (OCLIF), 352

Org62, 431
Org differences, managing
automatic replacements, 391
intentional and unintentional, 388
temporary differences, 388, 389
XSLT, 390, 391
OtherClass.doSomething() method, 118

P

Packages
depiction of, 136
Salesforce org, 135
sfdx-project.json file, 133, 134
Packaging
classic, 373–375
second-generation (*See* Second-Generation packaging)
Panaya, 392
Pareto principle, 296
Performance tests, 171
Platform as a Service (PaaS), 3
Process quality, 275
Pub-sub architecture, 122

Q

Quality
functional, 270
hidden levels, 271
process, 271
structural, 270

R

Red bead experiment, 277
Refresh Token, 156
Releasing by deploying, 396, 397
Restricted permissions, 432–434

S

Salesforce, 1–3
  background, 11
  business needs, 440
  click-based tools, 439
  delivery pipeline,
    changes, 435
  deployments, 440
  development lifecycle, 439
  DX, 3–5
  metadata, 435
  version update
    deploying, 197, 198
    early access, 196, 197
Salesforce admin, 411
  monitoring and observability, 420–425
  permission sets, 417–418
  scheduling jobs, 418–420
  security, 417
  user management, 416
Salesforce app builders, 427
sales force automation (SFA), 5
Salesforce CLI
  defined, 352
  hooks creation, 353
  NPM, 352
  OCLIF, 352, 353
Salesforce Core API, 358
Salesforce Data Loader, 351
Salesforce DX, 356, 360
  CLI, 25
  concepts, 20
  creation, 115, 116
  Dev Hub, 21
  development lifecycle, 67–70
  goal, 19
  managed packages, 22

  metadata API vs. SFDX source
    formats, 23, 25
  modular architecture, 22, 113–115
  modules, 22
  Scratch Orgs, 21
  second-generation packages, 23
  unmanaged packages, 22
Salesforce orgs
  API access, 155
  auth commands, 158
  bugs/issues, 174
  dangers in production, 147, 148
  Dev Hub, 154, 155
  developing new functionality, 169, 170
  environment strategy, 161
  mapping existing orgs, 167, 169
  OAuth 2.0 flow, 155–157
  testing functionality, 170, 171
  testing integrations, 172, 173
  training, 174
  types, 142
  user interface, 153
Salesforce packages, 133, 345
Salesforce platform, 65
Salesforce's Development Lifecycle
    Guide, 148
Sandboxes
  cloning/refreshing, 192
  creation, 192, 193
  definition, 145
  developing, 148–149
  disadvantages, 149–150
  DX team, 152
  login, 161
  planning, 194
  refresh process, 193, 194
  size, 145

Sarbanes Oxley (SOX), 342

Scratch Orgs, 146
  aspects, 181
  benefits, 150–152
  create additional user
     accounts, 186, 187
  creation, 154, 177, 179
  development, 189–191
  install, 183, 184
  pushing metadata, 185
  review apps, 191
  setup process, 188
  setup steps, 182
  shape, 180
  snapshots, 180, 182
  workflow, 176

Scratch orgs vs. sandboxes, 187

Second-generation package
  add and remove metadata, 378–379
  package dependencies, 378
  Salesforce DX workflow, 375
  unlocked
    AppExchange, 376
    branch flag, 377
    build and publish, 377
    Dev Hub, 376

Security model
  admin access, 101
  infrastructure, 99
  login and identity, 99–101
  user access, 101–103

Selector layer, 129–130

Separating deployments from releases
  branching by admissions, 403–406
  dynamic lightning pages, 400
  feature flags, 400–402
  layouts, 399, 400
  permission, 398, 399

Server-side programming
  Apex, 104, 105
  scripting and anonymous apex, 105, 106
  visualforce, 105

SFDX-Falcon, 354

sfdx force:user:create command, 186

sfdx-project.json file, 114, 183

Single-org vs. multi-org strategy, 163

single sign-on (SSO), 99, 416

Site Reliability Engineering (SRE), 45

Software delivery, 65, 139

Software Development
    Performance (SDP), 8, 40

Software/Platform as a Service
    (SaaS/PaaS), 5

Squashing commits, 214

Static analysis, 171

Strongpoint, 392

Structural quality
  maintainability, 272, 273
  performance, 274
  reliability, 272
  security, 274
  size, 274

Subject matter experts (SMEs), 332

T

Test-driven development (TDD), 272, 297

Testing, 275
  automated, 280
  business-critical customizations, 278
  code, API, and UI, 279
  commit-stage, 281
  components, 279
  continous, 281
  cost of fixing bugs, 276
  engine, 282

environments, 282
functional/nonfunctional, 279
integration, 279
KPIs, 275
manual, 280
red bead experiment, 277
shifting left cycle, 277
total quality management, 276
unit, 279
Testing functionality, 170
Tipping point, 54
Tracking issues and feature
    requests, 436–437
Trigger handler patterns, 132
Trigger management, 131–132

U

Unit testing
    Apex test runner, 292

aura lightning components, 293
creation, 296
data needed, 295, 296
lightning web components, 293
Salesforce org, 294, 295
TDD, 297
VisualForce, 292
Unit tests, 171, 279
User acceptance testing (UAT),
    269, 330, 332

V, W

Version control, 20
Visual Studio Code (VS Code), 73
Vlocity, 386

X, Y, Z

XSLT, 390

Printed in the United States
By Bookmasters